Pasco County Library System

Overdue notices are a courtesy of the Library System.

Failure to receive an overdue notice does not absolve the borrower of the obligation to return the materials on time.

Norse Warfare

ALSO BY MARTINA SPRAGUE

Sweden: An Illustrated History

Norse Warfare

The Unconventional Battle Strategies
of the Ancient Vikings

MARTINA SPRAGUE

Hippocrene Books, Inc.
New York

To my father, Sören
My late uncle, Lennart
And my aunts, Marianne and Agneta
You are the best!

For further information, address:
    Hippocrene Books, Inc.
    171 Madison Ave.
    New York, NY 10016
    www.hippocrenebooks.com

Library of Congress Cataloging-in-Publication Data

Sprague, Martina.
    Norse warfare / Martina Sprague.
        p. cm.

    ISBN-13: 978-0-7818-1176-7
    ISBN-10: 0-7818-1176-7

        1. Northmen—Warfare. 2. Northmen. 3. Vikings. 4. Scandinavia—
    History. 5. Europe—History. 6. Civilization, Viking. I. Title.

DL65.S76 2007
948'.022--dc22   2007026833

Printed in the United States of America.

CONTENTS

INTRODUCTION

— ❦ —

The focus of this book is a warrior race, the Vikings, who lived by a moral code different from that of their contemporaries in other parts of Europe. Norsemen of the Viking Age pursued a variety of occupations such as farmer, smith, merchant and explorer. Only 2 to 3 percent of the male population engaged in raiding and even they were peaceful when at home. But in battle they were ruthless and barbaric. Known for their savagery, the Vikings followed their own laws and defied those of other peoples. History is colored with the myths of these legendary Nordic warriors going berserk on hallucinogenic mushrooms and ignoring the rules of society by pillaging and plundering with no regard for God and human life. They refused to be dominated or bound by the precepts of others and took the fight to their opponents, invading and occupying many lands in northern Europe and Russia.

The Viking Age began in the late eighth century AD and spanned nearly three hundred years. Vikings inhabited the lands of northern Europe, mainly Norway, Sweden, Denmark and Iceland, and were known by the various names of Norsemen, Rus, Svear, Goths, Danes and Varangians (mercenary guards serving the Byzantine emperor), although peoples under attack frequently referred to the foreign invaders as Norsemen or Danes.[1] The term *Viking* is thought to stem from the Old Icelandic *vikja* (deviate or travel), or *vik* (bay), and to describe an individual who lurks in a bay area—a pirate. Viken, meaning "the bay," is the stretch of land between Oslofjord in southeastern Norway and Gothenburg on the west coast of Sweden. During the Viking era it was a heavily fortified stronghold and is mentioned extensively in the Icelandic sagas.

The Vikings frequently campaigned on home turf and fought their most ferocious battles against other Vikings, but they also traveled widely and engaged in conflict throughout most of Europe and Russia, whose leaders were in a state of almost continual warfare among each other. The Viking Age in general was a brutal time. Despite the lack of a centralized government, Vikings succeeded in terrorizing major civilized societies throughout the world for almost three centuries and their war history includes most of Europe where many of the battles were fought.

Skilled warriors both on land and at sea, Vikings reinforced their land warfare by attacking from the sea, and their sea warfare from the land. Combining land and sea battle was instrumental to their success. Most land battles were short, however, because the Vikings spent most of their time at sea where they were able to avoid other military organizations. The raids they mounted were on a relatively small scale, but their admirable seamanship, surprise attacks, highly developed ships and outstanding fighting skill created a disproportionately large impact. Their swift battleships, carved with frightening dragonheads on bow and stern, could be sailed into the shallow waters of a bay and quickly dragged ashore. Once on land the Vikings fought with determination and ferocity. To their victims they appeared to be an unstoppable force that rendered resistance pointless—better, if possible, to run away and be spared. Viking plunderers were like a plague to those under attack. Monks described them as stinging wasps, fanning out in all directions, wrecking, robbing and destroying.

The Norsemen were seen as simple barbarians, backward and under-developed, but dangerous.

While Vikings plundered far beyond their native northern territories and raided the coasts of England, Scotland, Wales, Ireland, France and Spain, they also engaged in exploring and trading, extending those activities to Russia, the Arab world and the Americas. Their trading activities were no less significant than the raids, although surviving accounts tend to focus chiefly on the latter because of their dramatic effect. Arabs welcomed the Vikings as trade partners, but Christians viewed them more negatively—understandably so, given the Viking penchant for killing monks and plundering monasteries. Vikings clung steadfastly to their pagan beliefs and for a long time gave no quarter to Christians trying to convert them. Alcuin of York, historian, scholar, churchman and one of the best information sources of the time, interpreted the Viking attacks as God's punishment for declining moral standards.[2] After the raid on Lindisfarne in 793, Alcuin said in a letter to Aethelred, king of Northumbria: "In nearly 350 years we and our forefathers have been living in this the best of countries and never before has such terror struck Britain as the one we now have to suffer from this heathen race. Nor was it thought to be possible that such an attack could be carried out from the sea."[3]

For her study, the author relied on a number of primary and secondary sources and researched museums in Sweden, Norway and northern Germany. Much of what is known about the Vikings is derived from Scandinavian finds, such as weapons, ships, jewelry and runes that paint the picture of a sophisticated trade culture, and from a few written records, chronicled for the most part by victims of the attacks. Apart from those who carved the runes, the Norse population was illiterate, so records written by Vikings from the period under study are few. The runes, written for posterity, reveal little more than the name of the person who raised the stone, the name of the person memorialized, social standing, praiseworthy deeds, if any, and cause of death. While they provide insight into the Viking value system and their notions of honor and heroism, they contain almost no information on Viking war strategies. Because the Nordic countries did not attain literacy until after Christianization was completed in the twelfth century, observations recorded in foreign chronicles provide most of what is known about Viking war history. These accounts include the *Anglo-Saxon Chronicle*, the *Nestorian Chronicle* (also called the *Russian Primary Chronicle)*, the *Alexiad* of Anna Comnena, and the *Gesta Normannorum* by Dudo of St. Quentin. The chronicles tend to be fairly consistent as to events, but were written by clergymen who, like most Christian Europeans, knew the Vikings only as plunderers and destroyers. It is therefore understandable that the chroniclers likely had a biased opinion of these marauding pirates and exaggerated the horrors they experienced on encountering a fleet of pagan Viking long-ships.

The Icelandic sagas are another source for information about the Vikings, but written some one hundred years after the Viking Age, they are said to contain more myth than fact and are characterized as being over laden with fanciful detail. The earliest sagas offer little help to military historians seeking such details, for example, as the prevalence of helmets and mail armor in battle, the shape of battlefield formations, the duration of a "standard" raid and frequency of military campaigning by an "average" Viking. Most scholars agree, moreover, that it is highly unlikely that the dialogues are accurate. The above notwithstanding, even the earliest sagas expand our notions of Viking life and the thoughts, feelings and mindset of the Norse population.

As they proceed into the tenth century, the sagas become more reliable. They establish a historical record, describe Viking principles and war tactics and highlight the role and importance of invasions and raids in Norse history. They commemorate mere soldiers, not just kings, and help to establish the family trees of men of lower rank—men who did not aspire to become leaders or kings, but who advanced their personal ambitions and displayed great valor in combat. It has been said that history often remembers only its kings, not its foot soldiers, but the sagas, which frequently shift from protagonist to protagonist, tend to depict heroic acts rather than the acts of heroes.

Embarking on a historical journey involves not just factual discovery or historical truth, but discerning the meaning of events and how they influenced society. War historians cannot limit themselves to battle dates, but must also ask why battles were fought and what influence they had on later generations of warriors. While archaeological evidence is often the historian's most dependable source, reliance on artifacts alone is insufficient. Tangible evidence frequently reveals specific events and customs in a given period, but does not necessarily disclose how people thought and reasoned. In the end, culture and ethnicity influence a society's myths. More important than their historical accuracy, the real value of the Icelandic sagas is the knowledge they provide of the culture and ideology of Norse society. The myths, sagas and eddas (narrated folktales of Norse mythology and Norse heroes), bolstered by archaeological evidence and eyewitness accounts, help form a more complete picture of Viking warfare.

Of the modern Scandinavian languages, Icelandic most closely resembles Old Norse. Though similar, minor linguistic differences existed between the east countries (Denmark and Sweden) and the west countries (Norway and Iceland). For the purpose of this study, the terms Norse, Danes and

Svear are used interchangeably with Vikings. The boundaries between the northern countries were poorly defined and Vikings commonly undertook joint ventures against foreign nations. To establish permanent bonds between families, Norse and Danes intermarried with the Svear, and vice versa. From the viewpoint of a raided country's population, however, the pirates coming from across the sea were all from one and the same geographical region; they looked the same, acted the same, seemingly spoke the same language and were therefore often described simply as Danes.

Achieving consistency with Norse names is difficult owing to alternative spellings and lack of a definitive standard. The different forms are, however, similar enough to be easily understood. The name "Olav" can also appear as "Olaf," "Anlaf" or "Olafr"; "Sven" as "Svein" or "Sweyne"; and "Knut" as "Knud," "Cnut" or "Canute." Unless quoting directly from a historical document, the author uses the Scandinavian version of the name rather than the common English translation. The Vikings had only one given name and surnames served to indicate patrimony only—whose son a particular Sven, Harald or Sigurd was. "Sigurdson" can also appear as "Sigurdsson" or "Sigurdarson." Most "surnames" referred to the person's father, but sometimes to the mother. The Danish king Svein Ulfson is usually known as Svein Estridsson, after his mother. Guthorm Gunhildson, an advisor to King Harald Hardrade, was also named after his mother. Spelling of names was sometimes linked to the country of the warrior's origin and was often a result of personal preference. Nicknames frequently reflected warriors' distinguishing characteristics in appearance or achievement, as in "the Tall," "the Great," "the Boneless," etc. Unless quoting directly from a historical document, the author has replaced nicknames such as Tveskaeg (Forkbeard) and Harfagre (Fairhair) with their English equivalents.

Chapter One provides an overview of the many Viking battles fought on foreign soil. Chapters Two through Nine discuss various aspects of Viking warfare, including motivation and leadership, ship building and seamanship, weapons and battlefield tactics, as well as the elite forces of Jomsborg and the Varangian Guard. Chapters Ten through Fifteen highlight prominent Viking kings and their most notable battles. In an attempt to illustrate the entire Viking period, the most renowned kings from Sweden, Norway and Denmark are featured. Supplemental information can be found in the accompanying footnotes and a glossary of terms.

Snorri Sturluson (c. 1178–1241), a prominent historian of the Middle Ages, considered the Norse king Harald Hardrade a great warrior, "bold in arms, strong and expert in the use of his weapons beyond any others. . . ." But Sturluson also cautioned against the indiscriminate, or wholesale, recording of Harald's feats, "owing partly to our uncertainty about them, partly to our wish not to put stories into this book for which there is no testimony. Although we have heard many things talked about, and even circumstantially related, yet we think it better that something may be added to, than that it should be necessary to take something away from our narrative."[4] This quotation is a reminder that historical research is not an exact science because it remains open—eternally—to the individual historian's interpretation and the particular prism through which the historian views events. So, while this book presents the author's view, it also seeks to encourage readers to pose their own questions and provide their own interpretation of the past.

Understanding the success of Viking raids and warfare requires knowledge of the forces that motivated these warriors. Were the Vikings' operating methods, battlefield tactics, strategies, weapons, communications, transportation system, military objectives and mindset more highly developed than those of other military organizations in that era? Were they ahead of their time? The pages that follow take the reader on a journey to far-away places one thousand years ago and trace the rise and fall of a great warrior race.

CHAPTER 1

RAIDS ON THE CHRISTIAN WORLD

*Fair-skinned, light-haired Norsemen ruled the
rivers, waterways and seas, casting their shadow
of destruction on the Christian countries of the
civilized world.*

◆—◆

They came in waves from the barren lands of the north—
young, energetic, adventurous men looking for a fight. The
surprise and fear felt by the monks at Lindisfarne, the monastery of St. Cuthbert on Holy Island on the Northumberland
coast in northeastern England, seeing a Viking fleet of long-
ships suddenly appear on the horizon can only be imagined. The
monks were men of peace who had been living and working
at this holy sanctuary since the sixth century; the destruction
they were about to witness was unimaginable. An attack on
God's church was not only unexpected, it was thought incon-
ceivable that a siege on such a scale could be carried out from
the sea. "This year came dreadful fore-warnings over the land of
the Northumbrians, terrifying the people most woefully: these
were immense sheets of light rushing through the air, and whirl-
winds, and fiery dragons flying across the firmament . . . and
not long after . . . the harrowing inroads of heathen men made
lamentable havoc in the church of God in Holy-island, by rapine
and slaughter."[1]

The Vikings came across the North Sea. When the long-
ships approached the coast, the monks went down to the
water to greet the arriving strangers, not realizing that this

was not a time to be trusting. Without warning, the crazed Norsemen beached their ships, robbed the monastery of its treasures, wrecked and shattered the precious altars and murdered the monks, leaving only blood and destruction in their path. By the time the sails of the Viking fleet disappeared over the horizon, the monastery stood in ruins. The situation was dreadful. If even God could not protect the monasteries, who could protect the rest of Britain?

The beginning of the Viking Age is said to have started with the raid on Lindisfarne in 793. It was, however, preceded by an earlier appearance of Norsemen in England when a smaller fleet of three long-ships arrived at Dorset in 787. A Saxon tax officer, mistaking the strangers for traders, asked that they face the king to pay a tax. The Vikings responded with displeasure at the request and killed the tax officer. "And in his days came first three ships of the Northmen from the land of robbers. The reve [steward] then rode thereto, and would drive them to the king's town; for he knew not what they were; and there was he slain. These were the first ships of the Danish men that sought the land of the English nation."[2]

Most early raids were comprised of small parties consisting of just a few ships, but the destruction was so great that the victims felt it was truly punishment from God. These early attempts at pirating the monasteries and convents along the coasts of England, Scotland, Ireland and Wales were ambitious, but because they were sporadic in nature, the great raid on Lindisfarne came as a shock to most of the civilized world. ". . . [T]he calamity of your tribulation saddens me greatly every day," wrote Alcuin of York to the bishop of Lindisfarne on hearing of the attack. The assault was so gruesome that Alcuin had to justify it by relating it to the sins of the people: ". . . when the pagans desecrated the sanctuaries of God, and poured out the blood of saints around the altar . . . truly it has not happened by chance, but is a sign that it was well merited by someone."[3] The Vikings, who embraced a polytheistic heathen religion that, by Christian standards, had few rules and fewer moral values and encouraged bravery in battle, must have laughed mockingly at the monks who, in their innocence, expected their Christian god to protect them.

Towns were often built along the coasts to provide easy access to travelers and merchants from the sea. But their location made them soft targets, especially vulnerable to piracy, and provided the Vikings with opportunity to raid. Location was a double-edged sword; ease of access was essential for a community to thrive, but a thriving community could also become a prime target for pirates. The Vikings targeted monasteries not because they were after Christians, but because these holy sites, known to store great riches, proved an irresistible temptation to pirates. The monasteries were poorly protected because Europe's organized armies were usually involved in conflicts among themselves and preoccupied with fighting wars in other parts. While Frankish, German and English leaders were busy resolving their internal squabbles, they neglected defense of the monasteries and coastal communities.

The Vikings, or Norsemen, were unlike other pirates of the sea who primarily raided common folk because they were seen as easy prey, defenseless and vulnerable. Instead, Viking strategy was to shift their piracy to places that housed the greatest treasures, namely the churches and monasteries. Holy sites, purposely situated in places inaccessible to ships, had previously been considered safe against looting. The Lindisfarne monastery on Holy Island, for example, was not reachable by land and thought to be secure against attack. But its so-called strategic location was a minor problem to the Vikings who overcame it through the particular construction of their ships that were built for speed, and the surprise of their attacks. Their ingenuity in ship design allowed the

Vikings to sail the length of a targeted country's coastline and pick off their prey one-by-one. Their broad-bottomed ships needed no harbor and could be sailed into shallow waters, enabling the Vikings to make landfall wherever they chose. The only way for a country to defend itself effectively against Viking attack would be for it to protect its entire coastline, an immense, infeasible task since military strongholds were generally located inland and forewarning, if any, was seldom sufficient to muster opposing forces.

The Vikings rarely traveled inland since their goal was to come away with booty, not to secure territory. Although greater riches may have existed inland, venturing too far from the water could have compromised their main military tactic which was a speedy, surprise attack, carried out by a small group who avoided land warfare against possible stronger armies, and a correspondingly swift departure. With the exception of short travels across terrain to reach a targeted village or monastery, and sometimes in order to transport the ship short distances on land from one waterway to another, long overland marches were generally avoided. Only small groups had the ability to execute quick entries and exits, and raids were often random and spur-of-the-moment. Huge fleets of several hundred ships required a different strategy. Although an individual Viking could arrange a raid and most men acted on their own initiative, great Norse leaders, such as Ragnar Lodbrok, Sven Forkbeard and Olaf Trygvason organized memorable campaigns that were large, well-planned and paved the way for later ones.[4]

The Vikings' rule of the seas and their ability to reach any island or penetrate any waterway left monks defenseless and unable to protect their treasures. Since Viking journeys originated in the little-known Nordic countries, most of Europe was generally unaware of the Norsemen's facility for planning and organizing raids and the superior technology of their speedy ships. The raid at Lindisfarne was a mere forecast of what would become a three-century reign of the unpredictable pillage, slaughter and plunder of Britain, Scotland, Ireland, France and the former Western Roman Empire. The prayers of the French would echo with the words: *Free us, oh Lord, from the frenzy of the Norsemen!*[5] Men, women and children began to live in fear, and it was rumored that half of the civilized world had fallen under the onslaught of heathen madmen from the north.

After the raid on Lindisfarne, England experienced a lull in the Viking raids that lasted almost a generation. In 833 King Egbert of Wessex fought thirty-five shiploads of Danes at Carhampton, culminating in a huge slaughter. Two years later, a large army of ships arrived at Cornwall, continuing inland on rivers and waterways where the Vikings targeted the British and Frankish Empires, sometimes mounting horses brought along for more rapid raids. The Baltic Sea, which surrounded the Scandinavian countries, connected to waterways that gave the Vikings direct access from the Baltic into rivers that ran through France, Russia and Arab lands. Along the way they destroyed towns and property, burglarized cities and monasteries and threatened the security of most of the well-established kingdoms of the western world.

The Danish Vikings set their sights primarily on England and France, but areas of modern Germany and the Netherlands also have long and bloody records of the Norse onslaught. The monastery of St. Philibert, founded about 680 on Noirmoutier, an island in western France, was the target of one of the earliest attacks. Between the years 814 and 819, Vikings sailed on the Loire River to the Bay of Biscay, sacking the monastery repeatedly, eventually taking it over and turning it into a headquarters for their operations; they even wintered in the monastery, depriving the population of the ability to recover and regroup before the next invasion. Having a base at Noirmoutier also enabled the Vikings to pillage the Loire region repeatedly.[6]

The Vikings also sailed close to shore and up rivers, raiding and devastating the rich towns and monasteries of northern France. Dudo of St. Quentin, a French historian, describes in his *Gesta Normannorum* how pirates came from the island of Scania, which was surrounded by the ocean, and then spread out over the vast Danube River which, with its streams and passages, rose from the apex of Mount Adnoa: "With Mars' forewarning, raging warlike peoples inhabit those tortuous bends of extensive size, namely the Getae, also known as the Goths . . . who live by cultivating the Baltic marshes . . . thus do they pillage all the places which stand against them."[7]

As reported by Paschasius Radbertus, abbot of the monastery at Corbey, it was not believed possible that a force so barbaric would dare penetrate the inner reaches of the sophisticated and far-reaching Frankish Empire, attack and burn churches and monasteries along the beaches of the Seine, carry away countless treasures and prisoners, and succeed in so completely humiliating the population. Their arrogance appeared boundless, for after attacking with fire and sword, the Vikings had the audaciousness to negotiate a peace treaty in exchange for huge sums of silver, placing a cash value on every living being. After concluding the contract, the Vikings returned to their ships with the booty. At other times, they found it more profitable to take up residence in the region. In 843, according to the Annals of St. Bertin: "Pirates of the Northmen came to Nantes, killed the bishop and many of the clergy and laymen, both men and women, and pillaged the city. At length they arrived at a certain island, and carried materials thither from the mainland to build themselves houses; and they settled for the winter, as if that were to be their permanent dwelling-place."[8]

Around the year 820, the Vikings invaded and attacked northwestern France, the area today called Normandy.[9] They sailed up the Seine River and then proceeded to sack the region for several consecutive years. Dudo of St. Quentin recorded how the Danes "have savagely landed with Duke Anstign where Francia extensively spreads out its tracts . . . [Anstign] this accursed and headstrong, extremely cruel and harsh, destructive, troublesome, wild, ferocious, infamous . . . brash, conceited and lawless, death-dealing, rude . . . rebellious traitor and kindler of evil . . . double-faced hypocrite and ungodly, arrogant, seductive and foolhardy deceiver . . . more monstrous than all the rest . . . ought to be marked not by ink but by charcoal."[10]

The Viking Anstign, so severely portrayed by Dudo, defiled nations, profaned the priesthood, raged around the walls of the garrisons, "as does a wolf around the pens of sheep," and butchered all living creatures until France became a desert and the Normans were "dreaded like the hidden rumblings of bellowing thunder." The king of the Franks lacked the means to resist the pagan temerity and was forced to ally with the "viler-than-the-vilest" Anstign. He concluded that to commence a war against the pirates did not seem wise: "If you by chance go forth to contend with them, oh! either you will die or they, extremely swift, will return to their ships, having slipped away in flight."[11]

But Anstign was not the only pirate to make a memorable impression on the Frankish people. In 876, Rollo the Pirate invaded Normandy with his army and reigned there for fifty winters.[12] Rollo, a ruthless Viking leader and son of a mighty Norwegian earl, received Normandy in 911 by the Treaty of Saint Clair-sur-Epte from the Western Frankish King Charles III (or Charles the Simple). Because King Charles III could no longer hold back the Viking advance he struck a deal with the Norse pirate, who pledged allegiance to him and promised to protect his land against further raids. In return, Charles III was obliged to concede his defeat to Rollo and hand over to him the area of the lower Seine. The acquisition of Normandy was a valuable strategic gain for the Vikings because of its proximity to the English Channel. The treaty permitted the Vikings to establish a more permanent foothold in the area, facilitating easy access to the British Empire. The Franks were as perplexed as the British had been previously over how God could allow such misery to befall good Christians; they explained the evil and misfortunes they experienced as God's just punishment for their faithlessness, wickedness, filth and treason.

As already noted, most raids were not aimed at taking territory or defeating an enemy army. For the most part they were small in scale at this time, but two, which took place in 845, comprised some six hundred ships and stand out for their size.[13] One attack was on Hamburg by the Danish King Horik, and the other on Paris, believed to have been led by the Viking commander Ragnar Lodbrok.[14] Lack of resources left France unable to monitor and protect its coastline and entry into its two major rivers, the Seine and the Loire. Ragnar Lodbrok, one of the most renowned of all Vikings, who claimed to be a direct descendant of the pagan god Oden, forced Charles II, king of the Western Franks (also known as Charles the Bald, grandson of Charlemagne and father of the aforementioned Charles the Simple), to flee Paris and take refuge in the abbey of St. Denis, where he prayed to a number of saints for a resolution to the catastrophe.[15]

King Charles II's mistake was dividing his army into two detachments, one of which fell to the Vikings. After Ragnar Lodbrok hanged 111 prisoners in full view of the second detachment of the Frankish army, the French were forced to pay a handsome *danegeld,* a ransom of seven thousand pounds of silver, in exchange for stopping the raid and saving their land and people.[16] In 857 Paris fell again, this time to

Björn Ironside, son of Ragnar Lodbrok. Almost three decades later, in 885, a large fleet of seven hundred ships, "not counting those of smaller size which are commonly called barques," and an estimated forty thousand Viking warriors mounted the most terrible raid to date, laying Paris under siege for a full year: "At one stretch the Seine was lined with the vessels for more than two leagues, so that one might ask in astonishment in what cavern the river had been swallowed up, since it was not to be seen."[17]

The occupation of a major city for such a long period of time likely caused fatigue and starvation in the population. Sigfrid,[18] the "sea-king" (a king without territory), commanded the expedition, terrorizing the French with poisoned arrows, famine and other forms of pestilence that he threatened to repeat yearly. Arrows mixed with stones and hurled by slings filled the air; the blood flowed until King Charles the Fat admitted defeat and gave the Norsemen the area of Sens to plunder. He then gave them seven hundred pounds of silver on the condition that they leave France for their own country.[19]

After his victory in Paris in 845, Ragnar Lodbrok continued plundering churches and demolishing towns along all the major rivers and coasts of the Frankish Empire. As described by the monk Ermentarius of Noirmoutier a decade later: "The number of ships is growing . . . Everywhere the Christians are massacred, burned and pillaged . . . A countless fleet moves up the Seine . . . Paris, Beauvais and Meaux are captured . . . and all towns besieged."[20]

The successful attacks on the monasteries encouraged the Vikings, giving them more than a taste of their capability. Bordeaux was captured in 848, and in 850 a large Danish fleet plundered along the Rhine. More destruction followed along the Loire in 853, including pillage of the two most famous monasteries in Tours. According to the Annals of St. Bertin:

"The Danish pirates, making their way into the country eastward from the city of Nantes, arrived without opposition, November eighth, before Tours. This they burned, together with the church of St. Martin and the neighboring places."[21] The Norsemen raided the abbey of Marmoutier and killed 126 monks. Only twenty are said to have escaped the massacre and were sheltered by the canons of St. Martin.

In 855, the Vikings, leaving their ships behind, marched overland to the city of Poitiers, "but the Aquitaines came to meet them and defeated them, so that not more than three hundred escaped." In 856, they sailed into the Seine, plundering and ruining the towns along both riverbanks, continuing their destruction in the monasteries and villages farther inland, before taking up winter quarters on Jeufosse Island near the Seine.[22]

In 859, they entered the Rhone, pillaged many cities and monasteries, and established themselves on the island called Camargue. These great successes set the course for future attacks on Spain, Portugal and Italy, where they captured and plundered Pisa and other cities. During the next two centuries, the Vikings attacked France 214 times; Great Britain and Ireland, 94 times; Spain, 9 times; Portugal, Morocco, Italy and Turkey, 6 times; and the Germanic lands, including the Netherlands, Belgium and Luxemburg, 34 times.[23]

Weak opposition and the Vikings' residence in winter quarters at suitable locations further strengthened their resolve. Since they lived in the occupied regions where their victims needed all of their manpower and energy to defend themselves, the Vikings did not expect or fear retaliation against their home countries. In fact, if the occupation was to be lengthy, they were frequently joined by their families. In 872, the Vikings took possession of the Frankish town of Angers within raiding distance of Tours; deciding it was a nice place to spend the winter, they sent for their wives and children, an act that further humiliated the rulers of the western kingdom.[24]

The Vikings' decision to winter in conquered territory shamed the Christian population and created a miserable existence for the inhabitants. Because both England and France lacked sufficient forces to oppose the occupations, the Danes were able to establish their own small kingdoms within the larger kingdoms and impose their own laws, known as *danelaw*, on the peoples in the occupied regions. For example, the entire eastern part of England fell to the Norsemen's command, but the colonization of land was more afterthought than planned military strategy. After campaigning in a profitable region such as England or France for a long time, it seemed only natural to set up camp, rather than return home to the north every winter. The laws of the Danes were enforced until the besieged king agreed to pay a large ransom to buy his people's freedom from continued occupation, attack and raiding.

For the first half of the ninth century, the Vikings were concerned primarily with daring and profitable raids in the Frankish Empire, but they began a fresh new wave of campaigns around the English countryside. The first attacks on England had been sporadic plunders of the monasteries and coastline cities. After the great raid on Lindisfarne and the approximately forty years of peace that followed, the riches in England tempted the Vikings anew in 837. Norse marauders marched inland and moved on to Canterbury and London. Alderman Ethelheim fought a pirate force in Portland, forcing an initial retreat, but the Danes subsequently killed the alderman and became masters of the field. For the next century and a half, the English were subjected to Viking raids almost every year. The country was heavily plagued by the Norsemen's advance for a period stretching from the late eighth century into the early Middle Ages, eventually resulting in the conquest of the entire country.

In 854, the Norsemen wintered for the first time on the Isle of Shepey. In 865, a Viking army overran all of Kent eastward, and in 866, took up winter quarters in East Anglia where the inhabitants made peace with them and supplied them with horses because Alfred the Great, defender of England from Viking invasions, feared that England would fall completely under Danish dominion. This invasion, led by three sons of the legendary Viking commander Ragnar Lodbrok, may have been the brothers' attempt to avenge the death of their father. They moved on to capture York, killing both of the English rival kings on the spot. They overran the country and destroyed all of the monasteries along the way, burning and murdering abbots and monks and wreaking such havoc that the monasteries, once full of riches, were now reduced to unrecognizable rubble. The *Anglo-Saxon Chronicle* reports that Hingwar and Hubba, two more sons of Ragnar Lodbrok, killed King Edmund at Thetford in 870.[25]

After the pillage of the Abingdon Monastery in Berkshire, probably during the Danish invasion of Wessex in 871, a monk wrote: "O what misery and what grief! And who is there of so dull a head, so brazen a breast, and so hard a heart that he can hear of these things and not dissolve in tears!" In Ireland a Celtic chronicler said: "In a word, although there were a hundred hard steeled iron heads on one neck, and a one-hundred sharp, ready, cool, never-rusting, brazen tongues in each head, and an hundred garrulous, loud, unceasing voices from each tongue, they could not recount or narrate or enumerate or tell what all the Gaedhil [Irish] suffered in common, both men and women, laity and clergy, old and young, noble and ignoble, of hardship and of injuring and of oppression, in every house, from those valiant, wrathful, purely-pagan people."[26]

In 886, a peace treaty was drawn up between King Alfred the Great and the Vikings after Alfred had retaken control of London. The treaty stipulated in part that any slain man would be compensated for by eight half marks of pure gold, regardless of whether he were English or Danish. This gave a monetary value to a man's life.[27]

Despite their victories, the Vikings were not immune to defeat. In 845, at the mouth of the River Parret, a huge massacre took place and Alderman Eanwulf was victorious over them. In 851, "the heathens now for the first time remained over winter on the Isle of Thanet. The same year came three hundred fifty ships into the mouth of Thames; the crew of which went upon land, and stormed Canterbury and London."[28] As they marched southward over the Thames into Surrey, Ethelwulf and his son Ethelbald at the head of the West-Saxon army made the greatest slaughter of the Viking army that had ever been reported in England. A Danish force was forced to flee at Sandwich in Kent, losing nine of its ships.[29] In 853, there was another fight on the Isle of Thanet. Here, too, the English won, but many men on both sides drowned or were killed. In France, the Vikings suffered a horrendous defeat at the battle of Saucourt in 881, when Louis III won and as many as nine thousand Danes were killed. More often than not, however, the Norsemen came away victorious and frequently in possession of huge sums of *danegeld*.

A century later when Aethelred the Unready was king of England, a second great wave of Viking attacks began. First, St. Petroc's-stow was plundered and a great deal of damage was done all along the seacoast, both in Devonshire and Wales. The major Viking chiefs responsible for the plunder of Wales were Erik Bloodaxe, Turf-Einar (Einar Ragnvaldson, earl of Orkney), Olaf Trygvason and Sven Forkbeard. In 982, three pirate ships came to Dorsetshire and plundered in Portland, the same year London was burned. In 987, Watchet was ransacked. A few years later, Olaf Trygvason came with ninety-three ships (at approximately one hundred warriors per ship, this was a force of more than nine thousand men) to Staines, which he raided before moving on to Sandwich, Ipswich and Maldon. Following the sacking of Folkestone and the battle of Maldon in 991, more than ten thousand pounds of silver were paid as ransom for the Vikings to stop the attacks and leave the area. The slaughter and ransom money were eye-openers to the English people who realized that they had become complacent and that their own forces were severely lacking in strength. In Lindsey and Northumbria large counter-forces were summoned, but when it was time for the armies to engage, the English generals ran away and the "king ordered Elfgar, son of Alderman Elfric, to be punished with blindness."

The Nordic kings Olaf Trygvason and Sven Forkbeard,[30] learned a valuable lesson from the raids and used it to their advantage. When the victimized societies gave in to their demands, the Vikings understood that they could blackmail the countries. They learned that it was more profitable to collect *danegeld* with a minimum of bloodshed and return a few years later for more, rather than plunder and take all they could at the moment. It is estimated that over the course of the Viking Age, between a quarter and a half million pounds of silver were paid to the Vikings.

Following the siege of London in 994, Trygvason returned to Norway and secured for himself the Norwegian crown. Forkbeard went to Wales and the Isle of Man and for several more years continued plundering in England. After a few years respite the Norsemen raided and slaughtered in Cornwall, North-Wales, Devon and Watchet. The Vikings came away with enormous booty and were continuously victorious against the English armies whom they always managed to force to flee.

In 999, the Kentish army encountered the Vikings in a close engagement, but they, too, were forced to retreat. In the meantime, the Danes continued to advance, dominating the battlefield, capturing the enemy's horses and overrunning nearly all of West-Kent. The *Anglo-Saxon Chronicle* reports that the English king resolved to proceed against the Norse army both with land and sea forces, but delays enabled the Danes to retreat inland from the seacoast with the English in vain pursuit. The English people were physically and emotionally depleted, their resources worn thin, but the resolve of the Norse pirates intensified.

Attacks against the English nation occurred almost every year as the Vikings relentlessly pursued greater riches and spread terror among their subjects, burning, plundering and ravaging the country. No fleet or army could withstand the formidable strength of the Norse invaders who moved so fast that they advanced as far as the town of Alton in a single march. These were indeed difficult times for England.[31]

In 1002, King Aethelred was forced to pay off the Vikings with food and a tribute of 24,000 pounds of silver. In 1003, Sven Forkbeard plundered and burned, first in Wilton and then in Sarum, before returning to sea and sailing his fleet to Norwich, which he raided and burned. He then repeated his actions in Thetford three weeks later. In Thetford, Earl Ulfkytel met the enemy with his army and many men on both sides were killed. Sven Forkbeard next set his sights on the English throne, a goal he eventually achieved in 1013.

In 1006, following the great famine that had struck England the previous year, and during which time the Danes had returned home for a short respite, a huge fleet of Danes came over to England. According to Florence of Worcester, a twelfth-century English monk and chronicler, the fleet landed at the port of Sandwich and the Danes destroyed everything in their path and took a large booty. King Aethelred summoned his forces, but spent the autumn in a futile campaign against the Danes. When winter came, the Norsemen retired to the Isle of Wight where they fortified their supplies. In mid-winter, they marched to Wallingford which they destroyed entirely, carrying off meat and plunder over a fifty mile distance back to the sea.

Although Aethelred encouraged his people to stand firm against the invading Danes, his call had little effect and Vikings still ventured forth on English soil as they pleased. In the end there was not a chief that would fight against them and all the work that had been done to secure the peace seemed in vain. So great was the English nation's fear of its formidable foe that the only way its leaders could think of driving them away was with bribes of provisions and tribute. In 1007, the Vikings accepted the terms offered them, were provisioned throughout England and received a tribute payment of thirty thousand pounds of silver.

In 1010, the Vikings were warned of an army that had gathered against them in London, so instead of raiding the big city, they stayed in motion all winter, then landed in Kent in spring where they repaired their ships, after which they descended on Ipswich. The inhabitants fought, but the Danes won, provided themselves with horses, and spent three months plundering in East-Anglia, northeast of London, killing men and cattle and burning Thetford and Cambridge. In 1011, they attacked Canterbury and set fire to it.

According to Florence of Worcester, the Norsemen committed terrible atrocities, hurling people off the ramparts, hanging them by their private parts and dragging women by their hair through the streets. Christ's Church was burned, and nine out of every ten men, women and children were slain. Aelfhea, archbishop of Canterbury, was thrown into prison and badly treated for seven months, and the Danes demanded three thousand pounds from the bishop for his freedom. When he refused, Aelfhea was killed with an iron-axe to his head. Then, to the relief of the English, "the wrath of God" brought upon the Danes an excruciating disorder of the bowels that killed two thousand of them.[32] When spring of 1012 came, King Aethelred sent messengers to the Danes to ask for peace, as a result of which the Danes collected the enormous sum of 48,000 pounds of silver in tribute.[33]

In 1013, King Sven Forkbeard, accompanied by his son Knut, set out to seize the English throne. Lasting support that he still enjoyed from his people facilitated his mission. He came with his fleet to Sandwich, and soon after all the peoples of Northumbria, Lindsey, Five Boroughs, Oxford and Winchester submitted to him and allowed him to take hostages. But when he came to London, King Aethelred was residing within the city and the population refused to capitulate. Sven was therefore unwilling to waste his troops on further assaults on London and instead sailed on to Wallingford and Bath where the populations submitted and gave him hostages.

When the English nation, mostly out of fear, could no longer resist in the south or in the north, there was no other course of action for the people than to subjugate themselves to the Great Dane and Sven Forkbeard was finally considered full king of England. However, his dominion over his newly won kingdom was short-lived, for in 1014 he died suddenly, and after a power struggle was succeeded by his eighteen-year-old son, Knut the Great.[34] With the succession of Knut to the English throne, the Viking triumph was complete. A Danish king ruled in England and the Danes were masters of the English lands and seas.

The Vikings attacked the Irish and Scots just as viciously as they attacked the English, plundering shamelessly and inflicting unspeakable pain on the population. The Irish were devout Christians and the monasteries and churches built along the long coastline of their country were a great attraction to the Norse pirates. The Norwegians arrived first and plundered among the islands before moving on to the western coast of Ireland, building fortified towns along the eastern coast, as well as at Cork, Waterford, Wicklow and Dublin. The many rivers in Ireland made inland travel easy. Waterford was raided in 914, and in 920 a combined force of Danish and Norwegian Vikings captured Limerick with an "immensely great fleet, more wonderful than all the other fleets," manned chiefly by Danes and commanded by Thorir Helgason.[35]

In 1014, at the battle of Clontarf, the Irish won an impressive victory, but when all was said and done, an estimated seven thousand Vikings and four thousand Irish had fallen. The losses were overwhelming on both sides of the conflict and although the Irish triumphed, it was a battle that cost them dearly. In Scotland and Orkney, Thorfinn the Mighty, one of the more notable of the Viking chiefs, became the Earl of Orkney and recognized ruler of all of northern and western Scotland in the early eleventh century. The Vikings also invaded the Faroe Islands in an attempt to escape the contemptible King Harald Harfagre (Fairhair) of Norway, driving away the Irish who had already settled there.[36]

While sea piracy had existed for centuries prior to the Viking Age, it was the Vikings' ability to cover great distances that distinguished them from other pirates of the sea and which contributed to their success at warfare. They also had the courage and daring to sail beyond the horizon, making it impossible for the target of their attack to sight them and ready a defense. The small and swift fleets, which the Vikings sailed up and down the coasts from one town to the next, gave potential prey little warning of the attacks to come. Success depended on knowing the precise target in advance, followed by a quick and fierce attack. The unpredictability of their raids helped the Vikings to guard against traitors or others who might otherwise have figured out their war strategies. They attacked day or night and without warning, but generally did not sail in winter. During these quieter times their victims relaxed their vigilance, believing the assaults had ended, only to be surprised again in spring.

Although Viking raids could appear disorganized and undisciplined to the enemy, who described the invaders as swarming bees spreading in all directions, Viking teamwork was good, enabling them to avoid confusion onboard ship. Their success was due also to their ability to wage unconventional warfare. Viking war strategies can be compared to those of contemporary Special Forces soldiers in the western world. Special Forces attack in small units with specific objectives, as did the Vikings; Special Forces, as did the Vikings, make use of certain tactics not practicable by larger armies that lack, for example, maneuverability, flexibility, speed, surprise and good communication. The enemy was up against considerable difficulty in uncovering and learning the strategies behind the small and seemingly sporadic attacks. In the end, the primary reason for the limited number of ships in most Viking war parties probably had more to do with the fact that the Norsemen came from an unorganized territorial conglomerate lacking united leadership, rather than from extensive, advance planning. In other words, the Vikings used whatever means were available to them and in the process discovered the natural benefits of maneuverability and surprise. Their *modus operandi* was: get in, raid, get rich, get out.

Viking conquest was due also to the fact that they came from afar to raid a village or monastery; they took the battle to their opponents, making it difficult for the enemy to mount an effective counterattack. The north—Sweden, Norway, Denmark and, later, Iceland—was too distant and out of reach for foreign armies. The terrain was inhospitable and the weather unpredictable. The Northern lands were considered uncivilized by the standards of most other countries. The people were regarded as backward and developmentally behind the rest of Europe. The Vikings therefore had little to fear from foreign invaders and no need of a standing army at home.

Although geographical location, the superiority of their ships and the Vikings' insensitivity to the moral standards of Christianity contributed greatly to the successes of the raids, much of the Vikings' strength had its roots in their imaginative and creative thinking. While other sailors dared not venture beyond their own horizon, the Viking world encompassed far more than the barren lands of the north. Vikings traveled widely, not just as pirates, but also as explorers and traders, and came into contact with peoples of many continents and nations. Raids started in waters close to home, but when the Norsemen discovered the capabilities of their ships, they set out on longer journeys covering hundreds of miles, across entire oceans and previously (at least by Europeans) unexplored lands. The Vikings became founders of new nations, such as Iceland and Russia. They even served as mercenary soldiers and guards to the emperor of Constantinople in the Byzantine Empire.

Their language still lives in a number of Irish place names, for example, Dublin and Wexford.[37] *Harald Harfager's (Fairhair's) Saga* reports: "King Harald gave ships of war to Thorgils and Frode, with which they went westward on a Viking cruise, and plundered in Scotland, Ireland, and Bretland [British Isles]. They were the first of the Northmen who took Dublin." In 842 a fort was founded as a refuge and trading place in Dublin. Around the same time, the Vikings also wintered for the first time on that land. Guthorm Gunhildson, an advisor to King Harald Hardrade, had his winter quarters in Dublin, was a great friend of King Margad and felt that Ireland was for him a land of peace.

Through their travels, the Vikings learned a great deal about their opponents. Personal experiences, face-to-face meetings with foreigners and the goods and weapons they acquired in the raids taught them about the technology, values and mindset of their adversaries. This knowledge, along with skilled seamanship combined with land warfare, placed them at the forefront of other military organizations. The Vikings established themselves as a continual threat to European countries, conveying to their victims the important lesson that the security measures of the past were insufficient. No longer could personal safety be assured by refuge in a church or monastery.

No longer could troubles brewing in the distance be known in advance. No longer was there time to prepare a defense.

The Vikings owed the success of their raids both to the method of attack and the very attacks themselves, rather than to planning, technology or weaponry. The Vikings' determination, boldness and undisputed courage in attempting what nobody before them had dared, including the raiding of holy sites normally regarded as safe havens, ensured them their place in history. Even if the enemy was often weak and disorganized, the Vikings' warrior mindset, seamanship skills and combat tactics were clearly superior and highly developed for the times. Moreover, Viking leaders were generally not content to rest on their laurels, but pressed forward towards ever-greater glory. Originally a set of tribes, the names of the people of the north are still known today the world over. Through repeated and relentless assaults on prominent and rich empires, these heathen people from the poor and barren north managed to distinguish themselves as formidable and mysterious warriors.

> *True wisdom, said a Viking poet, comes to one who "has traveled far and knows the ways of the world."* [38]

Depiction of a much anticipated return of a Viking long-ship from a raiding journey in England. Model displayed at the Viking Museum in Birka, Sweden.

The longhouse was a barn-like building that served as home to the Viking family. Some of the wealthier farms had several buildings and a large longhouse that also functioned as a meeting hall for the planning of raids and the celebration of festivities, such as Yuletide, (winter solstice). Model displayed at the Viking Museum in Birka, Sweden.

Pottery was produced locally or was of foreign origin and imported, displayed here at the Viking Museum in Haithabu, a stronghold for the Vikings (also called Hedeby or Heidaby) near the Danish border in northern Germany. Haithabu, "the heath-settlement" or "village on the heath," was the largest city in northern Europe in the Viking Age and at its height had around one thousand residents.

*Containers of various kinds used for storing food and drink.
A cooking plate of clay-covered stone was used for preparing
meals. Meat was smoked above the cooking plate.* Displayed at
the Viking Museum in Haithabu in northern Germany.

CHAPTER 2

LIVE HARD, DIE WITH HONOR

*The lands of the north were arid, the weather
hostile and the people poor. The great treasures of
the world lured young men to take to the seas in
the hope of bringing home bounties of wealth.*

———

The Vikings did not fight for country or province, for ruling
power or territory, for the glory of a king or god, but for
personal glory, material wealth, adventure and freedom. They
had no ties to any religion, government or king. Their rise
had more to do with greed and an unbounded enthusiasm
for control of the seas than with political plans and ideas for
territorial expansion or domination of other peoples.[1] Most
Viking raids were undertaken purely for economic gain and
often to fulfill the needs and desires of the individual men in
the raiding party. Ownership of tangible goods translated into
buying and trading power, that in turn translated into prestige
and a better position in society.

The north encompassed a large landmass, but had little
to offer other European nations in the form of valuables.
The land was cold, barren and covered in places by thick forests and poor soil. The climate was harsher than in the rest
of Europe, creating for the people an existence that required
hard work and considerable expenditure of energy just to stay
alive. Although there were vast forests, wildlife and waters
containing an abundance of fish, natural resources were still

too scarce to support the population, believed to have numbered about two million and growing.[2]

Taking to the seas was by far the easier way to get ahead in a society which offered men a choice only between hard labor with little chance for advancement and leaving for other countries in the hope of finding riches and warmer climates. Dudo of St. Quentin, tenth-century historian and dean of St. Quentin in France who wrote about the Viking invasion of Normandy, observed that if the Norsemen had continued living in their own deficient lands, they would have had little to bestow upon their offspring. Poverty, he said, led to savage in-fighting until those who reached maturity were brought together "into the realms of foreign nations to obtain for themselves in battle realms whereby they might be able to live in never-ending peace, as did, for instance the Getae, Goths who pillaged almost all of Europe up to where they now reside."[3]

Raiding and trade were activities that were frequently combined. Norwegian King Olaf Haraldson sent the brothers Karle and Gunstein on a merchant journey to Bjarmaland, the northernmost part of Russia near the White Sea, but when they arrived, they held a seamen's council and decided to advance on land to pursue booty. Although piracy presented an opportunity to amass wealth quickly, a longing for adventure and a desire to see the world also contributed to the Norsemen's drive to go a-Viking, especially when neighbors returned home from their travels with gold and silver, spices and slaves, as well as fascinating tales of strange lands and peoples.

The Vikings were of mixed Scandinavian nationalities from the geographical land area that is today Sweden, Denmark, Norway and, later, Iceland. The region of Russia where the Vikings, mainly the Swedish ones, settled was called Gardarike, or the kingdom of towns. Vikings colonized Ireland, France, the Faroes, Greenland and Russia and also founded the dynasty that led to the establishment of the Russian state.

They sailed to America before Columbus, conquered all of England, attacked Constantinople, and took large parts of the East Baltic lands. The Swedish Vikings, or Svear, sailed mostly east over the Baltic Sea to Russia and the Arab world, down to Novgorod (Holmgard, the islet town) and Kiev (Konugard, the king's town) through the River Dnieper, which opened the way for further exploration and travel to Constantinople (Miklagard, the great town or city) via the Black Sea. Although the Svear went east mainly to trade, their needs tended to change along the way and they often ended up engaging in raids more or less by chance, or were asked to assist in the conflicts among rulers of other nations.

The Danish Vikings, or Danes, took a different route.[4] In the second decade of the ninth century, they sailed with fleets comprised of more than two hundred ships along the northern coast of the Netherlands, then on to England and France where they threatened to besiege those prosperous countries and then established themselves as filthy, uncivilized barbarians completely lacking in moral standards. The Danes' travels to the west were primarily plundering voyages and colonizing attempts. In 820, a fleet of thirteen ships ravaged, burnt houses and stole cattle in Flanders before heading for the mouth of the Seine.[5] The Danes frequently stopped off at Orkney on their way to or from England, plundering and taking provisions and cattle from the coasts. Laden with rich booty, the ships returned home to the north. Since their society lacked political organization and the financial backing of a central government that could step in and protect the people, the Danes reasoned that they could establish their reputation as formidable fighters not to be opposed and terrorize the enemy. It was good strategy on their part and it worked.

The Norwegian Vikings, or Norse, sailed to the Orkney, Faroe and Shetland Islands. They also participated in raids on Scotland and Ireland and engaged in the exploration of

Iceland, Greenland and the Americas. Although the need for additional land eventually led them to colonize lands elsewhere, many of the Vikings who went to Iceland and the other Atlantic islands did so to escape the contemptible King Harald Fairhair of Norway. The Norse settlement of Iceland came about largely as a result of Harald's wars on his own people. According to his saga: "In the discontent that King Harald seized on the lands of Norway, the out-countries of Iceland and the Farey Isles were discovered and peopled. The Northmen had also a great resort to Hjaltland (Shetland Isles) and many left Norway, flying the country on account of King Harald." Legend has it that Harald Fairhair swore not to cut his hair or beard until he had succeeded at uniting Norway under a single king, himself. He made this promise in order to secure Gyda, woman of his dreams and daughter of King Eirik of Hordaland. When Gyda learned of Harald's desire for her, she said to the messengers: "Now tell to King Harald these words. I will only agree to be his lawful wife upon the condition that he shall first, for my sake, subject to himself the whole of Norway, so that he may rule over that kingdom as freely and fully as King Eirik over the Swedish dominions, or King Gorm over Denmark; for only then, methinks, can he be called the king of a people." Harald answered: "I make this solemn vow, and take God to witness, who made me and rules over all things, that never shall I clip or comb my hair until I have subdued the whole of Norway, with scat [taxation], and duties, and domains; or if not, have died in the attempt."[6] Ten years later when King Harald succeeded in subjugating Norway, he finally succumbed to a bath and a haircut. Since his hair was rough and matted from years of being unkempt, Earl Ragnvald, who had been entrusted to rid the king of his cumbersome coiffure, gave him the more noble, distinguished name Fairhair, so that everyone who saw him would agree that his was the most beautiful and abundant head of hair.

When King Harald Fairhair achieved his goal of defeating the last of the local chieftains in about 872, he increased the taxes on the common folk, until many of them grew tired of the oppression and left for Iceland, Greenland and the Orkney and Shetland Islands. Although the king eventually subordinated those islands to his rule as well, he failed to impose his oppression on Iceland and Greenland where the populations were prepared to fight to the last drop of blood. For the future protection of his country, Harald created a military system called *Leidgangr*, which gave him the right to levy ships for war and required that each man supply him with weapons and armor proportionate to his individual wealth.

Harald Fairhair's favorite son Erik Blodyx (Bloodaxe), a brutal man with an iron will, inherited the Norwegian kingdom in 933.[7] When Erik Bloodaxe was only twelve years old, his father gave him five long-ships with which he traveled in the Baltic, then southward to Denmark, Friesland and Saxland (the Old Norse name for Germany), spending four years on this expedition. He also plundered and ransacked in Estonia and Sweden. He spent another four years plundering in Scotland, Bretland, Ireland and Valland, before sailing "north to Finmark, and all the way to Bjarmaland, where he fought many a battle, and won many a victory." Eventually Erik obtained the kingdom of Northumbria, but dissatisfaction with his own limited power, as compared to that which his father had enjoyed, led him to continue plundering throughout the British Isles. Like his father, Erik Bloodaxe had his mind set on becoming king of all Norway. Dynastic struggles ensued, ending with the burning of a house containing his brother Ragnvald and eighty other men.

The Vikings spoke a common Germanic language, Norse, resembling modern Icelandic, and spoken all over Scandinavia. The north, however, was sparsely inhabited by a scattered population and was not unified under a single king.

Instead, several smaller chieftaincies existed, each with a different ruler: "There were many chiefs in the land at that time. There was Trygve Olafson [father of the famous Norwegian hero King Olaf Trygvason] in the Eastland, Gudrod Bjornson in Vestfold, Sigurd earl of Hlader in the Throndhjem land . . ." When there were matters of importance to be discussed, the kings met at Konungahella (King's Rock) by the Gaut River near Viken in the area surrounding Oslofjord. Towards the end of the eleventh century, after assuring each other safe conduct to the meeting, King Magnus Barefoot of Norway, King Inge the Elder of Sweden and King Eirik Sveinson of Denmark got together at Konungahella to enact a treaty by which each king would possess the dominions his forefathers had held before him. It was also decided that King Magnus would marry King Inge's daughter Margaret. Since young women were not forced into marriage and had the right to agree to the terms, King Inge's daughter became known as a "peace-offering." As for the kings, the once greatest of enemies became the best of friends.

Viking society as a whole had little class structure. There was equality at home, and broadly speaking, free men and women were held to be equal under the law. Women controlled their own destiny. If a man failed to fulfill his duties to wife and home, his wife could divorce him and vice versa. In 1049, a man by the name of Hakon Ivarson promised that he would settle an argument with King Harald Hardrade of Norway if the king permitted him to marry his relative Ragnhild, daughter of King Magnus Olafson. But King Harald, conscious of the power women enjoyed, told Hakon that he must make his own arrangement with Ragnhild, "as to her accepting thee in marriage; for it would not be advisable for thee, or for any one, to marry Ragnhild without her consent." Likewise, when King Gorm of Denmark wanted to marry Thyra, daughter of Earl Harold, the earl said that his daughter was to decide for herself "because she is much wiser than I."

Common laws were established and debated at the *ting* (a court or general assembly) where all free men could speak.[8] Gods were thought to have created the laws and passed them on to the people who were responsible for enforcing them. Since there were no written documents, agreements were oral, confirmed by a handshake and witnesses of appropriate social standing. Kings, for their part, were obliged both to obey and enforce the laws and could not impose laws that people would be unable to understand or to which they were not accustomed. To prosper, a king had to be true to his word. Since the king's power depended on the will of the people, his control was limited. If the people disliked the king or felt he had betrayed the law, they could oppose him by force, dethrone or even kill him, and elevate someone else to the throne. In the end, there was no obligation to acknowledge the king, which could be problematical in the event the king called the masses to war and his command was ignored.

Although a king was obligated by his position to take responsibility for the well-being and protection of the people, several kings failed miserably at this, usually out of greed, rather than lack of courage. Olof, son of a king of the Old Uppsala tribe in Sweden, decided to clear forests by burning them down; the common folk found this an ill-conceived act, especially on the part of a king's son who should have known that forests served as protection against future famine. It was customary for the people to attribute both good and bad years to a king's behavior; when famine struck, kings were known to have been burned in their homes and offered as a sacrifice to the god Oden.[9] King Harald Fairhair was renowned for his sense of humor and good disposition, especially in his youth; he honored the elderly and was therefore much beloved by the people. But as he grew older, he became greedy and forced submission to his rule, instigating shiploads of his people to flee from Norway to Iceland.

The Vikings acted in their own self-interest and did not feel they had to obey a call of duty to a higher lord. Loyalty could not be obtained through force; it had to be earned and sometimes bought. A chieftain had to treat his people with dignity and fairness if he wanted their support; he had to be generous with gifts and money. A leader had to offer the people concrete benefits. King Olaf Haraldson (ruled 1015–1028) awarded Sigvat Skald, the court poet who recorded the main events and composed verses for the king, with a golden ring on every "branch" of his hand.[10] But although both the king and his half-brother Harald Hardrade were bold and courageous warriors, they were greedy for power and property and poor at winning over the people.

King Erik Edmundsson Väderhatt (Weather Hat, c. 849–c. 900) of Sweden was of a different stripe; he was friendly and frequently listened to those in need. His name originated as a result of his great luck with wind and weather. It was said that he had only to aim his hat in the direction he wanted the wind to blow—a boon and great help when favorable winds for sailing to England were required. King Harald Gille (ruled 1130–1136) was another pleasing monarch—cheerful and so generous that he spared his friends nothing. He willingly consulted his people and took their advice, thereby obtaining their favor and enjoying a good reputation. King Olaf Kyrre, who ruled in Norway from about 1067–1093, was well received by his people because of the bountiful harvests during his reign. Olaf was jolly and said he had reason to be glad when he saw that his subjects were free and happy, for "your freedom is my gladness."

When literacy became more widespread, King Magnus the Good, who reigned in Norway between 1035–1047, and in Denmark between 1042–1047, was urged to observe the laws his father had established. He composed a law book, *The Grey Goose*, whose title originated from the color of the parchment on which it was written. *The Grey Goose* was a model, even by today's standards, for social and economic protection; it covered the poor and illegitimate, construction of roads and bridges, policing of markets and sea havens, the equivalencies of weights and measures, inns for travelers, wages of servants and support for sick servants, protection of pregnant women and domestic animals from injury and the treatment of vagrants and beggars.[11] By observing these laws, the king made himself popular and beloved by the common folk and received the name "Magnus the Good."

People's adherence to the law was important to the overall well-being of the community and clear codes existed for the treatment of criminals. For example, according to the Frostathing law, one of the earliest Norwegian laws, "Whoever kills a man without cause shall forfeit property and legal protection. Wheresoever he be found let him be declared an outlaw for whom compensation can be accepted, either by king or kin."[12] To be punished as an "outlaw," or criminal, was one of the worst sentences a man could receive and was one commonly ordered for murder or "secret killings." If a man took the life of another, he was expected to step forward and admit his crime so that proper punishment could be administered, unless it were determined that he had acted justly. Killing another man could be justified only in cases of self-defense or defense of family, property or reputation.

If a man were declared an outlaw, he lost his right to all legal help and protection and anybody could kill him without risking punishment. Erik the Red (950–1000), one of the most famous outlaws, was exiled to Iceland in about 982 for three years and later to Greenland. Erik's son, Leif Eriksson, has been credited with discovering America, and Erik's daughter and Leif's half-sister, Freydis Eriksdottir, is cited in Norse sources as notable among female warriors, with more than twenty-five killings to her name. Rollo the Pirate, the tenth century brigand who conquered Normandy, was declared an outlaw for committing "*strandhugg*," or plundering for provisions, in his own land. Many considered this unusually harsh punishment for just a little raiding that was, after all, necessary to finance his successful campaigns abroad.

King Olaf Haraldson of Norway was known for protecting the country against plunderers. He was especially intolerant of thievery within the country "and no offer of money-penalties could help them," even if the thieves were the sons of powerful men or rich in gold from overseas marauding. Crimes committed against a countryman could be punished by hanging from raised gallows near the water, so that those who traveled by sea could see the offender. In the twelfth century, Bjarne the Bad was sentenced to death by hanging and he was said to have uttered dreadful profanities during his execution, but soon "swung high on the gallows-tree, a sight all good men loved to see." Drowning was another favored way of execution. A certain Erling Skakke bound the villain Frirek to an anchor and threw him overboard. In about 1134, when King Harald of Norway was battling with his own brother, King Magnus, and took two men prisoner, he gave them a choice: one would be hanged, the other thrown into a waterfall. The elder of the two chose the waterfall, as this was the more awful death.

When Asbjorn Selsbane murdered Thorer Sel in 1023 with such a hard blow to the neck that Sel's head fell onto the table in front of King Olaf Haraldson, punishment took a different course. The king grew enraged beyond all measure, especially when he learned that Asbjorn was sitting outside under guard and had not yet been put to death for the offense. By both law and custom it was considered evil and a form of cowardly murder to put a man to death at night, no matter how guilty he was. Thus Asbjorn was chained and locked up for the night. When the king, who had adopted Christianity, went to mass the next morning, he continued to be outraged and complained to his house guest, the Icelander Thorarin Nefiulfson: "Is not the sun high enough now in the heavens that your friend Asbjorn may be hanged?" As it turned out, the king spared Asbjorn's life in return for his promise to undertake the duties of the man he had killed and agree to become the king's slave.

The Vikings confirmed their friendships by oath. When nearly sixty men in King Harald Gille's court fell in battle in 1134, Harald fled east to his ships in Viken and then on to Denmark where he was well-received by King Erik because the two kings had sworn to be brothers to each other. These "sworn brotherhoods" were a common practice of the time, they created war bonds between families and bound men by oath to aid or avenge one another. Treason, or betrayal of another man's trust and well-being, was considered to be one of the worst crimes a man could commit. Earl Toste said of King Harold Godwinson who had offered him peace and dominion: "I would be his murderer if I betrayed him; and I would rather he should be my murderer than I his, if one of two be to die."[13] A man who had betrayed another and was apprehended was expected to accept his punishment with courage and to feel such shame for his crime that death would be preferable to public flogging or humiliation. But to show any fear of death was, of course, completely unacceptable. The law also stated that if a man even attempted to take the life of another, that attempt should cost him his life.

Punishment for lesser crimes was of lesser magnitude. It could entail cutting off the offender's highly prized beard; since a long beard was the fashion, this was indeed a shameful punishment. Beards kept faces warm in winter and were a sign of masculinity. Many men had names in honor of their beards: Gulskeg (Yellowbeard or Goldbeard), Kolskeg (Coal-beard or Blackbeard), Tveskeg (Twobeard or Forkbeard), Treskeg (Threebeard), Skeggjason (Skegge's son or son of

Beard), Skeg (Beard), Jarnskegge (Ironbeard) and Luseskeg (meaning either Lushbeard or the less flattering Lousebeard). The famous Sigtrygg Silkbeard, who was the leader of the Dublin Vikings, fought in the battle of Clontarf and went on to found Christ Church Cathedral in 1038 (or 1028, according to some sources).

Hair and beards were often featured in the descriptions of the appearance of great men. Earl Hakon was "the handsomest man that could be seen. He had long hair as fine as silk bound about his head with a gold ornament." The Swedish *lagman* (lawman, or one who communicates the law) Thorgny was fine-looking and stately in appearance, and had a beard so long that "it lay upon his knee, and was spread over his whole breast." The warrior Sigurd had hair that was of a red-gold hue and fell in long locks and a thick short beard. King Harald Hardrade was a handsome man of noble appearance with a short beard, long mustache, and one eyebrow somewhat higher than the other. And King Magnus Barefoot, a stout man in a short red cloak, was easily recognized by his bright yellow hair that fell over his shoulders like silk.

His beard's appearance was also a sign of a man's wealth. King Halfdan Svarte had a peculiar dream one night (dreams were commonly interpreted and believed to tell the future).[14] He dreamt that he had unusually thick hair which fell in long knotty curls around him, some so long they reached to the ground, others to his knees, hips or neck. The curls were of a dazzling color. Thorleif, a wise man who deciphered dreams, said it meant the king's dynasty would grow to considerable size and spread over many countries. A man's hair could even save his life. When the Jomsvikings were captured by the Norwegians in battle, their feet chained to a log while awaiting beheading, a handsome man in the group twisted his exceptionally long hair over his head, stretched his neck forward and said to the executioner: "Don't bloody my hair."[15]

The executioner's assistant thought this a reasonable request and held the man's hair away from his neck. But the moment the axe fell, the doomed man jerked his head so violently that the executioner's assistant stumbled forward and the axe severed both of his hands. This trick was so admired by the enemy leader Earl Erik that it won the condemned man and his fellow warriors their freedom.[16]

Despite the beard's importance to a man's appearance, the wise warrior also had to consider its nuisance value in battle because "when the wind is blowing the beard can easily whip up into the face and jeopardize sight at the exact time when it was necessary to counter the chop of an enemy's weapon, and, therefore, it is a good idea to wear the beard braided."[17] The name of the Danish king Sven Forkbeard derived from the way he wore his beard—in two braids. A mustache was called a lip beard and a woman, much as she might adore everything about her formidable Viking warrior, often did not care much for the smell of his beard.

The Vikings' moral code for a happy life was to maintain peace with kin, defend the family honor and hope for a fair amount of luck. Defamation was one of the greatest threats to happiness. An insult against an individual was taken as an insult against the entire family and obligated the family to avenge the crime or live in disgrace, although many years might pass before a wronged man found the opportune moment to right the situation. A besmirched reputation was not easily forgotten, and the perpetrator faced the possibility of an agonizing death for the rest of his life. He could, if he were smart, choose to pay *wergild* (a sum of money) to the victimized family as compensation for his crimes. Asmund, a lawless individual, began to plunder both at home and abroad as soon as he reached maturity. Tired by his acts, the people complained to their king who advised them to go to Hakon Ivarson, the king's land-defense officer. Hakon went in search of Asmund and boarded his ship; in 1065 a horrific fight ensued, in which Hakon cut off Asmund's head and presented it to the king at the dinner table. The incident so upset the king that he ordered Hakon to leave his service immediately. "Tell him I will do him no harm," the king said to his messengers, "but I cannot keep watch over all our relations." The king's remark demonstrated the strength of family ties and the duty every man had to avenge crimes.

The bonds between families were strong because they were the only ones that united people. There was no church, no government or state with defined boundaries and no organized military or defense to unify them. Villages were small and scattered, making it necessary for families to stick together and assist each other. The Nordic countries, especially Sweden, were isolated and had few roads. For the population, it was a matter of survival in a harsh world, so in between voyages family came first. The family was so important that people were often named after a common ancestor, for example, the Skjölding dynasty after the ancestor Skjöld, or the Yngling dynasty after the ancestor Yngve. To bear the family name was an honor; Yngve's descendents, for instance, have since been known by the name Ynglingar.

Hospitality toward strangers was a feature of Viking life. Travelers were frequently offered a night's safe haven in the form of room and board. A woman by the name of Langholts-Thora was said to always have a dinner table ready for hungry travelers.[18] According to Ibn Rustah, a Persian explorer, the Vikings had "a most friendly attitude towards foreigners and strangers who seek refuge. However, they don't allow any visitor to insult or harm them in any way."[19]

Courage, strength and loyalty towards kin were the Vikings' strong ideals. They were ready to defend their family's reputation to the last drop of blood and ". . . win from the brave and honored name, and die amidst an endless fame." As stated in an old Viking poem: "Cattle die, families die, you too shall die; but a good reputation never dies, nor a good name."[20] Rune inscriptions further reinforced the value of family and the pride the Vikings felt at having served honorably in battle. In 1036, a large fleet of approximately thirty ships set sail from the Lake Mälaren harbor in Sweden. This was one of the last and largest Viking expeditions to the east and was carried out under the leadership of Ingvar den Vittfarne ("he who traveled widely"). The expedition made a daring voyage down the Volga, fighting battles on the way until it reached Särkland (the land of the Saracens) where Ingvar and his brother Harald met their unfortunate deaths in 1041. Ingvar was twenty-five at the time and only a few survivors returned home to deliver the sorrowful news to his family and the rest of the community. Approximately thirty stones were erected to honor the dead of the Ingvar expedition. "Tola let raise this stone after her son Harald, Ingvar's brother," says the stone at Gripsholms Slott near Lake Mälaren. "They traveled far to find gold and in the east they gave the eagle food. They died in the south in Särkland."[21]

According to the Georgian *Kartlis Tsovreba Chronicle*, the expedition, which encompassed three thousand men, reached Bashi, Georgia, near the River Rioni along the Caspian Sea. Some seven hundred men are said to have allied themselves with the king of Georgia and continued further inland to battle the king's enemies. Still the Vikings' primary aim was the acquisition of material wealth. Their strategy was to fight opponents who could easily be defeated and avoid offering a large fleet to foreign kings. Most successful raids were carried out in groups of three to six ships; a party of thirty or more ships was considered an exception.

All peoples have a need to be remembered in death and runes were the Vikings' vehicle for posterity. Although few in words, they are the most lasting written expressions from the Viking Age. Runes were often cut in memory of a family member, usually a father, brother or son who had gone on a raid and met his death. A stone by Fresta Kyrka near Stockholm, Sweden, says: "Gunnar and Sassur let raise this stone after Gerbjörn, their father, son of Vitkarl in Svalnäs. He was killed by the Norsemen on Åsbjörns knarr [ship]."[22] A stone in Edsvära in Västergötland in Sweden says: "Tola let raise this stone after Ger, her son, a very good young man. He died a-Viking in the west."[23] Most runic inscriptions, however, were carved to commemorate a mother or father who had died an uneventful death at home and provide little information aside from mention of the person for whom and by whom the stone was raised.

Some stones were raised by and for living persons, perhaps to draw attention to their personal wealth, courage and daring explorations of other lands. The stone by Eds Kyrka just north of Stockholm, Sweden, reads: "Ragnvald let carve these runes. He was in Greece. He was the chief of the warrior people." Ragnvald might have been a chief in the Varangian Guard, which was comprised of mercenary Norsemen loyal to the emperor of Constantinople. The Viking Jarlabanke in Täby, Sweden, carved in his own honor five stones, all carrying the same message: "Jarlabanke let raise these stones in his own honor while he lived. And he built this bridge for his soul, and alone he owned all of Täby. God help his soul."

Rune stones, usually carved out of hard granite, were supposed to last for eternity. They were often displayed near well-traveled roads and remain legible to this day. The Vikings understood the durability and value of these monuments and it has been estimated that it took a month to carve a rune stone using a sixteen-character alphabet.[24] Through a good name and great deeds, an individual could continue to live in esteem for generations to come, regardless of what the afterlife might bring. The opportunity to boast, as it were, on a piece of rock that had lasting value over time probably seemed more important than possessing land or riches.

Although the people of the Viking Age had communication needs similar to those of today's world, they also understood that some carvings simply were not appropriate for display. In the harbor in Bergen, Norway, hundreds of rune-inscribed sticks and bones have recently been uncovered. These smaller, graffiti-like pieces were probably not intended to withstand the effects of decay over time, but have miraculously survived. Some are obscene, out of place along a well-traveled road, with messages such as: "May I more often come in close contact with the beer house," and "Smed fucked Vigdis. She who belongs to the Sländeben people."[25]

Since the Vikings were generally illiterate, most accounts of their lives were taken down by Christian and Arab chroniclers. Viking society was comprised mainly of farmers, craftsmen and traders, but the warriors, through their extensive travels, came into contact with peoples of different lands. Ibn Fadlan, an Arab diplomat, writer and one of the best sources of information regarding Vikings in the Arab world, experienced Viking culture around the year 921 while traveling in a caravan from Baghdad to Bulghar. Since the Arabs were not concerned with religious conversion of the barbarians, a more peaceful exchange between them and the Norse could take place. Ibn Fadlan described the practices of the Vikings, perhaps with both disgust and awe: ". . . a man will have sexual intercourse with his slave girl while his companion looks on. Sometimes whole groups will come together in this fashion, each in the presence of others. A merchant who arrives to buy a slave girl from them may have to wait and look on while a Rus completes the act of intercourse with a slave girl."

The pale-skinned, blond, or worse, red-haired, uncivilized savages with large unkempt beards no doubt made an impression on travelers from Arab lands. In a less than flattering description, Ibn Fadlan finds the Vikings the filthiest and most disgusting of God's creatures: "They have no modesty in defecation and urination, nor do they wash after pollution from orgasm, nor do they wash their hands after eating. Thus they are like wild asses. Every day they must wash their faces and heads and this they do in the dirtiest and filthiest fashion possible: to wit, every morning a girl servant brings a great basin of water; she offers this to her master and he washes his hands and face and his hair—he washes it and combs it out with a comb in the water; then he blows his nose and spits into the basin. When he has finished, the servant carries the basin to the next person, who does likewise. She carries the basin thus to all the household in turn, and each blows his nose, spits, and washes his face and hair in it."

Since the chroniclers were most likely influenced by their own lives and circumstances, their emotions when coming into contact with the Nordic warriors must have been profound: "I have seen the Rus as they came on their merchant journeys and encamped by the Volga," recorded Ibn Fadlan in a contradictory statement. "I have never seen more perfect physical specimens, tall as date palms, blond and ruddy; they wear neither tunics nor caftans, but the men wear a garment which covers one side of the body and leaves a hand free."[26] The garment was the Norse rectangular cloak, pinned at the right shoulder, leaving the sword hand free to draw the sword worn on the left side, without risk of entangling hand and sword in the cloak.[27]

Going a-Viking was a great honor, an opportunity that would ensure a man a better place in the afterlife. Lacking centralized leadership, Nordic countries had little development of and support for a professional military organization (despite Harald Fairhair's creation of its forerunner, the *Leidgangr*). Raids were likely to start with a few local leaders, so the men who took to the seas had to maintain themselves with no hope of reinforcement from a king at home. The Vikings serving in the Byzantine Empire as guards to the emperor were the exception and probably come closest to today's professional soldiers. More commonly they arrived unannounced, took whatever they could and left in a hurry. At other times, as already noted, they negotiated large payments in *danegeld* in return for leaving the region.

Despite their brutal reputation, Vikings did not raid for pleasure alone. From the Viking perspective, to go a-Viking was an honor, undertaken by courageous warriors, not pirates. Their barbarism and the bloodshed of the raids came about as a result of battle, rather than preplanned strategy. Actual battle required face-to-face combat and a clash of men's spirits. Vikings lived hard and had the power and ambition to venture where others dared not. Through their voyages they established a sophisticated communication network with many peoples. Although the warrior's end objective in both thieving and raiding involved taking what did not rightfully belong to him, there was a clear distinction between the two. Theft or stealing from a neighbor was an act of cowardice, an unforgivable crime, while raiding a monastery abroad for booty was a heroic act that occupied the dreams of many young men, but was undertaken only by the best warriors. In other words, when a man fought bravely and won, he could justly take whatever he wanted from the losing party and would be admired and praised upon his return home. Battle gave a man an opportunity to prove his worth, build a reputation and walk away a hero, even if it ultimately meant death.

Almost all grave finds from the Viking Age include weapons such as swords, axes and spears, illustrating how important it was to live and die like a warrior. Hakon the Good's saga reports that when he died: "His friends removed his body to Saeheim, in North Hordaland, and made a great mound, in which they laid the king in full armor and in his best clothes." Viking leaders always took the front position in battle, so few lived to advanced age or died a natural death. For a warrior, no fate could be worse than to die in bed of old age. Of sixteen Norwegian kings, only two died in bed. The rest either fell in battle, were murdered, forced out of their country or died accidentally or naturally in office.[28]

The Norsemen who chose plundering did so out of their own free will, motivated to fight from a feeling of pride. This was a powerful incentive, often lacking in conscript armies, and contributed to the Vikings' reputation as powerful, dangerous and courageous warriors. Honor was acquired through bravery in battle, composure in the face of threat and fair play at home. When a threat was real and immediate, it was useless to show fear; better to uphold self-respect by maintaining composure and behaving as honorably as possible.

King Sverri of Norway (reigned 1184–1202), realizing that his troops were facing overwhelming odds, told them that a choice between two ways was sufficient—one was to attain victory, the other to die with honor:

> "Hear what a yeoman said who went with his son to the warships and gave him advice, bidding him be bold and hardy in perils. 'If you were engaged in a battle and knew beforehand that you were bound to fall, how would you act?' And the son answered 'What good would it be to forbear smiting right and left?' 'And now,' said the yeoman, 'if some one knew and told you of a truth that you would not fall in the battle?' The son answered, 'What good would it be to refrain from pressing forward to the utmost?' 'One of two things will happen,' said the father: 'in every battle where you are present, either you will fall or you will come forth alive. Be valiant, therefore, since all is determined beforehand. Nought may send a man to his

grave if his time is not come; and if he is doomed to die, nought may save him. To die in flight is the worst death of all."[29]

The Nordic countries often squabbled among themselves and the Vikings frequently ended up battling each other in the sharpest of conflicts, "for they are Norsemen like ourselves." This was said by King Olaf Trygvason upon meeting Earl Erik Hakonson, an ally of Sven Forkbeard, who had been placed in charge of Norway. Rebellions on home territory and between the Nordic countries were frequent and the Norsemen were attacked with repeated regularity, but hardly ever by non-Norsemen. The risk of a Viking death was far greater by a Norseman than by a foreign power. Olaf the Thick (Olaf Haraldson of Norway) and the Swedish king Olof Skötkonung quarreled about boundaries. Although the two kings were brothers-in-law, neither was willing to give up any of the dominions each thought to be rightfully his.[30] In 1030, after having lived in exile for some time, Olaf Haraldson resolved to go into Norway to reclaim the kingdom he felt had been taken from him and asked the then Swedish king Onund for assistance. But Onund said that the Swedes were little inclined to make such an expedition against Norway, because:

> **"*T*he Northmen are rough and warlike, and it is dangerous to carry hostilities to their doors."**

At the end of the tenth century, battles were fought in the Schleswig area, the most northern part of modern Germany. The Skarthi Stone displayed at the Viking Museum in Haithabu, founded by the Danish King Godfred in 808, near the Danish border in northern Germany, reads: "King Sven erected this stone in memory of Skarthi, his loyal follower, who had been in the West but then met his death near Haithabu." Sven was the Danish king Sven Forkbeard and "the West" refers in all likelihood to a raid on England.

Carved pottery displayed at the Viking Museum in Haithabu, northern Germany. The hooked cross or swastika-like symbol in the center of the pot is several thousand years old and has also been found on artifacts from ancient Chinese, Japanese and Indian cultures. The swastika symbolized Thor, the god of thunder, and represented favorable circumstances and was originally a sign of good luck and well-being. The swastika's positive connotations changed in the twentieth century after Adolf Hitler adopted it as a symbol for his Nazi Germany. Hitler also appropriated other Viking symbols; one was the Odal Rune, associated with wealth and prosperity and signifying the ancestral home, kinship and inherited lands belonging to a family, or the bloodline of an individual or tribe.

Runic graffiti on a piece of wood that reads: "A moderately wise person." Displayed at the Viking Ship Museum in Oslo, Norway.

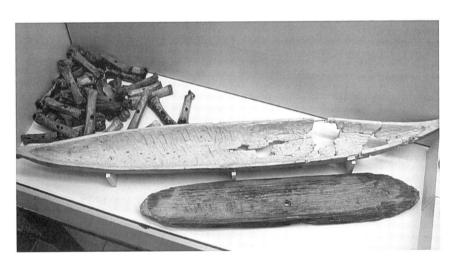

Young boys were given toys such as ships or wooden swords to play with in preparation for a possible life as a warrior. The small bones are from sheep and goats and could have been pieces used in a dice game. Displayed at the Viking Museum in Haithabu, northern Germany.

*Pendants of Thor's hammer (above) and a collection of Chris-
tian crosses (below). These amulets gave a warrior strength and
luck and protected him against evil powers. Many hammer pendants were made of iron. The one on the far right (above) is
made of amber.* Displayed at the Viking Museum in Haithabu, northern
Germany.

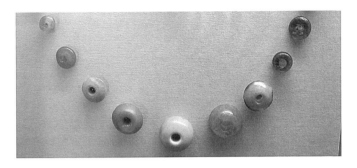

Amber, the fossilized resin of ancient trees found mainly around the Baltic Sea, was used extensively by the Vikings and traded in the form of jewelry for silver, gold, spices, silk and even slaves. It was also used to make game pieces. The peninsula north of Königsberg in East Prussia was considered the "Amber Coast." Displayed at the Viking Museum in Haithabu, northern Germany.

This stone pictures the symbol of the wheel and its importance in Viking life. The wheel signified the changing of the seasons, the rebirth of life at midwinter and the cycle of creation and death. When the wheel turned a full cycle, a new one began. At the winter solstice, death and rebirth became one. Displayed at the Museum of History in Stockholm, Sweden.

Prominent men were buried with their ships, though burning was usually the preferred way to dispose of the dead. This burial chamber, tent-shaped to imitate the tents pitched by men on shore for the night (although most slept in the open), is part of the Gokstad ship find from Norway. The burial chamber was built behind the mast. Displayed at the Viking Ship Museum in Oslo, Norway.

Gold carving of Yggdrasil, the tree of life. Displayed at the Museum of History.

King Harald Hardrade sent from Norway
to Iceland a bell for the church for which
Olaf Haraldson (the Saint) had earlier
sent timbers and which was built on the
Thing-plain. A similar church bell is displayed at the Viking Museum in Haithabu,
northern Germany, an indication of the
role of Christianity in the Viking Age.
A church was built in Haithabu in 850.
Christians used bells as protection against
pagan spirits. This bell may have been
part of a shipment of stolen goods from
Stockholm, Sweden.

Wood carving of a head from a wagon found in Oseberg, Norway. The wagon was most likely used for ceremonial purposes, as roads in the Nordic countries were scarce and difficult to travel. Displayed at the Viking Ship Museum in Oslo, Norway.

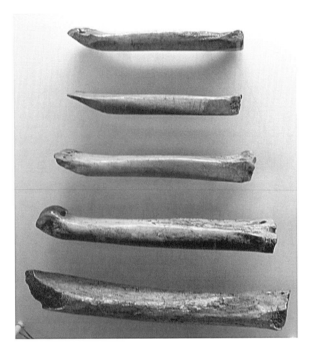

Antlers and bones were used to make tools such as needles, and grooming and musical instruments such as combs and flutes. The Vikings who lived near the water used these bones for ice-skating, binding them to the foot with straps; a stick was used to push off against the ice. Sometimes runes were carved in bone. Displayed at the Viking Museum in Haithabu, northern Germany.

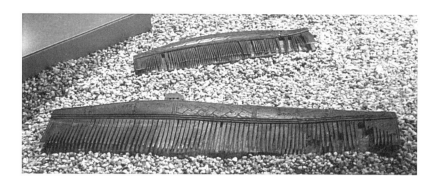

Combs made of bone or the hard antlers from elk or reindeer. The combs were decorated with patterns and the teeth were hand-sawn, one at a time. *Displayed at the Viking Ship Museum in Oslo, Norway.*

Women's and men's clothing as it might have looked in the Viking Age. Clothes were made of various weaves and were multi-colored and artistic in design. King Magnus Barefoot brought back clothing with him from the West, including short tunics and over-cloaks. Discarded garments were used to make paintbrushes, or were dipped in tar and stuffed between the planks on the ship as water sealants. *Displayed at the Museum of History in Stockholm, Sweden.*

Soft shoe made of calf hide (above), displayed at the Viking Ship Museum in Oslo, Norway. Leather was also used to make ropes, straps, pouches and knife sheaths (below), displayed at the Viking Museum in Haithabu, northern Germany.

CHAPTER 3

GOING A-VIKING

Many a young man would stand on the beach and look out to sea, dreaming of mastering the fury of the vast rumbling waters. The sea was the gateway to the world and he knew that if he could conquer the sea, he could conquer anything.

﹏

Sitting at home comfortably by the fire with family gathered around, holding a jug of beer in one hand and a slab of meat in the other was an experience no man wanted to miss. But to have the whole world to plunder and be able to journey several hundred miles across rough seas—what could be a better cure for old age and sorrow?

With little to do during the long winter months, the men would sit in the longhouse dreaming up adventures, and become restless and unruly. When they tired of the routine at home, they rigged out the ship, and as soon as the ice began to melt in spring, embarked on a journey to England or Ireland. Fierce warriors came out of the harsh north, men unaccustomed to luxury who had not grown soft from living in pleasant climates—fearless men itching to take the fight wherever the greatest riches were to be found.

Piracy seemed like a normal activity in an already violent world and was compatible with the religious beliefs of the times. Raiding increased the Norsemen's material wealth and helped to familiarize them with the availability of waterways for travel through Europe and the goods and weapons of other cultures. Vikings in droves challenged the perilous rivers of Russia, sailing all the way to Constantinople, capital of the Byzantine Empire and most splendid of cities. The first Norsemen to try these waterways were probably explorers, but information spread quickly and generations of formidable warriors soon followed in the tracks of the men who had preceded them.

Travel also exposed the Vikings to the political power struggles of European kingdoms. If blessed with strength and a strong constitution, the sons of Viking kings began to sail their fleets as soon as they were mature enough to fight, often about the age of twelve.[1] In the ninth century, Sigurd Hjort, king in Ringerike, a Norwegian province, was a good-looking twelve-year-old when he killed in single combat the berserk Hildebrand and eleven of his comrades. In 1049, Hakon Ivarson, a relation of Hakon the Great, distinguished himself in Norway and was sent very young on campaigns "where he acquired great honor and consideration, and became afterwards one of the most celebrated men." Olaf Haraldson, born in 995, embarked on a cruise in 1007, also at the young age of twelve, spent one summer and three winters in England, two summers and one winter in France, one winter in Normandy, returned home as king of Norway in 1025, was ousted from the country, killed and granted sainthood in death. Vagn Akesson, grandson of Palnatoke, leader and founder of the Jomsvikings, claiming he was as good in battle as any man eighteen or older, proved it when at the age of twelve he applied for admission to the elite fort of Jomsborg. Going a-Viking provided the younger generation with an opportunity for an education. To the old-timers not yet ready to settle down at home with family it was an opportunity to prove one more time their strength and worth.

The lands of the north, covered with forests, swamps and mountain ranges (especially Norway, though Sweden had vaster territories), were difficult to cultivate. Sigvat Skald reports it was "a hundred miles, and tree and sky were all that met the weary eye." Distances were frequently measured in time rather than in space. "Northward of the Black Sea lies Swithiod [Sweden] the Great, or the Cold . . . The northern part of Swithiod lies uninhabited on account of frost and cold . . . it is a journey of many days to cross them [the great uninhabited forests]." Norway and Sweden, the two most extensive kingdoms of the north, were practically unknown to the outside world. The mountainous and infertile lands of Norway extended farther north than any other land. "Norway could scarcely be crossed in a month while Sweden was not easy to get over in two," wrote Adam of Bremen, an eleventh-century cleric who befriended the Danish king Svein Ulfson.[2] Travel or movement of goods by land, legitimately acquired or pirated, was inefficient and simply too cumbersome to be practicable. The ship as a means of transport grew out of these harsh circumstances.

For the population in a cruel world, life demanded knowledge and an ability for self-defense. Norsemen were generally courageous and skilled at warfare both on land and sea, known for not retreating in battle and for fearing nothing, not even death. Although the image of the Vikings as brutal warriors is only part of the picture of Viking society as a whole, it is one that survives through the written records of those who experienced Viking barbarism and bloodshed. It is estimated that only 2 to 3 percent of the men embarked on sea voyages. Most of the Nordic population was illiterate. Only a small percentage of people were pirates and travelers, responsible for most of what is known about the Vikings' appearance, lifestyle and battle tactics. European kingdoms were politically split, had weak leadership, and were fraught with in-fighting. Internal squabbles undermined their ability to draw upon their resources and mount forces strong enough to counter attacks from the sea. The lands that endured the greatest sufferings under Viking raids may have been accustomed to war, but they were unprepared for the frequency and ruthlessness of the attacks and the Norsemen's unconventional war strategies. Although the Vikings were also explorers who founded towns in England, Ireland, Scotland and Russia, it is fair to say that they ransacked more than they discovered.

Because of warm summer temperatures, spring was a popular season to ready the ship and the crew for raiding. Winds were favorable in spring, blowing westward toward England and then favorable in the fall blowing eastward to assist in the return and bring the men home in time for harvest. Late fall was devoted to hunting. In winter, ships and weapons were repaired and plans made for the coming spring raids. The ships were pulled up on rollers and stored in boathouses by the water. King Eystein of Norway (ruled 1130–1136) used the best material to make large, heavily timbered dry-docks for his ships.

Some Vikings went on raids every year, others every few years. Fin Arnason "had been for some summers on a Viking cruise in the West sea," and Eyvind Urarhorn, an important man of high birth, went out on a Viking cruise every summer, "sometimes to the West sea, sometimes to the Baltic, sometimes to the Flanders. . . ." The great warrior-king Erik Edmundsson, Weather Hat of Sweden, went out in his warships every summer, subjugating parts of Finland and Estonia to his rule and forcing them to pay him taxes. In the twelfth century, Svein Asleifarson, who had settled in Orkney, would winter at home and entertain eighty men at his own expense. In spring he was occupied with planting crops. When this was done, he went off on what he called his spring expedition, plundering in the Hebrides and Ireland and returning home just after midsummer. He remained at home until the cornfields had been reaped and the grain was safely in, after which he set off once again on what he called his autumn expedition, returning only after the first month of winter.

Others were not concerned by winter and ice. While Magnus, son of King Harald Hardrade, set sail as soon as the ice was broken in the bay, Harald Hardrade himself spent nights on his ship, waking up one morning to find the ice so thick he was able to walk around the vessels. When he ordered his men to cut the ice, they chopped away like madmen. Those who hated this hard work found other solutions. King Eystein up in the fjord at Olso had his ships pulled for two miles over the frozen sea, "for there was much ice at that time in Viken."

A typical war party consisted of three to six ships with twenty to forty warriors per ship. Some parties grew in size along the way. When Gunnar and Kolskegg set out for abroad, they "went to the bay, took with them two ships and fitted them out thence." They sailed to one of the warrior's kinsmen, who "was a fine brave fellow . . . sure to get us some more strength for the voyage," and were able to add "two long-ships, one with twenty and the other with thirty seats for rowers." Fighting in such small parties gave them the ability to surprise. The narrow profile of the long-ships or *dragons*, as they were called, made them superior to other ocean-going vessels, rendering them extraordinarily fast and easy to maneuver both forward and backward with no need to turn the ship completely around to reverse direction. If pirates met a strong defense, they could simply go back out to sea.

Men followed leaders of their choosing and kings became kings over dominions freely granted them by the people.[3] Living under the rule of a small chieftain, rather than an important one, gave a man more freedom to pursue his own ambitions. Although the lack of a nationally sanctioned army and fleet had drawbacks, small self-ruled battle groups had greater maneuverability and the ability to pick only those battles they truly wanted to fight. Lack of motivation, mutiny or cowardice in battle did not occur among men not confined to a specific geographical location or bound to a particular king. Fighting for gain that was more personal than unifying a country or taking territory fortified the Viking spirit. But a warrior whose basic needs were ignored, who loathed his commanders and whose spirit was not nourished risked losing his mental focus and began to long for home. While threat to a warrior's spirit surely poses one of the greatest obstacles to victory, this threat was seldom faced by the Vikings who owed allegiance only to themselves.[4] Individualism, ambition and nonconformity were encouraged and fostered. Every warrior had the opportunity to come home rich, whether his wealth was measured in tangible goods, prestige or personal satisfaction such as adventure, freedom and self-rule.

A leader's quality was determined in part by his willingness to contribute to his crew's well-being. The king, either a real one who owned territory or a self-proclaimed "sea-king" in charge of a specific campaign, was expected to care for his men as he cared for himself, and to show leadership. He was responsible for keeping his men united in thought and action, for drawing strength and taking advice from the wisest among them who suggested raiding targets. In return, warriors stayed loyal to their leader and fought ferociously on his behalf. Although a king sought glory and wealth for himself, he shared his good fortune to attract a loyal following. The tenth-century King Hakon of Norway was the warrior's friend according to the skald Eyvind, and freely dispersed a "ransom of ruddy gold" to all bold men who had stood "against the arrow-storm."

To fight in a storm of singing arrows and ringing mailcoats, to win or die, was Oden's law. Norse gods were role models for warriors; their invincibility inspired them to fight well. Oden, the god of slain warriors, was the wisest and most valued of all, trusted by friends and dreaded by enemies. He had conquered many kingdoms and was truly a deity to emulate: "When sitting among his friends his countenance was so beautiful and dignified, that the spirits of all were exhilarated by it, but when he was in war, he appeared dreadful to his foes." Oden was said to "quench fire, still the ocean in tempest, and turn the wind to any quarter he pleased" with words alone. While Oden gave them wisdom for the battle, Thor, god of war, gave them power and fury, the will to fight until the bitter end, even if in vain. The Vikings were inspired by asa-gods whose feats they emulated, helping them to overcome hesitancy, to attack with fierceness and the reckless intensity for which they became famous. Their philosophy did not allow them to compromise pride in return for a long life. If peace lasted too long, a prominent man could begin to worry that he would die ignominiously of old age, rather than in the honor of battle, although men who outlived their military campaigns frequently died of illnesses such as ringworm and tuberculosis before the relatively (by today's standards) young age of forty.

A warrior, led by a good chief, confident that he was pleasing Oden and already practicing for Ragnarök, the final battle against the giants, became imbued with a focus and purpose so intense that he went forth with heart and soul immersed in the mission. A leader had to be unafraid to lead, reject cowardice, honor courage, proceed in battle with a singleness of purpose and emerge victorious.[5] When he was in the Varangian Guard, King Harald Hardrade distinguished himself by his wisdom and resourcefulness and fought fiercely to be victorious or to die. He had only one rule in battle: Success is half courage. "We shall rather all take the resolution to die with honor, or to gain England by a victory," said Earl Toste of King Harald's army when campaigning in England. King Harald was bold and lucky until his dying day.

While it was considered a glorious death to die in battle, to die in flight was considered shameful, the worst death of all. Thorkel the Tall made a vow to accompany his brother, Sigvaldi, in battle and not run away until he saw the stern of his brother's ship.[6] The worry of disgrace in defeat weighed so heavily on leaders that they dreamt about it. One night King Olaf Haraldson's sleep was so light he thought he was awake. He tossed and turned all night in anxiety over the enemy who had come to take his kingdom. Then Olaf Trygvason, Norway's hero-king, appeared to him in a dream and said that these tumultuous feelings came because he was thinking about laying down the kingly dignity that God had given him. "It is the glory of a king to be victorious over his enemies," Olaf Trygvason said, "and it is a glorious death to die in battle." Olaf Trygvason himself, in his final battle at Svolder against other Norse kings in the year 1000, exclaimed that God might dispose of his life, but never would he run away or ask his men to flee the dark cloud of weapons.

The warrior spirit lived on for generations past the Viking Age. Gregorius Dagson, son of Dag Eilifson, paid with his life assisting King Inge in battle in 1158. Before dying, he said that it was seldom necessary to encourage him to be brave and it would not be so now. When King Inge fought his own nephew, King Hakon Herdebreid, in 1161, some thought the risk to the king too great and suggested he avoid battle and instead send his brother, Orm, to lead the army. The king answered that had the brave Gregorius still been alive and able to avenge a fallen comrade, he would not hide, but would be in the battle. King Inge fought valiantly despite his poor health, and in a speech to the troops, said that in all his twenty-five years he had seen much misfortune and sorrow, but it was his greatest luck that he had never fled the battlefield. "God will dispose of my life, and of how long it shall be," he said, "but I shall never betake myself to flight."

Willingness to engage with the enemy in hand-to-hand combat, even against overwhelming odds, contributed to the Norsemen's reputation as unstoppable warriors. In 1066, King Harald Godwinson of England offered peace and quarter to the Vikings he had defeated in the battle of Stamford Bridge, but those warriors still alive called out that they would rather fall dead one across the other than accept quarter from an Englishman. After Guthorm Gunhildson and the Irish King Margad returned home (c. 1050) from a joint expedition against Bretland with immense amounts of booty, King Margad wanted all the silver for himself and told his former friend either to give up the booty and his ships or fight. Guthorm understood the futility in fighting Margad's sixteen ships with his own five, but considered it would be a disgrace to surrender his goods and ships without a single strike. He chose to conquer or die like a man, rather "than suffer disgrace, contempt and scorn, by submitting to so great a loss." His determination and courage, however, won him the battle against King Margad's much greater force.

The fortitude a man displayed on the warpath did not go unnoticed and kings were always in search of formidable warriors. But sometimes even the best intentions could go awry. Erling Skjalgson, the Brave, the Swift and the Bold, who fought against the Norwegian king Olaf Haraldson in 1029, defended himself manfully and no man attempted to flee or ask for quarter. Erling's stoic courage so impressed Olaf Haraldson that the king asked Erling to switch sides and enter his service. Erling agreed, removing his helmet and laying down his sword and shield. The king then struck Erling lightly on the chin with a battleaxe to mark him as a traitor to his sovereign. But seeing this, Aslak Fitiaskalle struck Erling in the head with an axe so that it "stood fast in his brain" and killed him. King Olaf, displeased at losing a courageous man who could have helped him reconquer the kingdom, confronted Aslak and said: "May ill luck attend thee for that stroke; for thou hast struck Norway out of my hands."

Only unlucky warriors, not cowards, were defeated in battle, because cowards were few among the Vikings. A story is told about the wife of Karl the farmer who was unable to sleep because of the shouting coming from kings who had been fighting all night. She asked her husband if, by chance, their own king had taken flight. Karl answered that he did not know if their king had run away or been killed. "What a useless sort of king we have!" said Karl's wife. "He is both slow and frightened." But their houseguest, Vandrad, answered: "Frightened he is not, but he is not lucky."[7] After Harald Hardrade fell off his horse fighting in England, the English king acknowledged him as a great man, handsome in his blue tunic and beautiful helmet, but also said: "I think his luck has left him." If defeated and driven to flight, some of these brave and gallant men would not easily be convinced to turn around. The Icelandic *skald* (poet) Thorarin Stutfeld composed the following insulting verse about a man named Arne Fioruskeif: "Of all his arms used in the field, those in most use were helm and shield."

Defense alone, without offense, was useless and not befitting of a Norse warrior. The brave Erling Skjalgson, brother-in-law of Norwegian king Olaf Trygvason, is said to have kept his courage hidden until the fight began, when he would step forward and outshine all others. If a quarrel arose on a campaign, a man could accuse another of cowardice simply to insult him. When Harald Hardrade asked Haldor (an ancestor of Snorri Sturluson, author of many Viking sagas) to carry the king's banner in the Varangian Guard, he answered: "Who will carry the banner before thee, if thou followest so timidly as thou hast done for a while?" Haldor's reply was spoken in anger, for it was known that Harald Hardrade was among the bravest of men in battle.

Flight, however, could be justified as long as it did not represent cowardice and was permissible, if for example, treachery was the cause. After Knut the Great of Denmark had assembled a large army to conquer Norway, the Norwegians fled because Knut had sent spies offering gifts to those who promised fidelity to the Danish king and agreed to join forces against their own country. King Knut's gifts made him popular with his subjects, but his generosity was shown principally to foreigners in an attempt to win them over.

Despite belief in the asa-gods and in the glory awaiting slain warriors in Valhalla, a man going to war knew that the possibility of death was very real and at some point must have felt fear. A leader's previous successes and the group's influence, however, gave men confidence and helped alleviate fear of death. Warriors were further motivated by promises of material wealth and financial security and knowing that the battle would be short—quickly in, quickly out.

Norsemen were loyal to their local chieftain, usually a man of their own choosing who could legally be dethroned if he failed to perform to their liking. Even acts of nature, such as good or bad crops, were held to count for or against the king. A chieftain who had the misfortune to rule during a time of great famine or distress had to answer to the population who considered it his fault. A king could be killed, his blood offered to the gods, to bring favorable seasons to the land. The opposite was also true. The first winter that Earl Hakon ruled in Norway, "the herrings set in everywhere through the fjords to the land, and the seasons ripened to a good crop . . ." People had hopes for a bright future. Likewise, during Olaf Haraldson's reign, the land smiled, "both mountain and cliff, and pebbly strand."

As commoners were drawn to their elected chieftain by his generosity, warriors were drawn to their leader by his courage and success in previous battles. A leader's success was not necessarily measured by whether or not the raiding party came back alive, as "few breakers of the peace grew old," but by how bravely the warriors had fought. Hjalte Skeggjason, who came from Iceland to Norway in 1017, said: "It is their lot who follow kings that they enjoy high honors, and are more respected than other men, but stand often in danger of their lives, and they must understand how to bear both parts of their lot." King Magnus Barefoot, ruler of Norway between 1094 and 1105, when accused by friends of recklessness on his expeditions abroad, retorted: "Kings are made for honor, not for long life," although good humor certainly helped. King Olaf Haraldson (ruled 1015–1028) was very cheerful and talkative on his campaigns which made those near him happy.

A leader's good reputation enabled him to recruit fine and courageous warriors who would contribute to even greater successes and inspire others to follow, both to acquire wealth and for the glory of serving honorably in battle. Once a leader had been chosen for his courage and luck in warfare, people stood by him and offered him their highest respect and assistance. Free farmers frequently became the chief's warriors. When the question of how to operate the ships arose, a Viking leader answered: "I will man one of them with my own house-carles [bodyguards] and the freemen around shall man the other." Norwegian king Olaf Trygvason was more careful in choosing the warriors for his pride and joy, the battleship *Long Serpent*, taking only men recognized for their strength and courage, no younger than twenty and no older than sixty. The crew of the *Long Serpent* became as famous among men as the splendid vessel was distinguished among battleships.

Since the Vikings set sail under their own rule and refused to be bound by a centralized regime, their compensation came in the form of spoils from the raids and depended on the success of the raid. Typical booty consisted of weapons, jewelry, clothing and slaves. The bodies of the slain were ransacked and the booty divided. How the booty was divided was decided beforehand to minimize the likelihood of disputes later. Each man got his share, but those who had worked especially hard, the leader or the rowers, for example, could receive more than the others. Disagreements among warriors still on a high from the raid or blinded by their own pride and skill in battle were, however, unavoidable at times. A story is told of Einar, a powerful man surrounded by many followers, who had taken possession of two parts of the country and was often out on marauding expeditions in summer, "but it went always unpleasantly with the division of the booty made on his Viking cruises." Although some may have been dissatisfied with their share, all men remained motivated by the promised treasures of the raids and made an effort for the crew as a whole, contributing their knowledge and physical skill in battle. Most raids followed a plan that was at least loosely developed, but if something interesting happened along the way, the possibility of greater riches or encounter of an enemy ship, the crew deviated from the original plan to make a spur-of-the-moment attack. While their method could make the warriors seem disorganized, it also enabled them to come away with more spoils than originally contemplated.

While some men were off on the raid, others had to stay behind to guard the ship. Ragnvald, the youngest Lodbrok brother, was left behind while others attacked the fortress in Hvitaby (c. 865). Thinking that his brothers had prevented him from taking part in the battle not because of his youth, but to take all the booty for themselves, Ragnvald left his guard duty and followed his brothers into battle. Although he fought hard, his inexperience resulted in his death.

The hard work of rowing was one of the crew's biggest problems. Men were especially ill inclined to row against the wind and would frequently think up other more clever solutions. Experiencing difficulties motivating his crew to row in the desired southerly direction, Erling Skakke decided to deviate from the plan, so he raised the mast, hoisted the sails and let the ship go north with the wind.

A Norse warrior's major strength was his ship that, with its long sturdy keel no more than three feet in depth, could be sailed into the shallow waters of a bay where it could do *strandhugg*.[8] This meant beaching the ship for a fast entry, a quick raid of a coastal community, where booty that included slaves was taken, and a speedy exit back to sea via the beach. When there was no wind, slaves were placed in chains on the rowers' benches and put to work. Wealthy Vikings kept some thirty slaves and other servants on their farms. According to Ibn Rustah, an Arab explorer: "They harry the Slavs, using ships to reach them; they carry them off as slaves and . . . sell them."[9] Escaping the tiresome work at the oars and good fortune in the raid helped to boost morale among warriors. But morale could easily be destroyed by a long spell of bad weather, high loss of life or goods, surprise attacks by enemy ships at sea, or feuds aboard, undoubtedly common among one hundred or so men living in exceptionally tight quarters.

After warriors did *strandhugg* and spent time in the cities along the coast where they restocked their ships with all the valuables they could carry, they continued to the next town or to greater treasure in England. Loss of men in battle lightened the load, further lightened by the men's appetites, and increased the ship's carrying capacity. Fresh food was generally readily available in the coastal communities as was mead, which was important as a morale booster for the rowers. It mattered little if food was scarce, so long as there was good beer and mead to drown fright.

Norsemen were known for their heavy drinking, and good social behavior dictated drinking up what was offered. Drinking in a large company was considered particularly pleasurable. Erling Skjalgson, brother-in-law of the Norwegian king Olaf Trygvason, had an entourage of ninety men who drank winter and summer; they stopped when a silver stud appeared above the liquor in the drinking horn or cup at the midday meal, but drank without restriction at the evening meal. Olaf Trygvason himself instituted a law forcing people to drink beer on the summer solstice.[10] Thorar, a *lagman* (lawman, or one who speaks the law) and person of high esteem, spent the Yule (winter solstice celebration) with his brother-in-law in 1027, taking part in the feast and challenging the peasants to drinking contests until men's tongues became loose and they couldn't remember a thing they had said. Vladimir, a prince of the Rus Dynasty (Vikings in Russia), when he was looking for a suitable religion for his pagan kingdom, rejected Islam because it demanded abstinence. Vladimir said: "Drink is the joy of the Rus. We cannot exist without that pleasure."[11] King Sigurd the Crusader saw things differently. He accused his son Magnus of knowing nothing of the customs of foreign people: "Dost thou not know that men in other countries exercise themselves in other feats than in filling themselves with ale, and making themselves mad, and so unfit for everything that they scarcely know each other?"

As a departure date drew near, the ships were readied with ornate weathervanes and dragonheads at bow and stern. The time had come to instill fear in the victims, to sail toward land with "yawning jaws and grimly gaping heads," to frighten whatever guardian spirits an enemy nation might harbor. Inspiring fear drained the enemy of their will to fight and mount a defense, making it easier to break them. Fear reduced strong men to inaction; it caused them to cower behind their shields, to look for a way out through flight, to stand on the sidelines doing nothing or attempting to bargain with their attackers. Shields, painted in colorful designs to draw attention to the mission and the crew's ferocity, were hung along the sides of the ships. War cries stirred up the crew, giving them unity of purpose, and also serving to overcome anxiety. Vikings who intimidated and frightened foreign women earned special bragging rights, because to frighten a woman was to insult her man.

The psychological interaction between warrior and victim was a cycle in which the stronger, more confident force overcame the weaker, psychologically disadvantaged one. Warriors understood the effects of fear and approached their upcoming battles with that knowledge in mind. The Vikings' reputation as unstoppable beasts was often sufficient for their disillusioned victims to run away before a single blow could be exchanged and convinced them that resistance was futile. Victims who fled created even greater fearlessness in Viking warriors, further motivating them in battle.

"Berserkers" were the most feared of Viking warriors because they fought with absolutely no regard for their own safety: "No iron could hurt them, and when they charged nothing could withstand them." When a man went berserk he fought with such unrestrained aggression that it was not unusual for him to howl, bite the rim of his shield and scowl like a madman. Since he felt no fear or pain, he attacked without worrying about his helmet or chain mail. In 962, after King Hakon Herdebreid (the Broad-Shouldered) received his death wound, his berserk men rowed with all their might against the enemy, "threw away their shields, slashed with both hands and cared not for life."

The role of the berserkers was to make the first attack and shock their victims into flight or submission; this opened the way for remaining warriors to follow. In land battle, berserkers were always at the front of the formation; at sea, they were placed slightly aft of the forecastle on the king's ship. King Harald Fairhair, the first king to rule all of Norway, fitted out his ships in spring "in the most splendid way, and brought his house-troops and his berserks on board. Such men . . . were remarkable for strength, courage, and all kinds of dexterity." King Harald had a court comprised of the most esteemed men in the country, warriors with the costliest clothing and weapons and wild berserkers who enjoyed special treatment.

Berserkers believed that Oden protected them so they could attack ruthlessly without fear of death and fight in any way necessary without considering the consequences. "Odin could make his enemies in battle blind, or deaf, or terror-struck, and their weapons so blunt that they could cut no more than a willow wand; on the other hand, his men rushed forward without armor, were as mad as dogs or wolves, bit their shields, were strong as bears or wild bulls, and killed people at a blow, but neither fire nor iron told upon themselves."[12]

Because the berserkers wore wolf-skins instead of chain mail, they were known as *ulfhedner*.[13] The dress of these fierce, savage, roaring mad warriors was almost as effective as armor against an enemy's sword.[14] Thorer Hund, who was involved in the killing of King Olaf Haraldson, journeyed to Lapland in the winter of 1029–30, traded various wares with the Laplanders and had twelve big coats made for him of reindeer skin "with so much Lapland witchcraft that no weapon could cut or pierce them any more than if they were armor or ring-mail." When King Olaf Haraldson struck Thorer across the shoulders, his sword would not cut, and "it was as if dust flew from his reindeer-skin coat." However, when Thorer Hund retaliated and struck the king with his spear, the weapon went under his mail-coat, into his belly, and along with another blow to the neck, killed the king.

Since the behavior of the berserkers could not be predicted, defending against their madness was nearly impossible. Some say the berserkers were social outcasts or men who had become psychotic from drugs, that their frenzied state was induced by consuming *fly agaric*, an hallucinogenic mushroom, drinking too much alcohol or simply tricking the mind into rage through self-induced or group stimulus.[15] Whatever the case, the berserkers were also feared by their own kinsmen. The frenzied state started with tremors and teeth-chattering, followed by a hunching of the shoulders and anger that grew into fury. The berserker's fists doubled up and he would roar like a wolf. At the height of his madness, he would bite his shield and hack away at everything and everyone in his path, friends included, not even feeling the effects of his wounds. Since he could not differentiate between friend and foe, he was a danger to all around him. Men were wise to stay out of a berserker's path, and wait to defeat him once the madness had left him and he was physically incapable of continuing the battle. When the berserk condition subsided, it was followed by extraordinary fatigue that could last for several days. A berserker who survived his ordeal remembered little, if anything, of what took place while he was in this state. Although the berserker was both admired and feared, he was also despised, because a Viking warrior was counted upon to remain a loyal and trusted friend.

These seemingly lawless Norsemen practically ruled the waters, waging war against the more civilized, more-developed British, Frankish, and Roman populations who should have been able to protect themselves better against the invaders who raided unchecked for almost three hundred years. The Vikings' versatility and their method of joining forces to achieve their goal, only to disband and disappear again into their former towns and chieftaincies, made them frightening adversaries, proving that "in the furious fight, none can withstand the Norsemen's might." With war preparations completed, men could look forward to the summer when all that remained was to wave good-bye to their wives and children, step aboard their ships and go a-Viking. Those foolish enough to engage a fleet of Viking long-ships had only themselves to blame for the misfortune that befell them.

And what glory it was to be "fighting against evil men ... if luck would have it that they would meet such men."[16]

Wagon wheel displayed at the Viking Ship Museum in Oslo, Norway. Combatants fought only if they were supplied with food and other necessities on their journey. The difficult terrain and under-developed land routes in the Nordic countries encouraged the Vikings to excel at sea where transport by ship was easier. A strandhugg *was a quick raid along the shore to acquire provisions for the journey.*

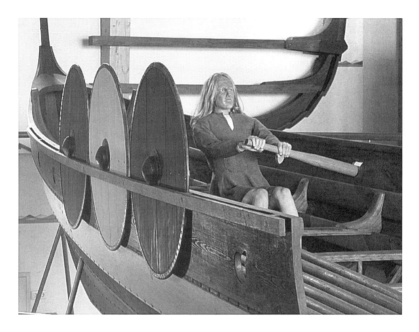

Oars were indispensable when traveling through narrow waterways. An oar could easily be broken if two ships encountered each other in a confined area. The shields fastened along the gunwales served as additional protection for warriors meeting an enemy ship at sea. Model displayed at the Viking Museum in Haithabu, northern Germany.

Nordic skalds *sang of "bright gold, glancing like the spray of sun-lit waves."* Skalds, *whose job it was to celebrate kings and warriors, were court poets and formed part of the king's entourage.* Sigvat Thordarson (c. *995–1045*), *a famous* skald *often called simply Sigvat Skald, belonged to the court of King Olaf Haraldson and was so skilled at his craft he could compose verse as quickly as others could talk.* Skalds *were rewarded with gold and silver rings: "King Olaf gave Sigvat as a reward for his verse a gold ring that weighed half a mark."*[17]

Men honored their wives and daughters with silver and gold rings and other ornaments. The ring as a symbol of fidelity survives to this day. Jewelry displayed at the Museum of History in Stockholm, Sweden.

Chapter 4

Building the Ship

The Norsemen's greatest weapon was their ship. Vikings did not march in armies, did not sail under a common flag, did not answer to a king or general and had no fear of God. They could not be defeated by conventional means. No fleet could track them down or cut off their escape routes.

Because land travel was time-consuming and great effort was required to penetrate the thick forests of the north, Vikings turned to the sea to reach their goals. The sea was not only highly accessible, opposing forces had no way of sealing if off. The many rivers and fjords running through Scandinavia and Russia facilitated transport of warriors, explorers, traders and goods and helped spread Nordic culture. The Viking long-ship derived its name from being long for its width; if the winds were favorable, it could sail across entire oceans at speeds of twelve to fourteen knots.[1] The development of the long-ship was the outgrowth of two factors: the Vikings' geographical location surrounded by the sea, and easy access to abundant building material from the nearby forests. When King Olaf Haraldson sent Thorarin Nefiulfsson from Norway to Iceland, a distance of nearly six hundred miles, the winds were so favorable that he sailed the stretch in just eight *dœgr*.[2]

Norse ships, "riding in pride upon the foaming ocean tide," packed with battle-hungry warriors eager to raid a monastery or coastal town, dominated the waters for almost three centuries. Thanks to their beautiful and efficient ships, perhaps the greatest achievement of that time, Vikings alone ruled and conquered the seas, inspiring alarm throughout the western world. Ships are often pictured on rune stones, attesting to their importance in Viking life; they were dexterous objects of beauty and might, both envied and feared—"weapons" which gave the Norsemen military advantage and significant tactical superiority over their foes. The ships were sturdy, roomy, flexible, fast and safe. They were symbols of Viking pride and prestige, but they were also their prime source of strength in battle, responsible for the ability of the Vikings to wage unconventional warfare.

The mere sight of a fleet of these magnificent, dreaded long-ships under sail was often sufficient to reduce the enemy to flight. The pride felt by a Norse king in command of his fleet has been retold in countless Viking poems. To lose a ship was disastrous and meant almost certain death. Even if he survived the ordeal, a sea-king who lost his ship was suddenly vulnerable and could be brought down in disgrace. Therefore, part of the crew usually stayed behind to guard the ship while the others went off raiding. The ships were so valuable that rich Vikings were buried with them and it is from these boat graves that many of the Viking finds have been recovered.

The ingenuity of the ships' designs gave the Vikings complete command at sea—power which they used ruthlessly, freely attacking wherever they pleased and plundering communities all along Europe's coastlines, before disappearing from enemy territory back to sea where they were safe from pursuit. Vikings were expert sailors simply because they sailed so much, whenever they needed to travel and for any reason. There were two main types of ships: *drakkar* (dragons or battleships) and *knörr* (merchant or trading ships). There was also a third type of ship, the *snekke*, a smaller warship of twenty or so benches of rowers. The *drakkar*, designed for superb maneuverability, could be either sailed or rowed. When the winds were favorable and the sails hoisted, the leader's luck was celebrated.

Warships were capable of carrying large crews of more than one hundred men. They were long, elegant, swift and completely open, exposing the warriors to the crashing waves and "oar-blades loud in the grey sea splash," an experience that required both physical and mental toughness, especially on long journeys. In contrast, the slightly slower and broader *knörr*, which had plenty of storage room in the middle for goods or animals to be sold or traded, carried smaller crews and traveled primarily under sail.[3]

Here, however, the focus is on the warships. The appearance of a fleet of *drakkar* sailing "mast after mast by the coast-side," multicolored sails striped and dyed in red like blood, gilded dragonheads at the bow and stern and with painted shields hanging along their sides, was an unparalleled sight that surely caused trepidation in even the most experienced and battle-tested warriors.[4] A monk at the monastery of St. Omer, France, described the sailing of the Danish fleet in 1013: "When at length they were all gathered, they went on board the towered ship . . . On one side lions molded in gold were to be seen on the ships, on the other, birds on the tops of the masts indicated by their movements the winds as they blew, or dragons of various kinds poured fire from their nostrils . . . But why should I now dwell upon the sides of the ships, which were not only painted with ornate colors but were covered with gold and silver figures? The blue water, smitten by many oars, might be seen foaming far and wide, and the sunlight, cast back in the gleam of metal, spread a double radiance in the air."[5]

King Olaf Trygvason acquired in battle a ship he called the *Serpent*, described as Norway's handsomest ship, with a dragon's head at the bow and a dragon's tail at the stern. The hoisted sail represented the dragon's wings. But the true pride of the Norse king was the *Long Serpent*, a ship he commissioned in the winter of 999–1000, and which outstripped all other sailing ships in northern waters. "Olaf Trygvason must be afraid, for he does not venture to sail with the figure-head of the dragon upon his ship," said King Sven Forkbeard as he lay in ambush together with Earl Erik and King Olof Skötkonung of Sweden, waiting for the mighty *Long Serpent* to appear. When they saw four ships sailing along, one of which had a large, richly gilded dragonhead, Sven Forkbeard stood up and said: "That dragon shall carry me this evening high, for I shall steer it."

The average warship had fifty to sixty rowers aboard, with one rower per oar. Each man brought his own chest with his personal belongings onboard, which he also used as his rowing bench. The ships had movable planks under the rowers, with plentiful storage room below deck for captured booty. Some of the larger ships could carry a double crew, allowing the men to row in shifts, half of the crew rowing and the other half resting. Shift work eliminated dependence on wind for travel, and since part of the crew was always resting, there was no need to set up camp for the night.[6] Double crews also made it possible to leave some warriors on the beach to guard against enemy attack while the others were off raiding. If a battle took place at sea, half of the crew could hold the shields for the other half who were busy throwing spears or shooting bows and arrows.

A ship that could be either sailed or rowed, or had a combination of both sails and oars, had the capacity to outrun other ships on the open sea and increase its strategic range. When King Olaf Haraldson sent the brothers Karle and Gunstein along with Thorer Hund on a merchant journey to Bjarmaland in 1026, disputes over division of the booty created bad blood between them. In a fit of anger Thorer struck Karle with a spear that went through him, killing him instantly. When Gunstein learned of his brother's fate, he retrieved Karle's body and left. Thorer prepared to follow, but "as they were hoisting the sail the fastenings to the mast broke in two, and the sail fell down across the ship, which caused a great delay." Thorer finally hoisted the sail anew and set out after Gunstein, using both sails and oars in an attempt to catch up with the other ship, but Gunstein also used sails and oars and Thorer was unable to close the gap throughout two days and nights of sailing.

The long-ships were steered using the rudder on the starboard side, but could also be steered by oars alone. The oars, approximately four to five and a half meters (thirteen to eighteen feet) in length, were placed along the sides of the ships after the wind picked up and the sail was raised. On some ships the oar holes, which were close to the water, were sealed with rotating covers to keep out the water. When the oars were in use, the masts were lowered, mainly for subterfuge. The Vikings could then travel beyond the horizon protected by the earth's curvature—a tactic that contributed to their success in warfare, as it minimized the enemy's ability to foresee attack and helped the Vikings make landfall at the time and place that suited them best.

The dual option of sails and oars made the ships highly mobile and reduced the Norsemen's dependence on good weather for their journeys. Their mobility also prevented the enemy from blocking the waterways or thwarting their attacks. The Norsemen had free rein to rob and plunder at will, then beat an easy retreat back to sea without fear of retribution. The sail increased the ship's range and was preferable to the oar. Rowing was hard work and the top speed of four to five knots when manually powered could only be maintained for a short time before the crew became exhausted. *Sjóvíka* or *víka sjóvar*, an Old Norse nautical term, is an ancient measure used at sea.[7] Although the distance covered varied depending on wind and currents, the measure corresponds to approximately seven to eight kilometers (four nautical miles), or one thousand strokes of the oar, which is the approximate distance a crew could row before it ran out of strength and had to be replaced by a rested crew. Good weather with favorable winds also helped preserve morale onboard.

Although sail remnants have not survived, sails pictured on rune stones show a crosshatched design, possibly symbolizing the interlaced ropes that were used to reinforce the bottom of the sail and perfect the curve of the cloth, allowing it to hold its shape and maximize its speed advantage. Ropes and riggings have not been found, but were likely made of linen, horsehair, tree fibers or animal hides such as walrus or seal. Literary sources indicate that the sails were often striped: "That is not the King's ship yet," said Earl Erik when waiting in ambush for King Olaf Trygvason, "for I know that ship by the colored stripes of cloth in her sail."

To create a single square sail required tremendous work. It is believed that the aspect ratio (width to height) was approximately three to one. A typical sail might have had a width of forty-eight feet, approximately half of the ship's length, and a height of sixteen feet. On a smaller ship, the sail would cover an area of 650 square feet; on a larger ship, it would cover 950 square feet and would require almost eighty miles of yarn, as much as four women could spin in a winter. The weaving of just one sail could take several years to complete. Spinning and weaving were believed to be year-round tasks, although women also spent the winter months equipping the warriors and readying them for raids, making both the sails and the clothes they wore during their journeys.

The sails were made of wool and coated with tar, animal fats, and oils to give them stiffness and make them water-resistant. Red dye was frequently applied to create a threatening and memorable impression, but other dyes were also used. Earl Hakon's dragon of forty rowers' benches was painted above the water stroke, and its sail was striped in blue, red and green. Knut the Great, king of Denmark, Norway and England, who together with his father, Sven Forkbeard, conquered the English king Aethelred the Unready, sailed his dragon in 1013 "with her sails of blue, all bright and brilliant to the view." The sail on the ship belonging to Harek of Thjotta was "white as snow, and in it were red and blue stripes of cloth interwoven."

No warrior would lose the opportunity to boast about his sail, the most distinguishing feature of his ship. When Sigurd the Crusader ventured to Palestine, he first sailed north to Cyprus, then to the Greek land where he lay low with his fleet for two weeks, ignoring the daily breezes favoring travel to the north. But Sigurd wanted others to notice his sail and therefore waited for a side wind, so that the sails on his ships stretched fore and aft, "for in all his sails there was silk joined in . . . and neither those before nor those behind the ships could see the slightest appearance of this, if the vessel was before the wind."

If a sail were damaged, or worse, stolen, and a king or leader had to return home by rowing, he would be expected to avenge the crime or risk remaining a laughingstock until he died. When King Olaf Haraldson decided to prohibit the export of corn, malt and meal due to a bad crop in 1022, a certain Asbjorn Selsbane concluded that the king's decision was totally unacceptable and ventured out on the seas in search of the necessary goods for his numerous feasts and drinking parties. He landed on the Island of Karmt and asked one of the king's bailiffs, Thorer Sel, to sell him some corn and malt. Thorer Sel dutifully informed Asbjorn that the king forbid transporting corn to other parts of the country. Disgruntled, Asbjorn returned to his ship, continued on to one of his relatives and with ten men standing guard was able to coerce the slaves into selling him what he needed. When Thorer Sel got the news and learned that Asbjorn's ship was laden with forbidden products, he caught up with Asbjorn and threatened to throw him overboard if he did not willingly go ashore and removed the entire cargo from the vessel. His final insult was to replace the magnificent sail on Asbjorn's ship with a smaller, shabbier sail.

Asbjorn's ship was said to have been easily recognizable by its high bulwarks, white and red hues and colored cloth woven into the sail. Returning home without the splendid sail, he indeed became a laughingstock and had to hide in shame for the winter. As soon as the ice began to melt in spring, he paid Thorer Sel a visit to avenge the dishonorable act that had caused him so much sorrow. When he arrived at the bailiff's house, he noticed that festivities were in full swing, and as he stood concealed in the shadows by the door, he overheard Thorer Sel recounting the humiliating story to his guests: "When we were taking out the cargo he bore it tolerably, but not well," Thorer Sel said, "and when we took the sail from him he wept." That comment ended up costing Thorer Sel his life. Asbjorn drew his sword, rushed into the hall, and struck Thorer Sel in the neck so hard that his head fell onto the table in front of the king, his body at the king's feet, soaking the tablecloth with his blood.

Some of the longer of the long-ships ranged in lengths up to 35 meters (115 feet) and had length to width ratios of up to seven to one. One advantage of the long-ships lay in the fact that their drag against the water (resistance to forward motion) was reduced. By increasing the length, only half a meter (less than two feet) of water was displaced when the ship was fully loaded. The shallow draft and broad bottom made the ship highly maneuverable (although less stable in high seas), able to penetrate any waterway in Europe and sail where other ships could not. The Vikings avoided long marches inland, confining themselves to raiding only those locations reachable by ocean or rivers, often in surprise landings on open coastline or islands with or without a harbor. This capability particularly shocked the Frankish Empire, whose rivers had theretofore been considered invulnerable to such large ships. The length of a ship also played a significant role in battle strategy, as a longship could carry more men at the oars.

One of the largest ships recovered, the *Gokstad*, excavated in Norway in 1880, dated to 850 and could hold seventy men. Built entirely of oak, the *Gokstad* measures twenty-three meters (seventy-six feet) in length, five meters (seventeen feet) in width and was found with the remains of twelve horses and other accessories, such as small boats, a large keg for drinking water, and a gangplank. The thirty-two oar holes and sixty-four wooden shields fastened along the sides provide an idea of the size of the working crew. The *Oseberg* ship, excavated in Norway in 1904, is thought to have been a royal ship, mainly representational in nature, and therefore not a true battleship. The mast on that ship is estimated to have stood about thirteen meters (forty-three feet) high. The one-meter, seven-kilo anchor made of iron and the rudder on the aft starboard side give further indication of how the ships were equipped. Typical warships were fifteen to twenty meters (forty-nine to sixty-six feet) long and two and a half to three meters (eight to ten feet) wide with room for thirty-two rowers, sixteen on each side, although the number of warriors the ships carried varied greatly.

Naturally, the most powerful kings and leaders owned the largest ships. Erling Skjalgson, known as the bravest man who ever held lands under a king in Norway, never went to sea with less than a fully manned ship of twenty benches of rowers. His largest ships had room for thirty-two benches and could carry a crew of two hundred men. But perhaps the most magnificent warship described in the Icelandic sagas was the mighty

Long Serpent, constructed by the master-builder Thorberg Skafhog by order of the Norwegian King Olaf Trygvason.[8] This ship, equipped with thirty-four rowers' benches (sixty-eight rowers), was the king's pride. At 55 meters (180 feet) in length and with a 45-meter (148-feet) long keel,[9] it was the biggest, most beautiful and most costly warship ever seen; it was both long and broad, but also high-sided—the bulwarks were as high as those on sea-going ships—and heavily timbered with gold-plated dragonheads at both bow and stern.[10] The *Long Serpent*, built during the millennium winter of 999–1000, was sailed by Olaf Trygvason in the battle of Svolder where he fought the united forces of Olof Skötkonung of Sweden, Sven Forkbeard of Denmark, and Earl Erik of Norway.[11] The splendid *Long Serpent* met its fate at the hands of Norse warriors. The ship was lost to the opposing force when Olaf Trygvason fell into the trap set for him by the Danish and Swedish kings.

The superiority that Norsemen battling foreign armies enjoyed was less keenly experienced by fellow Norse among whom disputes were common and the battles bloody. After the Norwegian king Olaf Haraldson's daughter mediated between her father and the Swedish king Olof Skötkonung in an attempt to make peace between them, the "Swedish king flew into a passion every time she named Olaf, so that she had no hopes of any peace." The two brothers, Jorund and Erik, known as great warriors, marauded one summer in Denmark where they battled with King Gudlog from Halogaland. The battle ended when the brothers cleared Gudlog's ship of warriors, took the king prisoner and later hanged him.

The Norse population had worked to develop their superbly crafted ships for hundreds of years prior to the Viking Age. They were flexible enough to withstand the force of the sea, lightweight enough to be transported on tree logs short distances across land, and simple enough to be built in a single winter. Wood was easier to work when fresh, so if construction of a ship had to be halted for some reason, the wood was stored in water to prevent it from drying out. In the autumn of 998, prior to his work on the *Long Serpent*, Olaf Trygvason built a ship he called *Tranen* (*The Crane*), a large long-ship, narrow and high in stem and stern, with thirty benches for rowers. His skilled crew of carpenters completed the ship by early winter.

Warships were streamlined and fast, yet capable of carrying a great deal of booty and supplies, including horses for land travel. These flat-bottomed ships capable of transporting horses became part of battlefield strategy, enabling raids far beyond coastal communities. Warriors could travel inland on horseback, return quickly to their ship and be out at sea again before their victims had time to mount a defense. Sigvat Skald, while riding up to Gautland, recorded: "Our horse-hoofs now leave hasty print; we ride—of ease there's scanty stint." Horses were also useful on peace missions. In about 1135, King Rettibur went to Konungahella, the place where kings met to discuss important matters, with 550 cutters, each carrying forty-four men and two horses. And then there was the question of what to do with the wounded: "All in the bottom of the ships the wounded lay, in ghastly heaps; backs up and faces down they lay under the row-seats stowed away."

The hiring of a shipwright (craftsman) was the first step in ship-building. The famous Thorstein Knarrarsmid was a master ship-carpenter, so expert that he worked without using drawn plans. The exact design the shipwright gave the ship depended on its primary purpose. If peaceful trade were the goal, carrying capacity was important, and trading ships were therefore normally designed with a large deck and big storage rooms. Crossing the Atlantic and discovering new continents required a ship strong enough to withstand the violent motion of the sea and with sufficient room to hold necessary provisions such as food and beer. Quick plundering raids required a ship designed primarily for speed.

Along with the shipwright came the laborers who felled the trees, carried the timber, cut the planks, shaped the wood, and manufactured the nails. Timber was plentiful in the nearby forests, oak and pine trees being common to the North.[12] Oak trees grew exceptionally tall and strong and were therefore widely used in shipbuilding, almost always for the keel which was formed first and constructed from a single piece of wood taken from the trunk of the tree: "Cross the East sea the vessel flew, her oak-keel a white furrow drew."[13] The keel, the backbone of the ship, the most significant innovation in Nordic shipbuilding, was already developed by the seventh century.[14] The keel, which was widest at mid-ship, ran the full length of the ship and was slightly curved and tapered at the ends; this design produced the greatest draught where the hull was broadest. By raising the front and rear ends of the ship from the water, the dynamics of the keel were increased and resistance to turning was reduced. The mast, bowpost, and sternpost were attached to the keel. The design made for speed and enabled the ship to hold out against the forces of the sea and cross entire oceans without breaking apart in a storm. In 1950, a Viking ship replica named *Ormen Friske* (*Serpent Friske*) broke apart in a storm in the North Sea, costing all fifteen crewmembers their lives. The accident was due to a construction error in the keel that had been built of laminated planks of weak knotty pine, that had ripped apart in moderate waves of only 2 meters (6.5 feet) or so, instead of the much stronger oak.

The keel was largely responsible for the amphibious nature of the ship. Only a few towns in the Nordic countries, such as Birka and Hedeby (Haithabu), were known to have had harbors, and archaeological evidence shows worn keels consistent with repeated beaching. It is therefore believed that the common method for embarking and disembarking the ship was by sailing all the way up onto the beach, or at least close enough to lay a gangplank.[15] Although iron and stone anchors were in use, they were not often needed because the design of the ship allowed the crew to jump into knee-deep water and immediately pursue the battle on land. Enemy ships with deeper keels were not as fast or as mobile and were no match for the Norsemen's swift ships.

When looking for timber for their ships, the Vikings selected trees with a physical appearance in the shape desired. The tallest and straightest trees were used for the masts and planks, while the biggest and thickest ones were used for the keels. Also, to preserve the natural strength of the grain and eliminate the need to cut the wood to form ribs, trees were selected for the way their branches naturally grew from the trunk, making iron nails, which were expensive, largely unnecessary. Whereas smaller boats were often carved from a single log, the long-ships were built by the clinker method, the lower edge of each plank overlapping the upper edge of the one below and bent to follow the shape of the keel. Iron rivets and nails were used to hold the planks together. Tree logs were cut by axe in radial splits to create planks. Splitting the wood along the natural grain, instead of sawing it, created planks that were exceptionally strong. Normally twenty to thirty planks, depending on the diameter of the trunk, could be split from a single tree. It is estimated that between ten and fifteen oak trees were needed to finish a ship. The planks were trimmed to a width of only two centimeters, approximately the thickness of a finger. The clinker method also made it possible to taper the bow and stern, which gave the ship its sleek and beautiful appearance. An old Norse song says: "As Norsemen row the serpent, riveted down the icy stream, it is like a sight of eagle's wings."[16]

Flexible planking enabled the hull to twist and absorb the motion of the sea and reduced the impact of the swells. But this elasticity also left cracks between the planks, making ships prone to leaks, especially in high seas. Since it was not practical or productive to wait for perfect weather conditions, animal hair, moss, or woolen yarn covered with tar was stuffed between the joints to make the planks watertight and seal them before they were nailed into place. But bailing was still frequently needed; drain plugs probably existed to empty the ship of water once it was dragged ashore. Finally, the finished ship could be rolled off the logs that had been supporting it on land during its construction and into the water.

The Viking ship represented the culmination of centuries of technical evolution and innovation in boat building in the northern countries. Although ships had existed for hundreds of years prior to the Viking Age, the great flexibility and carrying capacity of the Viking ships, together with the use of both sails and oars, made the Vikings famous throughout Europe, Russia and the Arab world. Several centuries would pass before their superiority would be challenged.

A well-known Swedish archaeologist wrote that the Viking ship was the only seaworthy amphibious landing vessel ever to be used by invasion forces. Even if this claim is an exaggeration, it is clear that the Vikings owed their military superiority to their ships, the way they were designed and the way they were used.[17] Without them, they would not have become a dominant force.

"Each war-ship, with its threatening throat
Of dragon fierce or ravenous brute
Grim gaping from the prow; its wales
Glittering with burnished shields, like scales."

The ship is the most noteworthy achievement of the Viking Age. Ships were built almost entirely of oak and had to be sturdy enough to survive ocean crossings and storms, but also lightweight enough to drag ashore or haul short distances across land. The Norsemen were able to reach all known parts of the world with their ships. Displayed at the Viking Ship Museum in Oslo, Norway.

Smaller craft, with or without sails, were sometimes used as supply ships for larger fleets. Models displayed at the Viking Museum in Haithabu, northern Germany.

Rune stone picturing a Viking ship with a square sail. "The square sail technique has been tested on a reconstructed Viking ship in Denmark. These experiments prove that this rig is well-suited to be trimmed to the wind in almost all directions. The Viking ships were able to set course into the wind, tack with their square sail rig against the wind, as well as sail with the wind abeam."[18] Rock carvings attest to the fact that ships were built and used in Scandinavia as early as 1500–500 BC. The Vikings, however, improved shipbuilding to suit their specific needs. Note the large steering oar on the starboard side. Displayed at the Museum of History in Stockholm, Sweden.

Stone carving of a ship with sail stowed. Since no sails have ever been recovered, exact dimensions of the sails and the height of the masts are unknown. The mast on the Oseberg *ship, excavated in Norway in 1904, is made of pine and estimated to have had an original length of thirteen meters (forty-three feet). Note the steering oar.* Displayed at the Museum of History in Stockholm, Sweden.

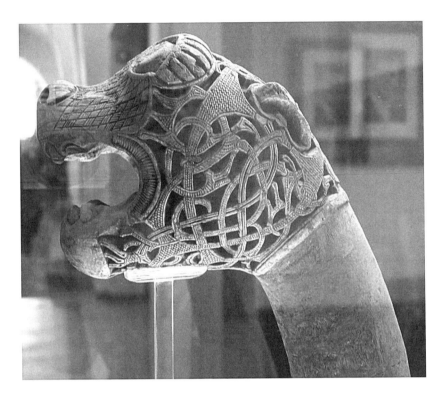

Not a single dragonhead decoration, widely described both in the Icelandic Sagas *and the* Chronicles *and commonly used on ships, has been found. This head post with gaping jaws was most likely carried for ceremonial purposes.* Displayed at the Viking Ship Museum in Oslo, Norway.

Spiraling serpents at the bow and stern were some-times carved as part of the ship and used in place of the dragonhead. The bow and stern were fastened directly to the keel and were often identical at both ends; at other times, the serpent's head was at one end and the tail at the other. Displayed at the Viking Ship Museum in Oslo, Norway.

Iron nails were used to hold the planking together. The wood was split along the grain with an axe, rather than a saw, to maintain the strength of the wood and protect the fibers. As the planks were nailed together, the ship was shaped and the hull widened with stones. Displayed at the Viking Museum in Haithabu, northern Germany.

The planks were joined together with iron nails driven through from the outside and secured by small clinch plates. Displayed at the Viking Ship Museum in Oslo, Norway.

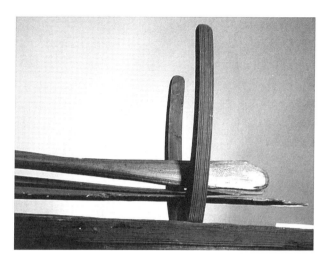

Oars made of pine and measuring between 3.7 and 4.0 meters (12 and 13 feet), depending on the distance between the oar holes and the water surface, were stowed in wooden forks when the wind was favorable and the sail hoisted. Some oars were even longer. Displayed at the Viking Ship Museum in Oslo, Norway.

Artwork along the keel of a Viking ship commonly pictured imaginary interlacing animal motifs. Displayed at the Viking Ship Museum in Oslo, Norway.

Clinker-building, with the lower edge of every plank overlapping the upper edge of the one below. Planks average about two centimeters thick, or about the thickness of a finger. Tarred wool was used for caulking to form a water resistant skin that was still flexible enough to give with the movement of the sea; bailing was still often required. Displayed at the Viking Ship Museum in Oslo, Norway.

The woodcarvings and high-rising bow of the Ose-berg *ship, excavated in Norway in 1904, gave the ship an elegant appearance, but one also capable of striking fear in the opposing force.* Displayed at the Viking Ship Museum in Oslo, Norway.

Ships frequently carried crews of one hundred men or more and conditions on board were crowded. Food and other necessities, as well as booty, were stored under the pine floor boards which were secured to the beams with nails; a few boards were probably left loose to provide easy access to the storage area and facilitate bailing. Shields were fixed to projecting cleats on a strip of wood running along the outside of the upper edge of the top strake. Model displayed at the Museum of History in Stockholm, Sweden.

Ship with floorboards. Warriors sat on their chests, which also contained their personal belongings. But "all in the bottom of the ships the wounded lay, in ghastly heaps; backs up and faces down they lay under the row-seats stowed away." Note the oar holes in the upper plank. Displayed at the Viking Ship Museum in Oslo, Norway.

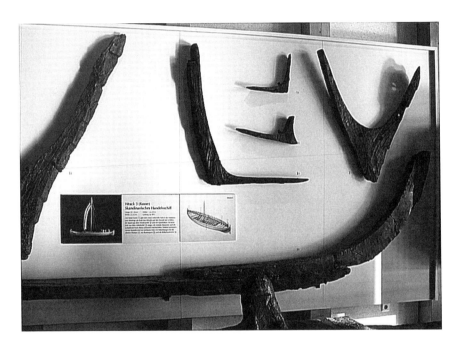

Pieces of a keelson (provided support for the mast and frame of the ship), ribs and knees. A wooden knee is the section of a tree where the trunk meets the root. The knee has great natural strength and was therefore used as a structural piece in shipbuilding. Ribs were secured to the planking either by binding them or with nails. Displayed at the Viking Museum in Haithabu, northern Germany.

The mast partner made of oak, from the Tune ship excavated in Norway in 1867, lay across the beams and supported the mast. The beams strengthened the ship and
formed the foundation for the deck. The height from the
bottom of the keel to the top edge of the hull on this ship is
1.2 meters (4 feet), estimated to be about 3 feet less than
the common ship height. This ship dates to c. 850–900. Displayed at the Viking Ship Museum in Oslo, Norway.

Some anchors were small in size. This is one meter (three feet) long and weighs only ten kilos (twenty-two pounds). Displayed at the Viking Ship Museum in Oslo, Norway.

Anchors were approximately one and a half meters (five feet) long and made of iron or stone. The anchor stock was made of oak and was significantly larger than the anchor. Although anchors were not usually needed because of the ships' amphibious nature, they were probably used during tides when waiting for favorable sailing conditions. Displayed at the Viking Museum in Haithabu, northern Germany.

CHAPTER 5

SEAMANSHIP AND NAVIGATION

*By a choppy sea, the chill breeze of a gray dawn cut
through clothing and flesh. The defining moment
when preparation and reality merged was finally
at hand. The planning was complete, the ship ready,
the provisions stored under the floorboards. The
warriors surrendered themselves to their fate. The
day to sail had arrived.*

⎯⎯

The Vikings traveled widely and covered vast distances.
Not all came back, but most did manage to find their
way home. Every voyage was fraught with difficulties and
threats to life and security, but also offered opportunity for
daring adventures and the acquisition of incomparable riches.
Despite the hardships, or perhaps precisely because of the
risks, Norsemen became the most accomplished of sailors.
When the winds were favorable their ships sailed briskly
through rain and shine, dancing gaily, as a Norse *skald* might
have said, with strong swelling sails across the waves. The
ships were sturdy and could generally be trusted in high seas,
but no amount of organization or shipbuilding technology
could replace or compensate for first-rate sailing and navigational skills, especially in the conditions under which the
Norsemen traveled. The combination of organization, skill at
the technical aspects of shipbuilding, and know-how at sea
enabled the Vikings to raid in nearby waters and even cross
the Atlantic in search of new continents.

When travel was restricted to well-known domestic waters, only the simplest navigational methods were needed and many campaigns took place by following the coasts and river systems. By using known landmarks along the easily recognizable coastlines of the Baltic Sea, and as long as the weather cooperated and night travel was avoided, the Norsemen had instant knowledge of their location at all times. Distances were counted in days at sea and sailing was normally limited to daytime hours. Since the Vikings had no obligation to be at any particular place at any particular time, travel speed had little meaning unless they wanted to avoid pursuit by an enemy ship. Part of their strength as warriors lay in the sporadic nature of the attacks. In order to make good use of their large ships, and for both safety and speed, they had to sail close to the wind; to calculate travel distances between landmarks, they often had to guess at the intensity of the currents. Their vast experience at sea and familiarity with weather, wind and currents on the most frequently traveled routes provided them with an almost instinctive feeling for their whereabouts and gave them confidence. If two or more ships sailed together, sight could generally be maintained between the ships and the crews could rely on each other to find their way around.

The Nordic people's experience at sea went back hundreds of years. Tacitus, an early Roman historian, described Swedes centuries before the Viking Age as men strong of arms, powerful at sea: "The form of their vessels varies thus far from ours, that they have prows at each end, so as to be always ready to row to shore without turning."[1] Their exploits extended from the nearby waters of Scandinavia through the Baltic Sea and down to the Mediterranean. Even before the ninth century, Swedes had sailed east down the rich and mighty Russian rivers, the Volga and the Dnieper, on their trading journeys to the Black and Caspian seas, before going on to Constantinople.

To the west were England, Ireland and Scotland and to the northwest lay the Faroe Islands, Iceland and Greenland. Led by Leif Erikson, the son of the exiled Erik the Red, the Vikings ventured all the way to Newfoundland in North America. Coastline navigation presented few problems for the Vikings. Extended journeys, however, over open waters without maps, clocks, compasses or other modern navigational instruments required knowledge of the ship, sea, sun and stars, weather in general, wildlife and natural landmarks. The majority of men who undertook such journeys had no access to drawn maps, and those who did lived with the inaccuracy of existing charts.[2]

The navigational charts that existed were unreliable and the magnetic compass as a navigational aid for ocean voyages was used for the first time several hundred years after the Viking Age. The sunstone has been cited as having been used to sense the polarization of skylight, but few other navigational instruments existed and the Vikings had to rely on astronomical observation and dead reckoning. So how did they do it? Several navigational methods were employed, with varying success. The preferred method was word-of-mouth. Personal accounts provided a clear mental map of their part of the world and helped them understand how the winds blew at certain times of the year. Landmarks, such as ocean wildlife or mountain ranges that could be seen at the horizon, were memorized and shared with others. The stories and practical knowledge passed on by those who had undertaken journeys and returned home safely to talk about them gave new generations of warriors a feel for where they wanted to go and what they could expect to find.

Trips to Iceland took about seven days at sea and by the tenth century had become fairly regular. These voyages, however, were often undertaken as trading missions, and as a result the crews often wintered in Iceland, returning to Norway the following spring. Sometimes winds and rough seas determined the final destination. The Swede Gardar Svavarsson is credited by some sources with having discovered Iceland accidentally in about 860, while on a voyage to the Hebrides to claim his inheritance (he was married to a woman from the Hebrides). He sailed into a storm and was blown off course, but eventually reached the eastern coast of Iceland. When he circumnavigated the landmass, he discovered that it was an island and named it after himself, Gardarholm. It is likely that the Irish monks who had settled Iceland prior to the Norsemen's discovery of this island also contributed to Viking knowledge of navigation across open waters. Although the Irish and the Norse were not on the best of terms, having confronted each other in battle in Ireland, stories on routes to Iceland circulated between them.

It is also speculated that hungry birds were brought along and then released to indicate the direction of land. Floki Vilgerdarson, nicknamed Raven-Floki, one of the first Norsemen in Iceland, is said to have brought three ravens on the journey from Norway. Whenever he thought he was close to land, he released one of the birds. The first raven flew over the stern of the boat and back toward the Faroe Islands. The second raven circled over the boat. The third raven flew in a straight line past the bow of the boat. When Floki followed this bird, he reached Iceland.

Accounts of personal experiences handed from one person to another were undoubtedly the most valued and might include how long it would take to sail a particular distance under specific weather conditions. Starting on the western coast of Norway, heading toward Iceland via the Shetland and Faroe Islands, the trip could be expected to take between seven and ten days. On such voyages, the Vikings followed the coast until arriving at the desired latitude, after which they headed straight west to their destination. On these longer trips, distant navigational landmarks, such as mountain ranges or sea birds, but also the migration patterns of animals such as whales or geese, which indicated proximity to land, were used. Land could also be ascertained by clouds which tended to form over it. The *Landnamabok*, the chronicles of Icelandic settlement, describes the trip from Bergen on Norway's western coast to Greenland as follows: "From Hernan (close to Bergen), sail west until you get to Hvarf on Greenland. Keep far enough from the Shetland Islands that they are barely visible in clear weather. Sail far enough from the Faroe Islands that you can see only half of these mountains over the horizon. Sail close enough to Iceland that you can see whales and birds."[3] Leaving from the northern part of England instead would have made the trip to Greenland considerably shorter; the Faroes, for example, could have been reached in only two days and two nights.

According to Adam of Bremen, an eleventh-century cleric, Norway extended to the most distant shores of the north, from which its name derives, and was the most infertile of all lands, suited only to beasts.[4] Ottar, a Viking chieftain from Halogaland, the northernmost of the Norwegian provinces, wanted to find out how far his land extended to the north. Later, in about 890, he recounted his travels to King Alfred of England: "Sail three days north with Norway on starboard and the wide sea on port, and you reach the end of the land of the whale hunters. Sail another three days north, and you can observe how the coastline turns toward the east. Sail four days to the east, and you can observe only the occasional Fin or fisherman. After waiting for due north winds, follow the coast to the south for five days and enter the mighty river, Dwina, across which is the land of the powerful and hostile

Bjarmer, where I did not dare set foot."[5] The crew never knew exactly what they would find when they made landfall. If the native population were hostile and the Viking forces inferior, a quick exit back to sea was often preferable over engaging in land battle.

Although most longer journeys involved traders and explorers rather than warriors, the ability to sail out of sight of land gave the Norsemen a tactical advantage and benefited them in warfare. The enemy could not spot the long-ships until the raid was upon them and had no time to mount a sufficient defense. Paradoxically, the number of war casualties during a raid had a positive effect in that the ship's carrying capacity was increased. The weight of the casualties could be subtracted and booty added in its place to be carried home to the Nordic countries.[6] But a smaller crew and more goods also meant fewer men at the oars in unfavorable winds. A ship heavily loaded with war treasures, but with fewer warriors to guard them, was safer journeying over open seas than traveling along the coasts where there was increased risk of meeting other pirates, largely other Norsemen. Asbjorn Selsbane, after returning to assassinate Thorer Sel who had humiliated him by stealing his beautiful sail and replacing it with a smaller shabbier one, at first sailed along the coast. Because of unfavorable wind, he steered his ship outside the rocks and the usual ships' channel, staying at sea until he could see the island he was looking for; its shape was "very long, but not broad at its widest part . . . It is thickly inhabited; but where the island is exposed to the ocean great tracts of it are uncultivated."

To navigate the open seas the crews must have had some knowledge of astronomy, or had at least one knowledgeable *ledhsagari* (navigator/guide) on board for the journey.[7] A man named Sigurd was said to have great talent and could not only interpret dreams, but also "determine the time of the day although no heavenly bodies could be seen." On clear dark nights Polaris, or the North Star, which lines up approximately with the North Pole and is stationary in the northern sky, could be used to determine latitude. The higher the star in the sky, the higher was the latitude and shorter the distance to the North Pole. Navigating by the stars, however, was possible only at night and only for one short month until the northern summer nights stayed too light for the stars to be consistently visible.[8]

In daytime the height of the sun could be used for navigational purposes. How the sun moved through the sky at different times of year was known and communicated from the elder to younger generations of sailors. A vertical stick or peg was used to measure the sun's shadow at noon. The length of the shadow was then marked off on a wooden disk surrounding the peg. If the shadow was too short, the sailor knew he had sailed too far to the south, if too long, he was too far to the north. It is also possible that latitude tables or sun charts that showed the motion of the sun were used in some way.

Another navigational device was the sun compass, or bearing dial, which determined the position of the sun and the moon, acted as a guide for north and south, and gave a rough estimates of longitude and latitude. The sun compass determined the ship's course through observation of how the shadow fell on a round disk. This instrument consisted of a rotational dial divided into the major directions of north, south, east and west and was perhaps marked with a scale comprised of thirty-two increments. Although the remains of what appears to be a bearing dial, with scratches thought to indicate the shadow of the sun at those latitudes, have been found in Greenland and dates to around the year 1000, it is unclear to what extent this instrument was used in the Viking Age.[9]

Another theory is that the Vikings used crystals of calcite that, when placed over a mark on wood or leather, gave a double image that aligned with the sun's position on cloudy days. Calcite, a mineral found in Iceland, changes color in polarized light and can be observed with greatest clarity around dusk and dawn. Because of its refractive properties, the sunstone may also have been used by Norse seafarers. The sunstone was probably made of feldspar, or Icelandic spar, a mineral with the capacity to polarize light. Looking through the sunstone and turning it until the color of the light changes from blue to pale yellow is an indication that it is pointing towards the sun. The farther north, the nearer the sun was to the horizon where it also stayed longer. Since the Vikings traveled extensively in the far north waters, this method would have worked well in enabling them to sense the polarization of light needed for navigation.

A more likely method, however, was dead reckoning, or observation of latitude with only a rough estimate of longitude. The longitude (east to west, or vice versa) was often equated to the distance sailed. Scotland and the northern part of England, for example, were located at roughly the same latitude as the Nordic countries, but at a longitude of ten to fifteen degrees farther west. By sailing due west from Denmark, it was likely possible, after a few days at sea, to reach Scotland or the northern part of England. The latitude could be checked against the sun or the North Star to prevent drifting too far off course.

If the ship encountered a storm, which happened frequently in the North Sea, it was in danger of getting lost and the crew had to rely on their leader's luck to bring them safely through the ordeal. In 1018, Thorarin Nefiulsfson was entrusted with taking a prisoner, the exiled King Hrorek, to Greenland and delivering him to Leif Erikson. He rigged out his vessel and considered what to do if, as often happened, the weather obliged him to land in Iceland instead. On departure, he caught a wind that enabled him to sail beyond the rocks and islands and into the ocean. When he saw the southern part of Iceland, he sailed west around it into the Greenland Ocean, encountering heavy storms that set him adrift for so long that summer came to an end. He managed nevertheless to make it back to Iceland where he disposed of his prisoner who then lived there for several years until his death. Hrorek is said to be the only Nordic king whose remains are in Iceland. In the summer of 1024, Thorarin made a second attempt between Norway and Iceland, this time with such favorable winds that the journey took him only four days.

Nothing mattered more than good winds and kind seas on a journey that was to last for the greater part of spring and summer. The Vikings disliked being out in their ships in autumn when evil forces were thought to be ruling over the seas. A leader whose luck brought favorable weather was therefore celebrated. A ship that returned home with booty, half of the original crew, and in need of only minor repairs was considered to have been successful.

As can be seen, navigation was an approximate science with limited application for the advancement and success of the journey, raid and return trip. In the end, skill and commitment were the determining factors. Although the Vikings were familiar with the speeds of their ships in stable weather and distances were often counted in days at sea, knowledge, along with physical and mental toughness, were required for sailing the world in a Viking long-ship. Although the ships were well-crafted and magnificent to the eye, the journey was still uncomfortable. Because of their flat and broad bottoms, the ships could easily capsize if the wind came from abeam. Shipwrecks due to foul weather, poor navigation, or enemy encounters were frequent. Many ships were lost at sea with all of their men and cargo. If a ship sunk, it might go unnoticed for months, perhaps forever, so that no search and rescue crews were dispatched to the scene. Of twenty-five ships that sailed from Iceland to Greenland in 985, only fourteen arrived.[10] In 1029, Earl Hakon of Norway went to England where he took a bride. When he was returning in autumn, he got lost in a heavy storm and "nothing belonging to the ship ever came to land." In about 1135, eleven of thirteen merchant ships were lost with all of the men and goods that were aboard. The twelfth ship was also lost, and although the cargo went to the bottom, the crew was saved. In Vallentuna, Sweden, a stone was raised in memory of Ingiberg's husband, who "drowned in Holm sea. His ship went down. Only three got away."

Comfort at sea was hard to come by, but important for maintaining morale. Sailing was preferably done in the summer during the day and in good weather, when the tide was favorable and the ship could land by nightfall on a beach where a fire could be lit, food cooked, and the weary warriors given a chance to enjoy a well-earned rest. If, however, the warriors wanted to stay on schedule and get on with the raid, rough seas could not be avoided. The Vikings challenged the roughest waters in the world with waves commonly rising so high that they hid sight of mountains and other landmarks. With the hull extending only a few feet above the surface of the water, there was no protection against the elements. Because of their clinker construction and flexible planking, the open ships took in considerable amounts of water and there was constant need of bailing. The warriors were probably wet and cold most of the time. A rune stone in Hønen, Norway, honors sailors at sea: "Out and far and lacking towel and food, wind-cold on ice. . . ." It took a tough and resilient man to find pleasure in the voyage alone.

"On shore the crazy boat I drew, wet to the skin, and frightened too," sang Sigvat Skald early in the winter of 1019, after leaving Sarpsborg, Norway, with two companions, going eastward over the moors to Gautland, Sweden, and running into difficulty crossing a river. If the weather was particularly bad, the crew could seek shelter under the sail. Animal hides, oiled to repel water, were used as raingear, but it is questionable how effective they were in high seas or heavy rain. Any opportunity to build a fire and warm up was welcome. The Danish king Harald Gormsson went ashore "accompanied by eleven others, and into the forest and kindled a fire to bask at. It was dark night by then. The king took off his clothes and warmed himself at the fire."

Night complicated such activities as lighting a fire for cooking, which was otherwise done in the evening when the ship was beached or anchored close to the strand, and camp was set up. Sigurd Slembe, a Norwegian king said by some to be only a pretender to the throne, carried a tinderbox with the tinder in a walnut shell encased in wax to make it impervious to water. King Magnus Barefoot did not bother to go ashore, sailing at night and pitching tents containing burning lights on his ships. King Harald Hardrade, sailing north along Vendilskage, encountered thick fog. When morning came and the king saw the sun shining down on the gilded dragonheads of the Danish enemy fleet, he told his crew to take down the tilts and use the oars. When a king was in a particular hurry to reach his destination or outrun an enemy pursuer, he ordered his crew to dismantle the tents, loosen the land ropes, hoist the sails, and depart hastily, regardless of the hour.

In general, however, the Vikings avoided sailing when visibility was reduced, or at night when known landmarks could not be seen. But if they were fortunate enough to have a double crew, they might continue rowing or sailing through the night, especially around the time of the summer solstice when the sun barely set below the horizon. Night sailing made it possible to outrun enemy ships and cover great distances across open seas in a shorter time. On such trips, there were no sheltered sleeping quarters, so the crew had to make itself as comfortable as possible on the open deck. The *Saga of Olaf Haraldson* suggests that the ships were decked fore and aft only, but not in the center where the rowers sat, making it impossible to put up a tent for shelter for a night onboard at anchor.

Escaping quickly with the booty after a raid required efficiency and the ability to sail in any weather conditions. In 1027, King Onund of Sweden, who raided widely in Denmark and took a lot of booty but no land, had three-hundred-fifty vessels when he left, but came back with less than one hundred. King Olaf of Norway, feeling sorry for the Swedish king, suggested that dead or run-away warriors were anyway worthless, so his loss was not really that great. In 838, a storm destroyed a Danish fleet, giving the Frisians it had set out to plunder good cause for celebration. In 877, when the Danish army was raiding in England, they "met with a great mist at sea, and there perished 120 ships at Sandwich." The Jomsvikings, the cream of the Viking elite, had to break off one of their battles because "it became so dark with nightfall that no one could longer see to fight."

The Vikings preferred to fight their battles on land, but if an enemy ship, most likely another long-ship, was encountered at sea, they had to be prepared for a furious fight regardless of location or weather conditions. Gaute Tofason went with five warships out of the Gaut River and fought a fleet of five large Danish merchant-ships. Although Gaute and his men managed to take four of the big vessels and came away with plentiful booty without losing a single man, the fifth vessel got away. Gaute turned around but the wind picked up and a storm came up so that Gaute lost his ship "with all the goods and the greater part of his crew." The Danes came with a new fleet of fifteen ships, caught up with the other four of Gaute's ships, killed Gaute's crew and recaptured the booty. According to the *Saga of the Jomsvikings*:

> "And right soon the weather began to thicken in the north and clouds covered the sky and the daylight waned. Next came flashes of lightning and thunder, and with them a violent shower. The Jomsvikings had to fight facing into the storm, and the squall was so heavy that they could hardly stand up against it . . . Nevertheless, no one needed to be urged on to do battle. But although the Jomsvikings hurled stones and other missiles and threw their spears, the wind turned all their weapons back upon them, to join the shower of missiles from their enemies."

Supply and logistics, too, had to be planned for and dealt with in preparation for long periods at sea. Food consisted of dried or salted meat, fresh fish, nuts, and beer or sour milk to wash it down. Barrels were used for the transport of liquids, such as water and beer, as well as for the protection of foodstuffs and other valuables against the saltwater spray of the ocean. "No drink but the salt sea, on board our ships had we," sang the skald Thiodolf when Magnus the Good and Svein Ulfson battled it out at Helganes. When King Harald Hardrade was marauding in Denmark and the lighter Danish ships pursued the Norwegian fleet, King Harald ordered his men to lighten their ships by throwing overboard malt, wheat, and bacon, and letting their liquor run out. Needing drinking water, the warriors went up into the islands, but found none.[11] The king, however, had a brilliant idea; he instructed his crew to find earthworms on the island and place them close to a fire to make them thirsty. He then ordered the men to follow the worms until they burrowed into the earth and to dig at that location for water.

River travel also exposed the Norsemen to danger and required knowledge of tidal effects on the river. For those sailing east, the river Dnieper posed perils deadlier than any other river. The terrifying rapids required the Vikings to transport their ships overland, hauling or carrying them on their shoulders. The Byzantine emperor Constantine Porphyrogenitus, in a manual written about 950, listed seven of these fearful falls, one of which he claimed was called *Aifor* (Ever Fierce) by the Rus. Landfall, however, required awareness against ambush by the local Petchenegs, a nomadic and warlike people of Central Asia who occupied the eastern lands in the ninth and tenth centuries.

River currents are strongest where the river is deepest. Sailing close to the center of the river was advantageous when the Vikings were traveling with the current. When traveling against the current, a position closer to shore was better. Knowledge of how to sail the Seine and the Loire, the major rivers of France, helped the Vikings in the ninth century to harass the Frankish population, in particular those in the monasteries and cities such as Paris. Sailing first up the Loire and raiding in the southwestern part of France, they next followed the favorable winds to the northwestern part of Spain. If they were unsuccessful in that region, they returned to France and plundered in Bordeaux and many other cities.[12]

Historical records confirm that the Vikings frequently sailed through areas that were experiencing tidal waters. For example, when Thorer Hund insisted that they go ashore and divide the booty the men had acquired in their raid in Bjarmaland, Gunstein, his companion, noted that it was time to sail because the tide was turning, so they began to raise the anchor.[13] Tidal oscillations are the effect of the sun and moon's gravitational pull on the earth and are highest when the sun, moon, and earth are aligned (at new and full moons). These tides are known as spring tides. Neap tides come in between spring tides, when the moon is at a 90-degree angle to earth.[14] Tides are most noticeable where there are large masses of water inhibited by land on one or both sides. The highest tides therefore occur in water that is shallow, such as in channels or near land. High tides have been found in the English Channel and along the coasts of Normandy, waters frequently traveled by the Vikings. Normandy, in fact, has one of Europe's largest tidal variations with currents up to ten knots.[15]

The ability to predict tides was important to pirates and other seafarers. Since both the earth and the moon rotate around the sun together, tides do not occur at exactly the same time every day. The tidal cycle is a little over twelve hours from one high tide to the next, with about a fifty-minute delay over the same point on earth per day. The time of high tide gets later as the day progresses—valuable information for knowing when to depart on a sea voyage. Accompanying the tides are currents. It was not until the nineteenth century, however, that tides and currents could be predicted with reasonable accuracy. In the Viking Age they were instead observed, memorized and then communicated to the younger generations.

To avoid getting stuck until the next tidal cycle, departures had to take place when the tide was ebbing. The appearance and disappearance of sea grass on rocks lining the shores and the sound of splashing waves and rising water were the warning signs of ebb and flow. Oars could have been used as sounding lines to find water depth and changes in the color of the water could also warn against running aground; if the wind were blowing, water was likely to break over sandbars and rocks. Viking ships, however, were built for sailing through shallow waters and were well-suited for river travel through France, Russia and the Byzantine Empire.

Out on the wide ocean, tide had little effect on the longships. Currents, however, experienced great directional changes due to the rotation of the earth, sometimes resulting in waters that flowed east to west, or vice versa. Such currents were advantageous for crossing the North Sea, but in a situation where there was no wind, a ship would not make headway if the current went against the direction of travel. Ways around this were to start rowing against the current, row towards land and wait for better conditions, or anchor the ship in place and wait. Rowing against the current was obviously an inconvenient alternative, since rowing was hard work even in favorable conditions. It was also difficult to row against a current stronger than three knots and little headway could be made. When Eyvind Urarhorn was sailing from Ireland to Norway in 1019, "the weather was boisterous and the current against him, so he ran into Osmundwall (in Orkney), and lay there wind-bound for some time." Rowing could also be disastrous from a military perspective. Around 1158, Erling Skakke advised King Inge not to row against the river current when attacking, because one out of three men would then have to be engaged in rowing while the others covered the rower with a shield, "and what have we then to fight with but one third of our men?" Men sitting at the oars with their backs toward the enemy were of little use in battle.

Most of the daring Norse sailors were men who lived peacefully when at home between raids; they owned farms and had wives and children. But the ship was an intimate part of Viking life and when on campaign, the Norse warrior bowed to no one. Disputes undoubtedly arose among the one-hundred or so free-spirited men stuffed into the cramped quarters of a long-ship with no place for privacy, sometimes for weeks at a time. To avoid problems and facilitate efficiency, men had assigned seats and duties. For example, King Olaf Trygvason, owner of the *Long Serpent*, organized his men as follows: Ulf the Red, the man who bore the banner, was in the forecastle together with Kolbjörn the Marshal, Thorstein

Uxafot and Vikar of Tiundaland; by the bulkhead were Vak Raumason from Gaut River, Berse the Strong, An Skyte from Jamtaland, Thrand the Strong from Thelamork and his brother Uthyrmer; then came the Halogamen, Thrand, Ogmund, Hlodver and Harek, together with the Throndhjem men, Ketil, Thorfin, Havard and his brothers. In the forehold were Björn, Bork, Thorgrim, Asbjörn, Orm, Thord, Thorstein, Arnor, Halstein, Eyvind, Bergthor, Halkel, Olaf, Arnfin, Sigurd, Einar, Fin, Ketil from Rogaland and Grjotgard the Brisk. In the hold next to the mast were Thorstein, Thorolf, Ivar and Orm Skogarnef, and Einar Tambaskelfer, who at eighteen was not considered to be as experienced as the other men. There were many more brave men, too numerous to mention, on the *Long Serpent*. In every half division of the hold were eight men, with thirty men in the forehold.[16]

There were established rules and disciplinary procedures. The elite Jomsvikings had laws stating that no one within the fort could start a quarrel, that all booty was to be carried to the standard, and that every man had a duty to avenge any other member as though he were his brother. On campaign, those failing to abide by the rules might be asked to leave the ship or pay a fine. Disciplinary action was taken for crimes that ranged from stealing or hitting resulting in injuries, either with or without visible bloodshed, intentionally throwing a man overboard, or killing another crew member. Communication problems also had to be resolved onboard the ships' noisy cramped quarters. The *Long Serpent* had gangways running along the sides of the ship to help the crew members move from bow to stern, or vice versa, and enable messages to be delivered.

It seemed that the Vikings knew how to get things done. But the constant work at the oars, "at sea beneath the ice-cold sky," the ocean's wild roar, the joyless weather, wind and rain, the pinching cold "and feet in pain," along with fatigue and sleep deprivation, eventually took their toll. A rune-inscribed oar uncovered in Iceland around the year 1530, speaks of the toil the men had to endure on the trip between Greenland and Iceland: "I was often tired when I pulled you."[17] When a safe beach was reached, the oars were placed along the sides of the ship and the ship was hauled up on land. After the fire was lit and the exhausted men were finally able to warm up, rest and satisfy hunger and thirst, the hard work was quickly forgotten and stories around the campfire began to flow as beer loosened the warriors' tongues. Camaraderie and a sense of belonging did wonders to heal battle-weary hearts.

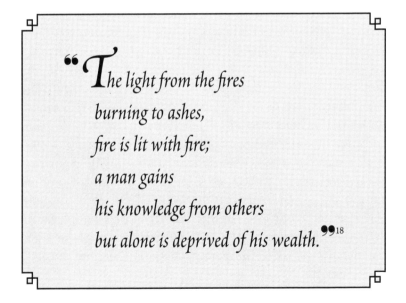

"*The light from the fires*
burning to ashes,
fire is lit with fire;
a man gains
his knowledge from others
but alone is deprived of his wealth."[18]

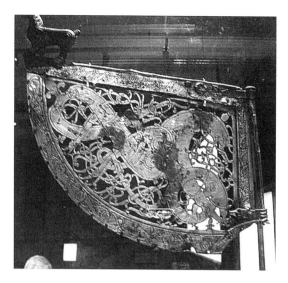

Ornate weather vane made of bronze. Weather vanes had unusual quadrant shapes, often mounted by an animal or creature from Norse fable, and were commonly used on Viking long-ships. Displayed at the Museum of History in Stockholm, Sweden.

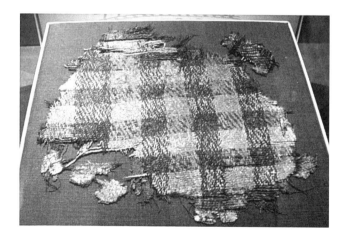

Clothing remnants. Viking women were skilled at spinning, weaving and embroidering and made clothes for the warriors as well as sails for the ships. Many fabrics were colored and had artistic patterns. Textiles were generally made of wool and silks and were most likely imported. Warriors needed at least one change of clothing for the journey, and if possible, a set of oil skins to keep them dry. Displayed at the Viking Ship Museum in Oslo, Norway.

Shoes were made of wood and leather and required considerable time to dry when wet. Displayed at the Viking Museum in Haithabu, northern Germany.

Hand millstone. Grain was coarsely ground and mixed with fine stone powder. Displayed at the Viking Ship Museum in Oslo, Norway.

Iron cauldron holding thirty-five to forty liters hanging from an iron stand, or tripod, which could be folded to save space when not in use. This cookware was probably used to feed the crew onboard the ship. Displayed at the Viking Ship Museum in Oslo, Norway.

Barrels were used to transport food and liquids, such as water, wine, beer and milk. On trading ships, delicate goods such as grain, clothes and furs were stored in barrels to protect them from the salt-water spray of the ocean. *Displayed at the Viking Ship Museum in Oslo, Norway.*

Barrels with the tops and bottoms knocked out were also used as wells on land. *Displayed at the Viking Museum in Haithabu, northern Germany.*

CHAPTER 6

WEAPONS AND ARMOR

When the message-token was sent out for war, young energetic men from all parts of the Nordic countries came together and crafted ships, swords, spears, axes, shields and helmets. An offering was made to Thor and the warriors' heads were sprinkled with blood.[1]

— ❦ —

Norse warfare was rooted in physical strength and courage. A warrior had to be in good health and be mentally strong. Physical ability was especially valued. A tall man, skilled at arms, was best-suited for triumph in war. Good weapons were the next requisite. Norse law held that every man should own weapons to protect himself and others. Weapons had to be affordable, durable, efficient and easy to handle. The warriors derived psychological strength from powerful weaponry that could threaten and intimidate the enemy. The mere sight of these tall fierce Viking warriors was sufficient to cause the enemy to run or hide behind their battle shields. When conflict started, spears and arrows flew so thick they blackened the sky. Axes were "hard driven, shields cleft and byrnies torn, helmets . . . shivered, skulls split . . . and many a man felled to the cold earth."

A warrior's weapons and shields protected him in battle, but were also a kind of status symbol, serving to enhance both his self-pride and respect for the chief under whose banner he was fighting. Axes and swords were personal objects, so highly prized that they were given commanding proper names. Because a warrior's life depended on them, it was important for him to give an identity to his weapons and armor. The name a warrior gave to his sword created a bond between him and his weapon, gave him confidence in his abilities, and allowed him to believe he was invincible in battle.

King Magnus the Good had a battleaxe that had belonged to his father which he called *Hel* after the goddess of death. In battle he swung it with both hands until shields, helms and skulls flew and it was said that never had there been such a massacre in the northern lands since the time of the Christianization. Skarphedinn named his axe the *Ogress of War* and once used it to hack at his opponent Thrain splitting his head open "so that his jaw-teeth fell out on the ice." After King Aethelstan gave his foster-son Hakon a sword with a superb blade and a golden hilt and handle, Hakon named it *Quernbite* (little millstone) after he had tested it to his satisfaction on a millstone. Earl Sigurd had a sword called *Bastard*, and Steinar's sword, named after Skrymir the Giant, was said never to have failed.

Ships, standards and mail shirts were also similarly honored. Earl Erik of Norway owned a ship he named *Ironbeard* because of its armored bow and stern.[2] Ragnar Lodbrok's celebrated *Raven* banner was presumably woven between dawn and dusk in a single day by three of his daughters.[3] In 878, Ubbe, Ragnar's son and brother of Ingwar and Halfdan, landed in Wessex with twenty-three ships, forcing King Alfred the Great to go into hiding in the woods. But Ubbe and eight hundred of his men were killed and the English took possession of the banner. King Harald Hardrade's banner, called *Land-Ravager* (also *Land-Waster*), was carried before him on the battlefield. It was his single, most-valued piece of property, as it was a common saying that "he must gain the victory before whom that banner is borne." In the battle of Scarborough, Harald Hardrade fought on the premise that the only choice an

Englishman had if he wished to live was to submit to him. In the battle at Humber, he ordered the Land-Ravager banner to be carried before him and assaulted so fiercely that the enemy gave way, leaping into a ditch that became so filled with the dead that the Norsemen were able to proceed dry-foot over the fen. The skald Stein Herdison spoke of this event in a song called "Harald's Stave": "Earl Valthiof's men lay in the fen, by sword down hewed, so thickly strewed, that Norsemen say they paved the way across the fen for the brave Norsemen." Harald Hardrade also had a coat of mail he called *Emma*; it was long, reaching the middle of his leg and looked like a dress, but it was so strong that no weapon ever pierced it.

The victims of Bolli's *Footbiter* should have been informed as to the name of their attacker's sword to safeguard their legs from the blows. Chopping off an enemy's limbs, the legs for example, could end the fight instantly, but it was also common to sever the head from the body. This brutality, mentioned extensively in the Viking sagas, seemed to be part of the strategy. Thorarin cut the leg from Thorir at the thickest part of the calf; Steinthor cut Thorleif Kimbi's leg from him below the knee; and Asgrim shot a spear at Skapti, striking him through both legs just below the fattest part of the calf.

Even if the attack missed and there was no physical damage, the victim was greatly frustrated. A skillful defender learned to anticipate these moves and avoid them. When Hall-bjorn aimed for Kari's leg, Kari leapt into the air so that the blow missed him. Orm was lying on a bench when his enemy raised a battleaxe against him; Orm drew his feet in and threw them back over his head so that the blow fell on the bench and the axe stuck fast in the wood. If a man took a mortal blow, he could succumb and die or attempt to take his opponent's life before his own ended. When Thorbiorn and Thorod battled it out, neither spared the other. The fight should have ended when Thorod hacked off Thorbiorn's foot at the ankle-joint. Nevertheless, Thorbiorn fought on and "thrust forth his sword into Thorod's belly, so that he fell and his guts burst out." A spear pierced King Magnus Barefoot through both thighs, but the king grabbed the shaft between his legs and broke the spear in two, saying that nothing could hurt him. He then encouraged his men to continue fighting. When a warrior lost his legs and had the stomach for it, he continued fighting on his stumps for as long as he could before finally passing out and dying from shock and loss of blood. Havard Hoggande was found standing on his knees at the ship's railing with a bow in his hand, "for his feet had been cut off."

The arm and the fingers on the hand that held the sword were also fair game. If a man lost a hand or injured it badly enough, the limb had no further use for offense or defense, severely crippling the warrior. Kormac's blow on his opponent Thorvard's shoulder was so severe that he could fight no longer because his collarbone was broken and his hand good for nothing. Gettir (or Grettir) the Strong (Asmundarson), said to be a descendent of Onund Treefoot (who had lost a leg), dealt his opponent Hjarrandi a blow that cut off his arm at the shoulder. When Gunnar battled it out with Gettir and his hands and shield were still inside Gettir's door, Gettir struck down between Gunnar and the shield, cutting off both of Gunnar's hands at the wrists. The fighters understood the importance their hands played in combat. Some even communicated their feelings at the moment the determining blow fell. After Helgi cut off Hrapp's arm, Hrapp said before he collapsed and died: "Thou hast done a most needful work, for this hand hath wrought harm and death to many a man." Norse defense strategy and the limitations of their weaponry were more obvious when Norsemen clashed with other Norsemen. At the battle in Stiklestad where King Olaf Haraldson fell in 1030, Sigvat Skald, the king's court poet who was in Rome at the time, still managed to record how "the clear blood ran beneath the feet of Swedes," who had come from the east to share in

Olaf's gain or loss. Olaf's younger brother Harald, still a child, insisted on taking part in the battle, "for I am not so weak that I cannot handle the sword; and as to that, I have a notion of tying the sword-handle to my hand." Fighting on foreign soil proved more profitable. King Olaf died in the battle, but young Harald, though severely wounded, escaped. He fled through the forests to King Jarisleif in Russia, made a remarkable recovery, worked as a mercenary for the Russian king, then sailed on and served for several years as a bodyguard to the emperor in Constantinople. After eighteen battles he returned home an immensely rich man, his body still intact, to reclaim the Norwegian crown.

Craftsmen skilled in metal-working were a feature of Viking culture and were highly regarded all over Europe. In addition to jewelry such as brooches and pins to hold clothes together, and weathervanes to decorate ships (most motifs were derived from nature and included ornate animal figures braided into complicated and artistic patterns), these craftsmen also constructed weapons such as swords (that were often artistic and pleasing to the eye), axes (made of iron, sometimes with inlays of silver), and spearheads.[4] Several sword finds reveal the names Ingelrii and Ulfberth, the sword makers, carved into the blades of the weapons.[5]

Although most warriors could afford only the bare necessities in weaponry, generally a sword and a shield, and sometimes just a shield and somewhat cruder weapons such as spears and arrows, some men were well-off and had weapons that, when viewed from a distance, gleamed like shining ice. King Magnus Barefoot, for example, "had a helmet on his head; a red shield, in which was inlaid a gilded lion; and was girt with the sword of Legbit, of which the hilt was of tooth [ivory], and the sword was extremely sharp." Most weapons, however, were sturdy and practical rather than decorative. The exact method by which weapons were constructed is not known, but it is believed that individual pieces were welded together. The central section of a sword blade consisted of several longer and thinner rods of iron that were hammered out and matched to form a pliable core. The edge was then welded to the core. In the 999–1000 millennium, Olaf Trygvason set out on his final battle in the *Long Serpent*. Seeing his men striking away with their swords but wounding few of the enemy, he called out: "Why do ye strike so gently that ye seldom cut?" After one of his men answered: "The swords are blunt and full of notches," Olaf Trygvason went down into the forehold of the ship, opened up a chest from which he took a number of sharp swords, and handed them to his men.

A warrior usually tested the strength of the sword before accepting it from the smith. Sigurd struck his sword into an anvil to test its strength, but it broke and he asked Regin, the smith, to forge a better one. Handing Sigurd a new sword, Regin said that if this one failed, he would not know how to make a better one. Sigurd tested it on the anvil which split. He praised the smith and went to the river with a piece of wool, which he threw up in the air against the stream to test the sharpness of the sword. He was very pleased when the wool fell into pieces. After acquiring their weapons from the smith, the warriors sharpened the blades, tested their strength and heeded the war horns when it was time to go on campaign.

A battle normally started at long range. Spears and arrows were fired from behind a shield formation, opening up a path for the close-range battle to follow. At sea, archers were positioned at the rear of the ship. During an uprising in Konungahella around 1135, a warrior among the Vindlanders was shooting with a bow and killed one man for every arrow shot; he protected himself behind two men who covered him with their shields.[6] The opposing Viking force fired at one of the shield bearers, displacing the shield so that when a second arrow was fired, it hit the archer in the forehead and came out his neck.

The Vikings were best known for their prowess with close-combat weapons—the sword and the axe. Although all free men were expected to carry weapons, swords, because of the amount of metal needed for their manufacture, were generally reserved for use by leaders or wealthy Vikings. Swords were sometimes traded abroad and sword blades were commonly imported from France and fitted with hilts made locally. "Each man has an axe, a sword and a knife and keeps each by him at all times," said Ibn Fadlan, an Arab chronicler of the time. He further described the swords as broad, grooved and of Frankish sort. The swords, used primarily for slashing or chopping, rather than as thrusting weapons, had blades tapered to a blunt tip. Lengthwise along the blade was a groove, called a blood groove or fuller, which made the weapon less expensive and lighter in weight, while maintaining strength.[7]

Swords were often stolen or stripped from the lifeless foe, along with shields, helms, ring-mail and plate-armor.[8] When Angle killed Gettir the Strong, he thought Gettir had carried his sword long enough and tried to pry it out of his hand, but the dead man's grip was so tightly locked around the hilt that eight men, attempting in turn to loosen it, all failed. When they recognized the futility of the situation, they decided that there was no need to spare a dead man. They placed Gettir's hand on a log and chopped off the hand at the wrist. When the hand was severed from the arm, the fingers straightened, enabling Angle to take the sword.

Swords had to be simple and functional. Although they were heavier than spears, they were also more durable. Swords were commonly one meter (three feet) long and ten centimeters (four inches) wide and could weigh one and a half to two kilos (three to four and a half pounds), light enough to be maneuverable.[9] Since combat with a sword involved a cut or a chop, the warrior was able to have positive confirmation of a kill. Killing an enemy with a sword was considered nobler than killing with a spear thrown from a distance. A distinguishing feature on a spear or arrow, such as a tip wound in gold, could sometimes give the finder of the weapon positive identification of the wielder.

The swords were devastating in power. Thorstein Midlang got into a fight with Bue of the elite Jomsvikings, cut him across the nose, severing the nosepiece of his helmet in half and inflicting a major wound. Bue countered by hacking at Thorstein's side and cut his opponent in half. Bersi took up his sword, two-handed, and dealt a deathblow to Thorkel, while Gunnar received his on the neck, his head falling off onto the board before the kings and the earls, "and the board was all one gore of blood, and the earl's clothing too." Guttorm drew his sword and pierced through the sleeping Sigurd so the sword point struck the bed beneath him. But Sigurd awoke and threw the sword at Guttorm, hitting him in the back, "and struck him asunder in the midst, so that the feet of him fell one way, and the head and hands back into the chamber." Thorer Lange drew his sword and struck his opponent Eilif on the neck so that his head flew off, and Thorarin rushed at Thorbjorn and "smote his sword into his head, and clave it down to the jaw-teeth." Gettir struck a blow at Thorbjorn with his sword "which severed Thorbjorn's shield in two and went into his head, reaching the brain," and Sigurd attacked Lyngi, the king, "and clave him down, both helm and head, and mail-clad body." Shields and armor were frequently split "like ice beneath the tread" by the power of a sword.

Swords were straight and double-edged (sharp on both edges) and because they could be turned over in the hand, or used with either hand, there was no need for a warrior to bother checking which side was the cutting edge. These types of swords are called *vandil* (*som man kan vända*, meaning "that which can be turned over"). Swords were normally wielded with the right hand; if a warrior were left-handed or used his left hand because of an injury to his right hand, the cuts would come from unusual angles and be unpredictable and difficult for an opponent to defend against: "Then Ogmund whirled about his sword swiftly and shifted it from hand to hand, and hewed Asmund's leg from under him." A skilled warrior could cut or thrust well with either hand. Gunnar could "cut with one hand and thrust with the other," and one warrior is said to have been so swift with his sword "that three seemed to flash through the air at once."

In addition to their use on the battlefield, swords and other weapons were also utilized to settle disputes. For example, a man who had been insulted might challenge the offender to *holmganga*, a duel of honor designed to resolve the differences between the parties. The *holmganga* took place on a small island (*holm*), or other carefully marked-off, restricted area. A square with sides ranging between nine and twelve feet would be set up for the purpose and an animal hide placed on the ground and secured with pins that were driven into loops at the corners. Each combatant was allowed three shields and a shield bearer, a helper who carried the shield during the duel and replaced a lost or broken shield. When a combatant lost all of his shields, he had to continue defending himself as best he could with sword alone. The person who had been challenged to *holmganga* was entitled to strike the first blow. His opponent would parry the blow and counter with another single blow; only one strike at a time was allowed. The blows continued until one of the combatants was injured. If blood fell onto the hide, the fight would stop and the wounded man would be required to pay three marks of silver to be set free and have his honor restored. If a combatant set a foot outside the pins, it was said that "he went on his heels," but if both feet were out, he was said "to run."

The battleaxe was another close combat weapon that made the Vikings valued mercenaries and infamous as far away as Constantinople. Axes were heavy, devastating chopping instruments whose blows laid many a man to permanent rest and caused the enemy army to fall "as thick as tangles heaped up by the waves on the strand." The axe clearly distinguished the Nordic marauders from the warriors of other empires. Although all European countries used an arsenal consisting of swords, spears and knives at the time of the Vikings, the sword generally surpassed the axe in European warfare. But for the Norse, the axe is considered their trademark in land battle. The Norsemen serving in the Varangian Guard in Constantinople, who took sworn oaths to protect the emperor to the death, went by the name "axe-bearing barbarians."

The axe was also used in disputes between Norsemen, either as a threat or to finish the adversary off in a fight. Uspak said to Alf: "Come not nigh, Alf; thin is thy skull and heavy my axe." When King Knut the Great of Denmark, who also ruled in England, threatened the Norwegian king Olaf Haraldson's dominions, King Olaf stood resolutely before the other Norse king and exclaimed: "I will defend Norway with battle-axe and sword as long as life is given me, and will pay scat [tax] to no man for my kingdom."

Axes were also popular because of the psychological damage they could inflict on the enemy. They ranged in size from a short single-handed version to the large Danish axe, which had a length of one to one and a half meters (three to five feet) and a cutting edge of up to fifty-six centimeters (twenty-two inches) and was wielded with both hands in a sweeping left to right motion. Thorgeir lifted his *Ogress of War* with both hands and "dashed the hammer of the axe with a back-blow into the head of him that stood before him, so that his skull was shattered to small bits." Most of the weight was concentrated in the head of the axe, so when launched in an overhead attack, it was a superbly strong hacking instrument that relied on gravity rather than muscle power. The axe was capable of cutting through an opponent's defense, which included his shield, mail armor and helmet, quickly killing him and splitting his skull in half all the way down to his shoulders so that his eyeballs fell out. The Danish axe was said to have a swing that could behead a horse with a single stroke.

Because of their size, axes were used strategically on the battlefield to cut through an enemy's shield wall outside of normal sword range. Once a gap had been formed in the wall, the remaining warriors had room to advance with their own shield wall and continue their heavy chopping assault from close range. A drawback of these big axes was that they could be wielded only by the strongest and most-skilled warriors and became impractical at very close range. The axe wielder needed considerable mobility in the arms and shoulders and lacked protection by his peers who had to stand several feet behind him, out of range of the swinging axe.[10] The psychological effect of this huge weapon on the enemy was great. Knowing that they could not protect themselves against these large axes, they had no choice but to retreat. The axe was therefore useful for breaking up enemy formations and paving the way for a raid.

On the battlefield, broadaxes of shining steel "rang on helm, and sword on shield." During a raid in Bjarmaland (Russia in the area of the White Sea), the battleaxe was also used, according to the account, to climb a fence to steal a gold ornament from the adversary's god. "Thorer went to the fence, stuck his axe up in it above his head, hauled himself up by it, and so came over the fence, and inside the gate." Once inside the fence, Thorer and his accomplice Karle found a mound in which gold, silver and earth were all mixed together and which was protected by the Bjarmaland people's god, Jomala. The Viking marauders decided to leave the god alone since nobody knew what powers such a strange god might have, but they could not keep their hands off the glittering stack of gold and silver. They took as much money as they could carry away with them in their clothes. But on their way back to the ship, greed got the better of Thorer. He decided to return to Jomala and steal the silver bowl full of silver money on the god's knee. Karle, unwilling to take second place in the plundering, also returned and cut a thick gold ornament from the god's neck with such force that "the head of Jomala rang with such a great sound that they were all astonished."

Smaller battleaxes wielded with one hand were the choice of weapon of some Vikings and were used primarily for heavy close-range fighting after the spear had been thrown to set up the attack. Shorter swords and knives, frequently worn both as weapons and utility tools, were used in much the same way as foot soldiers use the knife today. The *scramasax*, resembling a butcher knife or machete, was a single-edged knife or short sword carried across the back of the belt by the poor people of society, and was used primarily as a utility tool and defensive weapon by the Vikings and Saxons between the fourth and tenth centuries.[11] Knives served as excellent close combat weapons. "Thorir had a chain-knife around his neck, as the fashion then was." Hrorek conspired with his friend Svein to kill King Olaf Haraldson. When the king was ready to go to vespers, "Svein stood on the threshold with a drawn dagger under his cloak." As it turned out, Svein lost his nerve and was unable to commit the act. Later on Ascension Day when King Olaf was at high mass, Hrorek laid his hand on the king's shoulder to feel if he was wearing armor. When the mass ended and King Olaf was bowing before the altar with his cloak hanging down, Hrorek struck at him with a long knife. The king's clothes were cut, but he managed to escape injury. Rather than punishing Hrorek with death for the attempted murder, Olaf exiled him to Greenland.

Knives were also used as projectiles. Kalf Arnason invited all men with injuries to retaliate against King Olaf Haraldson by placing themselves under the banner advancing against the king and, in so doing, recall the distress the king had caused them. Kalf then went in search of his missing brothers, Thorberg and Fin, and found them, uninjured, on the battlefield. Rather than join Kalf in the protest, however, Fin threw his dagger at his brother, calling him "a faithless villain, and a traitor to his king." Poorer folk often had to wield whatever weapons were available to them in battle—arrows, spears, stones, sticks and staves. Ivar's brother Leif beat one of Steinn's men to death with the rib of a whale. Once when Gettir attacked, the victims defended themselves against his spear and sword with logs found lying on the ground. Some men were forced to take refuge in the boathouse and defend themselves with oars.

The spear and the bow were weapons of choice, more common than the knife, as projectile weapons from long-range. The spear was the favored weapon of Oden, the god of war, and is pictured extensively on rune stones and tapestries. The walls of Valhalla, the slain warriors' hall, were constructed of glistening spears, and the roof was a dome of golden shields. The splendor of Valhalla motivated the Vikings to use their spears in battle in the belief that if they died, Oden would honor them by adding their spears to the many others already supporting his magnificent hall.

Trees used for the construction of spears and other weapons, such as arrows and shields, grew in abundance in the Scandinavian forests. If a weapon could be manufactured from wood, it was; this included the ship, the greatest weapon of all. The availability of wood and the ease with which it was obtained allowed the Norsemen to craft a surplus of weapons between voyages. A surplus lightened the loss of an irretrievable spear thrown at an enemy or a shield chopped to pieces.

The spear was both efficient and inexpensive. It could penetrate most objects it hit, required little skill to use in battle and was easy to handle in piercing, slashing and throwing attacks. The only metal was in the twenty-five to fifty-centimeter-long tip (ten to twenty inches). The thin tip was fastened to a wooden handle of varied length, generally between two and three meters (six and a half and ten feet). The spear was also lightweight enough to be wielded with one hand, with the shield held in the other hand for defense. In close combat, this tactic provided the Vikings with sufficient reach without having to give up the safety provided by the shield. Some of the longer spears used for close-range thrusting or slashing attacks were probably wielded with two hands. They were devastating weapons that could penetrate both shield and mail armor. Thorhall thrust his spear at Grim the Red, right through his shield which split in two, and through his opponent, so that the point of the spear came out between his shoulders.

Although the spear was occasionally used in close-range thrusting attacks, it was primarily designed as a projectile weapon to be thrown from long range to open the line of battle, kill or harm as many of the enemy as possible prior to the hand-to-hand clash and prevent them from countering the attack. Shorter spears were used as javelins and have been found in great numbers in Viking graves in Scandinavia. When the combatant lines met, the warriors threw their spears before drawing their swords, axes or knives and moving forward amidst the bloodshed.

When spears, arrows and "all kinds of missiles flew as thick as a snow-drift," blackening the view, and when "spear torrents swept away ranks of brave men from light of day" and pursuit of the enemy continued all the way to the beach, the weaker ones who had not yet fallen sought refuge by throwing themselves into the water for protection. Man-to-man disputes were also settled with the spear. Asmund Grankelson vowed that he would make the blue cloak of Asbjorn Selsbane, the man who killed Thorer Sel, red with blood. He threw his spear with such precision and force that it hit Asbjorn in the middle of his body, tore through him and stuck fast in the upper part of the sternpost on Asbjorn's ship. Sigrid, Asbjorn's mother, recovered the feathered spear with the gold-mounted handle, gave it to Thorer Hund, Asbjorn's uncle, and asked him to avenge the death of her son.[12]

When it came to hurling spears, the Norsemen's natural physical height provided them with a built-in advantage compared to their shorter European counterparts. The Vikings' tall build and long arms (the Arab chronicler Ibn Fadlan described them as "tall as date palms") benefited them on the battlefield, enabling them to throw the spears from a greater distance or over the heads of other warriors in the same shield formation, than could shorter men. Arnjlot Gelline, who came to the assistance of King Olaf Haraldson on the battlefield in Stiklestad, is said to have been so tall that no one else stood higher than his shoulders. The warrior Sigurd had a wide, high-nosed, high-boned face with eyes so keen that "few durst gaze up under the brow of him," and shoulders so broad they looked like those of two men. When "he was girt with this sword Gram, which same was seven spans long, as he went through the full-grown rye-fields, the dew-shoe of the said sword smote the ears of the standing corn."[13] King Magnus Barefoot, also called Magnus the Tall, was distinguished by his height which was marked in Mary Church in the merchant town of Nidaros: "In the northern door there were cut into the wall three crosses, one for Harald's stature, one for Olaf's and one for Magnus's; and which crosses each of them could with the greatest ease kiss." King Trygve Olafson (son of Olaf Trygvason) took advantage not only of his height, but also of his skill. He was a man who slaughtered by throwing spears with both hands at once.

The problem with a projectile weapon was that, if it missed, the enemy acquired ownership of it and could return it with equal force. Thorstein took the spear out of Bruni's wound and hurled it back at his opponent. Kari saw the spear aimed at him in the air and threw his shield down so hard that the point stuck fast in the ground; he caught the spear and hurled it back at his opponent, simultaneously picking up his shield with his other hand. Gettir the Strong had great foresight; to prevent his opponent from returning the spear, he knocked out the rivet that fastened the spearhead, but the head was not as firm as intended and it loosened in flight and fell to the ground, rendering the throw useless.

After the spear was thrown, bows and arrows were employed, particularly in sea battles. Einar Tambaskelfer is said to have been the best archer in Norway. He could shoot with a blunt arrow through a raw soft ox-hide hanging over a beam. Bows were crafted of wood, sometimes strengthened with horn or iron. Bows ranged in size between one and almost two meters (three and six feet), could shoot over an effective range of 200 meters (660 feet), could easily penetrate a mail shirt from close range, and were especially successful when used in volleys. To be effective in warfare, the bow required a tension of at least thirty-five kilos (seventy-seven pounds), and often more. The warrior therefore needed considerable strength to wield the weapon and had to build up his physique so that he could shoot with power. Arrows were about seventy centimeters (twenty-eight inches) long and a strong, skilled warrior could fire up to twelve arrows a minute.

A warrior had also to think about defending himself against an enemy's weapons. Although wealthy Vikings could afford an iron helmet and some of the elite may have owned a mail shirt for protection against the piercing blows of an enemy's spear, the shield was the most widely recognized piece of Viking armor and was part of every warrior's equipment. The most common type of shield was the round version, approximately one meter (three feet) in diameter. An advantage of using round shields, versus the oval ones popular in the armies of other countries, was maneuverability. The drawback was a little less protection, making the legs especially vulnerable. Oval or kite-shaped shields, designed primarily to cover the legs of cavalry forces, did not become prevalent until the end of the Viking Age and were a prominent feature of the Norman Conquest in 1066. In addition to protecting the legs, another advantage of the kite-shaped shield was that the point could be thrust into the ground, freeing both of the warrior's hands, while simultaneously protecting him.

The shields were made of hard wood, often linden or ash, which were both strong and lightweight.[14] Oak, although used widely in the construction of ships, was too heavy, especially if damp, for use in shields. Shields were crafted of relatively thin planks, and therefore not expected to last more than one battle, and were too weak to withstand a direct blow with a heavy axe. They were therefore used mainly to deflect blows. A metal edge may have strengthened the rim of the shields against the chop of an enemy's sword or axe, and ox-hide covers over the full shields or just around the rims increased the durability and chances of surviving the arrow storms.[15]

In the center of the shields were cutouts for the hand and iron bosses for protection. The iron centerpieces could be used offensively when warriors advanced in shield formation.[16] Bearing down on the enemy with a wall of armor made resistance almost impossible. Thoralf "thrust his shield so hard against Eyvind that he tottered with shock." When King Magnus Barefoot fought the Irish in the early twelfth century, the Norsemen advanced in divided formation so that many of them fell.[17] When the king noticed the terrible lack of cohesion, he called his men together and had them make a rampart with their shields so they could retreat backward until they were in the clear and out of the bogs onto firm ground.

Shields were also used to disarm, ward off or even break the enemy's swords or spears. A warrior who managed to get an opponent's sword stuck in his shield could disarm his enemy by twisting the shield, and with it the sword, from his adversary's grip. When Gunnar fought Vandil, Gunnar gave his shield a quick twist just as the blow of the sword fell on it, which broke the sword off at the hilt. When Steinar and Bersi engaged in *holmganga* (duel of honor), Bersi hacked away, but his sword stuck fast in the iron border of Steinar's shield. Kormac, Steinar's shieldbearer, raised the shield up just as Steinar was striking out, so that when Steinar struck the shield-edge, "the sword glanced off, slit Bersi's buttock, sliced his thigh down to the knee-joint, and stuck in the bone." When a spear struck the shield, a sharp twist of the shield at the right moment could break the spearhead off at the socket.

"Across the Baltic foam is dancing, shields, and spears, and helms glancing!" sang the skald Ottar Svarte. When at sea, the shields were hung along the gunwales, or sides of the ships and served as protection against incoming spears or arrows from enemy ships. In King Olaf Trygvason's final battle aboard the *Long Serpent*, a cover of shields was set up. But the opposing force threw cutting weapons, swords and axes, as well as projectile weapons, spears and arrows, into the *Long Serpent* "and so thick flew the spears and arrows, that the shields could scarcely receive them." King Olaf mounted a defense by shooting with his bow for the greater part of the day and throwing two spears at a time. Blood ran down from under his steel glove, but he continued the battle relentlessly and without pausing so no one knew where he was wounded.

The shields that hung along the gunwales were painted in contrasting colors, often yellow and black, and were symbols of pride. A fleet of long-ships sailing down the Seine or Loire rivers through the Frankish Empire on its way to Paris, for example, was surely an impressive sight. Sometimes war shields were painted red as a sign of blood—the enemy's, it was hoped. Some shields brought from home were white and became red-stained in battle. White shields held aloft were peace tokens and may have been raised when meeting another friendly Norse ship at sea. Symbols were also used to communicate conversion to the Christian faith. King Olaf Haraldson wore impressive armor: a gold-mounted helmet on his head and a strong coat of ring-mail, an unusually sharp sword, a lance in one hand, and in the other a white shield with a holy cross inlaid in gold. "The most of his men had white shields, on which the holy cross was gilt, but some had painted it in blue or red." King Olaf also brought a shipload of one hundred men, each armed in a coat of ring-mail and wearing a foreign helmet, so that he could not be wounded.[18]

In their raids, Norse warriors acquired dead men's armor and weapons of value and also learned about the enemy's battlefield tactics. What was worn in the form of protective gear, however, often depended on the wealth of the individual. Arnljot Gelline, asking King Olaf Haraldson to accept his services on the battlefield in Stiklestad, was well-armed with a fine helmet, ring-armor, a red shield, a superb sword in his belt "and in his hand a gold-mounted spear, the shaft of it so thick that it was a handful to grasp." Iron, however, was a rarity. Few helmets have been found in Viking graves, suggesting that the Norse warriors either did not wear them, or they were made of leather and did not survive. The few helmets that have been recovered are made of iron, have a protective nose guard, and are reinforced with two crossed iron bands over the top. A leather hood was likely worn under the helmet as a cushion to reduce the shock of metal on metal.

Contrary to popular belief, the Vikings did not wear horned helmets that the opponent could have grabbed, controlling the wearer's head in the same way a bull can be controlled.[19] Because horned helmets would have restricted mobility, they would have been impractical for the efficient Norsemen. Horns, albeit of a different type, were, however, valuable in many other situations. War-horns, for example, were sounded prior to battle. When King Onund of Sweden saw the Danish fleet of King Knut approaching, he ordered the war-horns to sound. His people pitched their tents, put on their weapons, and rowed out of the harbor where they bound their ships together and prepared for the battle. King Harald Hardrade, when ready to fight the Danes, ordered the "war-blast to sound and the men to row forward to the attack." King Sigmund and Eylimi first set up their banners, then blew the horns for battle and the Vikings "rushed from their ships in numbers not to be borne up against." The horn was sometimes used as protective armor. When Steinthor struck Freystein on the neck with his sword, there was a loud clatter and no wound "for in a hooded hat of felt was Freystein, with horn sewn into the neck thereof, and on that had the stroke fallen."

In social settings, horns were used as drinking cups, with the biggest horns given to the best warriors: "When the first full goblet was filled, Earl Sigurd spoke some words over it, blessed it in Odin's name and drank to the king out of the horn." In the king's court, the king drank from a deer-horn, "and the ale was handed from the high-seat to the other side over the fire and he drank to the memory of any one he thought of." The chief of the Jomsvikings is said to have had the strongest drink from the largest horn that could be found. By contrast, the early Viking King On of Sweden was said to have lived to an extremely old age as a reward for sacrificing several of his sons to Oden. When at last he was incapable of walking and eating, he had to "turn his toothless mouth to the deer's horn" and suck his food "out of a horn like a weaned infant." Ever since, a man who died of old age without pain from war wounds was said to have On's disease. In rare cases, a horn was used as an instrument of torture. The horn was placed in the prisoner's mouth to hold the mouth open and a serpent was forced into the horn, down the prisoner's throat; the prisoner died after the serpent gnawed its way out through the body.

When deciding whether or not to wear armor, the Viking warrior had to consider his maneuverability on the battlefield and the weight of the protective gear. Mail shirts were often such nuisances that the warriors rid themselves of the cumbersome armor before the battle began. Earl Hakon found his mail coat so awkward that he flung it aside so that its steel rings rang loudly on the wet deck of his ship. King Magnus the Good, who had converted to Christianity, marched his army against the heathens and threw off his coat of ring-mail so that the red silk shirt he wore on top of his clothes was visible to all. Hakon the Good of Norway fully intended to go into battle with all the weapons and body armor he could find. He girded his sword, put a gilt helmet on his head, took a spear in his hand and a shield by his side, but threw off his armor before the battle began and went forward without helmet or mail coat, fighting the Danes boldly and winning the battle by driving the opposing force far up country. King Harald Gille was not as brave, for he wore two shirts of ring-mail. But his brother, the gallant Kristrod, wore no armor at all. Eystein and his men, however, had a different problem: they were in a hurry to leave their ships despite being exhausted and unfit to go into battle. In a last desperate attempt to save the situation, they threw off their mail coats, but many "fell down from weariness, and died without a wound."

And then there was the formidable King Harald Hardrade who fought in England. He had his men lay aside their armor because of the uncommonly fine weather with hot sunshine. The warriors were so merry that they went ashore only with their shields, helmets, spears and swords. But the approaching enemy's shining weapons and armor looked like glittering ice, and the nearer the opposing force came, the greater it appeared. Harald Hardrade, however, had no word for fear in his vocabulary and needed no skald to record his history in poetic verse, because he was himself blessed with the gift of lyric composition: "Advance! Advance! No mail-coats glance, but hearts are here, that ne'er knew fear," he shouted as he led his men into battle.

Chain-mail was not only cumbersome on the field of battle, it could also be a serious hindrance on return to ship after a successful raid. Swimming in chain-mail was not possible for the average warrior. Even wading back out to the ship under the weight of the heavy metal (it is estimated that a mail shirt weighed between thirty and seventy pounds, depending on size) was extremely difficult, especially if a warrior was tired or wounded. One warrior, however, is said to have been so strong that he "could leap more than his own height, with all his war-gear, and as far backwards as forwards" and swim like a seal and had no match.

Owning a mail shirt was a sign of wealth because of the large amount of metal needed to make the chains. It is estimated that more than thirty thousand iron links—each ring linked to four others—were required to make a shirt and that a single shirt could take longer than a year to construct. On some shirts, every other ring was solid. Most mail shirts reached to mid-thigh and had half-length sleeves. A good mail shirt could repel a slashing attack by sword or axe, but it is unlikely that it would have given sufficient protection against a heavy overhead blow by an axe. Spears and arrows were also capable of penetrating the links. When the spears were thrown "the ring-linked coat of strongest mail could not withstand the iron hail."

Leather or animal skins were worn under the shirt for additional protection and the chain-mail was sometimes fastened to the helmet or leather hood to protect the neck. In general, leather protection alone, not mail, was the common form of armor. Berserkers went into battle wearing only the shirt. Leather was readily available, was less cumbersome than chain-mail and generally effective against a slashing attack from a sword or axe, but did not give sufficient protection against a thrust with a spear or knife, especially to the face or neck area. When the site of modern Oslo was burnt about 1137, Thjostolf Alason threw his spear at a man named Askel, hitting him under the throat so that the spear point went through his neck. Thjostolf was extremely pleased by this spear cast, because no other flesh was visible aside from the small area hit.

In the end, the Norsemen's weapons differed little from those of other warriors of the time. All of the weapons used by them, with the exception of the axe, were also common to other armies. The weapons the Vikings chose to carry were not superior in themselves. Because warriors received little formal training, a weapon was only as good as the person wielding it. The successes the Vikings enjoyed, therefore, were due to the skill of the leadership and the fierceness of the attacks, their unstoppable nature, and strategy of overrunning the enemy. The Viking leader understood that "by heart and hand a field is won," but he did not expect his men to move boldly into battle without proper leadership. When the leader was intrepid, his whole body of men would be true to him. King Hakon the Good fought foremost in battle and hacked fiercely at the fleeing enemy. He wore a bright metal cap so that his men could recognize him and a body-coat of mail woven with iron. King Magnus Olafson, on hearing of Hardaknut's death, decided in the summer of 1042 to go with his army to Denmark to take possession of the Danish dominions to which he was entitled by an earlier agreement, "or to fall in the field with his army." He ran ahead of his men to the enemy army, cutting away with both hands at every man who came up against him. King Harald Hardrade, who was killed at the age of fifty, went into the fray where the greatest clash of weapons was, also cutting with both hands so that neither helmet nor armor could withstand him. He never fled from battle, but often tried cunning escapes when dealing with superior forces. His followers said that when he was in great danger, he always took the course that gave the best hope of a fortunate outcome.

Erling Skjalgson, seeing the enemy fleet rowing towards him with all their ships at once, stood on the quarterdeck of his ship with a helmet on his head, a shield before him and a sword in his hand. And when sailing the *Long Serpent* into his final battle against the Danish and Swedish kings, Olaf Trygvason of Norway stood on his ship's quarterdeck, high over the others—easy to distinguish by his gilt shield, helmet inlaid with gold and the short red coat he wore over his armor—and told his men to do exactly what they saw him do.

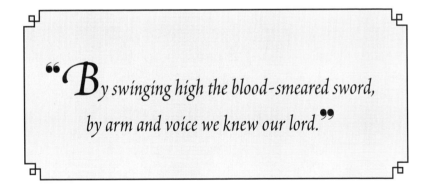

"*By swinging high the blood-smeared sword, by arm and voice we knew our lord.*"

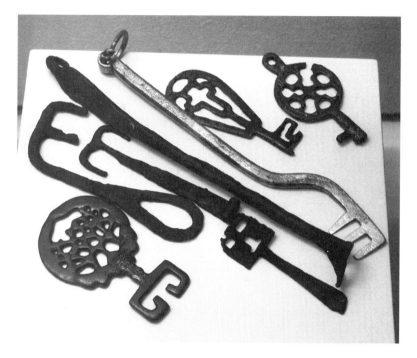

The blacksmith crafted weapons and tools, often richly orna-
mented, like these keys. Displayed at the Viking Museum in Haithabu,
northern Germany.

Note the ornamentation on the sword hilts. The guards were sometimes covered with silver plates and decorated with braided band motifs. Pommels were often three-sided and served primarily as a counterweight to the blade. *Displayed at the Viking Museum in Haithabu, northern Germany.*

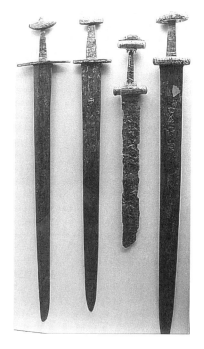

The sword reflected a warrior's social standing and was the most common weapon in the Viking Age. Swords came in varying sizes, but were commonly three feet long and up to four inches wide. Those containing too much iron did not hold an edge well. Note the relatively small pommels, grips and guards. Displayed at the Viking Museum in Haithabu, northern Germany.

Spear tips were between ten and twenty inches long and fastened to wooden handles of varied length. The spear was used both as a throwing and thrusting weapon and could easily penetrate mail armor. Displayed at the Army Museum in Stockholm, Sweden.

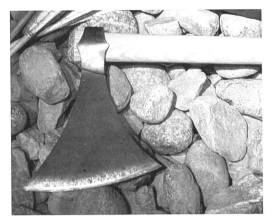

The axe was the most well-known Viking weapon. Vikings serving as bodyguards to the emperor in Constantinople were known as "the axe-bearing barbarians." Displayed at the Army Museum in Stockholm, Sweden.

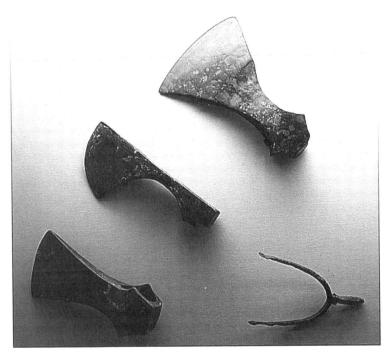

Axes varied in size from the short single-handed version to the large Danish axe that was wielded with both hands in a sweeping left to right motion capable of beheading a horse with a single stroke. Note the "bearded" cutting edge on the axe head in the center. Note also the stirrup, which allowed the warrior to fight on horseback. Displayed at the Viking Museum in Haithabu, northern Germany.

The shield was the most common Viking defensive armor. It was approximately three feet in diameter, covered with leather or reinforced with an iron edge with an iron boss in the center to protect the hand. The grip was fixed across the boss on the inside. The boss could also be used offensively to drive the enemy to the rear in a shield formation. The thin wooden shield was not expected to survive more than one battle. Shields attached to the sides of the ship were often fastened in such a way that they overlapped one another, with two shields between each pair of oar holes. Displayed at the Army Museum in Stockholm, Sweden.

Contrary to popular belief, Vikings did not wear horned helmets and only the wealthiest Vikings wore helmets at all. Their helmets had a protective nose guard and were reinforced with two crossed iron bands over the top of the head. Berserkers and Vikings who could not afford helmets wore leather hoods or went into battle bareheaded. Leather hoods were worn underneath the helmet to reduce the shock of metal on metal.

Mail shirts were expensive, requiring about thirty thousand iron links, and could take up to a year to construct. They were cumbersome to wear, so the Vikings frequently rid themselves of their mail armor in the moments prior to battle. *Displayed at the Army Museum in Stockholm, Sweden.*

CHAPTER 7

MILITARY ORGANIZATION AND BATTLEFIELD TACTICS

Victory was claimed by the boldest and bravest.
In the death struggle, shields clashed, arrows flew
as thick as snowdrifts, blackening the sky. Blood
dripped from every Norse spearhead until the
ships' decks were drenched in red gore.

— —

The Vikings employed basic war tactics. They had few formal weapons and little battlefield training, nor were they part of an organized and disciplined army that relied on extensive formations. But because they lived in a society built on warrior codes such as bravery and honor, when called upon, most adult males were prepared to pick up arms and fight. Basic weaponry skills were acquired at home or on hunting trips from a young age, promoted and taught by elders. Other skills were learned on a trial and error basis during the raids themselves. Paradoxically, the lack of a formal military organization was a contributing factor to Viking military success and enabled them to be unorthodox and unpredictable in their approach, especially in their combined use of sea and land warfare.

To form strategy, knowledge of the lay of the land was essential. A successful defense lay in an ability to anticipate the enemy and prepare for battle before the attack. This was not possible for most countries that needed time to assemble their troops. Countries targeted for raiding had no standing armies stationed by their coasts to warn of a Norse raiding party coming from the sea; but even if they had, they would not have been able to see the Viking ships advancing from afar. The Vikings were experienced sailors skilled at sea navigation and their ships could travel long distances safely and easily sail beyond the horizon to avoid detection from land. The Vikings were not unusual in their lack of unification around a single ruler. This was common to the world they inhabited and the countries they raided were similarly unorganized, making it impossible for them to build strong armies that could be called up for action the moment a threat came over the horizon. A further factor that worked in the Vikings' favor was that the kings of the foreign lands they invaded, mainly England, France and neighboring countries, had their own internal conflicts to deal with, most of which took place on land, not sea.[1] These foreign rulers had no means of shifting their strategy to defend their coastlines, but also no way of knowing when or from where the next threat would come.

Viking raiding strategy—bypass the enemy by entering from the sea, grab the booty and exit quickly via the beach before being attacked—was made possible because of the swiftness, maneuverability and design of the long-ships that were able to make landfall virtually anywhere. The Vikings could sail up any river and onto any beach where they suspected the defense to be weak, cities and monasteries to be unguarded, and riches to be found. The ship was their primary strength. Without it, venturing abroad to raid would not have been worth the risk involved. The speediness of the Viking ship also made pursuit at sea difficult, and each ship, though part of a fleet, was capable of advancing or retreating on its own.

Warriors too weak to defeat an enemy usually avoid initiating battle—not the opportunistic Norsemen. Despite the fact that only 2 to 3 percent of the population participated in raids, they still struck fear in their victims and made an indelible impression on those who encountered them and on the chroniclers who recorded their exploits.[2] Their views as to what constituted strength differed from those of the British, Frankish, and Roman Empires, who were in the habit of advancing in large formations. The Vikings' primary goals were personal glory and wealth, rather than the acquisition of land. They usually sailed in small parties, comprised of just a few ships, and subscribed to the philosophy that fewer numbers helped them to exploit their fierceness and element of surprise on the battlefield.[3]

Their attacks against European communities were generally successful, but the Vikings still had to consider the possibility of a failed attack and have a workable plan of retreat. When setting up camp for the night, they did so with the availability of natural escape routes in mind. Their ability to disperse in different directions at sea helped them avoid capture.

Defense at home was needed mostly to ward off other Norsemen. The strength of the Vikings' domestic military organization was counted in ships or ship-crews. In 950, after the battle at Ogvaldsnes, King Hakon the Good declared that "all the inhabited land over the whole country along the sea-coast, and as far back from it as the salmon swims up in the rivers, should be divided into ship-raths according to the districts." It was fixed by law how many ships each district should have and the population was obliged to participate whenever a threatening fleet came to the area.

There was almost no organization insofar as personal rank was concerned. Some warriors were as young as twelve years of age, but most were older and more experienced and able to act as advisors to the leaders. When hostilities were brewing between the Swedish and Norwegian kings, King Olaf of Norway sought the council of his chiefs and leaders of troops on what course to adopt. These powerful men argued: "Although we are a numerous body of men who are assembled here, yet they are all only people of weight and power; but, for a war expedition, young men who are in quest of property and consideration are more suitable." The chiefs agreed that ordinary men should be sent into battle ahead of those of influence and power for "the men do not fight worse who have little property, but even better than those who are brought up in the midst of wealth."[4]

The Jomsvikings were extremely particular in selecting warriors for their elite military organization. They required of each applicant tests of physical strength and endurance; of those applying for admission, generally only half were fit enough to pass. When the company of Bue and his brother, the sons of a man named Wesete who ruled over the island of Bornholm, were tested, "eighty of the men were considered up for the mark, but forty went back home."[5] The men had to be between the ages of eighteen and fifty. An exception was made for the twelve-year-old Vagn, the son of Palnatoke, founder of the Jomsvikings, because he was strong, handsome and accomplished in all manner of things. He claimed to be as proficient as a man eighteen or older, so in accepting him into the elite fort of Jomsborg the laws "would hardly be broken."

But most of the men who went a-Viking were not subject to "entry requirements." Rather, they contributed their own ships and weapons and sailed under the banner of whichever small "king" they chose. A chief was often called "king" as a courtesy and in recognition of his leadership, not because he was sovereign of a nation or owned land. Only in the eleventh century, starting with the attack on England in 1013 by the Danish king Sven Forkbeard and his son Knut did military organization become more cohesive, stable and permanent. By this time, a standing fleet of ships, along with other preparations, stood at the ready when the king made a call to war, because the people knew that they were required to supply manpower, ships, weapons and other equipment.

The *Leidgangr*, the Norse navy, was called out to war whenever the king felt so inclined.[6] The *Leidgangr* was conceived around groups of farmers who were responsible for specific duties including ship maintenance, stocking of food and other provisions, and personal participation in battle, generally on a "he who has been home the longest shall depart first" basis. A large crew with responsibility over a particular land area was responsible for providing the king with a ship when he called for war. The ship crews were further divided into smaller teams whose duty it was to supply the king with armed rowers.

Although in Norway participation in forays was thought to have been originally on a voluntary basis, King Harald Fairhair is credited with developing the forerunner to the *Leidgangr* as early as the ninth century. Denmark, in the eleventh century, is believed to have been the first Nordic country to require its people to supply the king with crews and other necessities for warfare. In 1030–31, King Sven, a son of King Knut the Great, introduced many new laws in Norway, modeling them partly along the lines of ones in Denmark, many of which were quite strict. He required that one of every seven males be taken for the service of war, "and reckoning from the fifth year of age; and the outfit of ships should be reckoned in the same proportion."

In 1048 King Harald Hardrade of Norway ordered a countrywide levy consisting of one half of the men and ships, then set off to Jutland, the mainland of Denmark, where he pillaged and burned all summer long. In 1062 the Danish fleet led by King Svein Ulfson came with three hundred ships upon the smaller, 150-ship Norwegian fleet led by King Harald Hardrade. After resolving to proceed in the summer of 1066 to England and conquer that country, Harald Hardrade sent a message-token to Norway and ordered out a levy of one half of all arms-bearing men.

Sweden also followed the call. In the twelfth century, Norway had more than three hundred ships set apart for the king, and Sweden had almost as many.[7] Håkan Röde (the Red) of Sweden was a known promoter of the *Leidgangr* during his four-year reign, 1075–79, and considered it his right to call out the fleet as he pleased to take part in attacks, raids, and later, crusades to the east, mainly to Finland.[8] The callout of a large fleet was time-consuming and could give the enemy enough warning to assemble their forces, but a swift callout of a smaller fleet, comprised of perhaps two hundred ships, could still mount a surprise attack.

The duties of the *Leidgangr* also included protection of the coastlines. The Vikings had little to fear in the form of foreign attacks from the sea, but because Norsemen frequently fought each other, some of the bloodiest battles in Viking history were internecine—Dane against Norwegian, Swede against Norwegian, Swede against Dane. When Earl Hakon fought the Jomsvikings, many men on both sides were killed, but the most by far on Hakon's side "for the Jomsborg Vikings fought desperately, and murderously, and shot right through the shields." A certain Gregorius Dagson expressed the view that the Norwegians were the most agile, most experienced of all Nordic warriors, but none were as bold under arms as the Icelanders.

Excavations at Birka in 1934, reinforced the idea that Sweden in the Viking Age had a professional army that included officers, garrisons and standardized military equipment.[9] This finding has dispelled somewhat the myth of the Vikings as a band of longhaired rogues traveling the seas, engaging in *strandhugg* and raiding without design or strategy. Forty Viking soldiers and their officers lived periodically in a building called "the Garrison" that was separated from the main city. The Garrison was Birka's largest building and measured approximately nineteen by nine meters (sixty-two by thirty feet). The warriors housed there were well provided for and supplied with their own weapons; they had the facilities of a smithy and a kitchen and were given fresh meat, a luxury, to eat year round. The weapons were primarily the spear and the shield. The higher-ranking officers had chain-mail, helmets and metal swords, while lower-ranking soldiers had to get by with leather helmets or hoods and wooden shields. Situated by the water, the Garrison at Birka is believed to have served as a harbor for both military and trading ships.[10]

In many battles warriors laid waste to large areas of land by burning—a way of making their point and also disposing of unwanted men. In the winter of 869, Earl Ragnvald surrounded King Vemund's house and burned the king together with ninety men inside. Two of Harald Fairhair's sons, furious that their father had refused to give them any part of the kingdom and had instead placed earls in every district, surrounded Earl Ragnvald's house and burned him and sixty men inside. King Harald Fairhair himself conquered five kings who coveted his dominions and set fire to two houses in which Hogne Karuson from Ringerike and Gudbrand were sleeping. King Harald then overpowered the dominions of Hedemark, Ringerike, Gudbrandsdal, Hadeland, Thoten, Raumarike and the whole northern part of Vingulmark.[11]

The Swedish king Ottar laid Denmark to waste because King Frode demanded a tax from the Swedes who disliked paying anything to a foreign king. When Frode, a great warrior, was denied the tax, he took his army to Sweden, pillaging, killing many families, taking others prisoner and carrying away enormous booty. The following year, when King Ottar learned that Frode had departed eastward for the summer and was not at home, the Swedish king departed with his ships to Denmark, where he sacked unopposed, burning and laying waste with his army until the country was utterly destroyed.

When King Olaf Haraldson asked his men counsel as to what should be done, Fin Arnason answered:

"I will say what should be done, if I may advise. We should go with armed hand over all the inhabited places, plunder all the goods, and burn all the habitations, and leave not a hut standing, and thus punish the *bondes* [farmers] for their treason against their sovereign. I think many a man will then cast himself loose from the bondes' army, when he sees smoke and flame at home on his farm, and does not know how it is going with children, wives, or old men, fathers, mothers, and other connections. I expect also that if we succeed in breaking the assembled host, their ranks will soon be thinned."[12]

The Jomsvikings were also notorious for setting land on fire. They assembled their fleet in Limafjord, went to sea with sixty ships and sailed north, plundering and burning all along the coast. Earl Erik set sail from Sweden in 997, forayed along the Baltic coast, pillaging and killing, burning dwellings in Valdemar's dominions and laying the country to waste. In 1015 Earl Sven and Einar Tambaskelfer gathered a large armed force of almost two thousand men and went to the king's town of Nidaros where they set fire to "rafters, root, and all" of the king's half-finished hall until the flames spread over the whole city.[13] In 1049 "all Heidaby is burned down! Roofs, walls, and all in flame high burning."

King Harald Hardrade also plundered and burned abroad. In Sicily, failing to gain entry into an exceptionally strong thick-walled castle, he caught some birds nesting in the castle, bound small splinters of tarred wood smeared with wax and sulfur to their backs and set them on fire. When he released the birds, they flew back to their young nesting under the reed and straw covered roofs and "the fire from the birds seized upon the house roofs," and one house after another caught fire, until the castle itself was in flames.

In sea battles, a different strategy was used. As soon as the ships came within fighting distance of one another, normally the range of a spear throw, the Vikings tied the stems and sterns of the long-ships together, broadside, with hawsers (ropes designed for this purpose) to strengthen their position and form a compact body, or platform, on which to fight and move from one ship to the next. The Danes bound their ships together all through the middle of the fleet. But the fleet was so large—nearly three hundred ships—that many ships remained loose and each commander advanced his ship according to his courage. During Sigvaldi's pursuit of Sven Forkbeard, Sigvaldi moored his ships by a tongue of land and turned them "so that their prows pointed away from land, and fastened them together broadside to broadside." Olaf Trygvason, sounding the war horns, ordered all his ships to line up close to one another. He then placed his own ship, the *Long Serpent*, in the middle of the line, and "on one side lay the *Little Serpent*, and on the other the *Crane*." Sigvat Skald composed a ballad about the fleet of King Knut the Great: "Mast to mast, all bound fast, his great fleet lies in ranks." King Olaf Haraldson gave a speech to his warriors prior to battle, urging them to be ready at their appointed posts and to row out the moment the signal was sounded: When "the battle begins, let people be alert to bring all our ships in close order, and ready to bind them together." Sweden's King Inge's men did not bind their ships together, but left them loose so that they could be rowed across the current to sway the large ships. Though in larger battles, some ships were lashed together and others were allowed to move freely. The ships could also be placed side-by-side to block a channel or narrow pathway during a raid.

When the distance between the opposing fleets closed, the warriors gathered their weapons and arranged themselves from stem to stern on the ship in a battle line so thick that shield overlapped shield all around the ship with a spear point poking out at the bottom of every shield. If the opposing force tried to enter the ship, the Viking warrior would throw his spear, shoot his arrows, and chop at his opponent with battleaxe or sword from over the railing. King Magnus the Good (1024–1047), a son of Olaf Haraldson of Norway, battled it out with Earl Svein Ulfson, fighting at the bows of the ships so that only the men located at the bows could strike. The men on the forecastle thrust with spears, while those farther out shot with spears, javelins and war-arrows. Stones and short stakes were also thrown; those who were aft of the mast shot with the bow. King Olaf Haraldson urged his men to spare themselves at the beginning of the battle and not cast their weapons into the sea or shoot them away needlessly in the air, but when the fight became hot, "let each man show what is in him of manly spirit." When the enemy began to fall aboard their ships and many appeared wounded, King Olaf's crew prepared to board.

The warriors moved swiftly and battle onboard was fierce, but the fleet's maneuverability was hampered by the ships being lashed together. When Palnatoke, the founder of the Jomsvikings, decided to undo all the ships from their fastenings and attack the king's fleet, "three swift-sailing ships in the king's fleet foundered and, of their crews, only those who could swim escaped with their lives." If a man were forced overboard, he attempted to strip himself of his heavy armor in the water and seek protection under his shield. With shields and spears, clothing and dead men floating all around the ships, nobody knew one shield from another and if a man had not been too severely wounded, he could cover himself in the water under a shield and perhaps escape with his life.

The ship was so highly prized that in sea battles a Viking force would try to take a ship from the adversary without damaging it. Building a ship required a considerable investment in time and goods, so the acquisition of an enemy ship that could be used in future battles was a sign of both wealth and prestige. If the opposing force had just returned from a raid, their ship was especially valuable because of the booty it contained. To capture an enemy ship without inflicting damage, warriors had to attack and kill the ship's crew, being careful to spare the ship, weapons, and armor, which were expensive and difficult to obtain, and any booty consisting of silver or gold. The crew was cleared off the deck in close man-to-man combat. At the battle in Hafersfjord in 872, Thor Haklan, a great berserker, battled against King Harald Fairhair's ship "until Thor Haklang fell and his whole ship was cleared of men." Erling Skjalgson and his crew, in their battle against King Olaf Haraldson, let the sails fall and seized their weapons, but the king's ship surrounded Erling's ship on all sides, the wounded lay all over the decks, and "the decks were slippery with red gore." If the opportunity arose, the inferior force might try to flee by jumping overboard, but not all could swim, and "dead men rolled in every wave . . . and skulls and bones were tumbling round, under the sea, on sandy ground."

Warriors who survived a battle at sea were left during the land battle phase to guard the ships while others scouted the area to ensure that the lines of communication were left open. Communication about the battlefield and the enemy took place mainly through word of mouth and shared information around the campfire. The Vikings acquired intelligence through preliminary espionage and exchange of information with others who had gone before them. When night was well advanced, King Inge's spies came to him and told him how King Hakon and his army were coming over the ice that covered the entire route from the town to Hofud Isle. The chiefs in Norway had their spies east in Svithjod (Sweden) and south in Denmark to find out if King Olaf Haraldson had come from Russia. Then the war message-token went around, and a huge army was summoned. King Hakon the Good ordered beacons to be erected on the hills "so that every man could see from the one to the other . . . and a war-signal could thus be given in seven days, from the most southerly beacon to the most northerly Thing-seat in Halogaland."

Since the Vikings generally wrote only in short runic inscriptions, mainly on stones, ambassadors between kings were accredited through presentation of a token—usually an article that could be recognized by the receiver of the message as belonging to the sender. Earl Hakon, for example, in order to save the life of Vandrad, sent his friend Karl as a token with the message that Karl should let Vandrad have the horse Earl Hakon had given Karl the previous day. King Olaf Haraldson took a gold-mounted sword and a gold ring and handing them over to Björn, his marshal, said: "This I give thee: it was given to me in summer by Earl Ragnvald. To him ye shall go; and bring him word from me to advance your errand with his counsel and strength . . . and this gold ring thou shalt give Earl Ragnvald. These are tokens he must know well."[14] Chiefs also lined their ships together to hold counsel and talk to their strongest and wisest warriors.

Since the Norsemen were traders as well as pirates and were constantly on the move, they heard about and saw for themselves the many riches they could expect to find in other countries and therefore had a good idea of where to attack. They learned a lot about their enemy's philosophy and warfare tactics during raids and through the weapons and other items they acquired. Their mobility both on sea and land allowed them to communicate vital information about the enemy's whereabouts, their weapons and strategy. Although they used horses as transport to and from the battlefield or village targeted for plunder, once there they preferred to dismount and fight on foot, with the leader at the center of the action.[15] The men of the Salmon-River-Dale "jumped off their horses, and got ready to fight." When Hawk and Arnkel battled it out, both men leapt off their horses and thrust at each other with their spears. When fighting foreigners though, a Viking commander had to be wary of the possibility that the opposing force might choose to stay mounted and sweep down on the flanks of a shield formation.

Time had to be spent forming the battle arrays. The battle itself was a clash of spirits, the enemy attempting to give back as much as they received. In the battle at Stiklestad in 1030, King Olaf received certain intelligence about the opposing forces and amassed an army of more than three thousand men, a huge army on a single battlefield. He spoke to his troops about how the force was to be drawn up, told them that his banner was to go forward in the middle of the army and that his court-men should follow it with the war forces. The banner, a symbol of leadership and pride, signaled to the troops the king's location and let them know that he was still in the battle. King Olaf Haraldson also stressed the importance of relations and acquaintances remaining together, "for thus they defend each other best, and know each other." Since King Olaf had adopted Christianity, he decided that all of the men should have a distinguishing mark upon their helmets and shields "by painting the holy cross thereupon with white color," and the battle cry should be: "Forward, forward, Christian men! Cross men! King's men!"

The opposing force, led by Kalf Arnason, raised their banner and drew up their house servants. Thorer Hund with his troops was at the head in front of the banner and to both sides was a chosen body of the most active and best-armed men in the forces. With so many banners flapping in the air, the warriors were ordered to take notice of their position and under which banner each man belonged, to note who was in front of the banner and who the side-men were so they could quickly find their place in case the formation broke apart in the course of march. Thorer Hund then advanced in front of the banner and raised the war cry: "Forward, forward, bondemen!" Despite the fact that the Vikings more commonly engaged in sudden raids, involving a relatively small number of warriors, they still had to protect themselves and be able to communicate on the battlefield. To do so, they remained close together, and especially close to their leader, chosen for his success in previous battles, who would take the front position and lead the charge. Although Norse forces had no particular method of moving the warriors efficiently across ground, the close formation in which they advanced gave every man confidence and the ability to draw upon his comrade's strength. A Viking warrior's strategy for success was to meet the enemy with force, be confident in his own strength and weapons, and trust his peers.

Varying design walls, shield joined to shield, were used for protection. The *svinfylking* (boar snout or boar formation), consisting of a wedge of twenty to thirty warriors with overlapping shields, created a strong defensive wall, its point facing the enemy, and was especially useful against spears launched from a distance. The shield wall also enabled those at the rear of the formation to launch their spears over the heads of those in front. In the battle at Stiklestad where King Olaf Haraldson was killed, the men who stood in front "hewed down with their swords; they who stood next thrust with their spears; and they who stood hindmost shot arrows, cast spears, or threw stones, hand-axes, or sharp stakes."

The main purpose of the *svinfylking* was to charge through enemy lines and break the opposing force with the point of the arrow formation. The strongest man led the formation, with the next two strongest behind him, followed by the next three strongest, and so on. The warriors would then launch their spears to open up the enemy for further attack, charging forward until the arrow-shaped formation penetrated the enemy troops' defense through the sheer momentum of the charge and concentration of force over a small area with a large and powerful back-up. As the *svinfylking* advanced, the warriors drove the enemy back with their shields, while hacking with swords and axes. The strategy worked even if the hostile force had also formed a barrier with their shields. The shields provided a relatively high degree of safety so long as the men remained in close formation, and provided physical strength as well as mental encouragement. The tactic worked well because of the Vikings' reliance on surprise attacks, which made it unlikely that they would be met with a strong well-organized enemy army, especially when fighting abroad.

Sometimes shield formations were formed by a single row of overlapping shields, which gave the formation length instead of depth. When fighting the English in 1066, King Harald Hardrade arranged his army so that the lines of battle were long but not deep, and bent both wings back so that they met together and formed a wide ring of equal thickness all round, shield to shield, both in the front and rear ranks. The king himself was within the circle with his banner and body of chosen men: "And our bowmen shall be near to us; and they who stand in the first rank shall set the spear-shaft on the ground, and the spear-point against the horseman's breast, if he rides at them; and those who stand in the second rank shall set the spear-point against the horse's breast."[16] Because of the Vikings' spears, it was no easy matter for the English to ride against the Norse. They rode around them. The fight remained loose and light as long as the Norsemen kept their order of battle. But when they broke their shield rampart, the English rode up from all sides and arrows and spears started flying.

In 1134 the brothers King Magnus and King Harald Gille divided the government of Norway and entered into a five-year conflict. When Magnus went into battle against Harald, he made his battle line so long that it could surround the whole of Harald's troops. But in the winter of 1135, when King Harald came with a large army to Bergen in Norway, Magnus abandoned the shield formation for something better. He erected a stone-slinging machine on a *holm* (small island) and had iron chains and wooden booms laid across the passage from the king's house with foot-traps in the fields. When King Magnus later attempted to flee to his ship, he fell into his own traps and the iron chains he had laid across the passage prevented his escape.

The shield formation also had its drawbacks because maneuvering with sword, axe, spear and shield became difficult with warriors standing so close together. Once enemy lines were broken, the warriors could split apart and fight on their own with axes and swords as best they could. Great risk of accidental injury was present within the ranks—"friendly fire" from large battleaxes swung frantically with both hands. At the battle in Stiklestad, confusion got the best of both armies. Because the men standing at the outermost wings of Thorer Hund's army repeated the opponent's war cry, they were mistaken by their own men for the king's men "and many were slain before they knew each other." And although the sun shone and the weather was splendid, "the heaven and the sun became red, and before the battle ended it became as dark as night." Men lay scattered in heaps on both sides of the conflict, severely wounded or so fatigued they could not move.

Another wall design with less obvious advantages was the zigzag shield formation. Because of the large number of shields required to cover the front, this type of formation placed more pressure on the men at the points, providing less protective force from behind after the initial charge had been absorbed.

The leader who had acquired his rank through skill in battle was expected to lead, together with his best men, from the front of the formation, to build morale and encourage the warriors to follow. In both land and sea warfare, commanders were often protected within the circumference of a circular shield wall borne by an entrusted party of warriors. Normally, the leader lived by the principle of taking charge and being the first to confront the enemy. Olaf Haraldson "came forth from behind the shield-bulwark, and put himself at the head of the army." At the battle of Aros, Norway, in 1044, King Magnus the Good, who at the beginning of the battle stood in a shield rampart on his ship, leapt over the shields when he thought that things were going too slowly, encouraged his men with a loud cheer, and rushed forward to the bow of the ship where the battle was going hand-to-hand. No matter how large and battle-hungry the army was, a leader was expected to move forward with courage and the resolution to win. If he was perceived to lack confidence in the cause and failed to marshal the troops behind him, the warrior spirit would leave the soldier's heart and "each will seek his own safety."[17] But when the leader was intrepid, the entire body of men would be true to him. One drawback of a leader's direct participation in battle was that it deprived him of the ability to oversee the action from a distance and communicate orders to the troops. Also, his high visibility, indicated by the banner, made him a strategic target to be killed by the enemy as soon as possible to deprive the warriors of their fighting spirit.

Night battle was generally avoided. The warriors spent nights lying under their shields, completely armed, changing watch with each other during the night. When they slept, the custom was for each man to wear his helmet, cover himself with his shield, lay his sword under his head, keeping his right hand on the handle. But if tension was high, battle could continue throughout the night, sometimes in horribly cold temperatures and driving snowstorms. In Nis-River, Harald Hardrade's bowstring, using the Laplander's *arrow-scat*, twanged throughout the night. King Hakon Herdebreid was encouraged to fight his own uncle, King Inge, at night, never by day, to obtain favorable results. The battle at Helganes between King Magnus the Good of Norway and King Svein Ulfson of Denmark began at about dusk and went on, man-to-man, all night at close combat, with King Magnus throwing hand-spears. The casualties were sizeable, and although many of King Magnus's men escaped death, most were severely wounded. Magnus, after ordering his men's wounds to be bound, found there was a terrible shortage of doctors and had to select men with the softest hands, hands he thought most suited for binding war wounds.

Battle wounds were gruesome and casualty rates high. Wounds and deaths increased by even larger numbers after fatigue set in and warriors became careless or too tired to defend themselves. Erling was wounded in the left side, but some say he did it himself in drawing his sword. Self-inflicted wounds easily happened when battles raged for several hours during which it is estimated that at least 20 percent of the warriors were dealt their deathblow, and more came away with severe wounds, including severed limbs. The Vikings suffered some of their greatest losses at the hands of their own. When Vagn of the Jomsvikings tried to escape with his men, having determined it was either that or wait till daybreak and be taken prisoner, they managed to get to a skerry, but "most of them were altogether done for, what with their wounds and the cold, and they could proceed no further. Ten men died there during the night."[18] Death from infection was also common. Earl Sigurd killed a Scottish earl called Melbridge Tooth and hung his head on his stirrup. But the teeth of the decapitated Scottish chief scratched the calf of Sigurd's leg, creating an infection in his leg that killed him.

Wounded men were carried to safety on battle shields or taken home to the farms so that every house was full and tents had to be erected over others. Vali received his death wound by the point of a halberd planted between his shoulders, after which his opponents Bersi and Halldor set his shield at his feet, his sword at his head, and spread his cloak over him.[19] In Stiklestad the battle raged so that "the one fell by the side of the other," those who still had enough strength to stand were severely wounded "and some retired to less dangerous areas, and others fled." An arrow struck Thormod Kolbrunarskald, who fought under King Olaf Haraldson's banner, in the left side, but he broke off the arrow and went back into battle. Near houses where the wounded lay howling and screaming, a man once came out and said: "A great shame it is that brisk young fellows cannot bear their wounds."

Unless the wound was life-threatening, most warriors did not even wince, bore their battle scars with pride, and showed them off as evidence of their participation in conflict. Thormod, listening to conversation in the barn, heard talk mostly about what men had seen in battle and their valor. As for his own wound, he pulled out the iron spearhead that had lodged itself into his chest with tongs and saw some morsels of flesh from his heart, some white and some red, hung on the hook. "The King has fed us well. I am fat, even at the heart-roots," he said, his final words before he leaned over and died.

The dwindling morale, desire to flee, longing for home when most warriors were bleeding to death or had already died from their wounds can only be imagined. After his battle with Fin Arnason, King Harald Hardrade sailed to Norway with his fleet. He went first to Olso where he granted all his people leave to go home if they so wished. King Olaf Haraldson also granted leave to many of his men who had farms and children to take care of, "for it seemed to them uncertain what safety there might be for the families and property of those who left the country with him."

Toward the end of the battle in Stiklestad, King Olaf Haraldson was so tired that he sat down, laid his head on the knee of Fin Arnason, one of his closest men, and after sleep overcame him, dreamt that he went up a ladder so high in the air that he came to the step closest to heaven. When Fin awakened the king to warn him of the advancing hostile force, Olaf said: "Why did you wake me, Fin, and did not allow me to enjoy my dream?" When King Olaf told his dream, Fin told him he thought it meant he was doomed to die. The king then recalled that, prior to the battle, Thorgeir of Kviststad had threatened him: "You shall now have such peace as many formerly have received at your hands and which you shall now pay for."[20] And indeed, this was Olaf's final battle.

As has been recounted, the Norsemen experienced their greatest losses on the home front, although they could have experienced even greater losses on foreign soil had they not focused on attacking the enemy's weak points. King Magnus fought three battles with King Svein Ulfson in order to regain the land that had been unjustly taken from him. But in 1042, when King Magnus finally gained possession of the Danish dominions he felt were his entitlement, he had the impudence to send a letter to King Edward of England stating that he considered himself owner also of England by a prior agreement made with Hardaknut, son of King Knut the Great. King Edward, of course, had no intention of giving up England and would not renounce his title. "If King Magnus come here with an army, I will gather no army against him," said King Edward, "but he shall only get the opportunity of taking England when he has taken my life." After King Magnus had reflected a while on this message, he said: "I think it wisest, and will succeed best, to let King Edward have his kingdom in peace for me, and that I keep the kingdoms God has put into my hands."

Loss to Vikings fighting abroad generally did not involve territory or entire armies. Rather, it was the loss of individual lives or a ship. Their goal was to get back to the bay and their ship with as few losses as possible and as much booty as they could carry and to disappear over the horizon before a counterattack could be launched. Although the Vikings fought on land and used battlefield tactics similar to those used by soldiers of other armies, their superiority lay not in their weapons or military organization, but in their ships, their imagination, and their unbreakable roguish warrior spirit.

"*They who the eagle's feast provide*
In ranked line fought side by side,
'Gainst lines of war-men under shields,
Close packed together on the fields."

CHAPTER 8

THE VIKING ELITE OF JOMSBORG

*They were men who knew how to die: "They look
death unflinchingly in the eye and with a jest on
their lips. They love life but would not be able to
survive the taunt of having begged for it."*[1]

The Jomsvikings, the most renowned of all Norse warriors,
were men committed to honor and courage. They lived
by a strict code of ethics and pledged total allegiance to their
leader. They were physically strong, skilled at arms, ever-ready
for battle, loyal to their peers, and unafraid of death. These
warriors formed a stronghold at the fort of Jomsborg, thought
to have been located near modern Wolin in the Baltic Sea just
off the Polish coast. But the existence of this elite fort, said
to have had a lifespan of only eighty years, has not been fully
corroborated by historical records, and some scholars claim it
may never have existed.

Legend has it that the three sons of a powerful man named
Toke from the Danish island of Fyen were in dispute among
themselves over their inheritance. On the death of their father,
two of the sons, Ake and Palner, took the entire inheritance,
leaving Fjolner, born of a different mother, embittered because
he felt he was entitled to a third of the property. He went to
see Harald Bluetooth (Gormsson), the ambitious king of Denmark, where he was well received, became the king's closest
advisor, and persuaded Harald to assassinate Ake.[2] "Ake is
a wealthy man who goes a-Viking with his ships every year,"

Fjolner told the king. "You cannot consider yourself full king of Denmark, so long as this man threatens your kingdom."[3] Harald took Fjolner's advice, readied a fleet of ten ships and five hundred men and killed Ake in a surprise attack at sea.

When he received news of the murder, Palner was so upset that he took to his bed.[4] Since he was too weak to avenge his brother's death, he sought the advice of his good friend and foster-brother Sigurd regarding the future protection of his inherited dominions. Sigurd suggested that Palner ask for Ingeborg, daughter of Earl Ottar of Gotland (the large island off southern Sweden), in marriage. Not only would this union strengthen Palner's wealth and social standing, it might also give him an heir who could avenge Ake's murder. Palner took Sigurd's advice, married Ingeborg and had a son called Toke, whose destiny it became to avenge Ake's death.

Toke displayed traits of courage and strength from early childhood and became known as Palnatoke or Palner's Toke. Considered the founder of the Jomsborg fort, it is around him, as the elite group's first leader, that much of the Jomsvikings' story revolves. Palner died before his son reached maturity and never witnessed the establishment of Jomsborg, and the subsequent harassment, kidnappings and threats to the Danish king's dominions.[5]

After his father's death, Palnatoke decided to make a name for himself by going a-Viking; he readied twelve ships, pillaged and plundered far and wide and became famous for his exploits. During a visit to England, he married Olufa, daughter of Earl Stefnir, acquiring half the kingdom and the title of earl. After a summer and winter had passed, Palnatoke left England and sailed back to Denmark with his wife, leaving Olufa's councilor, Björn the Welshman, to govern the English dominions. As a result of his growing wealth and success abroad, Palnatoke was considered by some to be the most important man in Denmark next to the king.

Palnatoke then prepared a feast to which he invited King Harald Bluetooth. Feasts frequently lasted for several weeks; at this one, the king enjoyed himself immensely and stayed a long time. Mead flowed freely, tongues were loosened, and few in the company remembered what transpired from one day to the next. One evening Harald Bluetooth, in a drunken state, bedded a poor servant girl who had been assigned to serve him. She became pregnant and the following summer, long after King Harald's return home, she had a son. When Palnatoke asked the woman who the father was, she told him it was King Harald Bluetooth of Denmark. The future suddenly became clear to Palnatoke who realized that he could use this information to entrap the king. He freed the woman from further duties, agreed to be the boy's foster-father and named him Sven.[6]

When Sven was three years old, Palnatoke felt the time had come to avenge his uncle's death. He decided to pay the Danish king a visit. Marching into Harald Bluetooth's hall, he reminded the king of the feast when he had drunk too much and of the servant girl with whom he had dallied. "Here is your son," he said, placing little Sven on the king's knee. "You shall now give him his inherited rights to the kingdom." King Harald was not pleased: "What is this horrible news you are bringing me? Take the boy, leave immediately and never set foot here again." By inspiring fear in the king, Palnatoke had taken the first step towards his revenge. Satisfied with his accomplishment, he sailed back home and continued to be foster-father to Sven.

The years passed, and when Sven turned fifteen, Palnatoke decided that the boy was old enough to sail alone to the Danish king and claim his rights. "But don't worry," he told his foster-son, "I'll stand behind you all the way." He gave Sven a ship and twenty men and sent him to King Harald. "It shows that your mother is of low birth and of poor reputation," the king grunted when Sven made known the reason for his visit. "I would have had a nobler birth," Sven said, "if the king of Denmark had only had the decency, common sense and foresight to provide me with such." King Harald smiled, taken aback by the impudent youngster, but agreed to furnish him with three ships and one hundred men. "Leave now and go a-Viking as you please," said the king, "but promise that you will never make that horrible request for my kingdom again." Sven accepted the warriors and ships and sailed back home. His foster-father Palnatoke gave him another three ships, and he now had his first fleet with which he spent the whole summer harassing the farmers and plundering in the Danish islands.

The following year he returned to King Harald and asked for six ships and crew. Feeling the growing threat to his kingdom, King Harald gave Sven what he wanted in the hope that the problem would eventually go away. Palnatoke matched the offer and added more ships to Sven's fleet. Sven then went out again to pillage around the Danish islands and spread havoc among the farmers; he killed so many innocent people that news of his notoriety traveled widely in the Danish dominions. Farmers complained to the king: "We have lived in peace for many years now and we are not about to be robbed and slaughtered by an impudent boy not yet old enough to carry a sword with pride. What are you going to do about it?" Harald had no ready answer because he had supplied Sven with the means to wage war on the farmers and he could not now reclaim his gift and place his kingdom at continued risk. Although King Harald's relations with his people deteriorated, he ignored the situation, hoping the problem would resolve itself by the following year.

Sven spent the winter with Palnatoke, and on his foster-father's advice, he returned to King Harald in spring for the third time, bringing with him his entire fleet and hundreds of armed soldiers who followed him into the king's hall. "Twelve ships I ask of you this time," Sven told the king, "or else, I will go to war against you." Harald had little choice but to give Sven what he asked for. Palnatoke once again matched the offer and Sven now had a magnificent fleet of twenty-four ships with which, again on his foster-father's advice, he continued to plunder in Denmark all summer, burning and laying waste to the country.[7]

In the meantime Palnatoke had business in England and sailed across the North Sea with a fleet of fifteen ships. With Palnatoke out of the way, King Harald took the opportunity to confront Sven at sea. He readied a fleet of fifty ships and met Sven outside the island of Bornholm.[8] A violent fight erupted and King Harald had so much help that Sven was overpowered. The fight lasted from early morning until afternoon when Harald managed to force Sven's ships into an enclosed area of the bay. By then King Harald had lost ten of his ships and Sven had lost twelve. Harald then anchored his ships across the bay to prevent Sven from escaping.

Palnatoke, on receiving news of the battle, returned home from England with a fleet of twenty-four ships. When he spotted Harald and eleven of his men warming themselves by a fire, he anchored his ship and went ashore, bringing his bow and arrows with him. He was one of the most skilled archers in the country and had once demonstrated his accuracy by shooting an apple off his son's head. He readied his bow, aimed and shot the king dead in the back.[9]

The battle started anew the next morning, but when the men learned of their king's death, they had little motivation to continue the fight. At the *ting* meeting that followed, Palnatoke suggested that Sven be celebrated as the new king of Denmark. There was objection at first. Sven had created such trouble among the farmers with his pillaging and burning, and caused so much grief that they had no desire to have him as their king. Instead they offered the kingdom to Palnatoke, who was much loved and admired, but Palnatoke refused the offer. "Either you will have Sven as your king or more battles will follow," he said. The *ting* ended and Sven was crowned king over all of Denmark.

Fjolner, Palnatoke's relation, who had served King Harald and convinced the king to kill Ake, now ended up in the employ of the new King Sven Forkbeard. When Fjolner recognized the golden arrow that had struck Harald Bluetooth in the back, he presented the arrow to Sven and encouraged him to avenge King Harald's death. "You have come here repeatedly and claimed that the king is your father," Fjolner said. "If that is really so, you will never be honored as our new king, unless you do what is right and avenge your father's death."

Sven agreed that even though King Harald had never acknowledged him as his son, it would be appropriate to honor his father with a memorial feast. He first invited Palnatoke to drink the funeral ale with him, but Palnatoke declined as his father-in-law, Stefnir, had just died: "I must go to England, take care of the realms, and protect my inheritance." Sven delayed the memorial feast until the following summer when he again invited Palnatoke. Palnatoke, who was in England, declined the invitation, "due to aging and ill health" and "the long sea voyage" which would "certainly be too much for me to endure." Sven delayed the memorial feast by still another year. When he invited Palnatoke for the third time, along with as many men as needed for the journey, he was angry. "You are dishonoring me by refusing the invitation," he said. "If you fail to come this time, then I will resent you, be forced to do battle with you and will show you no mercy." So Palnatoke prepared to depart England and attend the funeral feast for his enemy, King Harald.

On the evening of the feast, Sven seated himself with his men at the table, leaving room for Palnatoke on the high seat opposite him and one hundred of his followers. Palnatoke, who was traveling with three ships and three hundred men, arrived in Denmark in the late evening. He moored his ships with the bows pointing toward the sea and the oars still in the rowlocks for a quick getaway and walked into the king's hall together with his followers. Sven received him well and set up an additional table for the men. After some time had passed, Fjolner rose from his seat and whispered something to King Sven, whose face turned blood red. Talk about King Harald's death followed and Fjolner presented the golden arrow that had killed the king. Sven passed the arrow around among the guests. "If anybody recognizes this arrow, speak up!" he ordered. When the arrow arrived at Palnatoke, he stood up, looked Sven in the eye, and said: "The arrow is mine, King! Give it to me." He stared at the men seated around the table: "Or does anyone dare to imply that I am afraid to admit that I know this arrow?"

Sven rose. "Palnatoke," he shouted, "where did you part with this arrow?"

"If you really want to know this in the presence of so many men," said Palnatoke, "then I will tell you that I parted with the arrow when I shot your father in the back, so that the arrow pierced his body and came out through his mouth."

Sven yelled at his men to kill Palnatoke and his followers, for the friendship between them had ended. Nobody moved because Palnatoke was so beloved that no one wanted to lay a hand on him. Palnatoke drew his sword and swung it through the air so that the edge glittered in the firelight. The stroke, directed at Fjolner, split the man's head open and he fell to the floor. "Never again shall you speak badly about me before the king," said Palnatoke.

Now Sven was even angrier and again shouted for his men to kill Palnatoke, the man who had disturbed the peace in the king's hall during the memorial feast for Harald Bluetooth. But again, no one moved and the silence was deafening. Palnatoke finally stood up, walked out of the hall and motioned for his men to follow him to the ships that were ready to sail. He first went to England where he stayed for some time. After his wife died, he left his councilor Björn the Welshman to rule over the dominions and went a-Viking with a fleet of forty ships, raiding for three years in Ireland and Scotland, commanding respect for his wisdom and courage and amassing such wealth that he was considered the greatest Viking in all of the northern lands. After some time he landed in Vindland.[10] Palnatoke was not only a renowned warrior chief, it was said that he was almost always victorious in battle. Burisleif (Burislav), king of the Wends, felt the danger threatening his country and offered Palnatoke the Jome district on the southern coast of the Baltic Sea, on the condition that he settle there and defend the king's dominions. This contract resulted in a long-term friendship between Palnatoke and King Burisleif.

It was on the land received from Burisleif that Palnatoke set out to build the fortified stronghold he called Jomsborg.[11] He filled the fort with the strongest, fiercest and most courageous fighters of the Viking elite, each of whom was tested for valor before winning admittance. Within the fort's semicircular walls he built a harbor large enough to accommodate 200 ships (360 warships at anchor according to some sources), and a stone arched entrance with heavy iron doors that could be locked with iron beams from inside the harbor; on top of the arch he built a tower with catapults for defense. The main building was so protected that it was thought impossible to besiege it.

Palnatoke, together with his closest men, then established strict laws for the warriors living within the Jomsborg fort. The laws, based on courage and valor, were meant to distinguish the elite force within from those outside, further their reputation, and inspire them with the strength needed to endure the trials of war. No one younger than eighteen or older than fifty was admitted to the Jomsborg elite and each man had to supply the fort with two good warriors from among his own men.[12]

Total loyalty, even if it meant death, was expected at all times. No fistfights were allowed within the fort and a warrior had to avenge wrongdoing against another as if he were a father or a brother. Boasting or slander was not permitted and no warrior was to be honored over another. No man was allowed the company of a female other than his wife, and for no longer than one night at a time. If a warrior's father, brother or other close kin was murdered, Palnatoke alone would judge and settle all disputes. Warriors were not allowed to be absent from the fort for longer than one night (three nights according to some sources) unless Palnatoke had given his prior permission. All booty acquired privately, or in the company of others, had to be divided regardless of whether it was a large or small amount. Only Palnatoke announced news of importance. To be allowed in the fort, a man had to be prepared to endure hardship without complaint, never show fear and stand his ground in valor and arms. Nobody was allowed to pass through the fort's gates unless cleared by Palnatoke. Joining the elite force meant accepting its laws; there was no special consideration for fame or family name. Anyone who broke these rules was immediately banned from the fort, regardless of status or financial standing.

The warriors residing at Jomsborg were called Jomsvikings and came to be regarded as the northern lands' most hardened warriors, fortifying their reputations through their laws and deeds. They went on raids every summer and wreaked havoc in lands near and distant. They plundered in the English dominions of King Aethelred (the Unready), wintered on the Thames, pillaging inland in 1010 and sacking Canterbury in 1011. They joined in battles with other Norsemen, as in the noted battle of Fyrisvallarna in about 985, where Jomsviking Styrbjörn the Strong met his death against the Swedish king Erik Segersäll (the Victorious).

While Palnatoke was busy establishing Jomsborg, Ake, a son of Palnatoke and a rich and much beloved chief, was in charge of Palnatoke's dominions on Fyen. Sven Forkbeard valued his relationship with Ake, his foster-brother, and did not allow former bad blood to come between them. Around this time a man named Wesete also lived on the island of Bornholm with his wife, Hildiguda, and their three children. The oldest child was Bue the Strong, the second, Sigurd the Warrior, and the third, a girl, was named Thorguna. King Sven asked for Thorguna in marriage for his friend Ake and the wedding was celebrated on Bornholm in the presence of King Sven and many guests from Denmark. Soon Ake and Thorguna had a son they named Vagn. Vagn quickly grew big and very strong, but became so wild, unruly and difficult to handle that his family was unable to control him. The only person he obeyed to some degree was Bue, his maternal uncle. By the age of ten, Vagn had already killed three men and by twelve had strength matched by no other.

At this time Earl Harald ruled over Seeland and acquired the name Strutharald (Coneharald) because of his peculiar expensive hat into which ten gold marks had been woven. Strutharald and his wife had three children. The oldest was Sigvaldi, the second, Thorkel the Tall, and the third, a daughter, was named Thofa. The two brothers, having gained fame during their Viking expeditions, readied two ships and one hundred men for travel. After plundering Wesete of Bornholm, they sailed on to Jomsborg, mooring their ships outside the gate.[13] When Palnatoke asked why they had come, Sigvaldi asked to join the Jomsborg elite force, along with as many of his men who qualified. Palnatoke first read them the laws of the fort, then opened the gates and let the ships enter the harbor. The men were tested; half of them were considered fit for service and the other half were sent back home.

Bue and Sigurd, Wesete's sons, desirous of fame and an opportunity to enhance their reputation, sailed with two ships and one hundred men to Jomsborg.[14] But when Palnatoke read them the laws, he questioned how they intended to settle the disputes between the Wesete and Strutharald families. Bue explained that the families had already been reconciled through arbitration of the king. The gates to the fort were opened and the crew was tested, and eighty men admitted. From then on, Bue and his men went a-Viking every summer, raiding far and wide, with what was said to be unparalleled force.

Vagn Akesson was Bue's twelve-year-old nephew. Vagn's father, unable to keep the unruly youngster at home any longer, gave him two ships, let him choose one hundred men all about age eighteen and sent him off a-Viking, thinking that it would provide an outlet for the boy's energy.[15] He offered him weapons and provisions which Vagn declined, saying he could provide for himself. He sailed along the Danish coast and raided at will for weapons, provisions, clothes and anything else needed for his journey, until he showed up one morning at the gates of Jomsborg. When asked his errand, Vagn explained that he was the grandson of Palnatoke and had come seeking admission to the Jomsvikings. "I do not seem fit to be in the company of ordinary folks, and it is my parents' wish that I depart for a while," he said.

"Do you think you will be given free rein here in Jomsborg?" Palnatoke asked, turning to his closest men for advice. Despite his warm relations with Vagn, Bue advised Palnatoke not to let the wild youngster inside the walls of Jomsborg. Besides, Vagn was only twelve and the laws clearly stated that a Jomsviking must be at least eighteen. "So long as I am found to be equal to the older warriors in courage and ability," Vagn said, "the law would remain unbroken."

"Sail to Britain instead," said Palnatoke, "and I will give you half of my land." Although Vagn found this offer generous, he explained that he had not come for land, and had no intention of leaving: "I challenge Sigvaldi, son of Strutharald, to do battle with me. Each of us will have two ships and one hundred men. If Sigvaldi wins the battle, I promise to leave; if I win the battle, I expect to be admitted to the fort." Palnatoke turned to Sigvaldi: "If it is true what we hear of Vagn's courage, you are now in for a difficult test. But I ask you, do not kill him should you become his superior, but capture him instead and bring him to me."

Sigvaldi and his men put on their war gear and rowed out with their ships. Vagn made the first move by hurling a volley of rocks so forcefully at Sigvaldi's ships that Sigvaldi's forces were unable to counter the attack and had to defend themselves behind their shields to avoid being crushed by the barrage of rocks coming their way. When the rock supply was exhausted, the fight continued with bows and arrows. The young and battle-starved men on Vagn's ship fired the arrows so powerfully that Sigvaldi's warriors were unable to counter and again had to seek protection behind their shields. They were finally forced to jump from their ships and go ashore in search of more rocks. But Vagn attacked again and the clash began anew with swords. After Sigvaldi was forced to capitulate, Palnatoke declared the fight over. Both sides had suffered great casualties. Forty of Sigvaldi's and twenty of Vagn's men had fallen and many more were wounded.

The warriors agreed that Vagn should be admitted to the fort. From then on he went every summer with the Jomsvikings on plundering expeditions, commanding a large force of warriors and winning victory after victory, surpassing all other Jomsvikings in skill and courage.

When Vagn had lived for four years within the walls of Jomsborg, Palnatoke fell ill and called for King Burisleif of the Wends to advise him in choosing a successor. The two leaders agreed that Sigvaldi, the son of Strutharald, was the man best-suited for the duty. At this time Palnatoke also gave his grandson Vagn half of his dominions in England, governed by Björn the Welshman. Palnatoke's death was a great loss, both to the warriors of Jomsborg and to King Burisleif of the Wends. Sigvaldi assumed leadership of Jomsborg and continued fighting for the Jomsviking cause of freedom from the Danish king.

Although they fought with all those coming from the south, the existence of Jomsborg was dependent on the power of Sven Forkbeard. To bolster his standing after assuming command of the fort, Sigvaldi asked for Burisleif's daughter Astrid in marriage. Burisleif agreed, but only if Sigvaldi managed to free Jomsborg from the taxes imposed by the Danish King Forkbeard. Sigvaldi readied three ships, heavily soldiered with three hundred men, and embarked on a journey to Denmark. He turned his ships with their bows away from land and moored them broadside-to-broadside. Messengers then went to King Sven to inform him that Sigvaldi was severely ill and had important matters to discuss, so a meeting between the two would be prudent. Sven went with many men to the beach where the ships from Jomsborg were moored together in a long row. "Only thirty men are allowed to board the ships," the Jomsvikings told Sven. After Sven entered the first of the three ships, he was told that ten of his men were to stay on that ship and ten on the second, so that the last ship, where Sigvaldi lay on his deathbed, would not be too heavily loaded. When the king and the last ten men in his entourage boarded the third ship, the gangplank that acted as a bridge between the ships was hauled on board to prevent any others from entering.

King Sven found Sigvaldi so weak that he could barely talk. But when he bent down over Sigvaldi to hear what the Jomsborg chief had to say, Sigvaldi reached up and grabbed Sven's neck (some sources say Sigvaldi grabbed the king around his shoulders and gripped him under the arm), held him down, and ordered the ships to cast off. The rest of the king's men were left standing helplessly on the beach. Sigvaldi took King Sven prisoner to Jomsborg and forced him to make peace with King Burisleif "or else I will deliver you into the hands of the Wends." King Sven feared torture and death by the Wends and therefore had to settle in accordance with Sigvaldi's wishes. Sigvaldi was then able to marry Burisleif's daughter and a splendid feast followed in Vindland.[16]

Shortly thereafter Earl Strutharald died, and as was the custom, King Sven held a celebration in the dead man's honor, to which he invited the chiefs of all his dominions, including the Jomsvikings, to drink the funeral ale. Sigvaldi, Thorkel the Tall, Bue, Sigurd and Vagn, all excellent warriors, set out with a fleet of sixty ships. The tradition when a man of importance died was for those gathered to make impressive vows in the dead man's honor. The greater the vow, the more honorable it was considered.[17] King Sven started by filling the largest horns with strong drinks for the chiefs of the Jomsvikings. When the bowl was emptied, they drank to Christ's health and the largest horns were again filled with the strongest drinks for the Jomsvikings. They then drank the third bowl to the memory of Saint Michael, after which Sigvaldi drank a remembrance bowl to his father's honor. By then the men's tongues had loosened and the king stood up to make the first vow. He vowed that within three years he would conquer England, either by killing King Aethelred or by driving him from the country. He turned to the Jomsvikings, who had drunk heavily of the strong alcoholic beverages. "Now it is your turn, Jomsvikings," he said, "you, the greatest heroes of the north, will now find some honorable deed for which you will be remembered."

Sigvaldi stood up and drank. He was awed by the king's vow to conquer England and did not want to be outdone. "I vow," he said, "that within three years I will go to Norway, lay siege to the country and either kill Earl Hakon or drive him from the country, unless I will be killed myself." Then Thorkel the Tall, Sigvaldi's brother, stood up and swore that he would follow his brother in battle against Earl Hakon and not flinch or flee until he saw the stern of his brother's ship. "Well spoken," said the king, who then turned to Bue and Sigurd. "Now it is your turn. What great and noteworthy vow have you got in mind?" Bue and Sigurd too vowed to support Sigvaldi in his expedition to Norway and hold out, if they were not killed, until victory was theirs. The king then turned to hear the vow of young Vagn Akesson, Palnatoke's grandson. "I pledge that I will kill Thorkel Lejra in Viken and marry his daughter, Ingeborg, with or without the people's consent," said Vagn.

King Sven and all the chiefs were merry and drank to their vows, but when morning came and the men had slept off their drink, many felt they had taken on more than they could deliver. However, a vow was holy, and once made, had to be fulfilled. "It will not do for you to pretend that you made none," said Astrid, Sigvaldi's wife, "for to do so would bring you much dishonor." So the Jomsvikings had no choice but to ready a fleet of 60 ships (120 ships according to some sources), sail north and start marauding around the country and up the coastline of Norway, killing as many arms-bearing men as possible.

Earl Hakon of Norway, after hearing of the impending attack, sent war arrows around the country and spies onto the peaks and into the fjords and put together a fleet of 150 ships (360 ships according to some sources) with which he prepared to meet the Jomsvikings at Hjörungavåg.[18] The two fleets clashed, and the battle that followed was one of the bloodiest in the history of the Vikings. Sigvaldi displayed his banner in the middle of his fleet. His brother Thorkel was moored on one side and Bue and his brother, Sigurd, moored their ships to the north. Vagn and Björn the Welshman, who had come from England, were moored to the south. As the battle raged, many men fell on both sides. The many spears thrown at Earl Hakon split his armor, which he threw off so that the steel rings of his mail shirt clanged on the wet deck. It appeared at first as though the Jomsvikings, under Bue's leadership, were winning, but Earl Hakon grew worried and went ashore to make offerings to the gods and pray to his patron goddess, Thorgerd Holgabrud. To emerge victorious from the battle, he even went so far as to offer his own seven-year-old son to the goddess.

After the boy had been killed and the blood offering made, Earl Hakon felt sure of victory and urged his men on. The sky darkened and a terrible hailstorm erupted, with hailstones so large they weighed a "pennyweight." The storm confused the Jomsvikings and forced Sigvaldi to cut the hawsers that held the ships together. When Vagn saw Sigvaldi running away, he called: "Why do you flee, and leave your men behind? You will suffer disgrace from this for the rest of your life." Thinking it was Sigvaldi sitting at the rudder of the ship, Vagn aimed and threw a spear at the man. But Sigvaldi had become chilled in the hailstorm and had traded off with another man at the oars, thereby escaping unharmed. When all of the men except Bue and Vagn had fled, Earl Hakon moored his ships to the sides of Bue and Vagn's ships and the battle continued. Among the men fighting from Bue's ship was Aslak Holmskalle, Bue's foster-brother, who fought without a helmet; those watching thought that the iron swords being swung at him had no power over him, but Aslak finally received a blow from an anvil that split his head open, spilling his brains out onto the deck.

Then Thorstein Midlang of Earl Hakon's men entered Bue's ship and struck Bue across the face, slitting his helmet and cutting his nose. Bue countered by striking Thorstein in the side, cutting him in half. But the victory was short-lived, for Bue received a blow that severed both of his hands at the wrists. When he realized his loss, he stuck the stumps of his arms through the handles of two coffers containing gold, which he always carried with him and jumped overboard, calling to the rest of his men to follow; but most had already fallen on the ship.

Now the battle turned toward Vagn's ship, whose bulwarks were unusually tall and difficult to penetrate and provided good protection against the enemy's spears and arrows. Earl Erik of Norway drew alongside the ship and waited until it became too dark to fight and it was at last safe to enter the ship and clear it of warriors. In this way, Vagn and thirty of his men were taken prisoner and Earl Hakon was able to boast of a great victory over the notorious Jomsvikings. His only regret was that Sigvaldi, the Jomsvikings' chief, had gotten away with thirty-five ships (twenty-five of his fleet of sixty ships had fallen to the enemy).

Vagn and his men were brought on land and had their feet tied with a long rope to a tree log, leaving their hands free. These Jomsvikings would now be executed and it fell to Thorkel Lejra, the man Vagn had vowed to kill, to relieve Vagn of his life. Thorkel approached the prisoner with raised axe in hand. "You vowed to kill me," he said to Vagn, but it now looks as though I will kill you." One by one the Jomsvikings went courageously to their deaths, even, it was said, with a smirk on their lips, because by Jomsborg law a warrior was not supposed to flinch before death which would eventually be every man's due. One of the warriors was impudent enough to ask permission to pull down his trousers to relieve himself before being beheaded. The request was granted, and while the warrior was urinating in the grass, he told the earl that he wanted to bed his daughter.

As the executions continued, one of the doomed men turned to his friend and said: "We have often talked and argued about how long it is likely that a man can remain conscious after the head has been taken from the body. Now we will find out, for if I know anything at all after I have been beheaded, I will dig my knife into the earth." This was possible because his hands were not tied. Thorkel Lejra let the axe fall, the head was severed from the man's body and the knife immediately fell from the dead man's hand.

After eighteen prisoners had been disposed of, it was the turn of a magnificent, tall man with the longest and thickest hair ever seen, hair golden as silk. He wrapped his hair around his head and asked the executioner to hold the hair away from his face so that no blood would fall on it when the axe dropped. The executioner's assistant thought it a fair request and tied a rope around the hair so that he could hold it away from the doomed man's neck. Thorkel Lejra let the axe fall. But at that instant the golden-haired Jomsviking jerked his head violently to the side and the executioner's assistant fell forward causing the blow from the axe to land on his arms instead, severing both of them at the elbow. "Still live some of the Jomsvikings!" the man with the golden hair shouted. Earl Erik was so impressed he offered the doomed man his freedom.

When the man was freed from the ropes, Thorkel Lejra said to the earl: "Shall this man, who has in front of our eyes killed our comrades, really be allowed to live?" The earl reminded Thorkel who was in charge: "Don't you know that I have more power than you?" Thorkel was displeased. "That may be," he said, "but never shall Vagn Akesson escape with his life."

Thorkel Lejra ran with raised axe toward Vagn, but a man threw himself in front of Thorkel's feet so that Thorkel fell forward and had to let go of the axe in order to catch himself. Vagn grabbed the axe and cut Thorkel across the back of the neck with such force that the axe stuck into the ground.

In this way, it was said, he was able to fulfill at least half of his vow.

Earl Erik felt it was a shame to kill such a splendid warrior as Vagn and therefore offered him his freedom. "I would gladly accept your offer," said Vagn, "if all the men who are still living would also be granted their freedom. Otherwise I would rather share their destiny." The men were freed from the ropes, leaving twelve out of the original thirty alive.

Then a bowstring was heard twanging from Bue's fleet, and Gissur, one of the earl's men from Valders, was shot by an arrow fired from a ship closest to land; when the men hurried down to the water they found Viking Hovard Hoggande standing on his knees at the ship's railing with a bow in his hand, for his feet had been cut off. "Tell me, who was it that fell from the arrow?" he asked. When Hovard learned it was one of the earl's men who had fallen, and not the earl himself who was sitting on a log not far away, he said: "Then my luck was less than I had hoped; it was meant for the earl."

"The misfortune is bad enough," said the earl's men, "and you shall not make it greater," upon which they cut Hovard into so many pieces that had he had one hundred lives, he would not have survived.

Earl Hakon, having sacrificed his seven-year-old son to the gods for victory, was displeased that Earl Erik had given Vagn and his men quarter, but the decision stood, for it was said that he, Earl Erik, had contributed most to the battle. Vagn spent the winter with Earl Erik; the two took a great liking to one another and Earl Erik gave Thorkel Lejra's daughter, Ingeborg, to Vagn in marriage. Through this union, Vagn was able to fulfill the second half of his vow. The earl then bestowed on him a large and fully equipped long-ship for his return trip to Denmark.

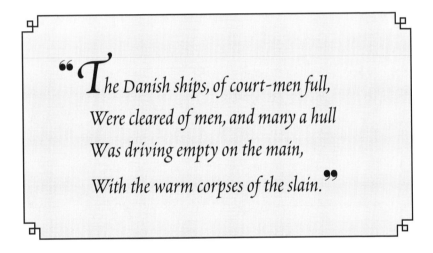

"The Danish ships, of court-men full,
Were cleared of men, and many a hull
Was driving empty on the main,
With the warm corpses of the slain."

CHAPTER 9

THE RUS IN THE VARANGIAN GUARD

*The Norse King Harald Hardrade fought so vio-
lently during his time in the Varangian Guard
that his battle code was victory or death. He lived
by the battle principle, success is half courage.*

———

Russia's extensive network of rivers and waterways extends
from the Baltic coast down the entire length of the country
to the Caspian Sea. Since the beginning of the Viking Age, Norse
adventurers had traveled across the Slavic lands via the rivers
that joined the north both to Russia and the Mediterranean,
enabling them to discover the wealth of the Roman Empire,
then continue southward to raid or offer their services to rich
countries needing mercenaries with military prowess. The
Norse-Russian merchants, whose origins were from Sweden
and Gotland, used the river systems to trade in Spain, Rome
and the Khazar world,[1] and were known for providing a continuous flow of goods between the Nordic countries and Byzan-
tium. The Danes and Norwegians invaded France and England,
but Swedes, known as Varangians, Rus, or Rhos, flourished in
Russia.[2] The Rus gave their name to the Russian Empire when
they organized the country, founding the first city in Kiev where
they ruled the state. Oleg of Novgorod, a kinsman of the Norse
warrior Rurik of the Rus, became the first prince of Novgorod
in 862, and is credited with organizing a military force of
Varangians who moved down the River Dnieper and took both
Smolensk and Kiev in 882, laying the foundation for a unified

Slavic state that became known as Kievan Rus.[3] In 901, Oleg organized a massive expedition of troops that sailed to the Black Sea and looted around the countryside, before working out a trade agreement by which Rus merchants would receive access to the Byzantine market.

The Rus were powerful men, known for their courage. They trekked into some regions on foot to raid, but also traveled by boat, seizing ships and plundering goods. It was said that they came from a forested island surrounded by water, "its extent being a distance of three days in either direction."[4] Great Svithiod, land of the Norsemen, was "reckoned by some as not less than the Great Serkland; others compare it to the Great Blueland."[5] Motivated primarily by hunger for wealth and adventure, the Vikings were helped in their journeys by their knowledge of river routes and confidence in their military capabilities. Viking warriors also realized that their host nation was weak and an easy target for pirates.

Miklagard, the great city of Constantine, fascinated the Nordic people with its wealth and magnificent buildings, a distant but powerful magnet that drew ships full of Norsemen through the River Dnieper and the Black Sea. The Swedish capital and trade city of Birka had only some one thousand inhabitants, but Constantinople, located on the border between Europe and Asia, had almost three hundred times that number. A raid on the splendid capital of the Byzantine Empire, center of world commerce, was a battle objective for Norsemen, providing an opportunity to achieve wealth by the sword as well as honor.

Norsemen traveling from Birka to Miklagard could start their journey over the Baltic Sea to the Gulf of Finland and on to Lake Ladoga in Russia, then through the River Volchov past Holmgard (Novgorod, a gateway leading to the River Dnieper) all the way down to the Black Sea, passing Konugard (Kiev) on the way. After reaching the Black Sea, it was easy to follow the coastline westward to reach Constantinople, a journey of about ten days. At settlements such as Staraya Ladoga,[6] which was reached by sailing to the tip of the Gulf of Finland then southward for some thirty miles, the Vikings switched from their larger ships to smaller boats for easier travel down the narrow waterways. Sometimes they spent the winter in Russian towns before venturing farther inland in spring, often with cargo consisting of furs, honey, amber, and slaves for trade in the Arab world in return for gold, silver, and silk.

There was danger in a journey covering several hundred miles of water and rough terrain. For a forty-mile distance, the River Dnieper was a gauntlet of hazardous rapids and seven major falls with names such as "Don't Fall Asleep," "The Islet of the Barrier," "Noise of the Rapids," and "The Boiling of Water."[7] The rapids were so powerful and rocky that men had to carry their ships overland, or drag them along the riverbanks. At times, men walked in the water by the bow, with others by the stern, and pushed the ship along with poles. Other rivers could be traveled only during times of high waters, which occurred no more than a few weeks out of the year.

Journeying through the trade routes also brought risk of encountering the hostile Slavic and Finnish tribes that dominated the lands and rivers leading to the Black Sea and beyond. Norsemen traveling the Russian rivers armed themselves with swords, knives and especially axes. The Arabic writer, Ibn Dustah (sometimes called Ibn Rustah from the Rosta district in Persia), a tenth-century explorer and geographer, describes the Rus as "bold and handsome barbarians, but dressed in dirty clothes, though the men wore heavy gold armlets; their sole occupations were fighting and bargaining . . . they were always armed, and were quick-tempered and pugnacious; they were excellent sailors, but rode little on horseback."[8]

There was safety in numbers, so the Rus traveled in groups, often with other family members, or people from their own land, sometimes joining up with another party going the same way. To overcome hostility, good health, a strong physique, and mental preparedness were required of all men in the group. In 972, Turkic Pechenegs (also called Patzinaks), a semi-nomadic people from the steppes, killed Prince Svyatoslav of the Rus "and made a drinking cup of his skull." These journeys required considerable planning and investment in provisions. The Volga River, the first trans-Russian waterway, which the Vikings started using in the ninth century, was an easterly route and an attractive alternative by which to sail far in a southerly direction into Serkland and all the way to the Caspian Sea.

The Black Sea became the scene of battles with the Byzantine navy between the tenth and twelfth centuries, a period marked by alternating armed conflicts and friendship treaties between the Byzantines and the Rus. The objective of these battles was to open up trade routes between Russia and the Byzantine Empire. The Byzantine capital was important to commerce because of its strategic location at the connecting waterway between the Mediterranean and the Black Sea. Although Vikings who went east were more often traders than pirates, some missions combined looting with trading. When temptation became irresistible, trading gave way to raiding and war, which kept the Byzantines in a state of continual alert from the mid-ninth to the mid-eleventh centuries.

On June 18, 860, a quarrel between Greek and Rus merchants resulted in a bold offensive by the Rus on Constantinople. This was the first attack by Swedish kings attempting to capture the great city. This audacious assault by a barbaric people sent shockwaves through the Byzantine Empire. The Norsemen's timing was perfect, as Emperor Michael III was busy fighting the Saracens and had temporarily left the capital. The Norse fleet consisted of two hundred ships, which had ravaged the coastal regions of the Black Sea before sailing within sight of Constantinople where it set ashore with sword-brandishing troops. The surprise attack forced the emperor to interrupt his war against the Arabs and return to the capital. Photius, the city's patriarch and one of the most learned men of his time, recorded that Constantinople barely withstood the spears thrown by the barbarous invaders, as he called the Norsemen, and was saved only because of a sudden storm that wrecked the Viking fleet. A truce was concluded a week later and the Rus began to leave, taking with them a large tribute payment in the form of gold, silk, fruit and wine.

The Rus impressed the emperor by their attack and established their reputation as fearless and formidable warriors. To stop the piracy, peace treaties were drawn up that gave the northern marauders greater trade privileges in return for a more peaceful relationship. He also capitalized on their ferocity by recruiting them into the Byzantine army as part of his elite bodyguard unit. The trade treaties, however, forbid the Vikings to carry arms when entering Constantinople. Black market dealings were punished by amputation of a hand. But the Vikings were used to raiding and taking whatever they pleased and their warrior spirit and military prowess made it difficult for them to submit to Byzantine rule, making a conciliatory agreement necessary.

Oleg of Novgorod's attack on Constantinople in 907, probably the consequence of an infringement of the earlier trade agreement of 860, is said to have consisted of two thousand ships and eighty thousand men, as well as additional cavalry for land warfare. Nordic warriors generally did not have cavalry, preferring to ride to the site of the battle, dismount and enter the fray on foot, a tradition they maintained during their stay in Constantinople. Fighting on foot gave them the freedom to wield their greatest weapon, the two-handed battleaxe that had a shaft of at least five feet and a long, "bearded" cutting edge. The new trade agreement resulting from Oleg's attack boosted the Kievan Rus economy and specified how the Rus were to be treated and supplied. The Rus, in turn, promised to end their raids against the Byzantine Empire. According to the treaty, the Rus were permitted to enter Constantinople through one city gate only and in small, unarmed groups of no more than fifty at a time and under official escort. In return, they were to receive a maintenance allowance of as much as they required, were absolved from paying taxes on their merchandise, were provided with bathing facilities on request, and were given supplies for up to six months that included bread, wine, meat, fish and fruit. For their return journey to Russia, the emperor was to supply them with provisions, anchors, sails and ropes.[9]

Some Vikings also served as volunteers in the royal armies of other nations. In 911, a second trade treaty to supplement the first one was negotiated; it allowed the Vikings to enlist as soldiers in the emperor's army. After Oleg, regent of Kiev, concluded the treaty of 911 with the Byzantines, the co-emperors Leo and Alexander are said to have kissed the cross in a binding oath, while Oleg and the Rus, as was their custom, swore by their weapons.[10] By the early tenth century, with more than seven hundred Rus serving in the Byzantine fleet, four hundred of them in seven ships assaulted southern Italy in a Greek-led invasion. In the tenth and eleventh centuries, five hundred Varangians were employed as the emperor's bodyguards.

In the summer of 941, Igor, son of Rurik, violated the agreement and suddenly decided to attack Constantinople with a fleet of one thousand ships when the Greek navy was away fighting the Saracens.[11] Igor's motives for the attack, which came after a long period of peace with the Greeks, are unclear. The Greeks defeated him by igniting the so-called devastating Greek Fire which could burn even on water, until the Norsemen fled, only to continue plundering in other provinces once they had recovered from their ordeal.[12]

In 988, the Varangian Guard appeared as an official force of six thousand Russian Viking warriors. They were dispatched by Kievan Prince Vladimir the Great in response to an appeal to serve Emperor Basil II against the Greek rebel Bardas Phocas, who marched against the capital and met his death in 989. In return, the Russian prince received the emperor's sister Anna in marriage. The emperor formed the warriors into a regiment to serve as his imperial bodyguard. The last Rus attack on Constantinople, led by Russian Prince Yaroslav I the Wise, took place in 1043. Although the Rus fleet of four hundred ships was defeated, the service of Norse people in the guard lasted until the fall of Constantinople to the Latins in 1204.

Mercenary soldiers have existed throughout history and were valuable for special skills lacking in a country's native soldiers. The Varangian Guard, comprised chiefly of Nordic and Anglo-Saxon mercenaries, became an elite force serving at the forefront of numerous Byzantine battles with the Turks, Crusaders, and Normans. The Byzantine Empire was often at war with the neighboring countries of Syria, Sicily, Cyprus, and the Khazar world and needed to recruit tough, loyal and dependable troops. Vikings serving in the guard were recruited directly from the Nordic countries and from Swedish settlements in Russia. They were one of the fiercest, most neutral, and most loyal elements of the Byzantine army and were used as shock troops because of their height, courage and quick tempers.[13] Quickly inflamed, they often fought without any particular strategy, but had formidable warrior spirit and remained devoted to the emperor as long as they got paid. The agreement was mutually beneficial. Norsemen in military service in Constantinople had many opportunities to acquire property and return home much better-off financially than when they left.

Vikings willingly served as soldiers to whoever paid most. Lacking allegiance to a specific Nordic king made it easier to be loyal to a foreign power, but hunger for wealth is what really drove them.[14] If a Nordic chief failed to pay his people or was not generous with gifts, a Viking warrior picked up and went wherever he could best fulfill his personal dreams and aspirations. Because the distance to his northern native land was great, there was minimal risk that he would be called upon to fight against his own people. Knowing little Greek, the Varangians did not mingle with the local population of Constantinople, and were not privy to, or affected by, any discontent the people might feel toward the emperor, which further contributed to the loyalty for which they became known.[15]

The word *Varangian* or *Varjager* is thought to stem from the Old Norse *var* which means loyalty, brotherhood or sworn men and refers to the "varar" or oaths, in this case, but in particular the pledges made by traders or warriors to a group or leader such as the emperor of Constantinople.[16] The value of these troops, who could be depended on to fight ferociously at a moment's notice, was not only in their courage and fighting skill, but also their zeal in fulfilling the duty for which they had been hired. These warriors were held in the highest esteem both by the population of the hosting nation and by their own kinsmen when they returned home to the north.

Viking mercenaries served for generations in the emperor's guard and fought under the Byzantine banner from Syria to Sicily. From the end of the tenth century and for the next two hundred years, Norsemen in droves joined the prestigious military service in Constantinople. The composition of the Varangian army was a conglomeration of different forces ranging from cavalry to sailors. The Vikings, known for their strength and use of intimidation, were called "the axe-bearing barbarians" or "axe-bearers" because of their enormous, two-handed axes (although they were also skilled swordsmen and archers).

Entrance into the guard was contingent on passing a test to prove strength and military prowess. The *Laxdale Saga* speaks of Bolli Bollasson, who had been in Constantinople only a short time when he managed to get himself recruited into the Varangian Guard and gained a reputation as the bravest Norseman ever to take war pay. A man of small build was deemed unfit for service, unless he could prove his strength by chopping off the head of an enormous bull with a single stroke, for example, as Thormondr is said to have done.[17]

The soldiers appointed to the guard protected both the emperor and his family. When summoned, they first went to the emperor's tent, some wearing their swords, others carrying spears or heavy iron axes on their shoulders. According to Anna Comnena, the eldest daughter of Emperor Alexius I and a major source of information about the reign of her father and the Varangian Guard: "Now when the Ambassadors from Persia arrived, the Emperor, a formidable figure, seated himself on his throne and the men, whose business it was, arranged the soldiers of every nationality and the axe-bearing barbarians in their proper order, and then brought in the ambassadors to the imperial throne."[18]

The Varangian Guard also served as escorts, performed garrison duty, and functioned as a police force within the city. When Robert Guiscard (the Resourceful), the Norman warlord who conquered southern Italy and Sicily and fought to expel the Byzantines in the mid-eleventh century, attacked the port of Dyrrakhion in 1081, paving the way for further exploitation of Constantinople, Alexius left Constantinople to face the Normans. To reinforce his military muscle, he took with him a unit of Varangian troops, leaving others at home to guard his palaces and defend the walls.[19]

The Varangian Guard was normally barracked in the uppermost part of the palace or in *varingiaskipt* (small barracks around the city), with other detachments near the Hippodrome and in the Saint Mamas quarter of the suburbs, although the guard was not granted the right to winter in Saint

Mamas. Every man was issued bedding in the form of a thin mattress and blanket which could be laid on the floor or on the benches in the barracks room. When the Emperor went on campaign and stayed in camp with his army, the Varangian men on guard remained out on the open plain, changing the watch with each other throughout the night. Those whose turn it was to sleep, lay down completely armed, with helmets on their heads, shields over them, swords under their heads, and right hands on the sword handles.

In order to increase morale and overcome language barriers in the guard, groups were kept together by district of origin and fought under their native leaders; they were allowed to carry the weapons they had brought along with them, especially favorite ones such as axes. Most Norse warriors arrived with little more military equipment than a shield, axe and possibly a helmet; mail armor was something Norsemen normally could not afford and shields tended to wear out quickly and needed to be replaced often. To the Vikings, full protective gear meant a helmet and shield, but often only a shield. Although historical records[20] do not indicate precisely the protective armor worn by the imperial bodyguards, it was probably fairly good, consisting of either chain mail or scale armor supplied by the empire and a helmet with an extra protection of mail for the neck, in addition to a shield and powerful weapon.[21] Weapons and equipment were checked regularly and replaced when broken. The round shield common to the Vikings was probably replaced with the larger kite-shield that better protected the lower body and legs. In the battle of Beroe in 1122, in which the Byzantine emperor John II employed Varangians to crush the Pechenegs, the Vikings were armed with single-edged axes and "very long shields."[22] For those fighting in the infantry, the weight of the armor had to be considered so that warriors did not grow fatigued too early into the battle. A good army also had to be sufficiently varied in skill and equipment, and possess a warrior's indomitable spirit.

The most notable Norse Varangian was Harald Hardrade (Hard-Ruler), son of Sigurd Syr and half-brother of Olaf Haraldson (the Saint) who fell in the battle of Stiklestad in 1030. The young Harald, fifteen at the time, was himself wounded in the same battle, but managed to escape together with other fugitives. In spring of the following year, Harald sailed east to the Russian king Jarisleif (known also as Yaroslav I, the Wise), where he remained for several years and traveled far and wide. Jarisleif, who had made important alliances with the Nordic countries as well as with Poland, France, Hungary, and Germany, and was married to the daughter of the Swedish king Olof Skötkonung, received Harald well. When Harald began his expedition to Greece and Constantinople in 1035 he was only twenty, but had already acquired a large retinue, who together with their leader, had the privilege of beholding the shining radiance of the mighty Greek city from the bow of their ship. Harald presented himself to Empress Zoe the Great, entered her service, and in autumn went out on the Greek sea with his own men and other troops and took part in the Arab wars in Asia Minor.[23] He fought in eighteen battles and before long was made commander of the Varangian Guard.

In the dominions of the Greek emperor, Varangians enjoyed freedom and independence from all but their own commanders. After Harald had served the empress for some time, he went west with his troops to Serkland, where he remained for many years and took eighty Arab strongholds, some that surrendered peacefully and some that he took by attacking, killing those who had not fled. (The gold, in the form of necklaces, arm rings and brooches, acquired in these raids was usually worn or carried, thereby resolving the need for storage or protection.) Harald, however, sent the valuables not needed to cover his expenses back to King Jarisleif in Novgorod for safekeeping, even though the treaty of 911 also included provisions for how to protect treasure accumulated by the Rus. If a Rus died before putting his affairs in order, his property went to his heirs in Russia; otherwise it went to whomever he had made heir by written testament.

The Varangian Guard was the best paid of all troops in the Byzantine Empire. Besides a regular wage, which their leaders collected and distributed to the men, the Varangians also received substantial bonuses and a share of captured booty. Leaders received large amounts of valuables that they could use as they saw fit, to pay motivational bonuses or improve the equipment. When a Greek emperor died, it was customary for the guards to plunder all of the emperor's palaces and keep what they wanted.[24] Harald Hardrade gathered a treasure so vast and extraordinary it made him the richest man in the northern lands:

"Then Harald had a large ox-hide spread out, and turned the gold out of the caskets upon it. Then scales and weights were taken and the gold separated and divided by weight into equal parts; and all people wondered exceedingly that so much gold should have come together in one place in the northern countries. But it was understood that it was the Greek Emperor's property and wealth; for, as all people say, there are whole houses there full of red gold."[25]

Harald Hardrade's later reign in Norway was financed with the gold he brought home from the Byzantine Empire. Acquisition of wealth was the prime motivation for joining the Varangian Guard, but the riches acquired by Harald Hardrade were highly unusual, even for a Byzantine guardsman.

Harald continued his travels, harassing and pillaging on both sides of Jordan, until arriving in Jerusalem to bring it under Greek command. Stuf the skald writes: "And by the terror of his name under his power the country came, nor needed wasting fire and sword to yield obedience to his word." When he returned to Constantinople, however, he longed for his native land of the north. Empress Zoe, hearing of his wishes to give up his command in the Greek service, accused him of misappropriating property, squandering the emperor's money, and acquiring more gold than the emperor had granted him and threw him into prison. As described in Snorri Sturluson's account of Harald Hardrade: Harald was saved by a "lady of distinction," who came in the night with ladders and rope and hauled him out of the prison tower. Although Harald was denied permission to leave Constantinople, he slipped away and eventually became king in his own land of Norway.

Norse involvement in the Byzantine Empire continued well into the early Middle Ages. In 1110, King Sigurd the Crusader sailed across the Greek sea to Palestine, Jerusalem, and Constantinople where he observed the land burghs, castles and country towns. When Emperor Kirjalax heard of the king's expedition, he ordered the city ports of Constantinople, called the Gold Tower (through which the emperor rode after a long absence or victorious campaign), to be opened.[26] King Sigurd remained in the emperor's service for some time and many Norsemen from this expedition entered the emperor's pay. When King Sigurd left Constantinople for his return trip to the northern lands, Emperor Kirjalax gave him horses and men to guide him through the Greek dominions. Sigurd, in turn, left his ships and beloved dragonhead, a superb work of Norse craftsmanship from the bow of his ship, as a gift for the emperor. Back home in the north, he was celebrated as a great king, who at the young age of twenty had made an honorable journey from Norway.

Most warriors serving in the Varangian Guard were young men easily energized and carried away by battle fury. What went through their minds as they faced an enemy army on the battlefield, as they were cut down by swords and axes on land and at sea, and when exhaustion from the weight of their armor overcame them? Were they ever afraid, did they long for home? These questions will never be answered. The Norse population believed that the *Norns*, three divine women representing past, present and future, decided man's destiny by weaving the fates of all people into the tapestry of life.[27] Since the time of death could not be changed, it was pointless to worry about it, and a strong man was expected to display fortitude and rise above his challenges with spirit and courage. While the unwise man thought he would live forever if he avoided battle, Vikings who had traveled far and learned the ways of the world knew that those who broke the peace rarely grew old. Age without accomplishment was meaningless and did not bring a man peace. An old Viking poem suggests that the best warriors did not brood over their destiny, but took life as it came:

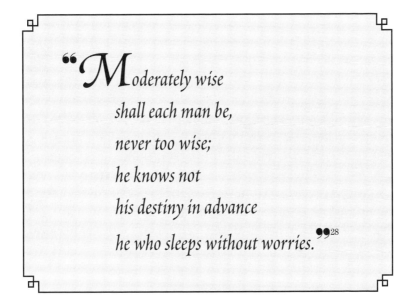

"*Moderately wise*
shall each man be,
never too wise;
he knows not
his destiny in advance
he who sleeps without worries."[28]

CHAPTER 10

RAGNAR LODBROK AND HIS SONS
C. 750–850

The infamous Viking commander Ragnar Lodbrok and his sons inspired horrific fear in the great empires of Europe. In over fifty battles, Ragnar Lodbrok was defeated only once.

T he story of the legendary Viking commander Ragnar Lodbrok, king of Denmark and Sweden, depicts the Viking view of life and death and the military mindset that prevailed in Viking culture. The exploits of Ragnar Lodbrok and his sons may not be factual, as it is not certain if or when they lived, although events chronicled in the sagas point to the end of the eighth century. Ragnar Lodbrok spent most of his life on the seas, raiding and plundering great cities along the coastlines. The earliest raids on the Baltic lands are frequently associated with him. Ragnar Lodbrok's favorite strategy was to attack Christian cities on holy days when most people were in church. His greatest accomplishments include leading the raid on Paris in 845, where he arrived with a fleet of more than five thousand men and was said to have forced Charles the Bald into paying a huge seven thousand silver-pound *danegeld* in exchange for sparing the city and its people from further massacre. It was from that raid that he learned that there were riches to be found in other important cities and he returned to attack other parts of France and demand huge ransom payments, most of which were satisfied. These forced payments eventually brought great countries like France and England to near financial ruin. In more than fifty battles, Ragnar Lodbrok was said to have been defeated only once, by King Aella II, the last independent Old English king of Northumbria.

The story of Ragnar Lodbrok and his sons is a tale of heroism and adventure from beginning to end. Ragnar's legendary death-song in King Aella's snake pit—a recapitulation of his many victories while snakes gnawed on his body—is a glorification of his life. His sons, after ravaging Europe's coastlines, cruised the Mediterranean, campaigning in Italy and Sicily, where with their last ounce of strength they fought bloody battles in the name of northern heathenism. Their heroic exploits in life were matched by the manner of their deaths. One son died on a bed of spears stuck vertically into the ground, another asked to be burned on a bed of his enemies' heads, and another had his mound raised on the side of his kingdom that was the most vulnerable to attack. Most of the stories surrounding Ragnar Lodbrok's life, however, should probably be taken with more than a grain of salt, although there may be some basis in historical fact here and there. Some scholars say the wars fought in England by Ragnar Lodbrok's sons following their father's death set the stage for the ongoing struggles between the Saxons and Vikings a century later.

Ragnar Lodbrok belonged to the Swedish Yngling Dynasty and claimed to be a direct descendent of the god Oden. He was unusually big for his years, brave, vigorous, friendly towards his men, and so powerful that he inspired dread and fear in his enemies. Born a pirate, he distinguished himself at the age of fifteen, having already been on the seas from a very young age. He succeeded his father, Sigurd Ring, who ruled as king over the Svear, but also conquered Denmark in about 750. Ragnar Lodbrok is said to have governed parts of Sweden, Denmark,

Finland and England, along with many smaller towns on the eastern seacoast. Swedish kings considered themselves rulers par excellence, though others did not necessarily agree with this so-called superiority.

Lodbrok's first wife, Thora Borgarhjort, known for her magnificence, was named after the *hjort* (buck), an animal superior to all others. Thora had two sons, Erik and Agnar, who took after their father in looks and accomplishment. His second wife, Kråka,[1] bore him five sons: Ivar Benlös (Boneless),[2] Björn Järnsida (Ironside), Hvitserk (White Shirt), Ragnvald, and Sigurd Ormöga (Snake-Eye). Sources also speak of Hingwar (possibly Ivar), Halfdan, and Ubbe, as well as three daughters who wove the famous Raven Banner between dawn and dusk in a single day.[3]

The name Lodbrok (*Ludenbyx* means Hairy Trousers) originates from the armor Ragnar wore when he defeated a huge *lindorm* (a mythical snake-like creature) and won his first wife's hand in marriage. The snake had grown so large that it surrounded the entire house in which Thora Borgarhjort lived. Ragnar made some soft clothes of animal skins, boiled them in tar, then rolled in them in the sand to harden them. He succeeded in killing the snake with his spear because his armor was impenetrable to the snake's venom. After he accomplished his deed, he took the spear shaft with him, but left the spearhead inside the snake. As proof of his feat, he brought the spear shaft to the *ting* meeting, and returning with the men to the dead snake, showed that it fit the spearhead perfectly. This accomplishment made Ragnar famous throughout the Nordic lands, despite the fact that he was only fifteen at the time and looked more like a troll than a man.

When Thora fell sick and died, Ragnar mourned her so deeply that he was unable to find peace at home. He went a-Viking, raided all over and was successful wherever he went. Ivar, the oldest son of his second wife, was called Boneless (or Legless) because his legs contained only cartilage and he had to be carried everywhere he went. Despite his handicap, Ivar grew to be big and handsome and masterminded many battles. He was considered the cruelest of Viking leaders, who killed Christians by torture. All of the boys followed their father's example. When Ragnar asked his sons Björn and Hvitserk how long they intended to stay at home doing nothing, Ivar asked his father to supply them with well-equipped ships and warriors so that they could travel far and loot all over the land. Ragnar complied and the young men took to the seas every summer, and became wealthy celebrated warriors with an impressive fleet.

Seeking new ways to win fame, Ivar suggested they look for more challenging opponents to truly show their valor. It was said they could be found in the city of Hvitaby. Since not even Ragnar had been able to take the fortress that protected that city, the brothers agreed that the opposing force must be quite skilled. They arrived at the battlefield carrying Ivar, a skilled archer, on a shield with his bow and arrows. Ragnvald, because he was the youngest (Sigurd had not yet been born), had been left behind to guard the ships. Suspecting that he had really been left because his brothers wanted all the glory for themselves, Ragnvald followed them and fought so hard that he soon fell. A warrior did not avoid battle even if he could, but sought it to enhance his honor and reputation. His brothers in the meantime gained access to the fortress, engaged in a violent fight and forced the opposing force to flee. They robbed the fortress of all the goods and riches they could carry, set houses on fire, destroyed the building and hurried back to their ships. When their mother, Kråka, learned of Ragnvald's death, she said that there was no greater honor than to join Oden in Valhalla, especially for one so young in years.

At that time Sweden was ruled by King Östen Beli from his domain in Upsala, where he made such frequent blood offerings to please the gods that few men had the courage to attack him. Ragnar Lodbrok and Östen Beli were great friends and visited each other every summer. During one visit, even though still married to Kråka, Ragnar asked for Östen's daughter, Ingeborg, either as his wife or mistress. When Kråka learned about the proposal, she managed to dissuade her husband from visiting King Östen again. As a result the friendship between the kings ended and Ragnar's sons felt empowered to fight the Swedish king.

The sons gathered their troops together and built new ships with which they sailed to Sweden. When the news came to Östen that a hostile force had landed in his dominions, he summoned a large army and marched toward the enemy. At nightfall he pitched his tents in a large forest and instructed his troops that when the sons of Ragnar Lodbrok arrived, only a third of his army was to come out of the forest to meet them. King Östen would then bring out the rest of his army and meet the Lodbrok army with an intensified force. This strategy was intended to make the enemy complacent and secure Östen's victory.

The plan worked as Östen had predicted. Seeing the small army coming out of the forest, Erik and Agnar, the two eldest sons, called out happily to their men. But when the rest of the force emerged and King Östen's mighty cow, Sebelja, was set loose among the warriors, the men became so bewildered they started fighting among themselves, and despite their reputation as formidable warriors, were unable to stay organized and withstand the onslaught of Östen's men. First Agnar was killed. Erik set out to avenge his brother's death, as was expected of a Viking warrior, but was overpowered and taken prisoner.

When King Östen got news of the capture, he called a stop to the fighting and ordered that Erik be brought to him. He offered Erik his life, but ashamed of his loss, Erik asked instead that his men be promised a safe trip home and that he be thrown onto a bed of spears planted upright in the ground.

When Ivar, Björn, and Hvitserk (Sigurd, only three at the time, was too young to fight) received news of their brothers' fate, Ivar took it badly, became sick and could barely move. He lay in his bed without uttering a word and his brothers feared he would die. This setback dispelled the myth surrounding them, making people think that Ragnar Lodbrok's sons were ordinary men, no better or more dangerous than others. It was now up to the brothers to set the record straight or live in disgrace ever after. Sigurd's foster-father readied five well-equipped ships to sail to Sweden. Within five days, Björn and Hvitserk contributed fourteen ships, and Ivar, ten. Some men were sent over land and ordered to kill everyone in their path.

When the Swedish king heard of these new ambitions by Ragnar Lodbrok's sons, he summoned all arms-bearing men. According to legend, Östen was very confident in the cow, Sebelja, to whom he made many blood offerings and who was so able to confuse the enemy they lost their focus and started fighting among themselves. When the two armies met for the second time, a horrific fight ensued. Ivar Boneless, carried on a shield, urged his men on, pressing them to be courageous in battle. He instructed his carriers to walk to the flanks of the formation so he could gain better perspective on the battle. When he saw Sebelja, he placed two arrows in his bow and tightened the string. The arrows hit Sebelja's eyes, but though the cow fell to the ground, she was not dead. Ivar then asked his men to throw him onto the cow's back so he could crush her with his great weight. With Sebelja harmless, Ivar was lifted onto the shield again and the bitter fight continued. Björn and Hvitserk fought so ferociously that King Östen was soon dead.

When the king had been disposed of, the brothers felt it was pointless to continue the fight. It was meaningless to conquer a land without a king, and they wanted greater challenges. They continued raiding along Europe's coastlines, burning one fortified city after another until Sigurd, the youngest, grew old enough to join them. The names of all the brothers became legendary and even children understood the horrors of meeting one of Ragnar Lodbrok's infamous sons whose match was unparalleled.

Ragnar Lodbrok's sons next set their sights on the capture of the ancient city of Rome. Rome, established seven hundred years prior to the birth of Christ, was the pride of the Roman Empire, and had at one time included all of the countries in Europe west of the Rhine and south of the Donau, in addition to all the countries surrounding the Mediterranean Sea. In 395, the great kingdom had been divided into the East Roman and West Roman Empires, but with time had diminished in size until only the capital with its surrounding areas remained. The city of Rome was a desirable target, not only because of its size and reputation, but also because it was the headquarters of the Christian population. Ragnar Lodbrok's sons had already traveled halfway across the world and now Rome beckoned in the distance. The city, they were told, housed a huge population and great riches.

The brothers never reached Rome, however, because a gray-haired traveler they met on the road showed them his iron shoes and they learned from him that: "The way to Rome is so long that these shoes, in addition to the ones I carry on my back, are completely worn out." The brothers decided it was more profitable to continue raiding in the waters around the northern lands.[4]

In the meantime, Ragnar Lodbrok himself was advancing in age and worried that his free-spirited sons would outshine him. Although neither he nor his wife knew exactly what their sons were up to or where they had traveled, news spread through the songs of the skalds, and Ragnar yearned again for the adventure of the battle he had so enjoyed in his youth and for the honor that came with it. He longed to hear his own name sung as loudly as the names of Ivar, Björn, Hvitserk and Sigurd. Deliberating over what glory and fame he could still achieve, he began building the two largest ships in the northern lands. When it was suspected what Ragnar was up to, word traveled far and great fear spread among the neighboring kings who had treasures and land to protect.

Instead of raiding in the Nordic countries, Ragnar confided in his wife Kråka that he had his sights set on England and would take only his two ships and as many men as they could carry. Kråka found his plan bold. "Better with a larger fleet comprised of many smaller ships," she suggested. "Winning in battle with many ships is easy," said Ragnar. "Nobody has yet heard of a man with only two ships defeating an enemy as great as England." He told her that if he lost the battle, there would be no dishonor to his name; people would say it was to be expected since he had only two ships.

When the ships were ready and manned, Ragnar waited for a favorable wind, ordered the ships to sea, and sailed toward England. But a violent storm erupted just as he was sighting land and the ships were thrown against the cliffs and broke apart. Ragnar and his men barely escaped death.

As soon as the men had solid ground beneath their feet, they advanced across the country, ransacking and destroying all the forts in their path. Aella, the reigning king of Northumbria, hearing of Ragnar Lodbrok's landfall, summoned his forces and placed spies all around the country. When he received the message of Ragnar's advance, he called together every man who could ride a horse and carry a shield. Aella spoke to his men before the battle, asking them to capture Ragnar alive, because if he were to be killed, his sons would most certainly wage a horrific revenge on the people of Northumbria.

When the two forces met, Ragnar entered the battle with sword and helmet, but no other weapon of defense. Although the fighting was fierce, the small size of Ragnar's army contributed to a quick end to the battle. His men fell and Ragnar himself was cornered behind a shield wall and taken prisoner.

When King Aella asked the prisoner's name, Ragnar refused to answer. "Much worse is the fate that will befall you, if you do not say who you are," said King Aella. He then ordered Ragnar thrown into the snake pit, where Ragnar uttered the famous words: "Grunt would the pigs do now, if they knew how the old boar is suffering." Ragnar had seen victory in fifty battles, and when he went a-Viking as a young man, thought there was no king bolder than he. Never did he think he would end his life in King Aella's snake pit—the same King Aella whose men had bled so profusely on the battlefield. But no one escaped the laws of the *Norns*. Ragnar Lodbrok in the snake pit sang: "Neither does the hero cry at his death in the wonderful Valhalla. Nor do I go in sorrow to Odin's great hall."[5]

When Ragnar died and King Aella understood that it was the renowned Nordic king whose life he had taken, he began to fear the repercussions that would most certainly come. The sons of Ragnar Lodbrok, who had been plundering throughout the northern lands, had heard no news of their father for some time. King Aella's messengers went to the northern lands, greeted Ivar Boneless and reported that Ragnar had fallen in battle. On hearing the details, Ivar's face turned color, first red, then blue and finally pale with anger. Björn Ironside, busy sharpening his spear, squeezed the shaft so hard that his hand left an imprint on it. Hvitserk and Sigurd Snake-Eye were playing *tafl* and let the game pieces fall to the floor after hearing the news.[6] Hvitserk squeezed a game piece so hard that blood squirted from underneath his fingernails, and Sigurd Snake-Eye, who was trimming his nails with a knife, cut himself all the way to the bone. Hvitserk jumped to his feet: "It will not be long before we avenge the death of our father, and let us start now with these messengers here." But Ivar intervened: "That act is not called for, brother, but let them go in peace."

After the messengers left on favorable winds back to England, the brothers discussed the revenge that by custom had to take place in a timely manner. They discussed the details of their father's death and started preparing their vengeance. But Ivar wanted no part of it because, he told his brothers, their father had no reason to attack King Aella. "It often happens," he said, "that he who is another's superior meets an unhappy end." The brothers, however, felt that to disregard the matter would be highly shameful. Avenging a dead family member was a duty for a Viking; not doing so brought disgrace. The fear of defiling their family's name left Ragnar Lodbrok's sons, brothers who had traveled the world and killed countless men, with no choice. They needed to ready their ships and ask all sword-bearing men in the Danish dominions to support them in the fight against King Aella. But Ivar would not be swayed. He suggested instead that King Aella pay them a *wergild,* a monetary payment that would make good the loss. "I'll stay here," he said, "with the ships that are mine." Because of Ivar's decision to stay at home, very few men gathered to follow the brothers into battle.

When King Aella heard the news of the approaching ships, he sounded the war horns and called together a huge army. Without Ivar to mastermind the expedition, however, the brothers' luck turned and they were forced to retreat. Ivar now took the opportunity to ask King Aella if he wanted to draw up an agreement, involving money, to prevent future wars between them. "You can act on this alone," Hvitserk told Ivar. "I do not want any part of this deal, nor any money that might be offered to us in order to resolve the issue."

"If we have to part, then," said Ivar, "you may keep what we own together, except that I want the part that rightfully belongs to me." And with these words, he bid his brothers farewell and departed for England.

Ivar met with King Aella and asked that, instead of risking more lives on both sides, the king give him all the land that could be covered with an ox-hide. "Around this land, I will build a fence. And I ask not for more," said Ivar.

Aella thought the demand paltry and granted it on condition that Ivar also promise never to fight him. Ivar agreed, obtained the ox-hide and softened it up with water to stretch it. He did this three times before cutting the hide into strips and spreading them on the ground. He used everything, even the hair, until the hide covered an area vast enough to support a huge fort. The fort, named Lunduna, was the largest in the northern lands. Ivar sat peacefully and became so wise and generous that many men, including King Aella himself, sought his advice.

When some time had passed, Ivar sent for all of his belongings. To ensure their loyalty, he gave of his wealth to the most powerful men in the country. When he had secured their loyalty, he asked them not to move, even if an enemy army came to attack the country. He then sent a message to his brothers to prepare themselves. The brothers quickly understood Ivar's grand plan and realized that the time had come to avenge the death of their father. They called together a large army with which they crossed the North Sea to meet King Aella in battle.

When King Aella received the news of the approaching Lodbrok brothers, he summoned his men, but few answered the call. Most of his former forces were now loyal and oath-bound to Ivar. Ivar informed the king that he would stay true to his promise and not attack him, but he could not answer for what his brothers might do.

The battle that followed was long and hard and the brothers, motivated to fight now that they had the upper hand, forced King Aella to defend himself against the Norse warriors. In the end the king's men fled and Aella was taken prisoner. "We remember the death you inflicted upon our father,"

Ivar told the king. "Now, you too shall die a dreadful death." So saying, Ivar carved a snake deep into King Aella's back and colored it red with the king's blood.[7]

After avenging their father's death, the brothers divided King Aella's dominions among them. Ivar Boneless stayed in England. According to legend, he invaded East Anglia in 866, and attacked York in 867. In 869, he captured King Edmund of East Anglia and killed him for refusing to renounce his Christian faith.[8] After the slaying, East Anglia had to submit to the heathen invaders. Björn Ironside, Hvitserk, and Sigurd Snake-Eye went back home to the North and divided their father's lands among them. Björn Ironside later plundered in southern Spain, sailing with a fleet of sixty-two ships through the Straits of Gibraltar and into the Mediterranean. He continued to northern Africa, called Blueland, taking slaves and selling them to Ireland. He lived up to his name because he was said to have never been wounded in battle. Kråka, mother of the Lodbrok brothers, lived long to hear about her sons' repeated victories.

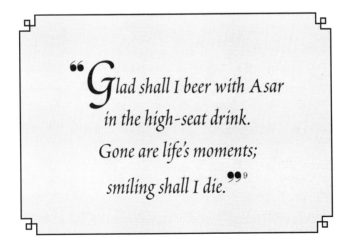

"*G*lad shall I beer with Asar in the high-seat drink. Gone are life's moments; smiling shall I die."[9]

CHAPTER 11

ROLLO THE PIRATE

c. 860–933

Rollo, son of a renowned Viking chief, spent most of his life plundering in England, Friesland and France. He was best known for his acquisition of Normandy in northwestern France, which he sealed in 911 by the Treaty of St. Clair-sur-Epte with the Frankish king Charles the Simple.[1]

———

The raid on Lindisfarne Monastery on Holy Island in 793 is the customary marker for the start of the Viking Age. After Lindisfarne, Vikings sacked cities and towns along all the major coastlines and rivers of England and France, which eventually led them to the shores of the area that is today called Normandy.

Raiding parties arrived in Normandy directly from the Nordic countries or came across the English Channel from Viking settlements in England, Scotland, and Ireland. Since Normandy's location in northwestern France required only a short hop across the water from England, the Franks were on constant alert against Viking attacks on their lucrative empire. Piracy and plunder of these dominions continued in the ninth and tenth centuries, starving the Frankish people and completely destroying the country, until the king grew resigned to giving up part of his land and entered into a peace treaty with the notorious Viking chief, Rollo.

Rollo's true origins are sketchy. According to Scandinavian lore, he was the son of the mighty Norwegian Earl Ragnvald of Möre, who lived during the reign of Harald Fairhair.[2] Dudo of St. Quentin, a historian of the first dukes of Normandy, claims that an old "man who never lowered the nape of his neck before any king, nor placed his hands in anyone else's hands in committing himself to service," lived in the region of Dacia (mainly modern Romania and Moldova, but also parts of Hungary, Bulgaria, and Ukraine, although Dudo describes it as Denmark), surrounded by many warriors. This powerful, arrogant man took possession of a large area of land and subjugated people to his rule through countless battles. He was known for his superior strength and many virtues. When he died, he left "two sons vigorous in arms, well-versed in warfare, in body most fair, in spirit most hardy." The elder brother was called Rollo, and the younger Gurim.[3]

Earl Ragnvald was an entrusted ally of King Harald Fairhair. The relations between the two men were close, especially during the time that Harald was struggling to bring all of Norway under his command. The earl won the king's favor and enjoyed his privileged lot. After the earl died, the leading men of his territory began to capture towns and encampments in an attempt to avenge the wrongs inflicted on them. Many of Rollo's men were killed in the conflicts. Among the fallen was his brother Gurim. Rollo, himself, was forced to retreat with six ships to Scania (today's southern Sweden), where he lingered for some time depressed, until he pulled himself together and outfitted his ships for an extended journey to England. His departure from the north was the start of his notorious reputation as a menace to the Christian world.

Rollo went a-Viking for many years on end, raiding both in England and Friesland, but his life seemed to be leading nowhere and he grew frustrated. He was in torment and vacillated "among three kinds of wandering, whether he should hit upon Dacia or proceed to Francia or should, through battle, strike and claim for himself the English land." Landing in the Hebrides west of Scotland, winter prevented him from leaving the area by way of the sea. He continued instead to England, where it is said that one night he had a vision that revealed the future. It urged him to campaign and plunder in France.

Having discovered his life's purpose, he prepared his ships for the journey and gathered an impressive force of "warriors in the flower of youth, Angles who had become his followers and were to travel with him," as described by Dudo.[4] In spring, he left England for the Frankish Empire. He was savagely battered en route by a storm, but managed to reach land, only to be ambushed by a peasant mob eager to attack the Viking chief the sea had carried to their shores. Rollo, "stirred up in his accustomed manner," advanced boldly against the peasants, killed many thousands and either captured or drove the rest away. He plundered and set the land afire. Victorious, he quickly pursued the Frisians and plundered them as well. After repeated victories, he collected tribute payments from Frisia before launching the canvas sails on his ships and setting back out to sea. He got as far as the coast of France, but King Alfred the Great, who was ruling in England at the time and with whom Rollo had established a friendly relationship by releasing a number of prisoners, asked him to return to England.

After a short stay, Rollo received supplies and men from King Alfred and again set out in pursuit of his vision. First he sailed into the Baltic Sea, then on to his homeland where he did *strandhugg* in Viken (the stretch of land between Oslofjord in southeastern Norway and Gothenburg on the west coast of Sweden) to provision his ships with necessities for his continued journey into France. King Harald Fairhair, who by then had united Norway under his power and ruled with an iron fist, prohibited plunder in his country. Rollo's act of *strandhugg* so roused the Norwegian king's anger that Rollo and his band of warriors were declared outlaws, an unusually harsh punishment for the crime of *strandhugg*, which normally involved stealing only food and necessities.

Around the year 876, Rollo, now amply armed with a large warrior band, finally arrived in France. Under his leadership his warriors pillaged in the countryside, plundered in Paris, and "burst forth in manifold variety like a swarm of bees from a honeycomb or a sword from a sheath, as is the barbarian custom." The sight of the fleet sailing up the Seine struck such fear in the inhabitants of Rouen that they went to Bishop Franco to ask his counsel. The bishop summoned his courage and begged Rollo not to harm the defenseless destitute population, most of whom were peaceful merchants by profession.

Dudo of St. Quentin reports that Rollo now secured his ships at the gate to the church of St. Martin. When he disembarked and saw the desolation and the monuments in ruins, he hesitated and questioned the value of further plunder in the region. But after returning to his ships and conferring with his men, he concluded that France, while plentiful in fruit and rivers full of fish, lacked armed men. He therefore decided to bring France under Norse rule even though the Rouen region had little to offer.

Rollo started by making Rouen his headquarters so he would have a place to return to between campaigns. He then continued up the Seine where the Frankish army was stationed. The Franks, astonished by the Norsemen's arrival, consulted with Charles the Simple, king of France. Also attending were Ragnold, prince of all Francia, and Earl Hasting, a former Viking invader of France, now resident there.[5] After conferring with his advisors, King Charles decided to send ambassadors to Rollo and his band of pirates to find out their purpose. He requested that Hasting, with his intimate knowledge of Norse warfare, act as mediator. Hasting and two skilled warriors went to the river to undertake the unpleasant task of questioning Rollo.

The ambassadors approached the water where they saw on the opposite riverbank Rollo and his men, who informed Hasting that they had come to take Francia by force. But Hasting, incited by his Viking past and curious about his own notorious reputation, could not resist asking Rollo what he knew of this former pirate who had once come to France with a huge army. "This Hasting," Rollo said, "always starts battle in a manly fashion, but has little honor left when it is over." Hasting was deeply offended, but ignored the insult for the sake of the Frankish king. He asked if Rollo and his men were willing to bow down before the king of France, devote themselves to his service and enjoy his good graces. "We will never subjugate ourselves to anyone," said Rollo, "nor cling to anyone's service nor take favors from anyone. The favor that would please us best is the one that we will claim for ourselves by force of arms and in the leadership of battle."

Hasting returned to King Charles with Rollo's message and advised the king that great peril would come to France if he attacked the Norsemen. Rollo's army, as Hasting had seen it from across the river, was comprised of young, strong, carefully selected warriors who were incited to destroy nations. If the Viking army were attacked, these pagans would continue to butcher defenseless Christians, killing everyone in their path and no one would be able to withstand the force of their arms. Hasting, as a former Viking pirate, spoke from personal experience.

But the Frankish king was not easily swayed and the words fell on deaf ears. He gathered his men and went across the river to Rollo's encampment. When Rollo heard of the coming attack, he fortified his position by building a circular bulwark from plowed-up earth. Then, as Hasting had predicted, Rollo defeated the Franks and took many prisoners. King Charles's poor judgment and disregard of Hasting's warnings gave Rollo access to free, unopposed travel throughout France.

Rollo started by attacking the inhabitants of Meulan, killing the leaders and destroying the entire province. He then sailed to Paris where he besieged the city, depending on booty taken in other far-off regions to prolong the siege. When the booty began to run out, he stormed and looted Bessin. After a year of rampaging in Paris, he went to Bayeux, which he took by force, destroying the entire city. Dudo of St. Quentin reports that he even brought along young Poppa, daughter of Prince Berenger, with whom he sired a son named William, born around 905.[6]

Rollo remained near Paris for some time, but sent his army to Evreux to capture the city and kidnap Bishop Sebar, who managed to escape. He finally returned to Rouen where he unleashed his energy on building a new town for the Norsemen. In the meantime, the terrified French population paid tribute to Rollo, and the bishops and abbots complained loudly about their excruciating suffering at the hands of the Norse pirate.

When Rollo left Rouen a second time and sailed up the Seine with a large warrior army, another war band of Vikings was simultaneously sailing up the Loire and Garonne, taking booty from the provinces along the riverbeds. King Charles was so terrified that he asked Bishop Franco to beg a three-month truce of Rollo while he considered his options. Dudo of St. Quentin says that King Charles failed to stop Rollo because his followers were being killed off on a daily basis: "Wherefore am I asking and deprecating your paternal holiness to obtain for us from Rollo a negotiated peace of three months and if, perhaps during that time he should wish to become a Christian, we will give him the very greatest favors and repay him with great gifts."[7] The truce, which Rollo granted, provided a brief respite from the invaders.

But the pact made with the Viking pirate brought shame to the Frankish Empire. The Burgundians accused the Franks of being militarily weak and womanish in their request for safety from Rollo, and sent Counts Richard and Ebalus to King Charles to offer assistance to the weakening empire. As soon as the truce ended, the Franks, annoyed by their weak king, readied their forces and waged war on the Norsemen in an attempt to reclaim their honor; as usual, they were quickly defeated. To make matters worse for the Franks, Rollo felt they had cheated him by using the three-month truce to build up their forces. Rollo retaliated by destroying the provinces and annihilating the population together with the Frankish and Burgundian fighting men.

The tide started to turn when a large army of foot-soldiers and horsemen came in pursuit of Rollo, who by now had made an enemy of the city of Chartres where he remained with a large army. The Franks and the Burgundians risked defeat a second time by attacking Rollo in Chartres. Although both armies lost a large number of men, the Franks were able to stand their ground. Then Bishop Uualtelmus, followed by the clergy and the citizens, started throwing spears and swinging swords at the Norsemen, forcing Rollo and his followers to flee to a nearby hill. When Ebalus, count of Poitou, arrived at the scene, he realized that he had missed the battle and started cursing the Franks and the Burgundians: "When you began the battle without me, you held me entirely of no account. I will be reviled by all nations who hear of these events. Ah, grief! I would have preferred to die with that host than to miss the battle."[8] Ebalus's disappointment drove him to attack the Norsemen on the hill. Missiles flew in both directions, until Ebalus concluded that he could not win. Weary and terrified of further hostilities, the Franks returned to their homes, and the Norsemen to their ships, after which they began to destroy and burn the entire territory.

Despite the Frankish army's near victory at Chartres, the Franks seemed unable to attain security for themselves. The state was in ruin, churches were abandoned and the land like a desert; the population had either been taken captive or lay dying of famine or battle wounds. Not having the strength to resist any longer, the Franks were united in purpose when they went to King Charles: "Why do you not aid the realm which you ought to rule and profit with your authority? Why is a peace, which we are unable to acquire either by war or by any obstacle of diligent defense, not being obtained through conciliation?"[9] The king asked the people to give him advice that would advantage the realm.

Charles sent Archbishop Franco of Rouen to Rollo with the message that Charles, with his followers' encouragement, wanted to give the pirate and pagan nations the maritime land from the River Andelle to the sea. He also wished to give his daughter, Gisla, to Rollo in the hope that their offspring would forge everlasting peace and friendship between the Norsemen and the Franks. In return for his generous offer, he requested Rollo to accept Christianity and protect France against nations opposing the empire, for Rollo was

> "born of the arrogant blood of kings and dukes, most beautiful in body, fiery at arms, prudent in deliberation, of handsome countenance, mild towards his followers, a trusty friend to whomever he has engaged himself, a cruel foe to whomever he opposes . . . versed in speech, easily taught about affairs, benevolent in his actions, respectable for his eloquence, filled full with manly virtue, humble in conversations, and most discreet in public affairs, just in judgment, circumspect concerning secrets, most rich in gold and silver, unremittingly surrounded by the thickest crowd of warriors . . ."[10]

Rollo, who found the terms agreeable, entered into another three-month truce with Charles the Simple and promised to subjugate himself to him. Since the Vikings wanted to stay in the land acquired by the treaty, they had an interest in defending it, which is why raids in the Frankish Empire eventually became less frequent.

King Charles met Rollo at St. Clair by the River Epte to finalize the agreement. Rollo was not only a hardened, skilled warrior, he was also a skilled politician. He realized that the land he was offered was untilled, stripped of cattle and too barren to make from it a livable existence, so he explained to the king that he would be forced to continue taking booty from other, wealthier regions. To arrive at a successful outcome, he demanded that additional land from the Seine by the River Epte to the sea be given him and that it remain his heritable estate from generation to generation for eternity.

King Charles mulled it over, but instead gave Rollo the Flemish land, which Rollo declined because it was too marshy. As a solution, Charles the Simple pledged to give him Brittany which bordered the land already promised him, but on the condition that he protect the coastline against attacks from other pirates, mainly Vikings coming from the British Isles.[11] Rollo then came to King Charles and sealed the treaty through his baptism and marriage to the king's daughter.

"In the nine hundred and twelfth year from the incarnation of our Lord Jesus Christ, archbishop Franco has baptized Rollo," reports Dudo of St. Quentin. The baptism took place in St. Clair, whose square by the church is still called Place Rollon in memory of the Norse pirate. Legend says that Rollo was forced to wear the white baptismal shirt for eight days to give the holy water sufficient time to wash away the horrible sins he had committed against France and the Christian people. Although many of Rollo's men also converted to Christianity at the time of his baptism, they later reverted to paganism.

After the baptism, Rollo was ordered to kiss the foot of King Charles in gratitude for the acquisition of Normandy and the king's daughter in marriage and as an acknowledgement of the king as his superior. As the bishops said: "Whoever receives such a gift, ought to kiss the king's foot," but Rollo decided to be difficult and refused: "I will never kneel before the knees of another, nor will I kiss anyone's foot."

The Franks were upset because the treaty could not be validated without the required kiss and Rollo's own advisors were split on the matter. To save the Frankish Empire from further destruction and save face, King Charles gave in and said that a kiss from one of Rollo's closest men would do. The Viking warrior ordered to kiss the king's foot was himself a man of high standing and was also highly displeased by the order. After some grumbling, he walked up to Charles and, refusing to kneel, stooped forward, grabbed the king's foot, brought it to his mouth and planted a kiss on it while standing upright. This caused Charles to topple backwards to the floor, but the ensuing uproar and laughter quickly eclipsed the embarrassing moment and the treaty went into full effect. Rollo prepared a splendid wedding and married the king's daughter according to Christian rite.[12]

Rollo was now officially a French duke, and Normandy became an autonomous dukedom with Rouen as its capital. Charles the Simple relinquished control over the region and was no longer able to collect tax, require military service, or approve rulers for the area. The designated land was to be bequeathed to Rollo's heirs and descendents from generation to generation for all time. During Rollo's reign, the boundaries of his land were expanded to include most of the region that is today called Normandy.[13]

Rollo ruled his country with wisdom and authority. He repaired the destruction, established rights and laws and guaranteed the safety of all people living in his dominions. The Nordic people's sense of self-rule was preserved, and although they soon intermarried with the rest of France's population, place names and the Norse mindset lived on. Many of the names of the villages and people of Normandy have their roots in Viking times: Quetil comes from Kettil; Troud, from Torvald; Anfrie, from Asfrid; Inguier, from Ingvar; Renouf, from Ragnulf.[14]

When he grew old, Rollo gave all the land to his son William by his mistress Poppa, and bound the leaders of his dominions to the new duke by a sworn oath of fidelity. Rollo died in Rouen and was buried in the chapel of one of the churches. The exact year of his death is uncertain, but is believed to be between 927 and 933, making him at his death, duke of Normandy for almost two decades.

The significance of the Treaty of St. Clair-sur-Epte and Rollo's achievements and contribution to world history have been overshadowed by the comic foot-kissing episode. It is worth noting, however, that in the eleventh and twelfth centuries the area of Normandy played an important political role and that through the Norman dynasty, whose dukes became future kings of England, Rollo was a direct ancestor of William the Conqueror.[15] Rollo became one of history's most celebrated Viking pirates and his name is still recalled with affection in the land he made his home.

> **"O**h Rollo, mighty Duke and most superior leader, through Christ's gift this town will flourish under your leadership ... This fatherland is to be built by your followers ...**"**[16]

CHAPTER 12

ERIK SEGERSÄLL, THE VICTORIOUS
945–995

Erik Segersäll, the most famous Swedish Viking king, triumphed at the battle of Fyrisvallarna, the biggest military conflict ever fought within Swedish borders in the Viking Age. The battle was the culmination of a power struggle that strengthened the standing of this king of the Svear.

E rik Emundsson Segersäll is the first Swedish king whose existence is confirmed by reliable records.[1] He is believed to have become king in 970, though the events and accomplishments of his reign remain sketchy. He ruled the kingdom jointly with his brother, Olof, until the latter's death in about 980, when Erik became sole regent of an area comparable in size to that of Sweden in the Middle Ages. Although the exact extent of Erik's dominions is in dispute, he managed to expand his kingdom, even bringing Denmark under his command. Friendly and articulate, he became known as an outstanding protector of his land and people. He was king of the Svear from 970 to 995, and also king of the Danes, but only for a year, approximately 992 to 993.

Erik's brother and co-regent, Olof, died suddenly during a ceremonial dinner in Old Upsala, headquarters of the Swedish kings. Björn, son of Olof (fostered by Earl Ulf, his maternal uncle), was technically heir to the Swedish crown after his father's death but because he was too young to rule, Erik assumed full control of the kingdom. Björn, an obstinate, unruly, strong child, acquired the name Styrbjörn Starke (the Strong).[2] Growing up, his violent temper and defiance of authority became more evident. After he jokingly threw a coat over one of King Erik's men at a dinner feast in Upsala and was reprimanded by a bump on the nose with a drinking horn, Styrbjörn became so enraged that he killed his chastiser.

At the age of only twelve, Styrbjörn began to pester his Uncle Erik for his birthright, half the kingdom, and to insist on taking his father's place as co-regent. His uncle advised him to wait until he was at least sixteen, but Styrbjörn refused to listen to reason, and while other young men took to the seas, he sulked on his father's grave for two years and demanded the kingdom of the ships sailing by. He then attended a *ting* in Upsala together with his foster-father, Ulf, and demanded assistance, but was told that he was too young and unruly to govern the kingdom. The people felt threatened by Styrbjörn's stubbornness and quick temper and drove him and Ulf away with rocks. Since the country needed a crown prince, King Erik decided that if his unborn child turned out to be a boy, he would make him co-regent. Erik's wife Sigrid Storråda (the Proud, or Arrogant), daughter of the renowned Viking Skoglar Toste, was pregnant at the time.

Styrbjörn felt he had a greater right to the kingdom than Erik's unborn son and Styrbjörn's final retaliation for his loss would be the battle of Fyrisvallarna.[3] But before that he demanded ships and men of Erik so he could go a-Viking as was expected of a king's son. King Erik thought that complying would provide an outlet for the young Styrbjörn's energy and obliged him with a fleet of sixty ships and warriors, telling him to stay away for at least three years. Styrbjörn readied his fleet and sailed eastward along the southern coast of the Baltic Sea where he raided. Few men wanted to risk meeting him on the open water and he became known as a man who feared nothing, neither war nor stormy seas.

At the age of twenty, Styrbjörn sailed with his fleet to Jomsborg, the elite Viking fort located near Wolin by the inlet to the River Oder in the southern part of the Baltic Sea. He decided to lay siege to the fort, built to protect the rich trading towns in Vindland. Despite the Jomsvikings' strength and resistance, Styrbjörn succeeded in establishing his authority at the fort and then continued with his fleet to Denmark where Harald Bluetooth reigned.[4] Styrbjörn continued raiding in Denmark until matters came to a head with Harald Bluetooth. However, as a gesture of thanks for conquering the Jomsvikings, who were a constant nuisance to the Danes, the Danish king gave Styrbjörn his daughter Tyri in marriage and Styrbjörn reconciled and allied himself with Harald.[5]

After the wedding celebrations, Styrbjörn returned to Jomsborg and readied a fleet of one thousand ships with which he sailed to Denmark and asked for an additional two hundred ships and troops to follow him north to Svithiod (Sweden). Harald Bluetooth gave his son-in-law a large fleet with warriors, and Styrbjörn sailed to Sweden to reclaim the land and the title he felt rightfully belonged to him. His plan was to dethrone King Erik, whose seat was in Upsala, and avenge his father Olof's death (rumor had it that Olof had died of poison at a dinner celebration). Among the men chosen to accompany Styrbjörn on the journey was King Harald Bluetooth himself.

When King Erik got news of Styrbjörn's advance and learned that his huge fleet had already entered Lake Mälaren, he sent messengers to muster troops. Erik's counselor Thorgny advised him to place logs in the water to prevent Styrbjörn's ships from reaching Upsala. But Styrbjörn declared that he would battle to the death, and to prevent deserters and encourage his men to fight to the bitter end, he ordered all ships burned. King Harald Bluetooth, enticed to fight by the promise of acquiring more land, became fearful when he saw the burning fires and the ships aflame and returned with his fleet to Denmark.

The plan was to attack from the northeast directly against the weakest side of the Swedish king's headquarters. Styrbjörn was near the harbor, but could not reach Erik because of the logs in the water and was forced to continue on foot to Upsala. When Erik tried to stop Styrbjörn's advance, Styrbjörn threatened to set the forests on fire. Eventually Styrbjörn and his men arrived at the fields along the Fyris River where King Erik and his troops had gathered for battle.

On Thorgny's advice, Erik tied his bulls and horses together with yokes to which he fastened sharp spears. When the war horns blared, the warriors shook their shields and held them aloft, shocking the poor animals into a frenzy and driving them into the enemy formation, where they created chaos and caused damage. But Styrbjörn, a highly skilled warrior, soon restored order among his troops, and the battle started anew and continued until late evening. After the first day of fighting, neither side declared victory and Erik spent the night bringing in fresh troops from the surrounding farmlands. The next day the battle started again, and once again neither side declared victory.

When evening came and it grew dark, both Erik and Styrbjörn, worried about the future, made blood offerings to the gods for victory. Styrbjörn called upon Thor, who is said to have shown himself to the warrior and was wrathful and predicted defeat. King Erik went to Upsala Temple and called upon Oden, whereupon a tall, magnificent one-eyed man, in a blue cape and silk hat came forward.[6] Erik promised Oden his life in ten years if victorious. The apparition in the blue robe then told Erik to shout out to the enemy warriors: "Oden wants you all!" On the third day of battle, arrows, said to be Oden's, flew so thickly that they blinded Styrbjörn's men, who began to beg for their lives. Erik's men formed themselves into a *svinfylking* (wedge, or boar snout formation) and stormed the opposing troops. When Styrbjörn felt his defeat imminent, he reminded his men of the loyalty oaths they had sworn and asked them to stay in the fight. Very few took flight and Styrbjörn rushed in among the enemy where he was killed together with his best warriors.

When the battle ended, King Erik went to Upsala and spoke to his people. He promised a great reward to anyone who could compose a war song about the impressive victory at the river. Thorvald Hjaltesson, an Icelander, came forward. Erik listened to the song with pleasure and rewarded Thorvald with a magnificent gold arm ring. The king then reached for his two-year old son Olof, held him up and encouraged the people to celebrate the new heir to the kingdom.[7]

Erik the Victorious is remembered for his expansion of the Swedish dominion "which he defended manfully." The victory at Fyrisvallarna also extended his rule beyond Sweden; he reigned in Skåne, conquered Denmark as revenge against the Danish king for his support of Styrbjörn the Strong, and forced Sven Forkbeard to go a-Viking in England. Erik's reign in Denmark was, however, short-lived because he soon fell ill and had to return to Sweden.[8] He died of tuberculosis in 995, as he had promised Oden he would, exactly ten years after his victory against Styrbjörn. His minor son, Olof Skötkonung, succeeded him. After Erik's death, Sven Forkbeard returned to Denmark and reclaimed his kingdom.

Several rune stones were raised to commemorate the men who fell in the battle of Fyrisvallarna. A stone in Skåne reads: "Eskil raised this stone after Toke Gormsson, his beloved master. He did not flee at Upsala."[9] Another stone reads: "He did not flee at Upsala, but fought as long as he had weapons." One of the most impressive stones is from the eleventh century and is three and a half meters high (eleven and a half

feet) with an inscription carved by Torkel that tells of the good
farmer Gulle's five sons, all of whom died: "The good farmer
Gulle had five sons. The brave warrior Åsmund fell at Föret
(Fyris). Assur met his end eastward in Greece. Halvdan was
killed on Bornholm. Kåre died by the cape. Dead also is Boe."
In Old Norse, adjusted from runic script for modern pronunciation, it reads:

"*Goðr karl Gulligat fæm syni.*

Fioll a Fyri Frøkn drængR Asmundr

ændaðis Assur austr i Grikkium,

varð a Holmi Halfdan drepinn,

Kari varð at Uddi ok dauðr Boi."[10]

CHAPTER 13

OLAF TRYGVASON
963–1000

"Kings are made for honor, not for long life." Olaf Trygvason, Norway's hero-king, had a short but glorious reign of only five years. He became known for never retreating in battle, a brave young king whose death weapons were the battleaxe and spearhead.

━━

Olaf Trygvason began his life in exile. He spent his childhood years in Russia and all of his adult life at sea under his own rule or in the service of foreign powers. Until his final years, he had never lived in Norway. He was a Viking first and a king second.

The time of Olaf's birth was a factor in his success. He was born in 963 (968 according to some sources), a period when one Viking expedition after another sailed west to do *strandhugg*, raid and attempt to lay siege to England. Olaf's destiny began with the murder of the chieftain Trygve Olafson of Viken, great-grandson of Harald Fairhair, by King Gudrod Björnson's men and Erik Bloodaxe's sons. Trygve left behind his pregnant wife, Astrid, to fend for herself, although her foster-father Thorolf Lusarskeg remained by her side and followed her into hiding.[1] When the time came for Astrid to give birth, she was taken to a small island in the middle of a lake. Thorolf Lusarskeg and other close friends stood guard against

Viking Campaigns in England, 991–1005. Arrows indicate the date and course of each raid. Among the campaigns depicted in this map is the Battle of Maldon (991 AD) in Essex, won by Olaf Trygvason.

her pursuers while Astrid gave birth to a baby boy, whom she named Olaf after the boy's grandfather and Trygvason (Trygve's son), after his father. Astrid and Olaf remained in hiding on the small island for the rest of the summer. When the days began to get shorter and the weather harsher, they journeyed on to Svithiod (Sweden) where they remained for two years with Håkan the Old, a wealthy, powerful man and good warrior friend of Astrid's father.

In 966, when Olaf was three years old, he sailed on the Baltic with his mother and Thorolf Lusarskeg, who hoped to establish contact with Astrid's brother Sigurd, who had long been abroad in Gardarike (the Viking name for Russia) where he was on good terms with the Russian king Valdemar. But the meeting was not to be. Estonian Vikings ambushed the ship, capturing both mother and child, and they separated Olaf from his mother and sold him and Thorolf as slaves to a man named Klerkon.[2] Thorolf was deemed too old to be of any value and was killed. Shortly thereafter, Klerkon sold Olaf "for a good cloak" to a man named Reas.[3] Olaf stayed with Reas and his wife, Rekon, for six years, and was evidently well treated.

When Sigurd, Astrid's brother, came to Estonia from Holmgard (Novgorod) on business from King Valdemar to collect taxes and rents, he noticed a remarkably handsome boy in the marketplace.[4] The boy's foreign appearance immediately caught Sigurd's attention and he asked the boy's name. When he learned that it was Olaf Trygvason, his nephew, he resolved to make a deal with Olaf's new parents and take him back to Holmgard where he would seek further protection from King Valdemar. Olaf was nine years old when he came to Russia, and he remained with King Valdemar for another nine years.

One day at the marketplace in his new home, young Olaf recognized Klerkon, the man who had killed Thorolf Lusarskeg. Enraged, Olaf advanced with a small axe and smashed Klerkon's head, splitting the man's skull to the brain and avenging Thorolf Lusarskeg's death. But there were several witnesses to the horrible murder and a crowd surrounded Olaf. The boy's natural strength and athleticism enabled him to break free, run home and tell Sigurd what he had done. Sigurd, who understood the customs of the country, knew that anyone who took the life of a man who had not been properly sentenced would himself be put to death. He took Olaf to Queen Allogia, who was married to King Valdemar, and begged her to protect the boy. The queen agreed that it would be a pity to kill a young man as handsome as Olaf and ordered her people to go out fully armed against the masses and demand that the boy be delivered to them. The matter was finally settled when King Valdemar agreed to fine Olaf for the murder and the queen paid the fine.

As Olaf matured, he became known abroad for his handsome appearance and strength. Muscular, but with a slender build, he was daring and excelled at every feat he undertook, including all kinds of physical sport and competition, including rowing. He was able to juggle three daggers while walking around the ship's rails. In battle, he was known for his skill with weapons and his ability to use both hands equally well; he was frequently observed casting two spears at once. Brave, well-spoken and meticulous in his dress, he was held in the highest esteem by King Valdemar and the queen. As his influence increased, people envied him and feared that this foreigner, so favored by the king and queen, would grow too powerful for them to control. When angered, he became violent and tortured his foes by setting them on fire or unleashing mad dogs to tear them to pieces. Olaf's enemies feared and despised him, but his friends found him sociable and generous. Everyone bowed to his will—his friends out of admiration, his enemies out of fear.

When Olaf was twelve, he went to sea in his Russian warships. He spent his youth waging campaigns, starting along the coasts of the Baltic Sea and later in the south, in Flanders,

France, and Greece and west, in England, Scotland, and Ireland. King Valdemar made Olaf chief over the soldiers he sent out to defend the land. As a leader, Olaf had luck on his side and his generosity and many successes built him a great following. He kept many troops at his own expense from the pay he received from the king. One day after leaving the Frankish coast and sailing toward England in bad weather, he drifted off course and landed in the Scilly isles, southwest of England. While regrouping for his continued journey, he visited a monastery and was baptized together with his men.[5] But when he returned to England, he longed for the Nordic countries where he and his family had held power for so many generations and was soon overcome with homesickness. He felt he had to go north to further his reputation. He said goodbye to the Russian rulers and the queen wished him luck and prosperity, assuring him he would be esteemed and admired for his courage wherever he went.

He sailed first to Borgundarholm (Bornholm) where he plundered. In the spring of 980, he sailed to Scania (the southern part of modern Sweden), conquered the people and made off with a large booty before sailing on to Gotland. He continued to the land of the Wends, remained there all winter, and married Geira, daughter of King Burisleif.[6] For the next three years he lived in Vindland, but after his wife died, he was overcome by grief and could not find peace. He readied his warships and left to campaign in Friesland, Saxland, and Flanders, then on to England, where he ravaged and plundered all the way from Northumberland to Scotland. Next, he marauded in the Hebrides and the Isle of Man, before sailing on to Ireland and Bretland, which he destroyed with weapons and fire. Olaf spent four years on this Viking cruise, guiding his fleet of ships around the British Empire. He became known as a brave young king who never retreated in battle and who brought death to Northumberland with battleaxes and spearheads.

Corpses lay thick on the fields and the Irish fled at the sound of his name. Olaf himself was once wounded so badly that his troops had to carry him back to his ship on a shield.

In 988 Olaf fell in love with Queen Gyda, daughter of an Irish king. But Alfvine, a great champion and single-combat warrior, also had eyes for her and challenged Olaf to *holm-ganga* (a duel of honor), as was the custom. Each warrior was allowed to bring twelve men to the event. During the duel, Olaf swung a large axe at Alfvine's sword and cut it out of his opponent's hand. With his next blow he struck Alfvine, then tied him up and carried him and his men off to a lodging. After proving his skill in man-to-man combat, Olaf married Gyda and thereafter lived either in England or Ireland.

England had already suffered heavily from repeated Viking attacks during the long thirty-eight-year reign of King Aethelred the Unready.[7] According to the *Anglo-Saxon Chronicle*, in the early 980s pirates from the north plundered Southampton, killing or imprisoning most of the population. There was great damage everywhere along the seacoast, in Devonshire and Wales and also Portland, where three ships of pirates plundered. Olaf Trygvason was too restless to let the splendor of battle pass him by. His campaign in England in 991 was the first for which reliable records exist. The *Anglo-Saxon Chronicle* recounts that Olaf was the leader of a large fleet of ninety-three ships that plundered Folkestone, then moved on to Ipswich before sailing to Maldon.

The battle of Maldon, which took place on August 10th or 11th of 991, was a decisive battle in favor of the Norsemen.[8] The conflict, a clash between Viking and Anglo-Saxon forces, was one of the most vicious battles since the Norsemen's arrival in England and was a disastrous defeat for the English whose leaders were overthrown. The battle was probably motivated by the Norsemen's desire to avenge their defeat at the same location in about 987 when, as the *Ely Book* (the twelfth-century *Liber Eliensis*) records, nearly all of their forces were killed "on the bridge." The few who escaped sailed to their own country to tell the news. According to the *Anglo-Saxon Chronicle*, the battle of Maldon was also the first time the English, because of Viking atrocities along the sea-coast, decided to pay tribute to the Norsemen. On the advice of Sigeric, archbishop of Canterbury, a sum of ten thousand pounds of silver was paid to the Danes to stop the plunder, burning, and slaughter.

Since the Vikings had been plundering throughout England for the greater part of a decade, the Saxons realized that it was only a matter of time before they were targeted at Maldon and had prepared their forces for the Vikings' advance. Olaf Trygvason, the future Norse king whose notoriety had already made the rounds of the British people, commanded the Viking fleet.[9] The Vikings chose Northey Island in the estuary of the River Blackwater east of Maldon as the base for their forces because it ensured a quick get-away. Byrhtnoth, alderman of Essex, a man of extraordinary wisdom and bodily strength (according to the *Ely Book*) and veteran leader of the English forces, stood ready with his men to confront the advancing foe.

However, high tide submerged the causeway (which is still in use today) from the island to the open pasture on the main-land and delayed the battle. In a failed attempt at diplomacy while the warriors prepared for battle, a Viking messenger attempted to negotiate, calling across the water to offer the enemy peace in return for gold: "I send to you from the bold seamen, a command to tell that you must quickly send trea-sures to us, and it would be better to you if with tribute pay off this conflict of spears than with us bitter battle share . . . we would be willing for gold to bring a truce."[10]

But this conflict would be resolved with arms, not gold, something both sides quickly understood. Byrhtnoth told the Vikings that their only levy would be spears, which would not bring them profit, and it would be shameful for the English if the pirates were to escape without a fight and sail away with English coins, especially since they had already advanced so far inland.

Byrhtnoth's men took up their shields and advanced to the riverbank, where spears began flying across the water, striking men on both sides. Because the tide still prevented the Norse warriors from crossing the causeway and facing the opposing force in the much-anticipated hand-to-hand clash, the atmosphere grew tense. As the tide began to ebb, the battle-hungry Vikings made another attempt to cross over to the mainland, but were only able to do so one at a time, instead of *en masse*. Byrhtnoth took advantage of the situation to order his fearless warrior Wulfstan, together with Aelfere and Maccus, men of great courage, to protect the causeway. The battle was at an impasse.

Growing frustration led the Vikings to request the English to permit their passage and allow the battle to get under way in a manly fashion. Byrhtnoth was motivated, knowing that if he shied away from the fight, he would be called a coward. He was confident in the strength of his forces and felt that he might at last teach the ruthless barbarians a lesson by defeating the glorious Trygvason, who would no longer be able to raid at will along the coastline, thus saving England from further destruction by the Vikings. Byrhtnoth realized that he had to win a decisive victory, but first had to get past the standstill and bring the Vikings to battle. He cleared the causeway and allowed them to cross: "Then advanced the wolves of slaughter, for water they cared not for, this band of Vikings."[11]

The Vikings carried their linden shields across the water and formed into battle array, ready to confront the enemy. Byrhtnoth, too, marshaled his troops, and when all was ready, dismounted among his men. Although his army was smaller in number, he refused to think that he could be overwhelmed by the greater Viking force. The time for battle had come. Boldly courageous, he marched his men forward.

Murderously sharp spears began to fly. As soon as the Vikings opened the lines of attack, they rushed forward and drew their swords for the hand-to-hand, close-quarters clash. The onslaught was fierce, shields were split apart, shield rims rang and corselets of mail sang under the heavy sword-blows. At first, the English stood firm against the marauders, but the Vikings centered their attack on Byrhtnoth who suffered wounds. He struck out with his sword in anger, but his arm was so damaged that his sword fell to the ground. He knew then that he was dying and for him the battle was over. Still he encouraged his warriors to advance bravely together. His army was not easily intimidated, nor were they fearful, and they pledged to fight as long as they had hands with which to hold their shields and broadswords: "An infinite number, indeed of them and of our side perished, and Byrhtnoth fell, and the rest fled."[12] As he lay dying in the arms of two Viking warriors, Byrhtnoth prayed to God for his soul's salvation and thanked the Lord for granting him all the joys of this world.

Now that Byrhtnoth was dead, the Vikings gained confidence in their strength and formed themselves into a wedge, rushing the enemy. A number of Englishmen chose to flee the battlefield in dishonor rather than risk their lives. Others remained loyal to their slain leader and stayed on the battlefield attempting to avenge his death. The Vikings also suffered casualties; many perished, exhausted by their wounds, and were barely able to man their ships afterward.[13] The weakened English forces were finally forced to give in to the Norse barbarians. Before departing the battlefield, the Vikings, in a final act of victory, cut off Byrhtnoth's head and took it as a war trophy to their own land.

Byrhtnoth, a seasoned skilled military commander, was due an honorable burial in the Ely cathedral where he was laid to rest with a round ball of wax in place of his head. The Norse victory at Maldon was an enormous psychological triumph, made even more rewarding by ten thousand pounds of silver. Aethelred, who was obliged to supply the Vikings with rations throughout their stay in England, was shamed and exposed as a weakling.

Olaf Trygvason, however, was not at peace. He returned to England three years later, and laid siege to London in collaboration with the Danish king Sven Forkbeard. The *Anglo-Saxon Chronicle* records that the two Nordic kings came "with four and ninety ships," causing great harm and unspeakable evil by burning, plundering, and slaughtering all around Essex, Kent, Sussex, and Hampshire. They obtained horses and continued raiding inland, until Aethelred offered them tribute, this time in the form of a *danegeld* of sixteen thousand pounds (roughly equivalent to seven and a half tons of silver), to leave the English kingdom in peace. After accepting the terms of the agreement, Olaf and Sven, with a full fleet, took up winter quarters in Southampton where they were well fed by the West-Saxon kingdom.

King Aethelred of England finally conceived a grand plan. He sent Bishop Elfeah and Alderman Ethelwerd to bring Olaf Trygvason to him. The bishops left hostages at the Viking ships and led Olaf with great pomp to the king, who received him well and honored him with royal presents.[14] King Aethelred convinced Olaf to accept baptism (an act many Norsemen considered a betrayal), break his bonds with King Forkbeard, England's most dangerous foe, and instead of continuing his campaigning in England, use his skills and strength to promote Christianity in his own land. Olaf decided to ally himself with Aethelred, who encouraged him to fight for the kingdom of Norway, and Olaf promised, "as he also performed, that he never again would come in a hostile manner to England."[15]

Olaf never fought for the Norsemen again, although he fought against them, and his alliance with King Aethelred eventually enabled him to return to his native land, defeat Earl Hakon, regent in Norway, and become Norway's chosen king. Earl Hakon had heard rumors that there was a man beyond the North Sea named Olaf who was looked upon as a king. Olaf, who had acquired the name *Ole den Gir* from Gardarike, Russia, was not known in Norway and most people, including his family and friends, had not had any news of him after he left the farmer Håkan the Old in Sweden. But Earl Hakon remembered that the chieftain Trygve Olafson had had an infant son who had gone to Russia and stayed with King Valdemar. Suspecting that Ole den Gir might be Olafson's son, Hakon began to fear competition for the Norwegian kingdom and sent his friend Thorer Klakka to Dublin to find out who this Olaf might be. If it turned out to be the highly reputed Olaf Trygvason, Thorer Klakka was to ensnare him through deceit and bring him under the earl's power.

When Olaf and Thorer met, Olaf inquired about news of Norway. Thorer told him that Earl Hakon was a powerful man against whom people dared not speak, but many wished that their king came from Harald Fairhair's race. This was Olaf's trump card as he was a descendent of Harald Fairhair from the Ynglinga Dynasty. He asked Thorer if he thought the people would have him. Thorer told Olaf that the best way to obtain a kingdom was to ask for it, and if that failed, to take it by force. This was a ruse on the part of Thorer Klakka, who did not actually intend for Olaf to become king of Norway; he believed that Earl Hakon would be powerful enough to defeat Olaf once he landed on the Norwegian coast, thereby putting an end to all threats to his kingdom.

Olaf accompanied Thorer Klakka back to Norway with five long-ships after having lived all of his life abroad. His raids in foreign lands had brought him wealth and leadership experience, which he wished to further by forcing Norway under his reign. His life's goal was to obtain the Norwegian crown and defeat heathenism in the Nordic countries.

As it happened, Earl Hakon and his servant Kark, hiding in a hole in the ground, overheard Olaf offer a large reward to whoever brought him the earl. That same night Kark beheaded the earl and brought the head to Olaf hoping to collect his reward. Instead of paying him as promised, Olaf beheaded Kark as punishment for betraying his master. He used the fort at Nidaros, today's Throndhjem, as the place for the execution, and afterwards fastened the heads of both Earl Hakon and Kark on top of the gallows.

In 996 (995 according to some sources), the *ting* at Throndhjem unanimously accepted Olaf as their king. Olaf was also able to bring Viken, the area from which he was descended, under his power. The skald Thord Kolbeinson "saw the son of Trygve stand, surveying proud his native land."

Olaf worked feverishly to establish Christianity in his kingdom, forcing it, if necessary, on the people. He was at first supported by the local population, but the smaller chiefs found him unreasonable and blamed him for taking even more *scat* (tax) than that levied by Harald Fairhair. They accused him of recklessly disregarding the wishes of the people, who complained that they had lost their freedom now that they could not even believe in the god of their choice. Olaf's relentless pursuit of the whole of Norway was also met with resistance from both the Danish and Swedish kings, and although Olaf was indeed well fit to be king, he was not able to enjoy his kingdom for long and was killed in the battle of Svolder.

Among Olaf's enemies were Sven Forkbeard (with whom he had earlier collaborated during his raids in England) and the sons of the beheaded Earl Hakon. Because the Danish king Sven Forkbeard had denounced Christianity and had been driven from his country several times, Olaf reasoned that he was more of a nuisance than a real threat and that he could drive the godless Dane away this time, too. The problem, however, was Sigrid, Sven's wife, once courted by Olaf who had struck her in the face with his glove in anger over her refusal to accept Christianity.[16] After the incident, Sigrid defiantly had told Olaf that she did not intend to turn her back on the beliefs she and her family had held for generations. Moreover, she had told him she did not believe he was true to the god of whom he spoke so confidently and that his behavior would some day cost him his life. So she now urged Forkbeard to fight Olaf; if Sven needed a kingdom, it was better to kill a Norwegian Viking than a Danish Viking.

Sigrid felt she had full control both over her husband and over her son, the Swedish king Olof Skötkonung, and was not afraid to encourage Sven to invite both the Swedish king and Earl Erik, Hakon's son, to Denmark with their fleets to help pursue Olaf Trygvason. Certainly, Olof Skötkonung would go with Sven and ambush the self-proclaimed King Olaf. After mulling it over, Sven Forkbeard met with the Swedish king and Earl Erik and the three of them plotted to take from Olaf his prized ship, the *Long Serpent*, during one of his trips from Vindland back to Norway. Sven had not seen the ship himself, but had often heard of its magnificence. When he boasted that he would himself steer the *Long Serpent* that evening, Earl Erik grunted: "If King Olaf had no other vessels but only that one, King Sven would never take it from him with the Danish force alone."

Sigvaldi of the Jomsvikings also saw a chance to win back his reputation, which had been badly damaged when he had fled in the battle with Earl Hakon at Hjorunga Bay a few years earlier. Since that time his relationship with both the Danish king and the Norwegian earl had remained tense; looking to smooth things over, he offered to deceive Olaf Trygvason and waylay him off the Island Svold near the cliffs of Rügen. He went first to Vindland, where Olaf was visiting, and delayed Olaf's return trip until he received the message that Sven and his troops were ready for him. But Olaf heard rumors of Sven's ill intentions. "Highly improbable," Sigvaldi told Olaf. "King Sven would not decide to sail against you alone, you who are so mighty."[17] To prove his allegiance to Olaf, Sigvaldi offered to sail ahead of Olaf back to Norway and clear the way of any hostile forces. Instead, he led Olaf directly into the ambush and scene of battle.

The Danish king Sven and the Swedish king Olof readied themselves for war. The weather was pleasant, so they lowered the sails, anchored their ships and climbed up on a cliff to look for Olaf Trygvason. A magnificent fleet of long-ships soon came sailing along, the first ship so splendid that they thought it was clearly the *Long Serpent*, but they were mistaken and each ship that followed was also magnificent. "Let us not attack until we see the *Long Serpent*," Earl Erik suggested. He reasoned that the more ships that were allowed to pass, the fewer they would have to contend with in the battle. When almost the entire fleet had passed in front of them, the kings grew restless, fearing they had missed their opportunity and would have to return home empty-handed in disgrace. But then three more ships emerged. The first was the *Crane*, the second the *Short Serpent*, so the third had to be the *Long Serpent*. The Norse king had certainly lived up to his reputation, for when they saw the ship, richly gilt with a serpent head decoration, appearing beyond the cliff, they could no longer deny that Olaf was a man of great strength and wealth. The water to the east was glowing as if gold had been scattered around the ship, which was so large that a good many moments passed before the stern could be seen. The kings stood in awe, admiring the *Long Serpent* with the tall bulwarks. A fearful hush fell over the men and Earl Erik said: "This ship is well suited for Olaf Trygvason, and now that we have seen it, we can agree that truth is well spoken when the people say that King Olaf is as distinguished among kings, as is his ship among vessels."

The Danish and Swedish kings and the earl now agreed that if they succeeded in defeating Trygvason, the kingdom of Norway should be divided into three parts, but that the booty on the *Long Serpent* should go to the king who first boarded the ship. Ownership of the other ships would likewise be given to the king who managed to take them into his possession. Drawing lots to decide who would get the first opportunity to battle the *Long Serpent*, Sven Forkbeard won the first try, followed by Olof, king of the Svear, and lastly, if needed, Earl Erik. The hunger for battle grew so intense among the Danish and Swedish kings and the Norwegian earl that they rushed down from the cliff, hurried onboard their ships and lowered the tents. Soon thereafter the Danish and Swedish fleets emerged from their hiding places and the sea was full of ships.

When Olaf Trygvason saw the opposing fleets approaching, he shouted: "Who is the chief of this fleet coming towards me?" Learning that it was Sven Forkbeard of the Danes, he sneered: "That man I know well and he is nothing to be afraid of, for the Danes never gained victory over the Norwegians; nor will they triumph today. But who is the other chief who is following him on the right?" When told it was Olof Skötkonung of the Svear, Trygvason said: "The Svear king would have been wiser to stay at home in Sweden, licking his offering bowls (Olof Skötkonung was still pagan), instead of coming here and spilling his own blood in pointless battle." Before battle, warriors commonly hurled insults at the enemy to show their manliness. "But who is that big skipper lying out there to the left of the Danes?" Olaf asked next. When he learned that it was Erik Hakonson, earl of Norway, he became less cocky: "I can see now that he has good reason to meet us." He turned to his men: "We have a tough battle ahead of us," he said, "for they are Norsemen like ourselves."

Thorkel Dyrdi, the man steering the *Crane*, advised Olaf Trygvason to turn around and retreat, that no one, faced with such a force, would consider it cowardly. "Let the sails fall," said Olaf, "for none of Olaf Trygvason's men thinks of flight. No real king succumbs to fear and flees from his enemies." Instead, he sounded the war horns and summoned his remaining eleven ships to either side of the *Long Serpent* and bound them together to prepare for the battle. But because of the ship's exceptional length, the *Long Serpent's* stern extended far past the *Crane* and the *Short Serpent* that lay on either side. "Let us move the *Long Serpent* farther forward," Olaf suggested, "for it looks bad if the king enters the fight behind the rest of his men." Ulf Röde (the Red) then said that if the bow of the *Long Serpent* stuck out too far, the ship would be easy for the enemy to board. "I didn't know," said the king, "that I have on my ship a man who is both *röd* and *rädd* (red and afraid, similar sounds in Swedish)." The king, angered by Ulf Röde's lack of courage, grabbed his bow and arrow and aimed at Ulf. "Better save the arrow for a greater danger," Ulf said. "I will do for you all that I am capable of doing. As you know, it is much anticipated that before evening not too many of your men will be left."

The *Long Serpent* was equipped with superb warriors, men of high standing, none older than sixty or younger than twenty. Eighteen-year-old Einar Tambaskelfer was the exception. He was Norway's most skilled archer and had been chosen to accompany Olaf based on his great skill in battle. The king himself stood in the stern, high above the others, with his gilded helm and shield and a red silk shirt over his coat of mail.[18]

Olaf Trygvason's fleet, however, was so greatly outnumbered that the battle is said to have been the harshest naval battle in Viking history, with greater casualties than in any other. The allied kings divided their ships into three separate fleets, with King Sven in the middle, Olof of the Svear to the right, and Earl Erik with his large ship *Ironbeard* to the left. The crews of the *Long Serpent, Short Serpent,* and *Crane* threw chains into King Sven's fleet, clearing the decks of as many warriors as they could and forcing King Sven to retreat aboard other vessels outside shooting range. The Svear king then moved into Sven's place, but he too was savagely beaten and forced to leave his position in a hurry. When Earl Erik's turn arrived, he had greater success. With sword and battleaxe he managed to clear many men off the deck of Olaf's ship, allowing the Danes and Swedes to reenter the scene of battle. They boarded the ships, taking the dead men's places, until all of Olaf Trygvason's ships, with the exception of the *Long Serpent,* were cleared of men.

Weapons began flying anew—arrows, spears, and rocks—and shields were scarcely sufficient against the onslaught of missiles. Olaf stood on the gangway of the *Long Serpent* and threw two spears at once, forcing Earl Erik to cover up behind his shield-burgh until all weapons had been cast. Several warships now surrounded the *Long Serpent* and defense onboard the Norwegian ship grew desperate. Olaf's remaining men, enraged, ran onto the ship's railing, cutting away with axe and sword, but the distance to reach their adversaries was too great and many fell into the water, sinking under the weight of their armor.

Einar Tambaskelfer, foremost among the Norwegian archers, stood at mid-ship with his bow. He aimed at Earl Erik and shot an arrow that hit the tiller end just above the Earl's head. The second arrow entered the stuffing of the Earl's stool. "Shoot that tall man at the mast!" Earl Erik ordered of Fin, a superior archer. Fin shot and split Einar's bow into two parts. "What was it that broke with such a noise?" Olaf Trygvason asked. "Norway, King," Einar answered, "Norway, from thy hands."[19] But Olaf refused to admit defeat. He handed his bow to Einar, who grabbed it and tightened the bowstring. "Too weak, too weak is the king's bow," said Einar, whereupon he grabbed his shield and sword and fought the enemy courageously in close quarters.

When Earl Erik saw how few men remained onboard the *Long Serpent*, he determined to board the ship. Olaf Trygvason made a final courageous attempt to defeat the earl, this time grabbing three spears at once and throwing them with all his might at Earl Erik. One spear flew closely past the earl's left side, the other barely touched his right side, and the third passed over his head. "So poorly have I never shot," said Olaf. "The earl has good luck today, and if God so wishes, he will gain the kingdom of Norway." Olaf, severely wounded in the battle, realized then that all was lost and jumped overboard. Earl Erik and his men tried to grab him and bring him back onto the ship, but Olaf threw his shield over his head and disappeared under the water. And so Earl Erik became the proud owner of the *Long Serpent*. He admitted that although he had fought many battles, this was the hardest and he had never before seen a ship so difficult to defeat.

The battle of Svolder, which took place on September 9, 1000, was said to have caused the death of Olaf Trygvason.[20] The Danish and Swedish kings and Earl Erik, as agreed, split the kingdom between them. Earl Erik got four districts in the Throndhjem country, along with Halogaland, Naumudal, the Fjord districts, Sogn, Hordaland, Rogaland and North Agder, all the way to the Naze, which he ruled until 1015. It is not known for certain what really happened to Olaf Trygvason on that fateful day, but legend has it that after jumping overboard, he cast off his coat of mail underwater, swam under the long-ships until he came to a Vindland cutter and survived. Olaf was said to have been sighted later in Constantinople. According to Halfred Vandredaskald: "From the far east some news is rife, of a King sore-wounded saving life." Others say he was so badly wounded that he could not possibly have come away alive.

Fifty years after the battle of Svolder, a certain Gaute came to a monastery in the Holy Land, where he made the acquaintance of an old man who resembled a Nordic warrior more than a monk: "Tell me," the old man said to Gaute, "do the people of Norway still remember Olaf Trygvason?"

"Holy is the king's memory," said Gaute, "for he raised the cross of Christ in the land of Norway."

The old man asked what happened to King Olaf after his defeat on the *Long Serpent* and Gaute answered: "The people have many different opinions regarding his fate, but most believe that when Olaf jumped into the water, the weight of his armor was too much and he sank to his death."

The old man wrinkled his brow. "That could not have been so," he said. "King Olaf was well-versed in all physical exercise and stronger than any other man. Tell me, is Einar Tambaskelfer still at life?"

"The richest man in Trondelage," said Gaute.[21]

"When you return to Norway," said the old man, "tell Einar that no one topped his courage in the fight on the *Long Serpent*."

According to saga legend, Olaf was the first king of a united Norway. Although his reign was short-lived and he never returned to his homeland, he is considered to this day to be the country's hero-king and is celebrated as one of the greatest Nordic kings. It is said that he once climbed the Smalsarhorn, at 850 meters (2,789 feet) high the tallest sea cliff in northern Europe, and hung his shield at its top.[22] His gold-plated ship was said to reflect in the water like a sunny street stretching across the entire ocean.

The few men who survived the battle of Svolder jumped overboard, were captured, taken to Earl Erik and then pardoned. Rumor was that Olaf's men bought their freedom through the intermediary of an unknown benefactor—most likely Olaf Trygvason himself. Others say: "What people wish they soon believe."

> "*Where arrows whistled on the shore*
> *Of Svold fjord my shield I bore,*
> *And stood amidst the loudest clash*
> *When swords on shields made fearful crash.*"

CHAPTER 14

KNUT THE GREAT
995–1035

With the Danish triumph over England complete, Knut the Great spent the rest of his life in conquest of a North Sea empire, which at its height encompassed Denmark, Norway, parts of Sweden and Scotland, and all of England.

K nut the Great,[1] son of the legendary Danish Viking leader Sven Forkbeard, had a bloodline that could be traced to Harald Bluetooth and Gorm the Old.[2] He was born in Denmark in 995 (997 according to some sources);[3] became king of England in 1016, two years after his father's death; king of Denmark in 1018, after his older brother Harald's death; and king of Norway in 1028, when he chased the reigning King Olaf Haraldson from the country without a fight. He ruled in all three kingdoms until his sudden and untimely death in 1035. Knut is first mentioned in the sagas when, at the age of sixteen, he accompanied his father to England. By then he had already been well-trained in warfare and had possibly had the opportunity to lead parts of his father's army abroad.

By the time Knut came of age, Sven Forkbeard had already long been on the rampage around the English countryside. He had plundered the lands of the Saxon king Aethelred, the Isle of Man and the Danelaw (areas of England that had earlier been placed under Danish command), and tested his strength against the English people and the self-governed Danish provinces. Almost twenty years had passed since Sven had allied himself with Olaf Trygvason, laid London under siege and discovered the city's great riches in silver and gold. Every year King Aethelred lived in fear of a return of the Viking raids that had so devastated his country. Aethelred's problems with the Danes were considered by many to be the consequence of his unwise decision to marry Emma of Normandy in 1002.[4]

Aethelred's marriage to Emma was political and to strengthen his ties to Normandy, he ordered the killing of all Danes in England. Sven Forkbeard's sister was among those condemned to death, which had wakened the Great Dane from his temporary slumber. Swearing revenge, Forkbeard then crossed the North Sea with his forces and raided in southern and eastern England, leaving death and destruction in his wake. Only when the big famine struck in 1005 and he could no longer supply his army with necessities was he forced to sail back to Denmark for a short respite. He returned to England a year later, however, and continued campaigning for several more years, ransacking Kent and other English towns and collecting from Aethelred huge sums of *danegeld*.

In 1013, Sven felt the time had come to fulfill the vow he had made many years earlier in front of an assembly of renowned Viking chiefs and warriors at the funeral feast for Earl Strutharald, father of the Jomsvikings Sigvaldi and Thorkel the Tall. He had vowed to attack the English throne either by killing Aethelred or driving him from the country. The bad blood between Sven and Aethelred resulting from the murder of Sven's sister only strengthened the Great Dane's resolve. Moreover, Earl Thorkel the Tall, who had managed many of Forkbeard's raids against England, had defected to Aethelred.

At the time of Sven's expedition, Knut, the second oldest son of Sven Forkbeard and Queen Gunhilde, was at sixteen deemed to be an adult, old enough to accompany his father to

England in pursuit of the English throne.[5] With the assistance of several long-ships provided by Knut's half-brother, King Olof Skötkonung of Sweden, they crossed the sea and landed their forces in southern England.[6] Their first goal was to win over the Danelaw area, where Forkbeard had earlier tested the Nordic people's character and felt they were likely to accept him as their king with little protest.

Forkbeard succeeded at gaining the people's support in the southern provinces and sailed his fleet to all the major cities in England, which submitted to him one after another. Aethelred, residing in London, the last city to fall to the Great Dane, could no longer resist the invasion and was forced to capitulate and flee to Normandy.[7] Sven Forkbeard had finally won all of England and fulfilled the vow made many years earlier, but he was not able to enjoy his victory celebration for long. He died on February 3, 1014, only a year after acquiring the kingdom. According to the *Anglo-Saxon Chronicle*: "This year King Sweyne ended his days at Candlemas . . ." Some believe that he was murdered. The *Saga of Olaf Haraldson* maintains that Sven died suddenly in the night in his bed, "and it is said by Englishmen that Edmund the Saint killed him, in the same way that the holy Mercurius had killed the apostate Julian."

Sven Forkbeard left two sons to inherit his riches, but also the war. Harald, the oldest, became king of Denmark, and Knut, in accordance with Sven's deathbed wishes, succeeded his father to the English throne. Sven considered the English inheritance appropriate for Knut and asked him to rule the land with prudence and justice.

The English advisors, however, disagreed, judging young Knut not suited and far too immature for the royal position. In addition, now that the formidable and fearsome Forkbeard was dead, the people of England became emboldened: ". . . whereupon advised all the counselors of England, clergy and laity, that they should send after King Ethelred; saying, that no sovereign was dearer to them than their natural lord." Messengers were sent to the exiled Aethelred in Normandy who, learning of Forkbeard's death, felt this was a good time to return to England to reconquer the land that had so unjustly been taken from him.

As soon as he returned to English soil, he invited men to enter his pay and join him in his pursuit to recover the country. He managed within a short time to muster a superior army under the leadership of his courageous son and successor Edmund Ironside (also known as Edmund the Strong), and rallied the people to rebel against Sven Forkbeard's army led by Knut. King Olaf Haraldson of Norway, who was also on bad terms with the Danes, came with a large army of Norsemen to assist Aethelred.

Aethelred's army went first to London, then sailed its fleet into the Thames, but was held back by Knut's army stationed inside the ditches and stone and timbered bulwarks built by the Danes. Knut's troops had barricaded themselves atop a wide bridge, but King Olaf devised a plan. He moored his ships under the bridge and along its sides, then built a roof for his ship with timber obtained by tearing down old houses; he then placed pillars under the roof for support, leaving enough room for his men to swing their swords.

Olaf's ship was now protected from the stones, arrows, and spears thrown by Knut's men from the bridge, but the missile barrage was so intense that many of his other ships were badly damaged and forced to retreat. King Olaf rowed up with the remaining fleet and laid cables around the pillars that supported the bridge. His ships then rowed off downstream, pulling on the cables and causing the bridge's base to break apart and give way under the weight of Knut's troops and the huge piles of stones and weapons placed on the planks. Many men fell into the river and others fled. Sigvat Skald relates the event: "At London Bridge stout Olaf gave Odin's law to his war-men brave—to win or die!"

After his success in London, King Olaf spent the winter with King Aethelred, fighting more battles and bringing the country, one part at a time, under the subjugation of the English king. Meanwhile, Knut remained with his army in Gainsborough until Easter, when Aethelred came with his forces and killed every man in sight, forcing the young Viking to take to the seas with his fleet and flee the country. Aethelred then proclaimed that all Danish kings would forever be outlaws in England.

Knut, greatly humiliated by his loss so soon after his father's triumph just a year earlier, proceeded with his fleet southward to Sandwich. To avenge the disloyalty he had suffered at the hands of the English people, he "landed the hostages that were given to his father, and cut off their hands and ears and their noses," returning them to England in a wretched, disgraced condition. Although this atrocity helped to compensate in part, Knut realized that a king without a kingdom had little to celebrate, so he sailed to Denmark and begged his older brother, Harald, to share his kingdom with him.

Harald had no intention of dividing his dominions with his younger brother. "I am happy for your safe arrival here, dear brother," Harald said, "but it bothers me greatly that you feel half of my kingdom should befall you. Our father decided, as you well know, that I alone rule in Denmark. It pains me, however, that you lost your inheritance, which was greater than the kingdom I now possess, and I will do what I can to supply you with new ships and warriors. But my kingdom remains mine alone."[8]

Knut needed both military equipment and manpower and eager warriors from Norway and Sweden answered his call for help. During his stay in Denmark, he reestablished his bonds with Thorkel the Tall of the Jomsvikings, who had earlier defected to Aethelred but had now switched sides again.[9] He also managed to convince Earl Erik of Norway to accompany him back to England. Erik had great military prowess and was well-known for his many successful campaigns and triumphs— the two most memorable being his victory over the Jomsvikings in Norway and his defeat of Olaf Trygvason at Svolder, when he acquired the *Long Serpent*. Earl Erik now resolved to be by Knut's side when the time came to take London. When Knut sailed westward and made a new attempt at England, it was at the head of an impressive fleet of two hundred ships and an army of ten thousand men.

The *Anglo-Saxon Chronicle* reports that after Knut arrived with a marine force of 160 ships, he plundered, burned and killed everyone in his path. He began searching for Aethelred's son Edmund Ironside, who by now had subjugated the Danelaw to him. Knut and Edmund wrangled for months, fighting hard and bloody battles throughout the autumn and winter, with victory alternating between sides. But Edmund gathered an army, which "could avail him nothing, unless the king was there and they had the assistance of the citizens of London." As one man after another in his ineffectual army left and went home, Edmund's frustration grew and he ordered, "under full penalties, that every person, however distant, should go forth," and that King Aethelred in London should meet his army with all the aid he could find. But facing Knut's forces, the English king was unsuccessful at motivating his own troops, and also soon learned that the men who were supposed to assist him would instead betray him.

Edmund then rode to Northumbria and on to his father in London, while Knut continued plundering in other parts of the country before following Edmund to London. Aethelred died when the ships arrived and the English council named Knut the new king of England. But the problem was not solved. London resisted and Edmund Ironside was chosen over Knut: ". . . all the peers that were in London, and the citizens, chose Edmund king; who bravely defended his kingdom while his time was."

Knut then proceeded to engage in several more battles with Edmund. In London his fleet could not pass London Bridge, so he "sunk a deep ditch on the south side . . . they trenched the city without, so that no man could go in or out." In the meantime, King Edmund invaded the West-Saxons, who submitted to him. At Bentford, many of the English drowned, supposedly by their carelessness. Edmund went into Wessex and summoned his army, while Knut returned to London and assaulted the city from land and sea; he then went into Mercia, "slaying and burning whatsoever they overtook, as their custom is."

For the fourth time King Edmund assembled what was left of the English nation and went into Kent, where he killed as many of the enemy as he could. Knut had by then managed to take control of almost all of England, with the exception of London. Knut's army returned to Essex, but Edmund overtook them at Ashingdon, where fierce fighting erupted and Edmund suffered one of his greatest defeats. The battle of Ashingdon in 1016 led to the downfall of the English nation's nobility. Knut's striking victory was achieved despite the fact that great parts of England fought against him. Knut continued his pursuit of Edmund Ironside into Glocestershire. By now the armies on both sides of the conflict were severely depleted and coun-selors advised the kings to make peace with each other, give up the hostages, and become allies. Knut and Edmund met on the Isle of Olney in the River Severn, where they agreed that a peace treaty calling for a partition of England was better than continuing the battle. They settled the army's pay and confirmed their friendship with pledges and oaths. The treaty, that was to be enforced until either Edmund Ironside or Knut died, at which time all land was to revert to the survivor, stipulated that Edmund Ironside would take Wessex south of London, and Knut, Mercia, the district north of the Thames, including London.[10] The two kings exchanged swords and promised to behave like brothers toward one another for as long as they lived.

When Edmund Ironside died suddenly on the feast of St. Andrew (November 30, 1016), Knut was left unchallenged king of all of England.[11] In 1017, he divided the English government into four earldoms, each with a separate ruler: Wessex and the Danelaw, formerly Edmund's part of the kingdom, for himself; East-Anglia for Viking chief Thorkel the Tall; Mercia for Alderman Eadric Streona who had helped him in the invasion; and Northumbria for Earl Erik, his Norwegian brother-in-law.[12]

King Aethelred's remaining sons went to Normandy and spent the winter in the company of King Olaf of Norway. They debated their future and agreed that, should they succeed at taking England back from the Danes, King Olaf would have Northumberland. *The Saga of King Olaf Haraldson* reports that Olaf and Aethelred's sons soon thereafter landed an army in a place called Jungufurda. Although they managed to take the castle, Knut's army was so strong that Aethelred's sons could not resist it and had to return to Normandy.

The stiff resistance Knut's forces had met in their struggle to conquer England had taught Knut a lesson. In order to rule his kingdom in peace, he had to erase any evidence that he was a foreigner in the country. His strategy was to strengthen his ties to England by marrying Aethelred's widow Emma, believed to have been fifteen years his senior. The marriage, a political move, was also an attempt to avoid bad blood with Aethelred's surviving sons in Normandy.[13] The agreement was sealed, and Knut was now truly part of English royalty.

As king, Knut had full control of the country's finances and became an enormously rich man. To satisfy the ransom demands of Viking marauders, he collected the unheard of tribute payment of "two and seventy thousand pounds, besides that which the citizens of London paid; and that was ten thousand five hundred pounds." He used this huge sum of money to pay the fleet that had followed him from Denmark and helped him to achieve his vision. He then sent them home to Denmark, but as security, retained an elite guard for himself consisting of forty of his biggest ships and three thousand of his best, most skilled warriors. Selected for their outstanding courage and wealth, they were equipped with expensively gilded axes and sword hilts in honor of their king. Knut kept his fleet magnificently equipped and ready to counter any possible attack against the English nation, which he suspected might come from either his brother Harald of Denmark or private Viking fleets. In 1018, he had to make use of his collective forces to defeat and kill the entire crew of an enemy Viking fleet of thirty ships. In the end, Knut's acquisition of England had a triple advantage: The English people were happy because they no longer had to fear Danish invasions; the Danes were pleased by the wealth they had acquired; and Knut was satisfied because he was finally considered the true king of England, not a conqueror.

In 1018, Knut's brother Harald, king of Denmark, died without leaving an heir, and in the winter of 1019–20, Knut went to Denmark with nine ships to secure the Danish crown for himself. He entrusted Thorkel the Tall with governing the English kingdom during his absence. But because Knut's ties to England were greater than his ties to Denmark, he soon returned to England in 1020, and sent Thorkel the Tall to reign in Denmark during his absence, and from that time on, traveled to his Scandinavian dominions only when there were problems that needed his attention. He was first and foremost an English king, and viewed England as the center of his empire.[14]

Over time Knut's great organizational talents allowed him to bring stability to a country that had been raided so relentlessly over many years. He respected the old English laws and attempted to right the many wrongs the people had suffered from generations of Norse raids. He built a church to commemorate King Edmund of East-Anglia and brought the body of the archbishop of Canterbury, who had been murdered in 1012, in great ceremony from London to Canterbury and gave him a proper burial. He also built a church on the battlefield in Ashingdon in an attempt to allay the memory of the bloody battle. It was said no one dared disturb the peace that he had established so well.

Knut was eager to expand his political power in England, even if this meant using the resources he had set aside for defending southern England against the Danelaw Vikings. To bolster his standing as king, he undertook harsh measures, including the murder or deportation of his most prominent English rivals. As soon as his place on England's throne was secure, he put together a large standing army of men found in Aethelred's court, as well as his own warriors, and paid them to fight for him. He would later give greater positions of power to the English nobility to stabilize his reign, although many from the old English aristocracy had either been killed for suspicion of treason or sent into exile. Knut reestablished the royal court in England, but accompanied it by new land divisions and other changes.

To keep the warriors residing in his court in their proper place and prevent rules from being broken, Knut established punishment orders. According to the Saxons, Knut was known for his uncontrollable anger and lack of restraint regarding both personal and political matters. He was often the first to break the rules and was known to have killed his own men after a violent outburst. The murder of Eadric Streona, the betrayer of Edmund Ironside, who had played a double role during Knut's struggle for the English throne and later became Earl of Mercia, is such an example. Knut also became an enemy of the Danish Earl Ulf, a great warrior who was accomplished at managing well what came into his hands. Ulf was married to Knut's sister, Estrid, but his continuous struggle for independence from Knut angered him. Knut was most dangerous when he perceived a threat to his kingdom. He eventually accused Ulf of treason and killed him at St. Lucius Church in Roskilde in southern Denmark, where the earl had sought refuge.

Knut stayed on good terms with the Christian Church in England and with the Roman pope. His ambition was to establish a Christian empire with himself as sole regent, for which he spent the 1020s on crusades throughout the Nordic countries. He soon began to covet Norway, which he felt should rightfully belong to him, a son of Sven Forkbeard, whose forefathers had ruled in Denmark and Norway for generations. "Canute the Great had conquered England by blows and weapons, and had a long struggle before the people of the land were subdued," reports the *Saga of Olaf Haraldson*. "But when he had set himself perfectly firm in the government of the country, he remembered that he also had right to a kingdom which he had not brought under his authority; and that was Norway."

The power base Knut had established in England helped him in his pursuit of Norway. In 1025, he sent messengers to the Norwegian king Olaf Haraldson (the Saint).[15] "King Canute considers all Norway his property and insists that his forefathers before him have possessed the kingdom," the messengers told Olaf in the *Saga of Olaf Haraldson*, "but as King Canute offers peace to all countries, he will also offer peace to all here, if it can be so settled, and will not invade Norway with his army, if it can be avoided." Knut offered a fiefdom to Olaf Haraldson provided he pay taxes, as earls before him had done. Olaf was not pleased by the proposition and replied that if Knut wished to rule over all the countries of the north and reduce England to a desert, "he shall do so . . . before I lay my head in his hands."

Olaf pledged to defend Norway with battleaxe and sword as long as he was alive and would pay taxes to no man for his kingdom.

In the summer of 1025, Olaf summoned all of his closest associates, for news had just arrived by way of merchant vessels that Knut had assembled a large army to sail from England to Norway. Spies were dispatched to learn more about what was going on in England, and in autumn Olaf sent messengers to his brother-in-law, King Anund in Sweden.[16] He reasoned that if Knut, conqueror of Aethelred, succeeded in subjugating Norway, the Swedish king would be most concerned as he would no longer be able to enjoy his Swedish dominions in peace. The two kings pledged to unite their forces and stand by each other with the strength of their kingdoms behind them.

Olaf and Anund felt that this was the moment, before Knut arrived from England, to invade and divide Denmark between them and they warned the Danish people of their intent. Farmers had no choice but to go into military service with Olaf to attack Denmark and rid themselves of King Knut. Olaf planned to conquer as much of Denmark as possible before Knut arrived and ravaged throughout the Danish countryside. However, Knut was told of the coming invasion by an informer and left England earlier than planned to protect his Danish dominions. He readied a fleet with an enormous number of men and "frightfully large" well-equipped ships, placing Earl Hakon second in command.[17] With his forces in order, Knut went aboard his ship that had sixty rowers' benches, positioned the gilt figurehead, and hoisted the blue, red and green striped sails.

When news spread of his arrival from the west, the farmers who had so willingly gone into King Olaf's service began to retreat, afraid of the mighty Knut, Aethelred's conqueror and son of Sven Forkbeard. As Sigvat Skald said: "Canute is on the sea! The news is told and Norsemen bold repeat it with great glee." Knut arrived in Denmark with a huge army and remained there all winter. He began his strategy to conquer Norway by sending lavish gifts to the Swedish king by messenger. If the Swedes agreed to sit by quietly and take no action during his battle with King Olaf, he promised to leave the Swedish kingdom in peace. But King Anund, who considered his friendship with the Norwegian king more important, was unwilling and rode across West Gautland in southern Sweden with an army of 3,600 men. He first imposed taxes and rampaged in Scania in southern Sweden. Meanwhile, King Olaf continued to commit atrocities in Denmark, plundering, tying up peasants and dragging them to the ships, killing some.

During Knut's residence in England, Earl Ulf Sprakalegson had been placed in charge of the Danish dominions, serving as the country's protector and also that of Knut's underage son, Hardaknut. Earl Ulf, tired of Knut's absence, believed no good came of a country left without a king and feared that the Norwegian and Swedish kings now felt free to pursue Denmark at will. With the support of many smaller chiefs, Ulf decided to remove the threat against the kingdom by making Hardaknut king of Denmark, despite his tender age and without informing Knut. Ulf's crowning of the seven-year-old Hardaknut, however, had less to do with fear of the other Norse kings and everything to do with his desire to rule the country through the boy-king, which was why he did not tell King Knut what he had done. Once he heard of Knut's arrival from England and of the alliance of the Norwegian and Swedish kings, Ulf understood that he could not fight them all and regretted having bypassed Knut, an act which would most certainly anger the king. Ulf therefore came forward and begged Knut for mercy for having placed the young child in charge of Denmark.

When Knut was informed of the power shift that had taken place in his absence, he commanded his son to come to him and relinquish the meaningless title, for obviously he had no power to stand against his father. Hardaknut went to his father, fell at his feet and laid the king's seal on his father's knee, while Earl Ulf prayed to Knut for mercy and reconciliation. Knut, known for his violent temper, said they would talk about the matter after his men and ships had assembled.

Meanwhile, King Olaf and King Anund were sailing east to Scania where they ravaged and burned the districts, then proceeded further eastward to the frontier of Sweden into the River Helga where they held council and remained for some time. It was agreed that King Olaf should go up-country to the forest, then on to the lake that was the source of the river. Olaf and his men spent many days there, building a large dam in the riverbed, until the lake became very high. But spies reported to Knut on the work of the two Norse kings and Knut sailed towards them with a mighty force said to be one half greater than those of both kings together. The time had come for the three kings to clash, this time in Helge å (Holy River) in southern Sweden. The battle took place in the summer of 1025 (though the exact year varies according to the source): "This year went King Knute to Denmark with a fleet to the holm by the holy river; where against him came . . . a very large force both by land and sea, from Sweden."

When King Anund's spies sighted Knut's fleet, Anund ordered the war-horns to sound. His men pitched their tents, readied their weapons and rowed out of the harbor with their ships bound together, as was customary when preparing for battle. But Knut, after looking over the opposing force that came to meet him, felt it was too late in the day to start a war, since his fleet was so great that it "required a great deal of room at sea, and there was a long distance between the foremost of his ships and the hindmost, and between those outside and those nearest the land, and there was little wind."

He brought as many ships as he could inside the harbor, and when morning came a great many of the crews went ashore to amuse themselves and converse with the crews of other ships. During this time King Olaf destroyed the dam he had only just built, releasing the water. Knut and his men remained unaware of what happened until the water from the dammed up lake came rushing toward them, carrying trees and other debris that damaged the ships and covered the fields with water. The force of the water drove Knut's ship out until it rested among Olaf and Anund's ships. But the big bulwarks and Knut's extremely fit and highly skilled crew made it difficult for the enemy to board the ship. Earl Ulf arrived a short while later, Knut's fleet gathered from all sides, Olaf advanced with a fleet of 420 ships, and the battle began.

Knut's losses were severe and many men, both Danish and English, were killed. Olaf and Anund retained possession of the battlefield. They let their ships retreat and allowed the fleets to separate. Although the Norwegian and Swedish kings had suffered few human losses, they knew that the next time they clashed with Knut, the odds would be in favor of Knut and they would have little chance of victory because of his superior power. Another vexing problem was that although they had taken a great deal of booty during their raids in Denmark, they had acquired no land. Olaf and Anund resolved to sail eastward to the Swedish king's dominions, distance themselves from the possibility of further battle, and return home with their forces intact.

Because of this retreat, Knut, despite his losses in men and ships, was considered the victor at Helge å. As the skald Ottar Svarte in *Saga of Olaf Haraldson* said: "For at Helga River's side they would not his sword abide." In a meeting in Sigtuna, it was said Knut was also named king of Sweden for this victory, although this remains historically unproven and his power in Sweden appears to have been in name only.[18]

After being driven from Helge å, King Olaf and King Anund went a-Viking all winter in the hope that Knut's men would grow homesick and return to England. They felt they had left a mark on the farmers through their raids all summer and that the villagers knew well whose favor to seek. When Knut's spies informed him that a large part of Olaf's fleet had returned home, rather than going back to England, he went to Denmark where Earl Ulf had prepared a great feast for him. Knut was in a sullen mood, possibly because of the indecisive victory at the river, which had resulted in great losses of men and ships, and got into an argument with the earl over a chess game. Ulf was a skilled chess player and tactician and when Knut perceived that he was losing, he cheated by replacing a knight that had been taken from him. Ulf grew miffed, turned the chessboard over and stood up to walk away. Knut called him a coward for running off, but Ulf reminded the king that he had not been a coward on the battlefield and had protected the king at Helge å, while the Swedes were bearing down. The next morning Knut was still stewing over the argument and Ulf, who sensed danger, fled to St. Lucius Church where Knut's chamberlain, Ivar White, tracked him down and pierced him with his sword, killing him on the spot.[19]

During his stay in Denmark, Knut continued increasing his wealth by collecting taxes from the richest people in the northern lands. He lived in magnificent houses and surrounded himself with pomp and splendor. He sent spies to Olaf's army, offering the men presents in return for their promise of fidelity to the Danish king. Knut managed in this way to build an army made up of many Norwegians, as well as English and Danes, who could help him bring the country safely into his hands.

In the spring of 1028 he fitted out an immense fleet and set out to conquer Norway from Olaf Haraldson, whom the people had come to despise because they felt they had lost their self-rule to the Norwegian tyrant. "This year went King Knute from England to Norway with fifty ships manned with English thanes and drove King Olave from the land, which he entirely secured to himself."[20] When news of Knut's approaching army arrived, the people were generally unwilling to offer their aid to King Olaf. Some of the Norwegians left the country; others went to Knut on seemingly innocent errands, told him of their hardships and delivered various presents to win his friendship. Sigvat Skald in the *Saga of Olaf Haraldson* says: "Our men are few, our ships are small, while England's King is strong in all." Knut used bribes to secure the fidelity of King Olaf's men who were not ashamed of switching sides. Flight could be justified, for King Olaf's small army had come about through treachery, not cowardice.

Knut sailed with his fleet to Norway where he summoned a *ting* and was everywhere welcomed as king. He placed men to rule over the districts, took hostages from among the farmers and was not opposed. At a *ting* in Throndhjem, he was chosen king of all of Norway. He placed Earl Hakon in charge and felt that the proper time had come to give his son Hardaknut the title of king.[21] Knut took hostages from among all the great men in Norway, their relations or close connections and was thereby able to secure their fidelity to him.[22] With the acquisition of Norway, he had reached the height of his career. Knut became known as the king who inherited the Danish kingdom, conquered England by force and Norway without a blow.

But he was not yet finished. His empire also came to encompass parts of Scotland and parts of southern Sweden, with ties to Iceland and Normandy.[23] He collected taxes from all the Nordic countries and renewed Danish control over a large part of Vindland. Olaf Haraldson's destiny took a different course. Realizing that the country had abandoned him, he fled to King Jarisleif in Russia and was received in the kindest manner. He returned to Norway in 1030, but was defeated by his own people in the battle of Stiklestad: "This year returned King Olave into Norway; but the people gathered together against him, and fought against him; and he was there slain, in Norway, by his own people . . ."

When Knut realized that he had finally attained dominance and become full king over the North Sea empire about which he had dreamt, he called himself emperor of Bretland, which included both England and Scotland. He remained in charge until his death at age forty in 1035: "This year died King Knute . . . He was King over all England very near twenty winters." Knut was buried in the cathedral in Winchester, the earliest capital of the Saxon kingdom of Wessex where he had spent much of his time. His death marks the beginning of the end of the Viking era in England. The stability England had enjoyed during his reign ended and the large empire he left behind split up and quickly reverted to the former royal lineage.

In Norway a rebellion immediately followed Knut's death. The Norwegians reclaimed their kingdom, disposed of Sven and placed Magnus the Good in charge. Hardaknut inherited Denmark, and despite great opposition from Emma, Knut's illegitimate son, Harald Harefoot, inherited England.[24] Knut's decision was based on the people's belief that Hardaknut, because of his long stays in Denmark, was too inexperienced to run the English kingdom. Around that time Emma's son Alfred, from her previous marriage to Aethelred, left Normandy for England but was killed. Emma herself was forced to flee.

When Harald Harefoot died suddenly in 1040, Hardaknut summoned an army and sailed to England to receive the English crown. But lacking the strength and political insight of his father, and after collecting huge taxes from the English people, he became generally unpopular. According to the *Anglo-Saxon Chronicle* for that year: "Then were alienated from him all that before desired him; for he framed nothing royal during his whole reign." In the meantime, Hardaknut's absence in Denmark prompted Magnus the Good, who was king of Norway, to conquer the Danish throne.

Hardaknut died in 1042, a mere two years after becoming England's king. The *Anglo-Saxon Chronicle* for that year states that while standing with a drink in his hand, "he fell suddenly to the earth with a tremendous struggle; but those who were nigh at hand took him up; and he spoke not a word afterwards, but expired on the sixth day before ides of June."[25] Since none of Knut's sons had produced any heirs, the English crown now passed to the former King Aethelred's son Edward. England would not be at peace for another twenty-four years, until William I of Normandy (William the Conqueror) defeated the English king Harold Godwinson at the battle of Hastings in 1066 and became England's new regent.

Knut had by all rights earned the honor to be called "the great" or "the mighty."[26] His had become the greatest Nordic empire in the history of the Vikings and he had been considered the most powerful man in all of Europe. He had been extremely rich and a skilled organizer who became known as the king who stopped the tides of Viking raids on England's shores, if not the tides in the ocean. Although Knut was a religious man, he was also a skilled politician. He made a point in having his throne carried to the water, where he would command the ocean to calm down. When it did not, it was proof to the people that, although his accomplishments as king were great, even the greatest king could not command the elements. It showed his powers were small in comparison to the greatness of God Almighty, who controlled the heavens, earth and oceans and who alone was entitled to be called "King."

In the end, Knut lived up to his name. Although he won the English kingdom by the sword, he governed the country with the help of the Anglo-Saxon earls and sustained twenty years of forced peace, during which trade, art and religion flourished. He was the first king to reign over a truly united England, free from internal and external strife and was one of the mightiest kings in the history of Christianity. An Icelandic poet composed a verse in honor of King Knut, the son of the Great Dane, Sven Forkbeard:

> "To Cnut the Dane I tune my lay;
> English and Irish own his sway,
> And many an island in the sea;
> So let us sing his praise that he
> Be known of men in every land
> To where heaven's lofty pillars stand."[27]

CHAPTER 15

HARALD HARDRADE, HARD-RULER
1015–1066

*Harald Hardrade was courageous in battle and
greedy for power. Lacking the diplomacy required
of a king to win the people's favor, he died at age
fifty in another king's dominion. He was the last
of the noteworthy Norse kings, and with his death,
the Viking Age ended.*

❧ ❧

Harald Sigurdsson, half-brother (by the same mother) of Olaf
Haraldson the Saint, who died in the battle of Stiklestad
in Norway in 1030, was a survivor.[1] At the age of only fifteen,
bloody and wounded from the battlefield at Stiklestad, he hid in
a farmer's house until he recovered the strength to continue his
flight out of Norway. With the help of the farmer's son, he was
escorted on horseback through the deepest parts of the forest,
far from the eyes and ears of the angered Norwegian population that had so recently disposed of Olaf Haraldson. Harald
maintained his belief that not only would he survive his injuries,
but that the day would come when he would be celebrated king
in the northern lands and that his mighty name would live on
through history.

Harald's travels first took him eastward to Sweden, where
many of Olaf Haraldson's defeated army had gathered. The
tired troops remained in Sweden over the winter, and in spring
1031, Harald acquired some ships and continued farther east

to Russia, to King Jarisleif in Novgorod, a long-time family friend who received him kindly. King Jarisleif had long associated with the Norwegians and Swedes and now gave Harald authority over the defenders of the Russian king's dominions, hiring Harald's men as mercenaries. His newfound power motivated the young Harald to remain in Russia for several more years during which he traveled throughout the country, learned the ways of warfare and built up his strength and fighting prowess. At age twenty he was already a fearsome warrior, driven by ambition and the desire to move on. With Greece, and more especially Constantinople, beckoning in the distance, Harald put together an impressive fleet and embarked on a new adventure that took him to the splendid Byzantine capital.

Immediately upon his arrival in Constantinople, he went into the mercenary service of Empress Zoe, sailed in the Greek islands, and fought battles against the corsairs.[2] With as many as five hundred of his own men under him, he soon became recognized as a chief and leader of the Varangians. One of his first campaigns was to Sicily where a Roman army was battling for the island. Harald remained in the imperial guard for several more years, fought in eighteen full campaigns, and gathered unparalleled riches.[3]

In 1045, Harald returned to Novgorod and King Jarisleif an extraordinarily rich man after his many successful campaigns in the service of the Byzantine Empire. After marrying Jarisleif's daughter Elisabeth (the Norsemen called her Ellisif), Harald set sail the following summer for Svithiod. First he met up with his longtime friend Svein Ulfson.[4] The two warriors had stories to share and egged each other on to the point that they outfitted their ships and gathered their forces for war. They sailed to Denmark where they pillaged and burned, first on Seeland and then on Fyen.

Harald's reputation as a stronger and wiser man than others, always victorious in battle, and who stopped at nothing, preceded him. Magnus Olafson, king of Norway and Denmark, hearing of the immense force his relatives Harald Sigurdsson and Svein Ulfson had amassed, quickly ordered a levy over all of Norway and brought together a large army to defend his kingdoms against the forces heading his way.

In an attempt to avoid fighting the fierce pirate, Magnus offered to partition Norway and give Harald half the kingdom "with all the scat and duties, and all the domains thereunto belonging, with the condition that everywhere thou shalt be as lawful King in Norway as I am myself; but when we are both together in one place, I shall be the first man in seat, service and salutation."[5] Harald accepted the proposal, the two kings thanked each other, agreed to divide all of their moveable property into two equal parts and sat down to drink and celebrate together. The following morning, after Harald was given the title of king at the general *ting*, the many caskets filled with valuables acquired during Harald's service in the Varangian Guard were brought in, spread on an ox-hide on the floor, and divided with King Magnus, as agreed. The two kings then had an equal share in Norway's real estate and an equal share in moveable goods.

But Harald's friend Svein Ulfson considered that Harald had only his personal interests in mind and felt cheated at losing the opportunity to fight and earn riches and a name for himself. "There are people, Harald, who say that thou hast done as much before as only to hold that part of an agreement which appears to suit thy own interest best," he said. When an assassination attempt on Harald went awry, the friendship treaty between Harald and Svein was broken. Svein was later proclaimed earl of Denmark, while Magnus and Harald continued to reign in Norway.

In spring 1047, Magnus and Harald ordered a levy. Co-rule proved difficult, particularly when the two kings were on campaign and quarreled over which of them should have first right to choose his place in the harbor. "I never forget what I have given, or what I have not given," Magnus reminded Harald. (They had agreed that when they appeared together, Magnus should be "the first man in seat, service and salutation.") The argument was settled and they sailed south to Denmark which they conquered and where they remained until late summer when King Magnus fell sick with ringworm disease and died after a long illness. Harald now became the sole ruler of Norway. According to the *Anglo-Saxon Chronicle* for the year 1048: "This year . . . Harold . . . went to Norway on the death of Magnus, and the Northmen submitted to him." Svein Ulfson was, in the meantime, still ruling in Denmark.

An underlying problem was Harald's belief in his hereditary rights to Denmark. He began motivating his forces, encouraging them as Norwegians to always demonstrate their superiority to the Danes. With funeral preparations for King Magnus interfering with his power struggle, Harald decided to return to Norway and secure that land first, before setting his sights on Denmark. The delay, however, enabled Svein Ulfson to bring all of the Danish dominions under his power and be proclaimed king of Denmark by the people.

In 1048, after Harald had reigned alone in Norway for a year, he ordered a levy and set sail for Jutland in the Danish dominions. The Danes watched the approaching fleet with dismay, understanding fully the horrors that were coming their way. They suffered greatly from Harald's plunder and burning, which lasted all summer and ended only after Harald returned to Norway in autumn with an immense amount of booty. King Svein, who had been quiet all winter and summer, now grew angered and sailed to Norway to repay Harald for the misery he had inflicted on the Danish population. He proposed that the two kings should meet and fight until their differences were settled, but Harald avoided battle with Svein and instead went south to the merchant city of Haithabu, which he burned to ashes. Harald then returned north with a fleet of sixty ships, all laden with the booty he had taken.

King Svein again challenged Harald to fight. This time Harald, who had only half the forces of Svein's huge fleet, agreed to battle him at sea. This, however, turned out to be a miscalculation and Harald tried to flee, but the Danish fleet pursued and caught up with the Norwegian fleet, which was so heavily laden with booty it could not escape. In a desperate attempt to lighten his ships and get away, Harald was obliged to throw all his goods overboard, including food, liquor and prisoners.

When Harald returned to Norway, he established himself as a wise and understanding ruler. He had proved himself a courageous warrior, expert in the use of his weapons, and he ruled his kingdom well. But with time, he became so proud and arrogant that no one dared to disagree or speak against him. Thiodolf the skald said that in King Harald's dominions, the common man had to follow orders, "should stoop or rise, or run or stand, as his war-leader commanded . . . nothing is left them, but consent, to what the king calls his intent." Einar Tambaskelfer, one of the most important farmers and most powerful lendermen (liegemen) in the Throndhjem land who knew the law well, informed Harald of the farmers' desire to follow the law of the land. They were tired, he told Harald, of tolerating the king's lawlessness. Subsequently, after King Harald murdered Einar in an argument about a thief who had once been in Einar's service, Harald became so despised that farmers and lendermen alike attacked him. Deprived of Einar, the farmers lost not only a great leader but also the inspiration and ability to rise united against the king.[6]

Fin Arnason, who had proved his fidelity to Harald's half-brother, Olaf the Saint, in the battle of Stiklestad, visited King Harald and consulted with him about the uproar over Einar's death. Fin Arnason spoke bluntly: the king had managed his affairs poorly, "first in doing all manner of mischief; and next, in being afraid that thou knowest not what to do." Harald listened, agreed that Fin had great insight into the matter and asked him to go to town and ask the people's forgiveness. In return, Fin would receive from the king whatever favor he desired. Fin asked Harald to provide Kalf, Fin's brother, with a safe haven in the country and to return his estates to him, which would restore his dignity and power.[7] Harald agreed and Fin went to town where he spoke long and well at the *ting*. He said that the king was now willing to pay a penalty, "according to the judgment and understanding of good men" for the murder of Einar Tambaskelfer.

In the summer of 1050, after relations with the farmers had settled down, Harald ordered a levy and went off to Denmark where he plundered widely throughout the summer. In the southern parts of the country he met a large Danish counterforce who pursued the Norwegian king with such vigor and determination that many of Harald's men were killed. Harald's next memorable battle came more than a decade later in 1062, when he built a huge ship, almost as splendid as the *Long Serpent* owned by King Olaf Trygvason. The ship, that had thirty-five rowers' benches, was outfitted with a dragonhead at the bow and a dragon tail at the stern. The sides were gilded and all the equipment, including the sail, riggings, anchors, and cables were of the highest quality. Harald was now once again ready to pursue the Danish dominions. He sent messengers to King Svein, asking him to come north in spring so that the two kings could finally meet, battle each other, and settle their differences. The winner, he said, would get both kingdoms.

To prepare for the battle, Harald assembled a huge force with which he sailed south, calling out a levy of men and ships wherever he went. When the Danes heard of the approaching forces, many fled. But King Svein remained with his ships and warriors in the areas of Fyen and Seeland and refused to meet with Harald's fleet. Once again, Harald was forced to let all but 150 ships return home. This was all part of King Svein's plan. Now that he knew exactly how strong Harald's fleet was, he sailed with three hundred ships toward the Norwegian king. Realizing they had been cheated and were outnumbered besides, many of Harald's men thought it better to retreat than fight. But Harald saw only ruin and no glory in flight. He urged his warriors on with the battle cry: "We will win or fall!"

When the two fleets met, King Svein positioned his ship against the side of King Harald's ship and a brutal battle ensued. King Harald's bowstring could be heard twanging throughout the night, until most of the Danish fleet broke apart and left. Harald was now able to board Svein's ships and clear them of most of their crews. Since the ships were tied together, they could not separate in time for the assault, which further complicated the battle for the Danes and they were forced to jump overboard in order to save their lives.

After clearing the ships, Harald cut down Svein's banners to communicate his victory. He had seized more than seventy of King Svein's ships and continued pursuing the remaining Danes who were still trying to row away. But the ships were so numerous and tightly packed together that there was no space in the water for the Danes to place their oars. Harald boarded and ransacked Svein's ships, one by one, appropriating immense amounts of booty. The casualties were many, but King Svein himself was not to be seen among the dead bodies on the captured ships. After the battle, Harald tended to his injured warriors and bound their wounds, and after this was done, he allowed the booty to be divided among his men. While they were working on this pleasant task, which took time because the loot was so plentiful, word arrived that King Svein had escaped alive to Seeland.

When the booty had been tallied up, divided, and everyone had received his share, Harald sailed home to Norway where he gave his warriors leave. Throughout that winter and spring there were many drinking parties at which the ale flowed freely, tongues were loosened and tales of bravery and heroism filled the warriors' hearts.

The Nordic population soon realized that quarrels between King Harald and King Svein would continue. Many casualties had already been sustained on both sides, so the wisest men were chosen to act as mediators between the two kings. After much talk and negotiation, it was finally agreed that Harald should have Norway, and Svein should have Denmark, in accordance with the former boundaries, and each should keep what was already in his possession without payment of reparations to the other. The peace agreement was to be in effect as long as both men remained kings. But Harald found little satisfaction in the deal and became frustrated with his lot. In the winter of 1065, he traveled in his dominions and accused the farmers of withholding taxes and other duties from him. Seeing no resolution to his problems, his anger grew and he maimed and killed people as a warning, he said, to those who dared to disobey him.

Harald's restlessness and inability to settle down finally drove him to set his sights on England. It was surprising, people said, that this great warrior, who had made such a big name for himself in the Varangian Guard and who was so immensely rich from his many successful campaigns abroad, had not attempted to take England, which lay open to him, but had instead been fighting for fifteen years for well-guarded Denmark. Earl Toste, brother of the English king Harold Godwinson, further influenced Harald Hardrade to invade England, having refused to be his own brother's servant.

Harald resolved to proceed across the sea to the English empire with the intention of conquering the country. Although some said that England was too difficult to confront because its people were such well-armed brave warriors, others thought that, if anyone could achieve this difficult undertaking, certainly Harald Hardrade of Norway was the right man for the job. In the autumn of 1066, Harald readied his forces and sailed to England with a large fleet consisting of nearly two hundred warships and an estimated ten thousand warriors.[8] He planned to take the northern parts of the country first, where the Nordic peoples' influence was the strongest. But he had a dream that boded ill and learned, after questioning those skilled at interpreting dreams, that he would not come away from this battle alive. He sailed nevertheless, leaving his son Magnus in charge of Norway, but taking along Olaf, his other son.

Stopping first in Shetland, he then sailed on to Orkney, which he captured, before continuing to Klifland, where he plundered and quickly subordinated the people to his rule without experiencing any significant opposition.[9] He continued his severe assaults on the English population, causing huge losses for his victims and conquering wherever he went, proudly carrying his banner, *Land-Ravager*, before him. When told of the news, the English king Harold Godwinson traveled northward day and night and as quickly as he could gathered his forces.[10] He swore that Harald Hardrade would get nothing more than seven feet of English soil, the space it would take to bury his body. When the forces met, the resulting slaughter was huge. Many of the English fell, drowned or fled, and the Norsemen retained possession of the battlefield.

When Harald Hardrade had several victories against the chiefs of the English forces behind him, he advanced on Stanford-bryggiur (Stamford Bridge), about seven miles east of York. Deeply distressed, the English submitted to Harald, giving him the children of important persons as hostages. Harald returned to his ships at nightfall to celebrate, and at the *ting* the next morning named officers to rule the town. In the midst of the victory celebrations, King Harold Godwinson, catching the Norsemen with their guard down, rode into the city from beyond the bridge with a huge army of cavalry and infantry and remained all night.

The English began the battle with a fierce assault, but Harald and his men stood their ground and countered the enemy forces with spears. To avoid the onslaught of missiles, the English rode in a circle around the Norsemen, then pursued them across the bridge. Severe fighting continued long into the day and grew into one of the sharpest conflicts of Harald Hardrade's reign. Men on both sides were slain in huge numbers. The English nearly took to flight, and for awhile it looked as though the Norsemen would triumph. But then Harald was struck with an arrow in the windpipe. Many of his brave warriors also fell in the battle, some from weariness, others from the heavy blows inflicted by the English. Those remaining kept on fighting to the point of exhaustion, throwing off their coats of mail, oblivious as to whether they lived or died, until almost all of the leaders and chief Norse warriors had fallen. Few managed to flee before nightfall when the battle ended: "The Normans that were left fled from the English, who slew them hotly behind; until some came to their ships, some were drowned, some burned to death, and thus variously destroyed; so that there was little left: and the English gained possession of the field."[11]

However, a remarkable, anonymous Norse warrior blocked the bridge, and taunted the English, accusing them of being feeble-hearted and unable to stand up to a single man, a man who was single-handedly preventing the superior English force from declaring victory. The English threw javelins at the obstinate Viking, but to no avail. They dared not close in on this man who so bravely defied death, until an English soldier managed to sneak up on the Viking from under the bridge and pierce him "terribly inwards under the coat of mail," giving the English king free access to the bridge. Godwinson proceeded with his forces and engaged in a massive slaughter of the Norsemen.

After the battle ended, King Harald Hardrade's body was transported from England to Nidaros, Norway, where he was buried in Mary Church, which he had himself built.[12] Olaf, Harald's son, who had accompanied him to England, survived the battle and received clemency from the English king, along with all those left on the ships, "who then went up to our [English] king, and took oaths that they would ever maintain faith and friendship unto this land. Whereupon the king let them go home with twenty-four ships."[13]

Olaf then sailed with his fleet to the Orkneys, where he remained all winter. In summer he proceeded east to Norway, where he was proclaimed king jointly with his brother Magnus. When King Svein Ulfson of Denmark learned of Harald Hardrade's death, he broke the peace agreement that was in effect between them. He insisted that there was no provision in the agreement to outlast their deaths and so called up a levy in both countries. But the Norwegians, tired of the endless strife between the two countries, sent ambassadors to Denmark with proposals for peace, threatening the Danish king with immediate war unless he let the old division of the countries stand. Friendship and peace were thereby restored between the Norwegian and Danish dominions.

Although Harald Hardrade, an experienced warrior, died at the age of fifty while trying to conquer another king's dominions, his accomplishments and wealth were still remarkable. The reputation he acquired while campaigning in the Varangian Guard would alone have been sufficient for his name to be remembered by posterity. The battle of Stamford Bridge was the last major battle fought by Norsemen and is often seen as the marker for the end of the era called the Viking Age. Despite his failure in England and motivated at the end by greed, the Hard-Ruler, Harald, nevertheless managed to leave his lasting imprint on history, exactly as he had wished.

> "*Our* Viking steed rushed through the sea,
> *As Viking-like fast, fast sailed we …*
> *Who knows, I thought, a day may come,*
> *My name will yet be great at home.*"[14]

AFTERWORD

—◆◆—

Most scholars date the start of the Viking Age in 793 with the raid on Lindisfarne, and end it in 1066 with the battle of Stamford Bridge that was followed by William the Conqueror's invasion of England. Others say that 1103 more accurately marks its end, because that was the year that Bishop Ascer became archbishop of all of the Nordic countries and colonies, which led to a widespread abandonment of heathenism for Christianity. Yet another view holds that the end was at hand already in the late tenth century, once the individual northern lands each became unified under a single king, Olaf Trygvason in Norway, Olof Skötkonung in Sweden, and Sven Forkbeard in Denmark.

The Viking reign lasted for some three hundred years and despite differing views, its concluding chapter was the result of an evolution rather than any single event. Viking kings continued fighting small battles for another hundred years after the battle of Stamford Bridge. The Norwegian king Magnus Barefoot crossed the North Sea with a large fleet in 1093, 1098, and 1103, and plundered and massacred in Orkney and the Hebrides, in western Scotland, and on the Isle of Man. Toward the end, however, the Vikings grew more intent on acquiring land than raiding and resorted to violence only in self-defense or to increase territory.

The Vikings burst onto the scene in a flash, startling the world with the reach and extent of their raids and the overwhelming destruction they wrought. Their unconventional war strategies, which left the enemy helpless and defenseless, built their reputation as brutal, bloodthirsty barbarians with no regard for God or human life. The reckless raiding of churches and monasteries was due in large part to their ignorance of the unspoken rules of warfare giving holy sites immunity, but it earned them the Christian world's contempt.

Christianity made slow inroads in the Nordic countries. It conquered gradually, with the followers of Oden and Thor continuing to show their pagan gods allegiance long after the masses had accepted baptism. Because of the many forced attempts to oblige people to denounce heathenism, Christianity was marked as an intolerant religion that gave rise to brutal rebellions for hundreds of years after the Viking Age was over. Many Norsemen were baptized and rebaptized, yet continued to live according to pagan rites. King Harald Bluetooth of Denmark, a notorious pagan, regretted his first baptism and reverted to heathenism. When he finally accepted Christianity in 962, he declared it the new state religion, greatly advancing its cause. When the conversion, which spanned several hundred years, became widespread, Norse raiding practices also came to an end. Accepting Christianity enabled Norse kings to end their relative isolation, control their populations more easily, and establish constructive relationships with other European countries.

While the brutality and violence of the Vikings is not contested, it is open to discussion whether they were in fact more brutal and more violent than their European counterparts. War atrocities are hardly a new phenomenon and have occurred throughout the history of most nations. The Viking period was one generally beset by war and during which European kings frequently fought one another in endless battles. But even centuries prior to the Viking Age there are examples of wars taking place every few years between competing kingdoms, such as Wessex, East-Anglia, Mercia and Northumbria, and during which churches and monasteries in Ireland were burned. Brutality was not, moreover, the exclusive province of non-Christian kings. In 782, Charlemagne, king of the Franks and a devout Christian, beheaded 4,500 Saxons in a single day after they continued to practice their pagan religion and refused to convert to Christianity. Einhard, a dedicated servant of Charlemagne, recorded that after these beheadings: "the King went into winter camp, and there celebrated mass as usual . . ."[1]

Despite the relatively small numbers—no more than a few thousand were involved in most campaigns—the Vikings prevailed because they engaged so aggressively and forcefully in the hundreds of battles that they fought both at home and abroad. They excelled militarily because they ignored traditional western fighting methods.[2] They had no respect for the church and flouted the norms and rules accepted by "civilized" societies that had their own ways of legitimizing violence. They did not bother to arrange a time and place for battle, as was often customary in Europe. Deception, attacking by stealth when the enemy was not fully prepared, or striking in a seemingly undisciplined manner was by no means considered cowardly or dishonorable from the Viking perspective. The Vikings, unconcerned by, indeed oblivious to, religious prohibitions, believed that war was worth any risk because it compensated so well in terms of adventure and spoils. Even the high number of casualties they suffered did not dissuade the Vikings from their lives as warriors.

The Vikings leave a formidable legacy as expert sailor-navigators of speedy pirate boats of their own design. Although European communities could prepare themselves for attack from their next-door neighbors, they had little opportunity to do so against the Vikings, who employed hit-and-run tactics from their boats and whose land was separated from England and France by the sea, precluding counterattack. At the same time, through their wide travels and daring adventures across rivers and seas, they established contacts with the peoples of many nations, which resulted in increased trade and commerce and stimulated the circulation of goods.

Although for almost three centuries the Vikings had been virtually the only predators and masters of western European waters, the time finally came when these free warrior spirits were replaced by others with different aptitudes and interests. Yet even today, at a distance of almost one thousand years, the Vikings remain vivid symbols of a culture that, despite its reputation for violence, still inspires admiration for its daring, mobility and dynamism.

GLOSSARY

—➤➤—

arrow scat   Annual tax paid in bows and arrows. An example: the Laplanders (the people of the northernmost area of Sweden and Norway) paid a yearly arrow scat to the king, which he used to equip his warriors and supplement his war expenditures.

Asar   Asa-gods, or gods of war, the most important of whom were Oden and Thor. Oden, god of slain warriors, gave living men the courage to face the enemy. Thor, noted for his strength and ferocity, reigned over thunder and lightening and fought the underworld giants by striking them with his mighty hammer.

Asatro   Name of the polytheistic religion of the Norse which means "those loyal to the gods" or "faith in the gods." Like most religions, it was an integral part of people's lives.

berserker   Also called a "berserk," a Norse warrior with sworn allegiance to the god Oden, in such a frenzied state he believed he was invulnerable. The pre-battle rituals may have included psychoactives (halluocinogenic mushrooms) mixed with mead which allowed the berserker to disregard pain and wounds in battle. The role of the berserkers was to make the first attack to shock their victims into flight or submission, opening the way for the rest of the warriors to follow.

bonde	Farmer or peasant. In the Viking era, many were poor and turned to raiding in the summer months to improve their financial situation.
danegeld	Land tax originally raised to buy off raiding Danish Vikings and later used for military expenditures. The English paid out large settlements during the course of the Viking invasions, some several times larger than those of the Franks.
danelaw	Small Viking kingdoms established within larger enemy kingdoms, specifically in England's occupied regions.
dragon	Name for a Viking long-ship which often had dragon-heads mounted at the bow and stern.
drakkar	Dragons or battleships designed for maneuverability that could be either sailed or rowed.
edda	A collection of poetic narrated folk-tales of Norse mythology or Norse heroes, originating in Iceland and divided into the poetic edda from the ninth century and the prose edda from the twelfth century.
futharken	Original rune alphabet, named after its first six characters. The older futhark was developed from a southern European alphabet around AD 200. In the Viking Age, the alphabet was simplified to sixteen characters, called the younger futhark.
go a-Viking	To embark on a raid. "Viking" was commonly used as a verb.
holm	A small island. The word is commonly found in many modern place names in Scandinavian countries, for example, Stockholm (the capital of Sweden), that is built on thirteen small islands linked together by bridges.

holmganga	A duel of honor designed to settle disputes, which took place on a small island (*holm*), or other carefully marked off and restricted area.
jarl	An earl, second only to a king in power. The jarl often served as the official ruler if a king was appointed at a very young age.
Jomsvikings	Elite Vikings from the fort of Jomsborg, thought to have been located near modern Wolin in the Baltic Sea just off the Polish coast. They lived by a strict code of ethics, were committed to honor and courage and pledged total allegiance to their leader.
knörr	Merchant or trading ships with capacious storage room in the middle for goods or animals to be sold or traded. These ships carried smaller crews than the drakkar and traveled primarily under sail.
Konungahella	King's Rock, or the place where kings met to discuss matters of importance.
lagman	Lawman, or one who communicates the law. Since the Vikings were illiterate, laws were declared, memorized and recited aloud by the lawmen.
landvaettir	Norse guardian spirit and mythical creatures in old Icelandic literature. They lived in the hills in Iceland and came in the form of dragons, birds, bulls and giants.
ledhsagari	A navigator or guide. After the Leidgangr, the first official military fleet, was established, a ledhsagari was hired to show the way.
Leidgangr	The first Norse navy, an officially sanctioned military fleet created by King Harald Fairhair of Norway. The

king had the right to levy ships for war, and required the population to supply him with weapons and armor in proportion to their individual wealth.

lenderman A liegeman, owing allegiance and service to a feudal lord.

Mimer The well of wisdom. The god Oden sacrificed an eye in order to drink from the well of Mimer and acquire wisdom.

Norns The three demi-goddesses of destiny, representing past, present and future. The Norns lived at the base of Yggdrasil, the tree of life at the center of the world, where they wove the tapestry of life.

Norse Name for the peoples of Norway, Sweden, Denmark, and Iceland before the Christianization of those lands.

Ragnarök Means "doom of the gods." This was the final battle that would end the world, waged between the asa-gods and their aggressors. It is perhaps more familiar by its later German name, *Götterdämmerung*, usually mistranslated as "twilight" of the gods.

rune A character in the runic alphabet used as a form of writing. The runes were said to have great magical powers. In return for learning the secrets of the runes, the god Oden subjected himself to a test that included hanging wounded in the tree of life, Yggdrasil, for nine days and nights.

Rus Vikings with roots in Russia. The Rus gave their name to the Russian Empire when they organized the country and founded the first city in Kiev.

scat Taxes, paid in the form of silver and jewelry, animals and weapons.

scramasax   A large single-edged knife or short sword used by the Vikings and Saxons between the fourth and tenth centuries. It resembled a butcher knife or machete, was carried across the back of the belt by poor people and was an excellent close combat weapon.

skald   Court poet, whose job it was to praise the king in verse. Skalds also often acted as councilors and warriors and were rewarded for their craft with gold and silver rings.

strandhugg   Stealing livestock and provisions to prepare for an extended journey. Norse warriors needed to be well-fed and rested at the start of battle and looked for provisions near the beach to avoid leaving the ship unguarded. Strandhugg, or "beach-chop," was frequently carried out among neighbors.

svinfylking   The wedge, or boar snout formation. Varying design walls, shield joined to shield, were used for protection. The svinfylking, consisting of a wedge of twenty to thirty warriors with overlapping shields, its point facing the enemy, created a strong defensive wall and was especially useful against spears launched from a distance. The shield-wall also enabled those at the rear of the formation to launch their spears over the heads of those in front.

tafl   Also *hnefatafl*, a popular board game simulating a raid. It is one of the oldest board games played by the Norse population.

ting   Court or general assembly where all free men could speak. Since there was no written documentation, agreements were oral, confirmed by witnesses of appropriate social standing and a handshake.

ulfhedner This is a term used for berserker which means *wolf men*, because they wore wolf-skins instead of chain mail.

Valhalla The god Oden's great hall of warriors. Valhalla was comprised of 540 doors and was wide enough to accommodate eight hundred warriors standing side by side. The walls were constructed of glistening spears and the roof was a dome of golden shields. In Valhalla, warriors would practice their fighting skills against each other all day long.

Valkyrie A warrior maiden serving the god Oden, whose job it was to find the greatest heroes for Oden's army. When a Viking warrior died in battle, it was believed the Valkyries would carry him to Valhalla.

Vaner The gods of fertility, most notable of whom were Njord and his twin children, Frej and Freja.

Varangians Vikings in the Varangian Guard, primarily Swedish Vikings serving the emperor of Constantinople. They were also known as Varjagi.

Vikings Men from Viken, the stretch of land between Oslo-fjord in southeastern Norway and Gothenburg on the west coast of Sweden. The Vikings were of mixed Scandinavian origins from the geographical land area that is today Sweden, Denmark, Norway and, later, Iceland, and are also known by the names Norsemen, Danes, Goths, Svear, and Rus.

wergild Money paid by a criminal to a victimized family as compensation for the crime. An insult against an individual was taken as an insult against the entire family and obligated the family to avenge the crime or live in disgrace. Unless the perpetrator paid wergild, he faced the possibility of an agonizing death.

Yggdrasil   The tree of life. The giants, a constant threat to Yggdrasil, forced the asa-gods to be on guard against the destruction of the world. A popular theory is that the Christmas tree evolved from this pagan tradition. Evergreens that didn't "die" represented rebirth and everlasting life, especially during the coldest, darkest and harshest time of the year.

Yule   Winter solstice celebration. *Yule* means wheel, the wheel of life, and death and rebirth. The recognition of this cyclic pattern goes back to prehistoric times in the Nordic countries, where rock carvings picturing ships and the sun disk symbolized the cycle of life and death.

Sources

Anglo-Saxon Chronicle, entries for the year 787, 793, 851, 877, 993, 994, 1014, 1018, 1025, 1028, 1030, 1035, 1040, 1042, 1066, translated by Rev. James Ingram (London, 1823), The Online Medieval & Classical Library.

Annals of St. Bertin, The, from Frederic Austin Ogg, ed., *A Source Book of Mediaeval History* (New York, 1907), The ORB: Online Reference Book for Medieval Studies.

Christiansen, Eric, *The Norsemen in the Viking Age* (Oxford, 2002), Blackwell Publishers, Ltd.

Dudo of St. Quentin's *Gesta Normannorum*, an English translation edited by Felice Lifshitz, The ORB: Online Reference Book for Medieval Studies.

Eyrbyggja Saga, translated by William Morris & Eirikr Magnusson (London, 1892), Bernard Quaritch.

Gettir's Saga, translated by G. H. Hight (London, 1914), The Online Medieval & Classical Library.

Griffith, Paddy. *The Viking Art of War* (London, 1995), Greenhill Books.

Heitharviga Saga, translated by William Morris & Eirikr Magnusson (London, 1892), Bernard Quaritch.

Jordan, Robert Paul, *Viking Trail East*, National Geographic, March 1985.

Kendrick, T. D., M.A., *A History of the Vikings* (New York, 1930), Northvegr Foundation.

Kormac's Saga, translated by W. G. Collingwood & J. Stefansson (Ulverston, 1901), The Online Medieval & Classical Library.

Laxdale Saga, translated by Muriel Press (London, 1899), The Temple Classics.

Njal's Saga, translated by Sir George W. DaSent (London, 1861), Northvegr Foundation and The Online Medieval & Classical Library.

Page, R. I., *Chronicles of the Vikings* (Toronto, 1995), University of Toronto Press.

Saga of the Jomsvikings, The, translated from Old Icelandic by Lee M. Hollander (Texas, 1955), University of Texas Press.

Smyser, H. M., *Ibn Fadlan's account of the Rus*, § 81 (New York, 1965), New York University Press.

Snorri Sturluson, *Hakon the Good's Saga, Heimskringla: The Chronicle of the Kings of Norway*, translated by Samuel Laing (London, 1844), The Online Medieval & Classical Library.

———, *Harald Harfager's Saga, Heimskringla: The Chronicle of the Kings of Norway*, translated by Samuel Laing (London, 1844), The Online Medieval & Classical Library.

———, *King Olaf Trygvason's Saga, Heimskringla: The Chronicle of the Kings of Norway*, translated by Samuel Laing (London, 1844), The Online Medieval & Classical Library.

———, *Magnus Barefoot's Saga, Heimskringla: The Chronicle of the Kings of Norway*, translated by Samuel Laing (London, 1844), The Online Medieval & Classical Library.

———, *Magnus Erlingson's Saga, Heimskringla: The Chronicle of the Kings of Norway*, translated by Samuel Laing (London, 1844), The Online Medieval & Classical Library.

Sources

————, *Saga of Hakon Herdebreid (Hakon the Broad-Shouldered)*, *Heimskringla: The Chronicle of the Kings of Norway*, translated by Samuel Laing (London, 1844), The Online Medieval & Classical Library.

————, *Saga of Harald Hardrade, Heimskringla: The Chronicle of the Kings of Norway*, translated by Samuel Laing (London, 1844), The Online Medieval & Classical Library.

————, *Saga of King Harald Grafeld, Heimskringla: The Chronicle of the Kings of Norway*, translated by Samuel Laing (London, 1844), The Online Medieval & Classical Library.

————, *Saga of Magnus the Good, Heimskringla: The Chronicle of the Kings of Norway*, translated by Samuel Laing (London, 1844), The Online Medieval & Classical Library.

————, *Saga of Olaf Haraldson, Heimskringla: The Chronicle of the Kings of Norway*, translated by Samuel Laing (London, 1844), The Online Medieval & Classical Library.

————, *Saga of Olaf Kyrre, Heimskringla: The Chronicle of the Kings of Norway*, translated by Samuel Laing (London, 1844), The Online Medieval & Classical Library.

————, *Saga of Sigurd, Inge, and Eystein, the sons of Harald*, *Heimskringla: The Chronicle of the Kings of Norway*, translated by Samuel Laing (London, 1844), The Online Medieval & Classical Library.

————, *Saga of Sigurd the Crusader and his brothers Eystein and Olaf, Heimskringla: The Chronicle of the Kings of Norway*, translated by Samuel Laing (London, 1844), The Online Medieval & Classical Library.

————, *The Ynglinga Saga, Heimskringla: The Chronicle of the Kings of Norway*, translated by Samuel Laing (London, 1844), The Online Medieval & Classical Library.

Volsung Saga, translated by William Morris & Eirikr Magnusson (London, 1888), Walter Scott Press.

NOTES

Introduction

1. Varangians, or Varjagi, are mentioned in the *Russian Primary Chronicle* (also called the *Nestorian Chronicle*) and refer to the people who came across the Baltic Sea.
2. Alcuin was born in York, England, in about 735. He later served at the Court of Charlemagne and died in 804 in Tours, France.
3. *A Part of Swedish History: The Viking Age*, Högskolan i Luelå (Luleå University, Sweden).
4. Snorri Sturluson, *Saga of Harald Hardrade, Heimskringla*. (Snorri Sturluson (or Sturlasson, spelling varies, 1178(79)–1241). *Heimskringla* means circle or ring around the world; in other words, it depicts happenings in the world by one who has encircled it.

CHAPTER 1: Raids on the Christian World

1. *Anglo-Saxon Chronicle*, entry for the year 793. The *Anglo-Saxon Chronicle* was originally compiled by order of King Alfred the Great (who defended Anglo-Saxon England from Viking raids) in approximately 890 AD. The *Chronicle*, a major source for details of naval and military glory, chiefly by eyewitnesses, is considered "the original and authentic testimony of contemporary writers to the most important transactions of our forefathers, both by sea and land."
2. *Anglo-Saxon Chronicle*, entry for the year 787.
3. Alcuin, Letter to the Bishop of Lindisfarne, *The Sacking of Lindisfarne, Northumbria 8th June 793*, The Open Encyclopedia Project.
4. In the beginning of the Viking Age, raids were not officially sanctioned. Large military campaigns were at first undertaken by Nordic kings who became prominent by successfully exercising their authority over smaller

kings and chieftains; these latter could then later choose to sail under the banner of a more renowned king.

5. *A Part of Swedish History: The Viking Age*, Högskolan i Luelå (Luleå University, Sweden). Author's translation from Swedish to English.
6. See Kendrick, *A History of the Vikings*.
7. Dudo of St. Quentin's *Gesta Normannorum*. The term *Goths* refers, in this case, to peoples who originated in Scandinavia.
8. Believed to be the Isle of Rhe near the town of La Rochelle, north of the mouth of the Garonne River.
9. The name Normandy is a reflection of *Norsemen* (men of the north), another name for Vikings.
10. Dudo of St. Quentin's *Gesta Normannorum*.
11. Ibid.
12. See also *Rolf, Gånge-Rolf, or Hrolf Ganger* (Rolf the Walker). Rollo's name is said to derive from his size; he was so big and heavy, no horse could carry him and he was obliged to walk everywhere.
13. Some sources say there were only 120 ships, a still significant fleet size. Most raiding parties consisted of 20 to 30 ships; several were comprised of more than 200 ships, while the great raid on Constantinople in 941 had a fleet with ships numbering in the thousands.
14. The accounts of Ragnar Lodbrok's life and the dates of his reign are based on Viking sagas and are somewhat sketchy. Most likely of mixed Swedish and Danish origin, he was known for attacking Christian cities on holy feasts, when most soldiers were in church, and requiring huge ransoms to leave his victims alone, only to return the following year.
15. See Kendrick, *A History of the Vikings*.
16. *Danegeld*, or Danish money, was a payment imposed by the Danes especially in relation to peace-treaties. The English paid out several settlements during the course of the Viking invasions, some several times as large as those of the Franks. England's ability and willingness to secure peace served instead to making the country an even more attractive target for pirates.
    According to the *Annals of St. Bertin*, the payment was seven thousand livres. The French livre is equivalent to approximately five hundred grams or one pound.
17. *Abbo's Wars of Count Odo with the Northmen in the Reign of Charles the Fat*, from Frederic Austin Ogg, ed., *A Source Book of Mediaeval History* (New York, 1907), The ORB: Online Reference Book for Medieval Studies. The distance of a league, a now obsolete measure of distance, can vary, but equals approximately three miles.
18. Names starting with *Sig*—Sigfrid, Sigurd, Sigvald, Sigvat, Sigtrygg— were common in the Viking Age and signified a person expected to be

victorious. In Swedish, the word *seger* (from sig) means victory. *Frid* means peace.

19. See *Abbo's Wars of Count Odo with the Northmen in the Reign of Charles the Fat*, from Frederic Austin Ogg, ed., *A Source Book of Mediaeval History* (New York, 1907), The ORB: Online Reference Book for Medieval Studies.

20. Jan Skamby Madsen, The Royal Danish Ministry of Foreign Affairs, Denmark, 1992.

21. *The Annals of St. Bertin.*

22. *The Annals of St. Bertin* state that the Danes "quietly passed the winter," though it is unlikely that France's population felt at ease during this time of raiding.The Aquitaines were horsemen living in southwestern France.

23. Arild Hauge, *From Trading to Plunder Raids*, Århus, Denmark, 2002.

24. See Kendrick, *A History of the Vikings.*

25. Possibly Ivar Boneless and Ubbe, two sons of Ragnar Lodbrok. According to *A History of the Vikings* by T. D. Kendrick, in 878, Halfdan's brother Ubbe arrived from Wales on the north coast of Devon with a fleet of twenty-three ships and an army of 840 men.

26. Kendrick, *A History of the Vikings.*

27. For more information on this treaty, see the *Internet Medieval Source Book*, The ORB: Online Reference Book for Medieval Studies.

28. *Anglo-Saxon Chronicle*, entry for the year 851.

29. See Kendrick, *A History of the Vikings.*

30. Svend Tveskaeg in Danish, Sveinn Tiguskaegg in Old Norse (tigu, see also ten), was a king of Denmark and a formidable enemy of England, who would later sit on both the Danish and English thrones. His name literally means "two-beard" or "split beard," most likely because he wore his beard split in two braids. The name is popularly translated as Forkbeard in English. Olaf Trygvason earned the title "Norway's hero King" despite his short five-year reign.

31. Alton is located southwest of Farnham and north of the Isle of Wight in southern England.

32. It is believed that a similar disorder of the bowels, although not quite as deadly as the one in England, struck the Vikings in France, having been caused by a combination of the unusually warm climate and consumption of too many unripe fruits.

33. For more information on the Viking atrocities in England, see the *Anglo-Saxon Chronicle*, entries for the years 1002–1012.

34. The literal translation of the name "Knut" is knot. Another possible meaning is kindness, attributed by friend rather than foe. In English the name is often written as "Canute," because in English pronunciation the letter "k" followed by the letter "n" results in a voiceless "k" (as in the word "knight"), whereas in Danish, "k" followed by "n" is hard, or voiced.

35. See Kendrick, *A History of the Vikings*. The Vikings' victory in Limerick turned out to be small against the powerful Irish kings.
36. See Kendrick, *A History of the Vikings*. "Faroe," from "Faereyjar" in Old Norse, means Sheep Islands.
37. The name *Dublin* is derived from *Dubh Linn* or *Dyflin*, meaning "black pool," and *Wexford* from *Weis Fjord*, "sandy harbor." The Vikings founded both of these towns as well as several others, although it is noted that lasting Viking colonies were for the most part established only in Iceland, the Orkneys and the outer parts of northern and western Scotland.
38. Priit J. Vesilind, *In Search of Vikings*, National Geographic, May 2000.

Chapter 2: Live Hard, Die with Honor

1. The conquest of territory, primarily in England, became important towards the end of the tenth century to the more prominent Norse kings. Rollo the Pirate may have been an exception, because the Frankish king Charles the Simple ceded Normandy to him in 911 as a strategic move to win him over. See Chapter Eleven for more information.
2. Some sources say the Nordic population was barely one million.
3. Dudo of St. Quentin's *Gesta Normannorum*. Goths refer to the people who originated in Scandinavia.
4. Although some distinction is made between the general areas of land raided by Svear, Danes and Norse, most raids consisted of a mix of Nordic peoples. For example, the raid led by the Dane Ragnar Lodbrok against Paris in 845 likely also included a considerable number of Svear.
5. See Kendrick, *A History of the Vikings*.
6. Ibid. Scat = tax. The modern Swedish word for tax is *skatt*.
7. There is speculation that Erik Bloodaxe's name derives from his having killed four of his brothers in a family quarrel.
8. The common English spelling of *ting* is "Thing."
9. The painting *Midvinterblot* (*Midwinter Sacrifice*) by the Swedish artist Carl Larsson (1853–1919) depicts the early Svear King Domalde, whose rule was marked by bad crops and starvation, willingly sacrificing himself at the Uppsala Temple in order to bring his people greater prosperity. This enormous painting, measuring 6.4 x 13.6 meters (21 x 45 feet), is displayed in the National Museum in Stockholm, Sweden, and can also be viewed on the Web.
10. The "branches" of the hand were the fingers, adorned with the generous king's "golden fruits."
11. See Snorri Sturluson, *Saga of Magnus the Good*.
12. Page, *Chronicles of the Vikings*.

13. Harold Godwinson was king of England, but he had Viking blood in his veins.
14. Halfdan was a common name in the Viking Age and is frequently translated as "Half-Dane." It is said that he was "the fifth down" from King Olof Trätälja of Sweden.
15. The Jomsvikings resided at the fort of Jomsborg on Wolin Island off the Polish coast in the Baltic Sea. The Jomsvikings were considered the most disciplined and greatest heroes of the North.
16. *Saga of the Jomsvikings.*
17. Frans G. Bengtsson, *Röde Orm* (Stockholm, 1941), P.A. Norstedt & Söners Förlag. Author's translation from Swedish into English.
18. Page, *Chronicles of the Vikings.*
19. Ibn Rustah, translated by Per Dahlgren, International College, Stockholm.
20. Karl G. Johansson, *Vikingarnas Visdomsord—The Wisdom Words of the Vikings* (Iceland, 1995), Gudrun Publishing. Originally translated into Swedish from *Hávamál*, a group of Icelandic poems approximately 1,000 years old from *The Poetic Edda. Hávamál* means "the words of the high one," in reference to the Norse god Óðinn or Oden, and contains wisdom on how to live well and deal with life's everyday problems, such as friendship, hospitality, loyalty, courage, moderation, worries, pride, poverty, riches, etc.
21. Inscription on the Ingvar Stone located at Gripsholms Slott near Lake Mälaren in Sweden. To give the eagle food meant to kill the enemy and leave his body on the battlefield for the eagles to eat. Särkland was the common name for Africa and the area around the Caspian Sea.
22. Amina Grill & Johannes Mårlöv, *DN, På Stan*, September 23, 2004. (Other rune translations are also from this source.)
23. Bengt Wadbring, *Bengans Historiasidor.*
24. The original rune alphabet, called the older *futharken* after the first six characters, was developed from a southern European alphabet around AD 200. In the Viking Age, the alphabet was simplified to 16 characters, called the younger *futharken.*
25. Although most runes were engraved in stone for posterity, those carved into bone, metal, or wood carried shorter messages that people could transport. When carved in wood, the runes were square rather than round because of the difficulty involved in carving rounded features against the natural grain of the wood.
26. Ibn Fadlan quotes are from Smyser, H.M., *Ibn Fadlan's account of the Rus*, § 83 (New York, 1965), New York University Press.
27. The sword hand was the right hand. In some depictions of the cloak, the sword hand is covered, but the sword, when sheathed, is not. In order to draw a longer weapon successfully, the warrior must do a cross-draw; that is, if right-handed, he wears the weapon on his left side, so

that he can draw it from across his body. With a shorter type weapon, such as a knife, a same side draw is easier.

28. See Paddy Griffith, *The Viking Art of War*.

29. *The Saga of King Sverri of Norway*, translated by J. Stephton (London, 1899), Northvegr Foundation. The origin of the word "bonde," from which "yeoman" is derived, means "commoner," or one who lives by cultivating the land; in other words, a farmer or peasant.

30. Sweden, Norway and Denmark were at war with one another throughout most of their history until 1905, when a forced Sweden-Norway union was finally brought about peacefully. Since then, the Scandinavian countries have remained the best of friends. Previously, Sweden, Norway and Denmark were joined in 1397 in the Union of Kalmar, from which Sweden declared its independence in the bloody liberation war of 1520–23, during the reign of King Gustav Vasa.

CHAPTER 3: Going a-Viking

1. It is doubtful that twelve year olds were in fact capable of fighting and commanding fleets. Knut the Great was sixteen when he accompanied his father, Sven Forkbeard, to England, but was still much too young and inexperienced to successfully control his English dominions after his father's death the following year.

2. Page, *Chronicles of the Vikings*.

3. A warrior typically became a leader of raids through his courage and battlefield prowess, but also through generous gifts to those he commanded. Many so-called kings were "sea-kings" who did not actually have a kingdom to defend. A man could be a king *in* Sweden, but not king *of* Sweden. Rollo the Pirate, answered the Franks demanding to know the origin of his war band and who was in charge: "We are Danes . . . we have come to take Francia by assault"; no one was in charge "for we are of equal power." See Dudo of St. Quentin, *Gesta Normannorum*.

4. Accounts of homesickness are rare, but according to the *Saga of Olaf Haraldson*, Swedish Vikings got homesick and sailed at night, which was a difficult and dangerous undertaking, not stopping until they were home.

5. When a leader was forced to battle other Norsemen at an unsuitable time, notions of courage were sometimes ignored. When they were deeply troubled or unable to devise good defensive strategies against threats from their closest neighbors, many great leaders took to their beds for long periods of time. Earl Hakon is said to have been so troubled over his war problems that he went to bed where he spent many sleepless nights, eating and drinking no more than was needed to support his strength.

6. When he was trying to conquer Norway, Sigvaldi turned coward and fled his enemy. He had to live with the shame and humiliation of his act for the rest of his life. His sorry state drove him to betray King Olaf Trygvason in the battle of Svolder in 1000, in an attempt to rectify his situation by befriending the Norse kings.

7. Snorri Sturluson, *Saga of Harald Hardrade.*

8. The literal translation is "beachchop," meaning landing and stealing livestock for food for the continued voyage. Norse warriors needed to be well-fed and rested at the start of battle and tried to find most food near the beach so as to avoid leaving the ship unguarded. Vikings frequently did *strandhugg* even among their own people. To provide the crew with enough food to sustain them for a journey to England, the ship's leader might decide to plunder a local farmer a few miles down the coast from departure point. The word *strandhugg* is still used in Sweden today to signal lunchtime, especially by families sailing the archipelago, but also by people traveling by car.

9. Jordan, *Viking Trail East.* Slaves could do much of the manual labor aboard the ship. The Swedish Vikings also went to Constantinople and traded slaves they had taken from Russia in return for spices and silk.

10. Daniel Ryden, *Olav gjorde ölintag till lag,* or *Olav made beer-drinking law,* Sydsvenskan, June 23, 2005. "Obligatory" beer drinking is to this day a valued activity in the Nordic countries. On no other day of the year is so much beer consumed as during the midsummer festival.

11. Jordan, *Viking Trail East.* In the nineteenth century, King Karl XIV Johan (Jean-Baptiste Bernadotte), one of Napoleon's marshals who had been imported to Sweden to strengthen the country's weak leadership, proclaimed that alcohol would be the ruin of the Swedish people.

12. Snorri Sturluson, *The Ynglinga Saga.*

13. *Ulf* = wolf; *hedner* = a man with a cloak.

14. The Swedish word for "berserk" is "bärsärk," meaning "in shirt only" or "unarmored." It has also been said to mean "in bear shirt" because the berserker took on the mental state of an animal and wore bearskins (although wolf-skins are mentioned in Gettir's *Saga*) impenetrable to an enemy's weapons. A berserker could go into battle with no fear of sustaining a significant wound.

15. The *fly agaric* is a poisonous, easily recognizable mushroom that grows in abundance in the forests of the Nordic countries. The most common type is four to eight inches in height, has a sturdy stem and a large red cap with white spots. Certain of these mushroom types have been used as intoxicating drugs in a number of cultures for over six thousand years. The red version is less poisonous than the white one which can be deadly even in very small amounts. The effects generally last between six and eight hours, during which time a state of intoxication,

likened to a mixture of alcohol and cannabis, is produced. As the effect wears off, the user becomes confused and can experience dry mouth, gasping breath and loss of feeling in the extremities, which is followed by a sleep-induced state of an hour or two characterized by euphoria and hallucinations. The red version of the mushroom can also induce paranoia, aggression and even blind rage.

16. Frans G. Bengtsson, *Röde Orm* (Stockholm, 1941), P.A. Norstedt & Söners Förlag. Author's translation from Swedish into English.

17. The mark, the common Nordic weight of the period, was roughly equivalent to 7 and 1/5 ounces, or two hundred grams.

CHAPTER 4: Building the Ship

1. Modern Viking ship replicas have reached top speeds of twenty to twenty-five knots, which would have placed England little more than a day's journey away. But it is unlikely that such speeds could have been maintained for any significant length of time. On longer ocean trips, a ship's effective speed has been estimated to be in the three to six knot range.

2. A *dœgr* is defined as twelve hours, half a day. When night was spent on land, travel would naturally be slower, even in good weather conditions.

3. Fewer casualties were expected onboard a merchant ship. The *knörr* could carry a smaller crew and leave room for more goods. It has been estimated that the largest of these transport ships could carry more than twenty tons of cargo. One of the *knörr* shipwrecks discovered in the harbor of Haithabu in northern Germany is estimated to have had a carrying capacity of forty tons of cargo. The presence of fewer men on these ships, however, also inhibited rowing on the open seas.

4. No actual dragonhead decorations have been found, but the Viking sagas describe them extensively. The *Oseberg* ship, the most well-preserved Viking ship found, has carved spirals at the bow and stern. King Olaf Haraldson built a ship he called the *Visund* (buffalo), that is said to have had a gilded bison's head on the bow and its tail aft on the sternposts. Olaf Trygvason's *Long Serpent* had a dragonhead with open throat, and King Harald Hardrade built a ship in 1062 with a golden-maned serpent head. In the early twelfth century, King Sigurd the Crusader presented the dragonhead from the bow of his ship, a superb work of Norse craftsmanship, as a gift to the emperor of Constantinople. The sagas also note that the dragonheads could be removed when sailing into a friendly harbor—perhaps the reason they have not survived.

5. Evan Hadingham, *Secrets of Norse Ships*, Nova Online.

6. Sailing in the dark was not common, but summer nights in the Nordic countries are predominantly light, making it possible to sail well into the night.

7. John Larsson, *Vikingen var shifteholdsarbejder—The Viking Was a Shift Worker* (Denmark, 1998). The Swedish city, Viksjö, (note the similarity between *vik-sjö* [also *veckosjö*] and *sjó-víka*) is located approximately one *sjóvíka* from the first Swedish city, Birka, a trading town and Viking stronghold. There is speculation that the term derives from the travel distance between the two cities. In other words, leaving Birka and reaching Viksjö, a Viking could expect to be relieved at the oars, also expressed as *vek vid årorna* (took turns at the oars). Other names in the Swedish archipelago that probably refer to the places where work duties were shifted are: *Ombyteshällen* (the changing rock) and *Växlet* (the trade-off).

8. The dragon, or dragon ship, was associated with the snake. Ships without removable dragonheads often had spiraling snakes at the bow and stern. Carvings of snakes are also commonly found on rune stones. In 1157, King Eystein Magnuson set sail with his ship, the *Great Dragon*, modeled after the *Long Serpent*.

9. King Olaf Trygvason's *Saga* says the keel was seventy-four ells when resting on grass, though this may be an exaggeration. An ell is approximately 1.14 meters, which would have made the length of the keel 84 meters (276 feet) at the start of construction. In another account, a man's height is described as five ells, with an ell equal to six handbreadths. An ell is also described as approximately twenty-two inches. According to this description, a keel of 74 ells would have measured approximately 136 feet. The keel of the *Gokstad* excavated in Norway in 1880 was built of a straight grown oak, approximately 25 meters (82 feet) in height.

10. The ship was unusual in that the bow and the stern were identical in construction (although the placement of the serpent head and tail ornaments often were not). The ship's design allowed for quick reversals in direction in narrow waterways, eliminating the need to turn it around or execute complicated maneuvers.

11. The exact location of Svolder is unknown, but thought to be in the Strait of Öresund between Denmark and southern Sweden.

12. Pine was used more extensively towards the end of the Viking Age, when many of the magnificent oak trees had already been felled.

13. In Sweden, it is said that an oak tree grows for five hundred years, lives for five hundred years, and dies for five hundred years.

14. Ship and boat building did not originate in the Nordic countries during the Viking Age, but predate it by several hundred perhaps even one

thousand years. The Vikings, however, perfected the design to meet their specific objectives.

15. The gangplank found on the *Oseberg* ship excavated in Norway in 1904 measures 6.9 meters (22.6 feet) long and 30 centimeters (12 inches) wide, with twenty-three rungs cut from the upper side.

16. Sons of Norway, Gyda Varden, Lodge # 21.

17. See Arne Emil Christensen, *The Vikings*, Nytt fra Norge, produced for the Ministry of Foreign Affairs.

18. *Wikinger Museum Haithabu, Text of the Exhibition*, translated by Peter A. Mott.

CHAPTER 5: Seamanship and Navigation

1. Tacitus, c. AD 55–AD 117, *Tacitus' Germania*, translated by Thomas Gordon, The ORB: Online Reference Book for Medieval Studies.

2. The Vikings lived five hundred years prior to the discovery of America by Columbus. Although they did not always end up where initially intended, they never got quite as lost as Columbus, who thought he had arrived in India.

3. Johan Kock, *Om Vikingarnas och Nordbornas Navigation (On the Vikings' and the Nordic People's Navigation)*. Author's translation from Swedish into English.

4. See Page, *Chronicles of the Vikings*.

5. The Bjarmer were people living along the White Sea who engaged in trade, mainly fur, in Finland and northern Sweden. Johan Kock, *Om Vikingarnas och Nordbornas Naviagation (On the Vikings' and the Nordic People's Navigation)*. Author's translation from Swedish into English.

6. Sometimes the dead were stored under the floor boards and brought back home, but at other times they were left behind, since home could be more than a few days' journey away. For example, a Viking crew might decide to be gone most of the summer, sailing up and down a country's coastline and plundering several towns before returning home for the winter.

7. *Ledh* means way, *sagari* means sayer. Later, with the establishment of the *Leidgangr*, the first official military fleet, a guide was hired and paid to show the way.

8. The Scandinavian countries are located at a north latitude of approximately sixty degrees. Above the Arctic Circle in the northernmost parts of the area, there is no nightfall at all in the summer. Slightly farther south the summer nights are overwhelmingly light and approach a state of dusk for only a few hours between sunset and sunrise. Most of the

Viking travels around Scandinavia took place between north latitude fifty and seventy degrees.

9. See Johan Kock, *Om Vikingarnas och Nordbornas Naviagation (On the Vikings' and the Nordic People's Navigation)*. Stjärn-Oddi Helgason (*stjärn* means star) worked up a chart in Iceland for the motion of the sun in the twelfth century, so this method of navigation could only have been used during the later part of the Viking Age or Early Middle Age.

10. See Griffith, *The Viking Art of War*.

11. The North Sea consists of undrinkable salt water. The Baltic Sea is made up of brackish water, a mixture of salt water from the North Sea and fresh water from rivers and rainfall, and is also not good for drinking.

12. The Franks felt that it was only in the power of God, not humans, to defeat these Nordic sailors. To this day, one of the few successful victories over the Norsemen is celebrated in Tarbes, near the Adour River in southwestern France. See Bengt Wadbring, *Bengans Historiasidor*.

13. This is the same raid described in Chapters Two and Four, where Thorer ended up killing Karle in a dispute over the booty.

14. Tidal atlases and nautical almanacs find that at Dover mean high water springs are 6.7 meters (22 feet) and mean high water neaps are 5.3 meters (17 feet). See Hugh Tucker, *English Channel Swim*, August 2004.

15. According to Fredrik Koivusalo, skipper on the *Heimløsa Rus*.

16. Snorri Sturluson, *King Olaf Trygvason's Saga*.

17. Bertil Daggfeldt, *Vikingen Roddaren*, Fornvännen # 78. Author's translation from Swedish into English.

18. Karl G. Johansson, *Vikingarnas Visdomsord—The Wisdom Words of the Vikings* (Iceland, 1995), Gudrun Publishing. Originally translated into Swedish from *Hávamál*, a group of Icelandic poems approximately one thousand years old from *The Poetic Edda*. *Hávamál* means "the words of the high one," in reference to the Norse god Óðinn or Oden, and contains wisdom on how to live well and deal with life's everyday problems, such as friendship, hospitality, loyalty, courage, moderation, worries, pride, poverty, riches, etc. Author's translation from Swedish into English.

Chapter 6: Weapons and Armor

1. The war-arrow, a symbolic token, was sent from farm to farm to instruct men owing military service to appear for muster. In Sweden, a *budkafveln* (message roll, also called *härrör*, translated literally as "army tube") was sent out when the king wanted to marshal his troops for war or had other important news to tell the people. The message roll was a staff on which the names of those who failed to convey the message or refused

to obey the muster were marked; offenders were punished by hanging or the burning of their houses. The message roll was supposed to "proceed forward," never backward; if it arrived from the east, it had to continue to the west, if from the south, to the north. Since the Swedish countryside was sparsely populated, it was not difficult to figure out which house to deliver the message to next; if the designated recipient was not at home, it was left above his bed or above the door to his house.

According to Dudo of St. Quentin, a tenth-century historian and Dean of St. Quentin in France, it was the Norsemen's custom to smear their heads with sacrificial blood before setting sail.

2. Because the Vikings could sail their ships backward and forward without turning around, an armored bow and stern could be used for ramming other ships at sea.

3. According to the Annals of St. Neorts, if the Vikings marched in victory, the raven in the center of the banner looked as though it were flapping its wings; if defeated, the raven dropped motionless.

4. Some of the Norsemen's inspiration may have come from foreign works of art. Carvings were also made in wood on church doors, few of which have survived. Ornamentation can also be seen on rune stones, often depicting a slithering snake.

5. See Lee A. Jones, *The Serpent in the Sword* (United Kingdom, 1998), The Fourteenth Park Lane Arms Fair.

6. Vindland was the land of the Wends, a western Slavic people who occupied the southern Baltic region. Some scholars speculate that Vindland was Finland.

7. The blood groove was thought to promote bleeding without removing the sword from the wound. Although according to legend the groove was for poison, a more probable function was to make the sword lighter in weight; on smaller swords and knives, blood grooves were often purely decorative.

8. Ring-mail is mentioned more often than plate-armor in the Icelandic sagas. An exception was Ivar, son of Hakon Mage, who fastened a boathook to Gregorius Dagson's body, but because he was wearing a platecoat of armor, he was only slightly wounded. See Snorri Sturluson, *Saga of Hakon Herdebreid*.

9. Swords that appear to have been shortened by a few inches have been found in children's graves.

10. See Mike Knibbs, *The Dane Axe*, Anmod Dracan History Reenactment Society.

11. The first part of the word—*scrama*—is derived from the Indo-European root of score, or *sker*, which is related to cutting or slicing; for example,

shear, scissors or skirmish. The Old English word *sceort* means to cut. It is also related to the German word *schirm*, meaning to shield or protect. The second part of the word—*sax*—means scissors in Swedish. Thus the *scramasax* was an object that cut, sliced, divided, shielded and protected.

12. The incident of Thorer Sel humiliating Asbjorn by stealing his sail had now resulted in the death of both men, with more slayings following as family members avenged their dead. Although it was considered more honorable to kill with the sword than with the spear because a sword killing gave the combatant and any witnesses positive confirmation of the kill, in this case the distinguishing feature of a projectile weapon gave the finder positive identification of the wielder, allowing the finder to avenge the crime.

13. A span is a unit of length based on the width of the spread-open human hand, from the tip of the thumb to the tip of the little finger; one span is equal to approximately nine inches. The "dew-shoe" may be part of the handle, hilt, guard or sheath of a sword, perhaps even the tip of the sword when the sword is stood vertically on the pommel. The Old Norse/Icelandic term for the word is *döggskórinn*. In Scandinavian languages a word can have more than one meaning and sentence context is used to determine exact meaning. In breaking down the word dew-shoe, the first part of the word could possibly mean either *dagg* (dew) or *dagger*—in other words, a short sword or knife. The second part of the word, although it means shoe, could also mean a protective casing, hence it is possible that the dew-shoe is the dagger or sword casing or sheath. But it could also be the guard, the "dagger protection," or what protects the hand from the opponent's dagger blade.

14. Linden shields are mentioned in the poem of the Battle of Maldon in 991.

15. The existence of a metal rim remains speculative because in most shield finds only the iron centerpiece remains.

16. Shield-walls with overlapping shields to strengthen the defense was a battlefield tactic used to protect against arrows and spears in land warfare.

17. The Viking period is generally said to have lasted between 793 (raid on Lindisfarne monastery) and 1066 (the battle of Stamford Bridge), but smaller battles were waged for some time thereafter.

18. The Vikings commonly acquired enemy armor in battle, but Olaf Haraldson might also have engaged in trade for the foreign helmets.

19. The notion of horned helmets, so often depicted in literature, may have been a historical mistake stemming from the find of a Celtic helmet with horns. Horned helmets may also have been used for ceremonial

purposes. For example, the Oseberg tapestry, uncovered with the *Oseberg* ship in 1904 and which can be viewed at the Viking Ship Museum in Oslo, Norway, depicts in the upper left corner a man wearing a horned helmet who is leading a funeral procession. Monks who were robbed by the Vikings considered them to be the most satanic of peoples, with the horns symbolizing the devil.

CHAPTER 7: Military Organization and Battlefield Tactics

1. The Vikings' opponents were many: Franks, Bretons, Scots, Irish, Romans, Italians, Russians, Slavs and last, but not least, other Norse.
2. Harald Hardrade, during his campaigns in Serkland, Sicily, Constantinople and Jerusalem, is said to have fought eighteen battles but even the most experienced warriors seldom fought more than three to four battles in their lifetime.
3. Although most raids were comprised of just a few ships, several smaller parties sometimes joined together and formed larger fleets; for example, in the Paris raids in 845 and 885, said to have comprised fleets of six hundred and seven hundred ships respectively, the fleets stretched across the Seine for more than six miles.
4. The poor had an opportunity to improve their lot through battle which probably motivated them to be good fighters.
5. Some accounts say that one hundred men went to Jomsborg, of which eighty were sworn and forty went away. The "one hundred" composed of eighty and forty referred to here was, in fact, what was known as the "long hundred" of 120. The *Anglo-Saxon Chronicle* and the Old Icelandic Sagas use numbers and totals with a factor of twelve, which explains how a base unit "decade" of "100" becomes 120. See Carol F. Justus, *Numeracy and the Germanic Upper Decades* (Washington DC, 1996), Journal of Indo-European Studies # 24. The Saga of Olaf Trygvason describes how King Harald Gormson ordered a levy of men from all over his kingdom and sailed with 600 ships, in reality 720 ships, if counted in "long hundreds."
6. *Leidgangr* means warfare at sea.
7. See Per Åkesson, *Ledung och Lotsar* (Stockholm, 1996), Sportdykaren.
8. See Bengt Wadbring, *Bengans Historiasidor.*
9. Birka, Sweden's first city built in the mid-700s, was located along several important trade routes on Lake Mälaren by the Baltic Sea.
10. See Micke Jägerbrand, *Här bodde Sveriges första yrkesarme (Here lived Sweden's first professional army)*, Aftonbladet, August 8, 2001.
11. Ringerike was a dominion in Norway. Because the Nordic countries

were not united under a single king, many smaller "kingdoms" existed in the region.

12. Snorri Sturluson, *Saga of Olaf Haraldson.*
13. Nidaros Cathedral is in the historic city of Trondheim by the Nid River where King Olaf Haraldson, also known as St. Olaf, was buried after his death in Stiklestad in 1030.
14. Snorri Sturluson, *Saga of Olaf Haraldson.*
15. In general the Vikings preferred to fight on foot rather than on horseback, although one account tells of how Otkell put spurs on his feet, rode up to his opponent, Gunnar, and drove a spur into Gunnar's ear, causing a huge gash.
16. Snorri Sturluson, *Saga of Harald Hardrade.*
17. Kalf Arnason at the battle in Stiklestad against King Olaf Haraldson.
18. A skerry is a small island common to the waters around the Scandinavian countries.
19. The true halberd is a medieval weapon that first became prominent in Europe in the fourteenth century, but variations of it, designed primarily for use against mounted warriors, existed even in the Viking Age and earlier.
20. Dreams were commonly interpreted and said to determine the future.

Chapter 8: The Viking Elite of Jomsborg

1. *The Saga of the Jomsvikings.* The *Saga of the Jomsvikings* also discusses the elite force's recruiting practices.
2. According to the Jelling stone which he raised for his parents, Gorm and Thyra, Harald Bluetooth "won Denmark and all of Norway and made the Danes Christian." Harald and his brother Knut raided in England during King Aethelstan's reign, 925–940, but Knut was killed by an arrow and Harald became sole successor to the Danish throne.
3. The dialog in this chapter, translated by the author, is based on information from a number of sources, primarily the *Saga of the Jomsvikings* and *Berättelser ur svenska historien (Stories from Swedish History)* by C. Georg Starbäck and P.O. Bäckström (Stockholm, 1885), A.L. Normans Boktryckeri-Aktiebolag.
4. The Icelandic sagas record that great warriors and kings frequently took to their beds, sometimes remaining to the death if life became too much to handle.
5. Disagreement surrounds the founding of Jomsborg. Although there is archaeological evidence of a ring wall and harbor in the area, some scholars say that Palnatoke and the Jomsborg fort are purely fictional,

that King Harald Gormsson (Bluetooth) founded it as a rampart against the Wends, that the Jomsvikings were part of the king's warriors, that Styrbjörn the Strong, not Palnatoke, was the first leader and that the deciding battle in Hjörungavåg was fought during King Harald's reign, not King Sven Forkbeard's.

6. As for a number of Norse kings, it was common for children to be brought up by foster-parents. Fostering another man's child strengthened the bonds between families and lent prestige and security, which is why kings and other men of high standing often parented one another's sons. Though foster-fathers frequently grew quite attached to their foster-children, the practice, which could be seen as a "friendly hostage" situation, was sometimes used as a means of deterring threats to country or security.

    This was the boy who would become the much-reputed Sven Forkbeard and later set out to conquer England.

7. Some accounts say thirty ships, presupposing that Palnatoke did not match the last gift of twelve from King Harald. *Jomsvikingasagan* from *Berättelser ur svenska historien (Stories from Swedish History)* by C. Georg Starbäck and P.O. Bäckström (Stockholm, 1885), A.L Normans Boktryckeri-Aktiebolag, states that Sven had twenty-four ships. There are other instances in this story when sources differ as to the number of ships and men in a fleet.

8. According to Lee M. Hollander's translation of the *Saga of the Jomsvikings*, the confrontation took place on the east coast of central Jutland, since it is unlikely that the island of Bornholm had the capacity to harbor such a large fleet.

9. This event is recounted in the *Saga of the Jomsvikings*. After Palnatoke had proven his skill by shooting the apple off his son's head, the king questioned why he had another arrow hidden in his waistband. Palnatoke answered: "It was meant for you, king, had the first shot missed the apple."

    The facts about the Jomsvikings are sketchy. Some scholars say that a man named Toke (unrelated to Palnatoke) shot the arrow that killed the king in 986 or 987. Other sources state that King Harald Gormsson Bluetooth died in exile at Jomsborg, driven away by his illegitimate son, Sven Forkbeard. After Bluetooth's exile, Sven became regent of Denmark.

10. Vindland was in all likelihood the land of the Wends, a Slavonic people who had come to fear the power of the Danish kings. It has been said that in about 960, Harald Bluetooth Gormsson tried to take this profitable dominion by force.

11. As previously noted, historians disagree on whether this fort ever existed, and if it did, who built it, whether Palnatoke and his warriors

took control of the fort after it was already in existence, or if Styrbjörn the Strong, nephew of the Swedish king Erik Segersäll (the Victorious) later drove Palnatoke from the fort. Others say that the founding of Jomsborg was an attempt at independence from the Danish king, for whom the Jomsvikings had little respect.

12. According to *Jomsvikingasagan* from *Berättelser ur svenska historien (Stories from Swedish History)* by C. Georg Starbäck and P.O. Bäckström (Stockholm, 1885), A.L Normans Boktryckeri-Aktiebolag, no one younger than fifteen could join the fort. The *Saga of the Jomsvikings* claims eighteen was the minimum age.

13. Wesete and his sons later avenged this act, ransacking Strutharald's farms and parading around in his famous hat. In order to avoid further battle, King Sven was made to act as arbitrator between the parties.

14. According to some sources, there were 120 men, probably because the counting was in "long-hundreds" (100 equals 120).

15. Some sources state that Vagn's father gave him one ship and sixty men, that Wesete, his maternal grandfather, gave him one ship and sixty men, and that the crew chosen by Vagn was between the ages of eighteen and twenty, except for Vagn who was twelve.

16. Some sources say that this was the second time the Jomsvikings kidnapped King Sven Forkbeard. The first time, they asked for the king's weight in gold to release him and many people from the Danish dominions scrambled to supply the king with the money, selling their gold ornaments and buying the king's farms. The second time, the women of Denmark had to give up their jewelry to buy the king his freedom.

17. It was considered manly to make a grand vow and keep it. King Erik Edmundsson Väderhatt (Weather Hat) of Sweden once vowed that he would not rest until he had won a kingdom in Viken as large as the one owned at one time by King Sigurd Ring and his son, Ragnar Lodbrok. King Harald Fairhair once promised that he would not cut his hair until he had subjugated all of Norway under his power.

18. Also Hjorunga Bay. This battle, thought to have taken place in 986, is considered the one at which the Jomsvikings were defeated, although many survived and returned home to Denmark.

Chapter 9: The Rus in the Varangian Guard

1. The Khazar world was near the Caspian Sea. The word *Khazar* is of Turkish origin and means wanderer, to describe the semi-nomadic people of Central Asia, many of whom converted to Judaism.

2. The Varangians or Varjagi are mentioned first in the *Russian Primary Chronicle* as having arrived from beyond the Baltic Sea around the middle of the ninth century.

3. Rurik's kinsman, Oleg (from the Norse name Helgi), founded the grand principality of Kiev around 860 (880 according to some sources), and Oleg's successor, Igor (from the Swedish name Ingvar), believed to be Rurik's son, is considered the founder of the Russian Rurik dynasty which remained in power until 1598. Some scholars believe that it was the Danish King Rorik, who reigned in Denmark 853–873, not the Swedish Rurik, who founded the Russian state. One theory, still unproved, is that the Slavic tribes were torn with internal strife and therefore petitioned the Vikings for strong leaders who could reestablish order. The Slavs are said to have told the Norsemen: "Our land is large and fruitful, but lacks organization. Come rule over us." The word Rus is believed to be derived from the Finnish word for Sweden—*Ruotsi*—meaning rowers or seamen, derived in turn from *Ro(d)slagen* (the "d" has since been dropped), a district in the Lake Mälaren area, the third largest lake in Sweden with outlets to the Baltic Sea, to this day a popular destination for boating enthusiasts. *Roslagen* translates as "row beats," or oars beating against the water. Others say Rus simply means fair or ruddy, as the Arab chronicler, Ibn Fadlan, described the Norsemen in his account of the Rus.

4. The water referred to was probably the Baltic Sea, also called the Varangian Sea, and the island, Gotland, the larger of two islands east of the south tip of Sweden. Finds from Gotland account for over half of all the silver discovered in Sweden and includes more than 140,000 silver coins. Most of the coins date to around AD 900 and are of Islamic, German and English design. Gotland is therefore believed to have been a supply stop for the Vikings and an important link to seafaring and trade.

5. Svithiod is another name for Sweden, also identified with Russia or Oden's kingdom. Serkland was the land of the Saracens, North Africa or any Arab land. Blueland was Saharan and sub-Saharan Africa, so called because of the "blue men," or Berber/Tuareg nomads who wore blue garments and long blue scarves around their heads and faces. Most Varangians did not come directly from Sweden, but from the Swedish settlement at the southern end of Lake Ladoga.

6. Archaeological evidence points to the establishment of a Swedish colony/ stronghold on the southern shore of Lake Ladoga, for which the Norse name was Aldeigjuborg. The settlement, believed to have been established in the late 700s, was destroyed by fire, then rebuilt and fortified.

7. Page, *Chronicles of the Vikings.*

8. Kendrick, *A History of the Vikings*, from the account of Ibn Rustah, approximately 912.

9. See the *Nestorian Chronicle*, Bengt Wadbring, *Bengans Historiasidor*.
10. See the *Russian Chronicle*, Radio Islam.
11. Some historical accounts say the fleet numbered between ten thousand and fifteen thousand ships, though this seems excessive.
12. Greek Fire was "liquid fire," a secret weapon which Eastern Roman emperors hurled at enemy ships. It is thought to have consisted of liquid petroleum, naphtha and burning pitch. It is similar to modern-day napalm, as the fire continued burning under almost any conditions. Greek Fire is believed to have been used against Viking fleets in the Black Sea in 860, 941 and 1043.
13. Although the people of this era were generally smaller than today (verified through the smaller sword grips), the Norsemen were considerably taller than the warriors of most other nations.
14. The Varangian guardsmen were paid forty "gold pieces" a year (according to Eric Christiansen, *The Norsemen in the Viking Age* [Oxford, 2002], Blackwell Publishers, Ltd.), or ten to fifteen "gold solidi" per month of service (according to Kendrick, *A History of the Vikings*), as well as other benefits, such as quarters, food and special bonuses. These attractive salaries are believed to be responsible for the later requirement that foreigners pay for their commission in the guard.
15. The Norsemen's unshakable loyalty to the Varangian Guard has been questioned because of mutiny in the reign of Alexius' predecessor, Nicephorus III Botaniates (1078–1081), and fear of a transfer of allegiance to the northern kings accompanying the warriors, who could address the troops in their own tongue.
16. In *asatro*, the Norse pagan religion, oaths were sworn to the goddess Var, who punished those who broke them.
17. See Graeme Walker, *Everyday life with the emperor's varangians*, Varangian Voice, issue 38.
18. From the *Alexiad of Anna Comnena*, Book XV, translated by Elizabeth A. Dawes (London, 1928), The ORB: Online Reference Book for Medieval Studies. Anna Comnena is considered the world's first female historian.
19. More information about Robert Guiscard and the Battle at Dyrrakhion can be found in the *Alexiad of Anna Comnena*, Book IV, translated by Elizabeth A. Dawes (London, 1928), The ORB: Online Reference Book for Medieval Studies.
20. Historical records, both chronicles and runes, speak of the Nordic people's presence in the area. For example, the Piraeus lion, a Greek sculpture made of marble and originally stationed at the Piraeus harbor at Athens, displays runic "graffiti" carved into its flanks dating to the second half of the eleventh century: "Hakon, combined with Ulf, with Asmund, and with Orn, conquered this port . . . Egil was waging war, together with Ragnar, in Romania and Armenia." It is believed that

Harald the Tall (Hardrade), who worked as a mercenary for the Byzantine emperor, ordered the inscription. (See Eric Mader, *The Lion from Piraeus*, September 2003.) Runic graffiti also scars a balustrade in Istanbul's Hagia Sophia, but only the name "Halvdan" remains legible. (See Robert Paul Jordan, *Viking Trail East*, National Geographic, March 1985.)

21. Mail shirts were commonly knee length with wide sleeves. The Byzantines had two types of armor: scale, made of small plates of iron, horn or hardened leather attached to a backing and overlapping downward, and the lamellar, *klibanion*, made of similar plates, but overlapping upward and more complex than chain mail. The plates of the lamellar were fixed to a backing and were originally laced to each other and later riveted, with leather strips between horizontal rows to protect the laces from wear. Helmets normally did not have nose guards, but a layer of mail hangings or padded cloth protected the back of the neck and the face except for the eyes. (For more information, see Steven Lowe, *The Armour of the Varangian Guards.*)

22. Steven Lowe, *The Armour of the Varangian Guards.*

23. The Greek sea is mentioned in Snorri Sturluson's account of the Norse in his *Chronicle of the Kings of Norway*. It is not clear as to whether the Greek sea refers to the Black Sea, the Sea of Marmara or the Aegean Sea.

24. The custom of the Varangian Guard to plunder the palaces was called *"poluta-svarf."* *The Chronicle of the Kings of Norway*, by Snorri Sturluson, states that Harald Hardrade plundered palaces three times during his service in the Byzantine Empire, 1035–1043.

25. Snorri Sturluson, *Saga of Harald Hardrade.*

26. Kirjalax was the name by which the Varangians knew Emperor Alexius I.

27. The Norns, *Urðr, Verdandi, Skuld* (past, present, future) were three wise maids, keepers of Yggdrasil, the tree of life, which was rooted in a spring, but stretched from the underworld to the heavens and created tension between the gods and the giants. *Urðr* is fate, or that which was or has been; *Verdandi* is the present, or that which is in existence; *Skuld* is what will be, or that which is destined. What the Norns wove into the tapestry of life and cut into the runes of fate could not be changed.

28. Karl G. Johansson, *Vikingarnas Visdomsord—The Wisdom Words of the Vikings* (Iceland, 1995), Gudrun Publishing. Originally translated into Swedish from *Hávamál*, a group of Icelandic poems approximately one thousand years old from *The Poetic Edda*. *Hávamál* means "the words of the high one," in reference to the Norse god Óðinn or Oden and contains wisdom on how to live well and deal with life's everyday problems, such as friendship, hospitality, loyalty, courage, moderation, worries, pride, poverty, riches, etc. Author's translation from Swedish into English.

CHAPTER 10: Ragnar Lodbrok and his Sons, c. 750–850

1. *Kråka* means "crow." She was given this name by an ugly poor couple who adopted her after killing her foster-father. Her real name was Aslög.

2. The name popularly translates as "Boneless," although the Swedish word *ben* can be translated as both "bone" and "leg." Ivar was most probably legless (or lacked use of his legs), rather than boneless which is why he had to be carried to the battlefield on a shield, but could still shoot with a bow and arrow. Although some imply that he acquired his name because he "lacked backbone" or was "spineless," there is no evidence for this.

3. According to the legend of the Raven Banner, the standard belonged to Ragnar Lodbrok's son, Ubbe, who was killed at Ubbelaw in 878 and buried by the Danes in a huge mound in Yorkshire. On his death the banner was captured. The Raven Banner also appears in stories about King Knut the Great (Danish regent of England from 1016) at the battle of Ashingdon, Essex. The Danes had a banner with a peculiar characteristic: there were no figures embroidered on the simple light-colored silk. However, during wartime a raven could always be seen on the banner. According to the Annals of St. Neorts, if victory was at hand for the Vikings, the raven in the center of the banner would become restless and spread its wings, but when defeat seemed likely, it would hang motionless. Ragnar claimed to be a direct descendent of Oden whose ravens, Hugin and Munin, flew far, reporting to him everything they had seen. The verb "raven" (*röva* in Swedish) means piracy or plunder.

4. The dialogue in this chapter is author's translation/interpretation based on information found in a number of sources, mainly from *Berättelser ur svenska historien (Stories from Swedish History)* by C. Georg Starbäck and P.O. Bäckström (Stockholm, 1885), A.L. Normans Boktryckeri-Aktiebolag.

   Some sources say the brothers mistook the city of Luna in the ancient part of Italy for Rome, and this is why they never actually invaded Rome.

5. Ragnar Lodbrok's song in the snake pit from *Berättelser ur svenska historien (Stories from Swedish History)* by C. Georg Starbäck and P.O. Bäckström (Stockholm, 1885), A. L. Normans Boktryckeri-Aktiebolag. Author's translation into English from Swedish: "Ej gråter hjelten för döden i det härliga Valhall. Ej kommer jag sorgbunden till Odinssalen."

6. *Tafl* (also *Hnefatafl*) was a popular board game played in the Viking Age simulating a raid.

7. This may be the origin of the myth of the "blood eagle" (*rista blodörn* in Swedish). Since no other evidence has been found to show that this was a common practice among the Vikings, the eagle may simply be metaphorical. The year of King Aella's death was 867. Sources say the Danes

killed him and it is unclear as to whether indeed Ragnar Lodbrok's sons committed the act.

8. According to some sources, it was Hinguar (Hingwar, possibly Ivar) who ordered King Edmund beheaded.

9. Ragnar Lodbrok's song in the snake pit from *Berättelser ur svenska historien (Stories from Swedish History)* by C. Georg Starbäck and P.O. Bäckström (Stockholm, 1885), A. L. Normans Boktryckeri-Aktiebolag.

CHAPTER 11: Rollo the Pirate, c. 860–933

1. See also Rolf Ragnvaldsson, Gånge-Rolf, Rolf Ganger, Rolf the Walker, Hrollaugr in Old Norse, and sometimes, but rarely, Robert, a name he might have received at his baptism. Scholars are at odds over whether the historical Rollo, the first Duke of Normandy, is the same person as the legendary, partly historical Rolf the Walker, who had to walk whenever he traveled by land because his size and weight were too great for a horse to bear.
    Friesland is the northwestern region of the Netherlands that borders the North Sea.

2. Conflicting sources say that Rollo's origin is either Danish or Norwegian and that his father was named Carillus (from Kettil). Most historians are in agreement, however, that his army was comprised primarily of Danes.

3. Gurim was possibly Guthorm.

4. The Angles were a Germanic people from the Schleswig area who settled in East Anglia, Britain.

5. See also Hastein and Anstign. Dudo of St. Quentin describes this same episode while referring to Anstign, "himself formerly an invader of France." Hasting, Hastein and Anstign may be the same person. With the exception of the runes, the Vikings had no written language and names were learned according to how they were pronounced.

6. This is William Longsword, who succeeded Rollo as Duke of Normandy in 927.

7. Dudo of St. Quentin's *Gesta Normannorum.*

8. Ibid.

9. Ibid.

10. Ibid.

11. Charles the Simple lived up to his name by giving the Vikings more land than had any other European king. Some historians say that there is no evidence that Rollo was involved in the battle of Chartres, which may explain why Charles agreed to cede territory to the pirate. Others believe that the Norse settlement of the area now called Normandy and the treaty were not meant to be permanent and that the Franks

intended to recover their losses later. It is also possible that the land was given to Rollo because the Franks were unable to control it. It was clear, however, that Rollo took whatever and as much as he could and the king, a diplomatic strategist, saw an opportunity for protection by not opposing his acquisition of the region.

12. Some modern historians question Rollo's marriage to Gisla.

13. Rollo is referred to as the first duke of Normandy, sometimes also as Count of Rouen, probably a more accurate reflection of his area of authority, until the region expanded to include all that is today Normandy.

14. According to Herman Lindqvist, Swedish journalist, historian and author.

15. William the Conqueror became king of England through the battle of Hastings in 1066.

16. From Rollo's vision and how he recalled it when descending from his ships in Rouen and seeing the desolation of the country. See Dudo of St. Quentin's *Gesta Normannorum*.

CHAPTER 12: Erik Segersäll, The Victorious, 945–995

1. According to some sources, Erik was the son of Björn Eriksson (making his surname Björnsson, not Emundsson) and ruled together with his brother, Olof Björnsson. It is possible that Emund and Björn were also co-rulers, just as Erik and Olof would become. Erik Segersäll was the grandson of Erik Väderhatt (Weather Hat), who was so lucky with weather that he only had to remove his hat and point it in the direction he wanted to sail for the wind to blow his way.

2. Björn's real name was Björn Olofsson. The name *Styrbjörn* derives from his unruly nature; he was told that he must learn to control himself and be patient until he turned sixteen (*styra sig*), though *styra* also means "lead," perhaps because he later conquered the Jomsvikings and became their leader; *ostyrig* means "unruly." He acquired the epithet *the Strong* for obvious reasons.

3. See also battle of Fyris Wolds, derived from the Old Norse *Fyrva* ("to ebb"). Fyrisvallarna was a marshland near Old Upsala, seat of the Swedish kings and reachable only on foot. Around 985, Erik and Styrbjörn met there with their armies and fought a three-day battle in which Styrbjörn was killed and Erik won, earning him the name *Segersäll* (a form of "victorious").

4. According to the *Saga of the Jomsvikings*, Jomsborg was not established until after Harald Bluetooth had been killed by Palnatoke's arrow and Harald's son, Sven, was the Danish king.

5. Tyri was the half-sister of Sven Forkbeard and later married Olaf Trygvason of Norway.

6. Oden had sacrificed one of his eyes for the privilege of drinking from the well of wisdom.

7. Olof acquired the name Skötkonung, believed to mean "treasure king," as it was during his reign that Sweden minted its first money.

8. It is believed that Erik was baptized into the Christian faith by Bishop Poppo, who had come to seek Erik's protection of the Christian parishes in Denmark. Bishop Poppo demonstrated his faith by carrying burning irons in his arms without sustaining any injuries, a feat which convinced King Erik to adopt the "true" faith. After Erik returned to Sweden, however, he reverted to his pagan beliefs.

9. It is possible that the chieftain Toke Gormsson was a brother of Harald Bluetooth.

10. From Riksantikvarieämbetet (The National Heritage Board), Sweden.

CHAPTER 13: Olaf Trygvason, 963–1000

1. The sources are unclear as to whose foster-father Thorolf Lusarskeg was. According to King Olaf Trygvason's *Saga*, he was Olaf's, not Astrid's, foster-father.

2. Astrid was taken to the land of the Wends and sold as a slave to a wealthy man from Viken, her native land. She ended up marrying the man, whose name was Lodin.

3.. Olaf was first traded for a goat, then traded a second time for a shirt and a cloak to Reas.

4. Other sources say Olaf was playing with some boys outside of a farmhouse when Sigurd took notice of them.

5. From *Berättelser ur svenska historien (Stories from Swedish history)* by C. Georg Starbäck and P.O. Bäckström (Stockholm, 1885), A.L. Normans Boktryckeri-Aktiebolag. Other sources say that Olaf agreed to be baptized first in 995, after his siege on London.

6. Olaf made a number of dangerous enemies along the way, which was why he pushed the alliance with Burisleif of the Wends.

7. Aethelred was normally called by the less than flattering name "The Unready," thought by some to be a pun on his own name which meant "ill-advised" or "of no counsel" because his advisors often took advantage of his ignorance.

8. The name "Anlaf" or "Unlaf" is used for Olaf Trygvason in the *Anglo-Saxon Chronicle*, and in one version of the account, the year mentioned is 993. Some scholars believe that the chronicler took the events that took place between 991 and 994 and compressed them into the single year, 993. It is also possible that the events were confused and that two separate battles took place, one in 991 led by Olaf Trygvason, and

another in 994 led by Sven Forkbeard. *King Olaf Trygvason's Saga* in Snorri Sturluson's *Chronicle of the Kings of Norway* makes no mention of the Battle of Maldon, although Olaf's many plundering expeditions to England are cited. A treaty between Aethelred and the Vikings, whose leaders were Olaf, Justin, and Guthmund, gave the Vikings twenty-two thousand pounds of gold and silver in return for peace.

9. Some scholars believe the battle of Maldon was a joint effort between Olaf Trygvason and the Danish king Sven Forkbeard and that the warriors were a mixed group of Nordic men.

10. From the Anglo-Saxon poem of the Battle of Maldon, translated by Douglas B. Killings. The important historical event at Maldon inspired this famous poem, which was composed shortly after the battle and is one of the main sources of information on it. Even though the poem's beginning and end have been lost, it nonetheless provides a detailed account of the battle from the English perspective and reveals how they felt about their pirate enemies. Whether the Viking negotiator could speak Old English as well as portrayed is doubtful.

11. From the Anglo-Saxon poem of the Battle of Maldon, translated by Douglas B. Killings.

12. *Byrhtferth's Life of St. Oswald*, a Latin text written towards the end of the tenth century (London 1968), UK Battlefield Resource Centre.

13. The forces are estimated to have been between three thousand and six thousand on each side. The actual number of casualties is unknown, but was high. Although the fight is said to have continued for a fortnight, the actual duration of the battle is also unknown.

14. Hostages, often the most valuable army members, were frequently left as security.

15. *Anglo-Saxon Chronicle*, entry for the year 994. King Aethelred knew how to take maximum advantage of men born with a warrior spirit and was able to channel Olaf's great energy into a benefit for England.

16. Sigrid, also known as "The Haughty," had once burned a small chieftain, whom she considered unworthy and his men to death for having had the temerity to ask for her hand in marriage. Sigrid, who considered herself too wealthy and fine for the smaller king, was insulted by his proposal. Shortly after the incident with Olaf Trygvason, she married King Sven Forkbeard of Denmark. Sven may have considered the marriage to Sigrid as a political union, since she was the widow of the Swedish king Erik the Victorious and was thought to be the mother of King Olof Skötkonung of Sweden. Olof and Olaf are the Swedish and Norwegian spellings, respectively.

17. All dialogue in this chapter is the author's translation/interpretation based on information from a number of sources, mainly *King Olaf*

Trygvason's Saga by Snorri Sturluson and *Berättelser ur svenska historien (Stories from Swedish History)* by C. Georg Starbäck and P.O. Bäckström (Stockholm, 1885), A.L. Normans Boktryckeri-Aktiebolag.

18. At this point, it is said that Queen Tyri, Olaf Trygvason's wife and sister of Sven Forkbeard, who was on the ship, burst into tears when she realized that the fight was inevitable. The king tried to comfort her, telling her that times were good because he could finally obtain for her the riches she had been promised. Tyri is said to have died of sorrow nine days after Olaf's defeat. As in other parts of the world, political marriages were also common in the Nordic countries, but these royal relationships often became entangled and resulted in feuds between otherwise closely knit families.

19. Snorri Sturluson, *King Olaf Trygvason's Saga.*

20. The place of the battle of Svolder is unknown, but is believed to have been either in the Baltic Sea or in the Strait of Öresund.

21. Einar Tambaskelfer survived the battle of Svolder and is believed to have fled to King Olof Skötkonung, the king of the Svear, where he received quarter. In 1028 when Knut the Great took Norway from Olaf Haraldson (the Saint), he gave Einar Tambaskelfer back all of his former fiefs and promised to make him the greatest man in Norway. In the *Saga of Harald Hardrade*, Einar Tambaskelfer is described as the most powerful lenderman (liegeman) in the Throndhjem land.

22. See Verner von Heidenstam, *Svenskarna och Deras Hövdingar*—the *Swedes and Their Leaders* (Sweden, 2004), Project Runeberg.

CHAPTER 14: Knut the Great, 995–1035

1. Though the accepted English translation is Knut the Great, the Danish *"Knud den Mektige"* is more literally translated Knut the Mighty.

2. If Sven Forkbeard were in fact a son of Harald Bluetooth, Gorm the Old (originator of the dynasty led by Knut the Great) was then Knut's great grandfather. Gorm, or Guthorm, is said to have lived to be one hundred; even if exaggerated, such longevity was unusual among Viking leaders who typically did not live past their fortieth birthday. Harald Bluetooth was one of the first Viking kings to embrace the new religion and is known for having Christianized the Danes.

3. The year of his birth is in question, as is that of Knut's older brother, Harald. If Erik Segersäll the Victorious, king of Sweden and husband of Sigrid the Proud, actually died in 995, Sigrid could not already have been married to Sven Forkbeard and by 994 and 995 have given birth to

Harald and Knut. A further case for the later birth date of 997 was that Knut was said to be sixteen when he accompanied his father to England in 1013.

4. Emma was the sister of Richard II, duke of Normandy, and a descendent of the notorious Viking outlaw Rollo the Pirate who, some one hundred years earlier, had wrested Normandy from the Franks.

5. Sigrid the Proud (or the Haughty), after being widowed from the Swedish king Erik Segersäll (the Victorious), married the Danish king Sven Forkbeard, took the name Gunhilde and bore him three children. The first son, Harald, born c. 994(5) became king of Denmark after his father's death, and Knut, the younger of the two boys, succeeded his father to the English throne.

6. Knut and Olof Skötkonung had the same mother, Sigrid the Proud (Queen Gunhilde), who married Sven Forkbeard after her husband Erik Segersäll died in 995.

7. According to the *Saga of Olaf Haraldson*: "The Danes had spread themselves so widely over England, that it was come so far that King Ethelred had departed from the country, and had gone south to Valland." Valland was Normandy, just across the Channel from England. The Norman earls were descended from the notorious Viking pirate Rollo and were generally on good terms with the Norsemen. The *Saga of Olaf Haraldson* says: "Every Northman found a friendly country in Normandy, if he required it."

8. Author's translation/interpretation of the conversation that took place between Knut and Harald.

9. Aethelred had paid Thorkel the Tall 21,000 pounds of silver to ensure his fidelity in helping to protect London from Sven Forkbeard, but the payment turned out to be of little use and shortly thereafter Thorkel defected back to Knut.

10. Sources differ on the Treaty of Olney. According to *World Wide Illustrated Encyclopedia*, 1935: "By the treaty of Olney, Edmund received Wessex, Essex and London, while Canute held Northumbria and Mercia." According to the *Anglo-Saxon Chronicle*, "King Edmund took Wessex and Knute, Mercia and the northern districts."

11. The circumstances surrounding Edmund Ironside's death are unclear. Some scholars presume that he was murdered by Eadric Streona on the orders of Knut. Later, when Eadric demanded a reward for the murder, Knut had the alderman's head lopped off, considering him a future threat to the throne. Knut questioned how a man who had let down his own lord could be true to a new king. Knut told the men in his court that Eadric's beheading was in fact a reward for the murder, for Eadric

had now received the ultimate position of honor—his head on top of a pole for all to see.

12. Alderman Eadric Streona had betrayed Edmund Ironside in 1015, taken forty ships from him and submitted to Knut the Great.

13. The decision to marry Emma would prove to have great consequences for the future of England. Since none of Knut's children had heirs who could inherit the kingdom, Edward the Confessor, son of Aethelred and Emma, returned from Normandy in 1042 to seize the English throne.

14. After Thorkel the Tall died, Earl Ulf, who was married to Knut's sister, Estrid, reigned in Denmark. Ulf was also the foster-father of Knut's son Hardaknut.

15. Olaf the Saint was called Olaf the Thick (meaning "fat") while he lived. He was one of the first Christian Viking kings and became a saint after his death in 1030 in the battle of Stiklestad in Norway.

16. King Olaf, close friend of the Swedish king Anund (or Onund) Jacob, was married to the king's sister, Astrid.

17. According to Sigvat Skald, Earl Hakon tried to spread discontent among the Norwegian people so that they would rise up against King Olaf.

18. There is no mention of Knut the Great in the Swedish royal lineage. Anund Jakob was the reigning king from 1022–50. Some coins found in Sigtuna, Sweden, attest to Knut having been king of all Sweden, but in a letter to his subordinates in England, Knut called himself king over part of the Svear, possibly because for a short time he managed to conquer the most southern parts of Svea Rike.

19. Knut's murder of Earl Ulf possibly came about as a result of the perceived threat to the Danish kingdom after Ulf had crowned Hardaknut king in Knut's absence. The argument over the chess game could have been the event that triggered the murder, although not the real cause of it.

20. *Anglo-Saxon Chronicle*, entry for the year 1028.

21. Earl Hakon died at sea in 1030. On his death, Knut promised the Norwegian kingdom to his illegitimate, underage son Sven (by his mistress Aelfgifu). Hardaknut was to succeed Knut to the Danish and English thrones, instead of the Norwegian throne.

22. Hostage-taking was a common part of the process for validating agreements and treaties. The role of hostages, who were treated honorably, was to ensure that the parties would stand by their oaths of fidelity. For example, two kings might agree to exchange their sons as hostages and become their foster-fathers, thereby strengthening the royal ties between different territories or nations.

23. Some scholars claim that Knut's empire included all of Iceland.

24. Knut and Emma's oldest son Hardaknut was born in 1018, and supposedly at the request of Emma, Hardaknut, rather than the sons she had left

behind in Normandy, became the rightful heir to the throne. Knut also had two other sons, Harald and Sven, by his English mistress, Aelfgifu.

25. It is theorized that he died of poison placed in his drink.

26. Knut became known as "the Great" only after his death. According to some scholars, this was an attempt at church propaganda; in other words, the king was great because he was granted his office by God, who was great.

27. Alfred J. Church, *Stories from English History*, The Baldwin Project. "*Knut*" is also written *Cnut*, Canute or Knud.

CHAPTER 15: Harald Hardrade, Hard-Ruler, 1015–1066

1. Olaf Haraldson was forced to give up the throne to King Knut the Great and flee to Russia. When he tried to regain his kingdom, he was defeated and killed in the battle of Stiklestad. He became known as Olaf the Saint after his death in the battle at which his young half-brother, Harald, was present and barely escaped with his life.

2. Corsairs were pirates commissioned by a government to attack another country's ships.

3. For a more detailed account of Harald's adventures in Constantinople, see Chapter Nine on the Rus in the Varangian Guard.

4. Also known as Svein Estridson after his mother.

5. Snorri Sturluson, *Saga of Harald Hardrade*.

6. Einar Tambaskelfer had served with King Olaf Trygvason in the battle of Svolder in the year 1000, almost fifty years earlier.

7. In the battle of Stiklestad, Kalf Arnason had become known as a traitor to the king.

8. Two hundred ships in addition to provision ships and other smaller crafts. The *Anglo-Saxon Chronicle* describes Harald, king of Norway, as arriving with a very large sea-force of three hundred ships or more.

9. Klifland is possibly Cleveland in northeastern England.

10. In 1065, Edward, son of Aethelred the Unready, was king of England, having acquired the kingdom after the death of Hardaknut, son of Knut the Great. Edward and Hardaknut were half-brothers, born of the same mother, Emma, daughter of Earl Richard of Rouen, Normandy. Knut the Great had married Emma, widowed after the death of Aethelred. King Edward died of an illness after he had reigned in England for twenty-three years, 1042–1065. He left no heir, so Harold Godwinson, son of Earl Godwin, one of the most powerful men in England, was elected to succeed him. His period of tranquility ended quickly, and he held the kingdom for just forty weeks and a day when William the Conqueror came from Normandy and conquered England.

11. *Anglo-Saxon Chronicle*, entry for the year 1066.
12. Nidaros, the old name for Throndhjem in Norway, became an important Christian pilgrimage site.
13. Of the original Viking fleet of two hundred ships, only twenty-four remained.
14. Harald Hardrade was skilled at verse, and although he had several skalds traveling with him, composed many verses himself, including this one.

Afterword

1. Arthur Kemp, *March of the Titans, A History of the White Race* (1999), Ostara Publications.
2. Western warfare generally relied on decisive battle in open terrain and did not employ ambush or hit-and-run tactics. The Vikings were successful because they were mobile and did not approach war in the traditional sense—that is, one nationally sanctioned army against another. The location of the Scandinavian countries together with the free-spirited nature of the Norsemen who had a direct stake in the outcome of a raid which could make them instantly rich, contributed to the Vikings' success as unconventional warriors.

INDEX

Note: All references to illustrations are in bold face.

ACKNOWLEDGMENT

The author would like to acknowledge her editors, Linda Saputelli and Samantha Edussuriya at Hippocrene Books. Thank you for your hard work and dedication to this project.

evaluates processes and criteria of research allocation in light of the ends of medicine, the common good and fairness. Similarly, the prophetic perspective "can function to jar institutions from blind acceptance of the status quo" (Gustafson, 1990b, p. 141). In this spirit Gustafson questions the tendency of biomedicine to deny the unavoidability of disease and death.

To understand Gustafson's analysis one must recall that it was written in the midst of a macroallocation crisis. By 1984 it was clear that costs would prohibit using the solution reached in the case of hemodialysis—namely, making it available to all who needed it—as a precedent for new forms of treatment. In light of these facts, Gustafson proposes two significant but fairly uncontroversial alterations in the research process. One is that questions of the cost and criteria of distribution of the final results of such research—the new therapy—should be considered not only at the end of the process when the new therapy is available but earlier in the process when decisions are made about whether to fund the research (Gustafson, 1984, pp. 257–258). Of course, as Gustafson no doubt recognizes, there are problems with this recommendation. It is not always possible to give accurate estimates of the cost of a final product in an early stage of research. Such estimates require comparisons with total costs (including risks) of current alternatives, calculation of savings from cost-saving "spin-offs," and a host of other factors. A second recommendation concerns the disease process itself: At what point in this process should research be directed? Gustafson argues against directing research toward costly end-stage interventions and in favor of prevention of severe diseases and therapies targeted to early stages of a disease (Gustafson, 1984, pp. 257, 261, 267, 276). His reasons are consequential: these interventions are less costly in economic terms and they allow for more physical and social functioning over a longer period of time. Again, the economic argument is questionable if one counts, as health economists do, the costs of future health care and pension payouts for those who live longer due to effective preventive and early-stage care.

The consequentialism indicated in the second recommendation pervades Gustafson's entire analysis. Its primacy is announced in the opening sentence: "The ultimate justification of all stages of medical research and health care is the benefits they will have for persons and for a human community" (Gustafson, 1984, p. 253). Of course nobody denies the necessity of consequential judgments for macroallocation, but for Gustafson they assume a priority that they do not have in many other accounts. Allocation decisions are judged by their outcomes. Measuring outcomes requires judgments about what wholes are to be taken into account. As Gustafson recognizes, determination of which wholes are relevant is difficult, but his theocentric perspective gives more weight to the common good or the goods of larger wholes (Gustafson, 1984, pp. 264, 271–272, 275–276).

> Individual persons are not of absolute value, and thus continuation of physical life is not of ultimate value. Physical life, while the indispensible condition for all human values, is not an end in itself. . . . From my perspective individuals are interpreted in their relations to other persons and to the communities of which they are a part. . . . Interdependence carries mutual responsibilities so that persons and policies have to take into account how the consequences of the pursuit of particular valid objectives of research and therapy affect other persons and other objectives. (Gustafson, 1984, pp. 275–276)

Three controversial conclusions follow. First, Gustafson rejects the orientation of research toward merely extending physical life. Hence he accepts medical criteria that emphasize not only the importance of physical functioning but the capacity for social functioning as well. Of the six medical criteria he discusses—frequency of the disease, mortality, severity, age at onset, the point in the disease process, and the state of research—three (severity, onset age, disease process) are justified at least in part on these grounds, and Gustafson's account seems on the whole to favor these three criteria, though not to the total exclusion of others. Questions of justice occur almost entirely within these criteria rather than determining them (Gustafson, 1984, p. 264).[22] Beyond this, Gustafson recognizes that extension of physical life often creates both individual and social problems, including loss of the sense of the worth of one's life, the aging of the population, and the loss of resources that could be directed to other worthwhile ends (Gustafson, 1984, p. 273). Second, ever mindful that neither the common good nor the goods of individuals is free from occasions of moral conflict and tragedy, Gustafson is able to envision circumstances under which risks are taken with some for the benefit of others. For example, experimentation might justifiably occur without the fully informed consent of the participants (Gustafson, 1984, p. 272).[23] Third, the common good is a substantive notion and thus "is not achieved simply by aggregative benefits to particular individuals with particular needs" (Gustafson, 1984, p. 276). Gustafson is not a utilitarian. To determine the common good requires a normative account of what larger individual and social goods health serves.

It is precisely here, as Gustafson realizes, that this account is incomplete. While it is clear that research and therapy should serve the goods of wholes larger than the physical life of individuals, it is not clear what these personal and social goods are or how particular therapies or states of health are related to them. The result is an argument that is sufficient to criticize research oriented to the mere extension of life but not sufficient to answer questions of how to weigh the various medical criteria or costs and benefits, or to resolve conflicts between them. Nor is it sufficient to respond to the questions posed by gene therapy which we discussed in chapter two. Gustafson realizes the importance of what he has omitted. He notes that the burden of his entire analysis of research funding is on "the need for more careful forethought about the social and individual ends to be served by biomedical research and medical care" (Gustafson, 1984, p. 273). But he gives no indication of what these ends are or how to inquire regarding them, only a reminder of what they are not.

> Does the pursuit of health and the extension of physical life tend to become an idol—an idol whose worship skews other valid ends both for individuals and for societies? . . . Yet in the end the powers that create and sustain human life also bear down upon it and destroy it. Nature and God will not be defied; disease and death come to each and to all whether we consent to them or not. (Gustafson, 1984, pp. 276–277)

In characteristic Protestant fashion, Gustafson leaves us with an eloquent prophetic warning rather than a reflection on the ends of human life.

EVALUATION

In my discussion of his accounts of suicide and allocation of biomedical research funding I pointed out in that in both cases Gustafson's descriptions of what is normatively human are too thin to address the most pressing questions in both areas. Accordingly, my first set of criticisms raises the question of why Gustafson's account of the ends and goods of human life is so sparse and whether a richer account is possible within his scheme. The reader will recall that for Gustafson claims about nature can support certain presumptions and provisional orderings of values and moral principles relevant to what is normatively human, but cannot supply a single order that offers moral certainty and resolves conflicts between different goods or ends. The reader will also recall that the human good must be placed within a broader context within the divine ordering. Do these conclusions necessarily constitute a barrier to a robust view of the good?

If Gustafson has failed to supply a thick view of the normatively human it is not for lack of attention to the issue. It is fair to say that for at least twenty-five years no issue has occupied him more. He became convinced early on that the chief moral issue in the biological sciences (especially behavioral and genetic research) is what is and ought to be valued about human life (Gustafson, 1974, p. 232). In order to probe this question he has sought to explore the relations between scientific descriptions and explanations of human nature and human valuations of human nature (cf. Gustafson, 1974, pp. 229–244; 1992b; 1994, pp. 750–753). In both clinical and research medicine, for example, judgments about what is biologically natural or normal in a functional or statistical sense are used as grounds for intervention into natural processes to restore or enhance a natural process or to refrain from intervening in the case of an abnormality that resists cure (Gustafson, 1984, pp. 273–274; 1994, pp. 752–753). I have already indicated the major point of Gustafson's own response, but his comments can be summarized in three points. First, scientific descriptions and explanations are necessary but not sufficient since nature changes due to its own processes and to human intervention and since biological requisites and capacities can be fulfilled in a wide variety of ways. Second, reflection on human experience is likely to disclose a wide range of things people value about life. Third, the appropriate response to this indeterminacy of nature and pluralism of experience is for various "communities of moral discourse" representing various perspectives and interests to engage in these issues in the confidence that agreement can be reached on some moral presumptions and provisional orderings.

Of course, it would be a mistake to expect Gustafson to provide an exhaustive description of the goods and ends of life. As Aristotle and Aquinas both recognized, any such description would have to be highly general since specific determinations depend on knowledge of particular circumstances and contingent conditions. But it is also true that any such description would fall into a particular tradition of inquiry in which the indeterminacy of nature is given some determinacy, and the pluralism of experience is given some specificity. Gustafson is fully aware of the particularity involved in any effort to construe the world. The problem is that the less nature itself can tell us about what is the normatively human, the more we must rely on there being people trained in the skills of discernment in communities of moral formation and moral discourse. But any adequate description of these communities and their moral and intellectual virtues is bound to be highly particularistic, as are their views of the normatively human.

A desire to avoid this kind of particularity may be a major reason why, despite the appeal to communities of moral formation and discourse, Gustafson seeks to determine the normatively human by the sciences and common experience more or less apart from the virtues and practices of particular communities. Hence it is not surprising that in the end faith is ultimately piety and the relevant church is the community of scientific research and practice. Gustafson thus follows the trail blazed by Charles S. Peirce, for whom faith and church were, respectively, "musement" (reflective piety) and the community of inquirers.

The question is whether Gustafson's commitments require him to follow that trail. Must a theology that takes its cues from nature resist a strong appeal to moral traditions or communities? Gustafson recognizes that nature and culture can never be distinguished sharply since culture itself is what humans do with the indeterminacy of nature and since culture also shapes nature. If this is so, our descriptions of human nature—for example, of the biologically "natural" or "normal," of "normal human functioning," and their negative counterparts—will reflect the discourses and practices that embody what our culture values. Of course, Gustafson is fully aware of this. But it also seems reasonable to expect that an adequate description of our "nature" would have to refer to the way it is formed and shaped by the way of life of a culture or tradition. In other words, while every tradition or way of life both forms and is formed by "nature," there is no adequate description of the natural that is not at the same time a description of the goods and ends that comprise a particular way of life.[24] This move would, I believe, be consistent with Gustafson's enterprise, though it would call for major alterations in the precise relationship between tradition and the sciences—alterations, I am convinced, that would be more adequate to the way both sources should and actually do function in practice.

A second set of criticisms concerns two sets of opposing pairs or binary oppositions that structure Gustafson's ethics of vocation or participation. One opposition is between the participant and the prophet. We have seen how Gustafson distinguishes policy discourse from both ethical and prophetic discourse. This by itself is innocent enough but it becomes a problem when Gustafson distinguishes the participant as an insider from the prophet as an outsider. On the one hand, as a participant a theologian "is actively involved in the shaping of events and in the development and reordering of institutions" and "is one partner among many in the human conversation that determines uses of knowledge and power and resources" (Gustafson, 1974, p. 84). The prophet, on the other hand, is defined in terms of distance from the arenas of life in which this conversation occurs. "The prophetic distancing of the moralist from persons and institutions is not impossible within theocentric ethics but theocentric ethics always takes more cognizance of the need to affect presently existing valuations and social institutions and how they can be directed toward more appropriate ends" (Gustafson, 1984, p. 9).

Once again my criticism must be focused carefully since the emphasis on participation is bound up with legitimate concerns. Gustafson wants to avoid both rationalistic moral theories that abstract morality from nature and history and prophetic critiques that deal in generalities. He rightly argues that moral reasoning should begin in the concrete, with the question of what is going on. And he rightly challenges those who criticize the ethos of, say, medicine to show the specificity of the ethos they criticize. "If they cannot address the specific and concrete manifestations of the ethos (if it can be said to exist independently) in the particularities of cases and policy choices, if they cannot show how their theologies address the issues as they arise out of specific activities, conversation never gets off the ground" (Gustafson, 1987, p. 39). Finally, Gustafson rightly points out that those "who have responsibility for particular spheres of interdependence and action must be accountable for the choices they make," so that it is appropriate for moral inquiry "to broaden and deepen [their] capacities . . . to make morally responsible choices" (Gustafson, 1984, p. 315).

However, a concern with the concrete can easily become a general acceptance of institutions and practices as they are given. Ethics then has the task of advocating incremental changes within the given or calling for changes around the edges where limits are recognized, all the while omitting fundamental criticisms of those institutions and practices themselves. Similarly, Gustafson shifts from requiring prophets to specify their criticisms to requiring them to accept the insiders as the final judges of the appropriateness of their criticisms. But this rules out criticisms that question the grounds on which those judgments are made. Finally, helping participants make morally responsible choices can obscure the prior question of the grounds of their authority to make those choices.

The problem is that Gustafson reifies his ideal types and thus forces us to choose between criticism and involvement. The result is that an ethics of vocation for which morally worthy activity is found in participation in institutions and practices will necessarily consider criticism as a marginal activity. But the choice between criticism and involvement is a false choice. It obscures a form of moral inquiry that helps participants become more aware of how they describe events and exercise their agency. Gustafson is well aware that events and cases are constructed by agents; they do not come with labels and a set of instructions for interpreting them. Accordingly, one task of moral inquiry is to point out alternative descriptions that bring neglected factors to the fore and allow for alternative courses of action. For example, in his discussion of possible means of population control, Gustafson points out that there is a wide range of responses between pure rational autonomy and outright physical duress and thereby challenges descriptions that reduce the alternatives to voluntariness and state control (Gustafson, 1984, p. 248). But such inquiry would also seem to require criticisms of the ways in which participants construct cases and events: How are actions and events described? What is assumed to be given or necessary? How does the narrator construct her own agency in interaction with other participants and with the audience? To use Aristotelian categories, Gustafson's "points to consider" constitute a "topics" for moral discernment; what is needed in addition is a "rhetoric."

Gustafson is aware of the importance of institutions in shaping moral action. He is also critical of ethical analyses that restrict their focus to particular acts and the voluntariness and intentionality of actions in part because they attend to moral quandaries without analyzing and criticizing the pervasive and usually unself-conscious ethos that has profound effects on agents and communities (Gustafson, 1990a, pp. 184–185). One of Gustafson's own examples, as we have seen, is the ethos that makes avoidance of death the end of medicine. Yet curiously he deals with institutions mostly as conditions for human life and well-being and as setting limits to the realization of morally worthy ends but not as constituting sets of discourses and practices that radically shape agents.

The second opposition that structures the ethics of vocation is between two forms of practical ethics that Gustafson, in a discussion of genetic engineering, connects with two images of the human. One form presupposes a static human nature from which fixed principles and prohibitions are derived. The other form views human nature as constantly developing new ways to determine human life. Rather than fixed rules and prohibitions the requisites for human life "can become the guidemarks and the lights of intention which give direction to the course of future human development." Gustafson's choice between these alternatives is clear.

My basic point, then, is that the procedure for thinking ethically about human experimentation ought not to begin with a fixed image of what was, is, and always ought to be, from which are derived authoritative and unalterable rules which govern experimentation. Rather, the weight is on human initiative, human freedom (if you choose) to explore, develop, expand, alter, initiate, intervene in the course of life in the world, including his own life. But this does not mean there are not guidelines and lights of intention which can give direction to the uses of new knowledge. It does not mean that there is nothing to give warnings against certain possibilities, and to give positive support to others, or to set certain limits beyond which man cannot go. (Gustafson, 1974, p. 285)

Once again the problem is that Gustafson sets up his opposing types in such a way that a certain kind of moral activity is excluded. His alternatives reflect the kind of choices the Baconian morality of ordinary life forces on its adherents. Moral inquiry will either take the form of rules and prohibitions that give a false certainty based on an unpersuasive image of human nature or it will restrict itself to guiding the activities of man the intervener. What is excluded is moral inquiry as the activity of a community critically reflecting on its own discourses and practices regarding the good to determine what place interventions should have in its life and the lives of its members. It is no accident, then, that Gustafson chooses the biomedical researcher over the clinician as the paradigmatic figure for his bioethical reflections. But for all the power and profundity of his limitation of the Baconian project, one wonders whether this choice has not already given a tacit endorsement to technological curative medicine and its effort to relieve the human condition.

In conclusion, Gustafson's theocentric ethic constitutes a powerful critique of the technological utopianism of the Baconian project. He criticizes both the view of nature that supports it and the primacy of human well-being in the divine ordering that it assumes. Perhaps most significantly, Gustafson affirms the inevitability of moral conflict and tragedy that the Baconian ethos denies. Relief of the human condition of subjection to necessity is a pretentious and ultimately idolatrous goal; one, moreover, that is perilous to human beings and to the rest of nature. Nevertheless, Gustafson's ethics of vocation includes some of the most characteristic features of the ethics of ordinary life that forms the background to the Baconian project. To be human is primarily to intervene into nature. Gustafson accordingly accepts the technological self-understanding of medicine as intervention rather than as caring or the wisdom of the body in service of a morally worthy life. He therefore diagnoses the problem of technological utopianism as a matter of pride, that is, the Greek notion of hubris, for which theocentric piety is the cure. But if I am right that the Baconian project is linked with the loss of a moral vocabulary regarding the meaning of the body and its place in a morally worthy life, then Gustafson's acceptance of the ethic of ordinary life, like any ethic that stops short of retrieving such a vocabulary or replacing it with a new one, will be unable to overcome the Baconian project. It is true that Gustafson calls for reflection on the common good and the ends of life and questions the orientation of medicine and other forms of human activity to mere preservation and extension of physical life, but he lacks the moral vocabulary to describe the virtues, practices, and discourses that would allow us to identify and pursue those goods and ends. As his analyses of suicide and biomedical research funding indicate, Gustafson goes beyond contemporary secular bioethicists in recognizing the limits of the standard principles of bioethics in resolving or even adequately articulating the deeper problems raised by technological medicine. But ultimately the task of moral inquiry for him is to articulate the possibilities and limitations of technological medicine, not to challenge its hegemony.

If our task is to bring technological medicine into the service of our moral projects rather than vice versa, these shortcomings indicate that Gustafson may not be able to speak the final word for us. But he has argued eloquently and persuasively against the Baconian project from within the general moral tradition that spawned it, and every effort to go beyond this tradition will remain deeply indebted to him.

CHAPTER 5

Medicine as a Moral Art

The present chapter marks an important transition in our inquiry. We have seen that Jonas and Gustafson concentrate on the threats and (in Gustafson's case) the promises biomedical research holds for human beings and for the natural world. They then try to develop normative conceptions of the human to determine proper uses of the new technologies and to limit the utopian ambitions that accompany them. Leon Kass and Stanley Hauerwas, the principal subjects of the following two chapters, shift the focus to the ends and moral convictions that characterize medicine as a practice and to the ways in which the new powers available to medicine support or hinder our pursuit of a well-lived or morally worthy life. This does not mean that Kass and Hauerwas are uninterested in technology and its effects or in guiding and limiting its uses. Rather, they believe that any effort to address these questions misses its mark unless it concentrates on the practices (especially medicine) that care for the body, the forms or traditions of inquiry that articulate the meaning of bodily life, and the kind of institution or community that can foster the virtues needed to sustain the care for the body and fulfill the meaning of bodily life. Because of their emphasis on tradition, community, virtue, and practice, Kass and Hauerwas depart further from standard bioethics than do Jonas and Gustafson, and are by the same measure closer to the issues I have identified as crucial for bioethics, namely the place of the body and technological control over it in a morally worthy and responsible life.

Kass is best known for his controversial positions on reproductive technologies, physician-assisted suicide, and health as the *telos* of medicine. I address some of these issues below, but I believe Kass's work on such issues is best understood by following his advice to view the new technologies in terms of "the great wave upon which each of these technologies is but a ripple. All of the technologies arise from and are part of the great project of modernity, the 'conquest of nature for the relief of man's estate'" (Kass, 1985, p. 69.) Kass observes, no doubt with Bacon in mind, that the implicit goal of such technologies is the reversal of the curses laid on Adam and Eve or the restoration of the tree of life by the tree of knowledge (Kass, 1985, pp. 34 n., 131). Taken alone, the tone of his comments seems to confirm the initial impression most readers have of Kass: that he is a straightforward opponent of the technological transformation of medicine who would like to return to a pretechnological era. But although Kass would like to retain many of the virtues and norms that characterized pretechnological medicine, his attitude toward what I have described as the Baconian project is complex. In the first place, his primary concern is not technology at all, but modern science and "the consequences for belief, for self-understanding, for our sense of our place in the world" it engenders. As with Jonas, the problem is that the (in Kass's view) value-free methods of modern science foreclose any attempt to find in nature the answers to questions of human flourishing by disclosing a natural world that is indifferent to all such concerns. Modern science thereby opens a large gap between nature as human beings experience it in their ordinary lives and nature as science interprets it (Kass, 1994, pp. 4–6). This gap creates severe problems for ethics because the latter, as Aristotle taught, is concerned with the way we live, and is ultimately grounded in our ordinary experience of life. But if modern science leads us to adopt a view of nature that discounts, ignores and abstracts from ordinary experience, then our ethically freighted ordinary experience will appear to have no connection with nature and thus to be pure convention—all *nomos* and no *physis*, all invention and no discovery. The problem, then, is not technology per se, but that the capacity of modern technology to intervene into and reorder human nature through control of the body comes at a time when the cumulative effects of the methods and results of modern science have made it virtually impossible for us to determine from nature what constitutes human flourishing. Convinced that any customary morality must therefore be purely conventional, we welcome the new technologies and their control over the body as tools of our desires and wishes, which are untutored by any conception of natural human excellence. Lacking a substantive view of natural human flourishing, we have no way to ensure that our technological capacities will serve human nature rather than erode or destroy it.

Medicine occupies a strategic yet vulnerable location in this landscape. As Bacon and Descartes foresaw, biomedical advances play a major role in the effort to overcome natural necessity. But for Kass, because these biomedical advances have entered society through the practice of medicine their dangers have been less apparent. For medicine has traditionally been "an art with relatively clearly defined ends and norms of conduct" that implicitly bears the moral wisdom that is lacking in modern science (Kass, 1985, p. 11). Hence medicine by its very nature as a moral art is poised to connect the new technologies with a view of human flourishing and thus assure their proper use. But as an art, medicine's knowledge is implicit (and, I will argue more strongly than does Kass, incomplete) and therefore in need of articulation by a biology that is more attuned to the kind of ordinary knowledge of human nature medicine and other practices presuppose. But if medicine instead remains wedded to *modern* biology it is in danger of losing its identity as a moral art and, devoid of intrinsic norms and ends, of becoming merely a means of fulfilling arbitrary preferences and relieving whatever humans find unsatisfactory about their natural and social conditions.

This indicates that it will not be the new technologies per se but the practice of medicine that for Kass will demand the most urgent attention. As the conduit of biomedical advances, medicine marks the point at which a moral framework for these advances must be maintained. But medicine stands in need of a biology which can bridge the gap between nature and convention and thereby provide standards for the uses of new biomedical technologies. This suggests an argument that moves from (1) the struggle of medicine to maintain itself as a practice defined by a distinct end and governed by intrinsic norms to (2) a more adequate biology that grounds what medicine implicitly knows and supplies a bridge between nature and convention to (3) a moral ordering that enables us to determine whether and how the new biomedical technologies may serve rather than hinder genuine human flourishing. These three stages will be taken up in order in the following three sections.

THE MORAL TOPOGRAPHY OF MEDICINE

If medicine is to play any role in directing the new biomedical technologies to genuine human flourishing, Kass will have to overcome the view that medicine is a morally neutral set of skills and services whose only internal standard is technical competence and whose moral standards, which are of general applicability, must come from outside. Kass realizes that moral neutrality can be avoided only if medicine can identify a distinct end that it serves.

> If the art of medicine is defined primarily in terms of its powers,
> its techniques or skills, then the argument for its moral neutrality
> is hard to refute. . . . Only if an art is more than know-how, only if
> it is also know-what-and-what-for, and, further, only if that knowl-
> edge of ends informs the choice of means, could one begin to look
> to the art for its own inherent ethic. (Kass, 1985, p. 226)

The technological capacities of modern medicine make the need for
clarity about ends even more urgent. Technology greatly expands control over the body. As the profession legally licensed to touch the body
and intervene in its processes, medicine is in a position to be pressed
into the service of whatever individual and societal desires and interests, from the modest to the utopian, are attainable or believed to be
attainable by control of the body. Hence while standard bioethics concentrates on the moral quandaries posed by the new biomedical technologies, for Kass these new technologies force a question that medicine
for centuries could take for granted: the question concerning the purpose of medicine itself. No longer do the limited capacities of the art of
medicine delimit its purposes. Since medicine as an art or *techne* can
now be used for almost any end, clarification about its true end becomes
urgent.

   In short, if medicine can be shown to be directed to a limited but
vital end as a partial component of human flourishing then it would not
be a morally neutral art but would possess a standard for its control of
the body. Kass occasionally confuses this concern about human flourishing with a concern to maintain the authority and status of the medical profession, so that his call for medicine to articulate its purpose
reflects a fear that medicine is becoming a mere service industry. "For
without a clear view of its end, medicine is at risk of becoming merely a
set of powerful means, and the doctor at risk of becoming merely a
technician and engineer of the body, a scalpel for hire, selling his services upon demand" (Kass, 1985, p. 158). However, despite these remnants of a Doctor's Club mentality that appear in some of his essays
(especially those where physicians are the intended audience), Kass's
more explicit claim—that the role of medicine is to enable patients to
secure a limited but vital good amid tendencies to use the powers of
medicine in ways that ignore or threaten that good—is separable from
this implicit claim about the status of medicine.

   In this context Kass presented his initial claim that medicine is a
techne directed toward health as a natural, nonrelative good (Kass, 1985,
pp. 157–186). The claim that medicine aims at health is an old one—
Aristotle takes it for granted in his *Nicomachean Ethics* (Aristotle, 1094a,

1097a)—which nevertheless has generated considerable controversy. Proceeding by negation, Kass distinguishes health from the use of medical skill for the pursuit of individual pleasure or convenience, the enforcement of civic or moral virtue, the alteration of human nature and the prolongation of life—all of which give a green light to medical imperialism over the whole of life (Kass, 1985, pp. 159–162). These uses of medical skill often take refuge in expansive definitions of health that equate the latter with well-being in general, as in the well-known WHO definition of health as "a state of complete physical, mental and social well-being" (World Health Organization, 1981).

Kass is equally concerned to avoid definitions that reduce health to the absence of disease. According to one such definition diseases are treated in biostatistical terms as "internal states that depress a functional ability below species-typical levels" (Boorse, 1977, p. 542). Kass believes this kind of narrow definition is responsible for the errors of the expansive definitions.

> Indeed, the tendency to expand the notion of health to include happiness and good citizenship is, ironically, a consequence of, or reaction to, the opposite and more fundamental tendency— namely, to treat health as merely the absence of known disease entities and, more radically, to insist that health as such is nothing more than a word. (Kass, 1985, p. 164)[1]

The last comment indicates that in some definitions, concepts of health and disease refer to subjective or culturally relative valuations rather than to natural states. This has the effect of subjugating the physician to whatever the individual or society decide health is. Not surprisingly, Kass is a realist rather than a nominalist about health; health refers to a natural state rather than to a subjective evaluation or a social agreement. "Disease-entities may in some cases be constructs, but the departures from health and the symptoms they group together are not. Moreover, health, although certainly a good, is not therefore a good whose goodness exists by convention or by human decree" (Kass, 1985, p. 168). Kass accordingly concedes a certain relativism with regard to disease—namely, that disease classifications and explanations vary among cultures—but holds to a universalism with regard to health.[2]

What then is health? Against these rival definitions, health is a nonrelative natural good concerned with the body. Kass recognizes that the conception of health will always be imprecise and not definable in strict terms (Kass, 1985, p. 169). But like Aristotle he does not demand more precision from his subject matter than it allows. Taking his cue from the etymology of words for health in Greek and English, he argues that health involves the wholeness and well-functioning of organisms. Wholeness is a key concept in Kass's biology, where it is connected with notions of teleology and form that I examine below. But medicine knows this wholeness implicitly in its awareness of "the remarkable power of self-healing" possessed by organisms and their pain response and immune systems (Kass, 1985, pp. 171–172). These capacities of the organism to act as a whole also indicate its healthiness or at least its natural tendency to maintain the health of the whole. But wholeness gives us an incomplete conception of health. Health is revealed not primarily in structure but in activity and therefore consists in the well-working of the whole organism in accordance with the standards of excellent bodily functioning for that organism (Kass, 1985, pp. 173–174).

If medicine were to direct itself to health along the lines Kass suggests, the implications for its practice would be far reaching. It would substitute an emphasis on health promotion and maintenance for its current preoccupation with restoration and remedy (Kass, 1985, pp. 165, 179–80). It would orient its epidemiological research around healthiness rather than morbidity and mortality (Kass, 1985, pp. 180–181). In support of these changes Kass invokes the emphasis of the Hippocratic Oath on dietetic measures as the principle mode of treatment, for this emphasis signals a recognition that "[t]he *body is its own healer.*" Medicine is therefore "a cooperative rather than a transforming art, and . . . the physician is but an assistant to nature working within . . ." (Kass, 1985, p. 233). But because human beings are capable of ruining their health due to aspirations beyond self-preservation that make them human and, moreover, must maintain health by effort and discipline, instinct and self-healing are not sufficient; the body's natural powers of self-healing must be joined by the virtue of moderation (Kass, 1985, pp. 174–176). Yet moderation alone is not enough; it must be informed. "The physician, the ally of our body and of those inner powers working toward our own good, supplies needed knowledge, advice, and exhortation" (Kass, 1985, p. 233). The respective roles of patient and physician in this model are therefore clear: On the one hand, because a healthy body is much more the result of discipline and lifestyle than of medical treatment, the patient's habits and environment are more important factors in her health status than is the physician (Kass, 1985, pp. 180–181). Despite his obvious concern with maintaining the authority of medicine, Kass's emphasis on personal responsibility for health gives patients a much greater role in attaining the end of medicine than they are given when medicine is dedicated to the elimination of disease or to an end that requires technological control of the body. On the other hand, since the physician treats the body and not the patient's wishes and desires, and since the physician, not the patient, is the expert on the body, in the clinical setting the patient and his or her opinions have value only as clues for the physician (Kass, 1985, p. 167).

Does this account of medicine as a *techne* directed to health as its end succeed in overcoming the view that medicine is morally neutral? The viability of Kass's argument depends heavily on whether or not the conception of health as a natural, nonrelative good is valid. I return to this issue in the final section. Assuming for now its validity, medicine does seem to be a moral art. First, the orientation to health means that medicine for Kass can not merely deliver whatever services its technical competence enables it to deliver, nor can it reduce the body to an instrument of the arbitrary will. As a cooperative rather than a transformative art, its business is not manipulating the body and its processes according to personal whim but rather promoting and maintaining the body as a whole and well-functioning organism and helping it resist obstructions from outside. Moreover, if medicine primarily assists the body's own healing powers then the Hippocratic Oath's prohibitions against physician participation in ending patients' lives and in abortion would seem to be integral to medicine, for these activities are inconsistent with the essence of medicine as assisting the body's own healing powers. "Is it not self-contradictory for the healing art to be the killing art— even in those cases in which we might all agree that killing is not murder (i.e., that it is legitimate)?" (Kass, 1985, p. 234)

Nevertheless, several limitations pertain to Kass's description even if his view of health as an end is defensible. The first is that while we know abstractly that the orientation of medicine to health means that medicine is more than a skill for hire and that its control of the body is subject to a standard of bodily excellence, without a more complete account of bodily excellence we still do not know what that standard is and how to determine it.

A second limitation follows from the very nature of a *techne*. Kass knows that according to Aristotle the action of a *techne* results in a product distinct from the action— unlike, say, virtuous action, whose end is the action itself (Aristotle, 1140a; Kass, 1985, pp. 216–217). This does not mean that the *technai* are morally neutral: any *techne* requires virtues to perform it well. But the necessary virtues are enabling virtues rather than constitutive virtues; they simply facilitate competence in the art. This raises the vital question of whether medicine is dependent on other virtues and practices in order to determine the proper role or use of its product, namely health. Kass recognizes that in Aristotle's account the product of a *techne* is useful for a further good that the practitioner of the *techne* presupposes. In other words, these purposive human activities serve goals other than themselves, and thus derive their meaning and worth finally from the contributions they make to the ultimate goods of human life. Thus, even if the physician as physician could discern that and why health is good, he may not be able, as physician, to assess how health stands relative to justice, learning, pleasure, or freedom, especially in concrete cases where these goods are in conflict. (Kass, 1985, p. 217)

Medicine therefore plays a vital but limited role in human flourishing. Health, Kass argues, "cannot be the greatest good, either for an individual or for a community," primarily because "it is not mere life, or even a healthy life, but rather a good and worthy life for which we must aim" (Kass, 1985, pp. 185–186). The goods of the body (healthy functioning) are distinct from the goods of the soul (a virtuous life) and the former are ultimately for the sake of the latter (Kass, 1985, pp. 165 n, 186). While bodily health is a good in its own right, it is ultimately because health is necessary, or at least helpful, in attaining virtue that the pursuit of health is a duty. The physician dispenses advice and dietary regimens to make the body function well; directing the healthy body to virtue is the task of the patient, for which the guidance of a physician of the soul, as Moses Maimonides called them, may be necessary.[3] The authority of medicine over health does not, therefore, translate into authority over these other goods or over the relation of health to these other goods. For Kass this means that "medicine cannot be a simply autonomous profession." Instead "the ruling character of the political must be conceded, even if with fear and trembling" (Kass, 1985, p. 194). The reason is that, following Aristotle, politics for Kass is the art that orders the goods of the community relative to their proper place in human fulfilment. But to the question of whether politics may go beyond establishing the place of medicine in the broader pursuits of a society and qualify the doctor-patient relationship itself, Kass's answer is an emphatic "no": medicine must be free to exercise its loyalty to the patient whatever role medicine itself is given amid the various pursuits of a society (Kass, 1985, pp. 194–195).

The previous two paragraphs discuss limitations medicine faces precisely because it is an art and does not, *qua* medicine, possess the knowledge to articulate the standards of bodily excellence it presupposes or the authority to judge matters beyond health. These limitations threaten to trivialize the claim that medicine is a moral art since medicine appears to possess neither the standards to specify its end nor the authority to determine the importance of that end relative to other ends. The following four paragraphs discuss various aspects in which medicine must be more than a *techne* if it is to exercise the moral role Kass ascribes to it.

On the surface there certainly seems to be something wrong with reducing medicine to a *techne* that produces health as an end. The problem is that medicine seems to be directed to the patient rather than to health. Medicine does not simply produce health as a shoemaker produces shoes, not only because health lacks the specificity and concreteness of shoes but primarily because medicine is directly concerned not with health but with patients, that is with human beings who bring to the clinical setting a wide range of desires and wishes, disruptions of valued life-functions, varying capacities for achieving health, and senses of vulnerability and disruption that accompany illness as a reminder of finitude. Each of these facets requires virtues and skills that go beyond what a mere *techne* would demand and beyond the complex "helper of nature/leader and teacher of the patient" role delineated above. In later essays Kass expands and qualifies his description of medicine as a *techne* and his concept of health to respond to this kind of objection. (I argue below that he abandons his original concept of health.) First, he qualifies his hard-line stance against physicians indulging desires and wishes of patients that have little connection to what he regards as the pursuit of health. He now seems to recognize that the exclusive orientation to health that for him characterizes the traditional practice of medicine has its own dangers.

> Thus, while it is true that the physician has been rightly committed more to patient good than to patient rights, to patient need than to patient wish, it is also true that physicians frequently now hold too narrow a view of need and of good, too shrunken a view of the integrity of the human organism, and almost no view at all of the riches and mysteries of the human soul. (Kass, 1985, p. 199)

The task is not to aim at health as a *techne* aims at its product, but to distinguish needs from desires, reasonable desires from unreasonable ones, and reasonable desires that deserve the attention of a physician from those that do not. To make these distinctions well requires of the physician (apparently the patient does not participate in this process of discernment) virtues of moderation, gravity, understanding of the human aspects of illness, courage to resist unwarranted demands, and prudent judgment (Kass, 1985, p. 199). Clearly, these virtues surpass the enabling virtues required to carry out a *techne*, but they also raise the question (which I address in the final section) of whether the distinctions Kass mentions require a view of the good beyond medicine itself.

Second, Kass recognizes that the concentration on somatic functioning or bodily excellence ignores the crucial fact that patients seek bodily functioning for the purpose of continuing various valued life-functions that illness threatens. The question now is: "Which are the functions of the well-working human organism *as a whole*, in relation to its *proper human environment?*" Kass lists such things as "the patient's powers and desires for work, friendship, love, learning, awareness, mobility, thought and memory, self-command, and the sheer enjoyment of life. . . ." Neither the clinical setting nor the usual techniques of medicine are ideally designed to assist the physician in assessing the level of this sort of functioning or in improving and maintaining it (Kass, 1985, p. 202).

Third, since patients come to the clinic with capacities to achieve varying degrees of health, physicians must do more than simply apply health as a standard. Kass eventually comes to view medicine not simply as an art aimed at health as an end but as a complex practice that mediates between health as a universal standard and the fact that it is attainable by individual patients only provisionally and temporarily. The task of determining what level of functioning is possible for a particular patient requires detailed attention to life-functioning and also life-situations, especially for the chronically ill (Kass, 1985, pp. 202–203).

Finally, unlike other *technai* medicine deals with the mystery of human embodiment, which means that the quest for health is bound up with the vulnerability of human beings to illness and decay and with the fears and disturbances of the immediacy of our relation to the life-world that accompany illness.

> The physician, who is a knower of health and the numerous forms of its absence, who seeks to assist the healing powers in the human body, also must tend particular, necessitous human beings who, in addition to their symptoms, suffer from self-concern and often fear and shame—about weakness and vulnerability, neediness and dependence, loss of self-esteem, and the fragility of all that matters to them. (Kass, 1985, p. 219)

Here the asymmetry of the physician as knower/leader/teacher and the patient as needy is complemented by an equal and mutual sharing in finitude (though the physician remains a figure of strength and support while the patient is needy and vulnerable). Once again, this dimension of medicine transcends what is involved in a *techne* and entails additional moral duties and virtues. Discussing the so-called decorum paragraphs in the Hippocratic Oath (having to do with the doctor's behavior when he or she enters the houses of the sick), Kass observes that illness upsets the network of relations that constitutes the household of the patient and forces on all a recognition of the precariousness of the human. "All our hopes and aspirations, our ways and achievements, and all our loves are at the mercy of this fragile body. This grim truth, as well as our particular degradations, are confirmed and ratified when the doctor enters a house" (Kass, 1985, pp. 237–238). The prohibition against sexual relations with patients recognizes the exploitation possible in such a situation—but also the injustice already done to the patient's humanity by reducing his or her body to the objectifying gaze of medicine; the obligation to confidentiality recognizes the need to protect the reputations and self-esteem of the ill—but also the importance to the patient and family of maintaining "protective shame" against exposure of the indignities of illness to outsiders, a need that has already been compromised by the necessary intrusion of the physician (Kass, 1985, pp. 238–240). In both cases, the very activities by which the physician ministers to the finitude and vulnerabililty of the sick threaten also to exacerbate the indignity and degradation inherent in illness. Hence the need for duties with regard to justice and shame. "These professionally imposed restrictions on deed and speech grow out of the recognition that illness is inherently degrading and dehumanizing, and that it exposes and threatens the sick person's body, soul, and intimate relationships. The physician pledges himself not to aggravate degradation or exploit weakness" (Kass, 1985, p. 222). However, finitude and vulnerability do not involve only degradation and indignity, they also provide the occasion for courage and for resistance to fear, shame, and despair. Hence an additional duty of the physician is to instruct and encourage the patient in the cultivation and exercise of these powers (Kass, 1985, p. 222).

The result of these observations is that the moral fabric of medicine is actually a very complex pattern. What appeared to be a relatively straightforward *techne* directed to health turns out to be a rich practice "with its own special norms and duties flowing from (1) the dignity and precariousness of the goal—health; (2) the human meaning of illness; and (3) the mutually shared self-consciousness of the doctor-patient relationship" with its asymmetry in regard to the sick patient and the treating physician who yet share equally "in the gift of life and in its unavoidable finitude" (Kass, 1985, p. 213).

Where does all of this leave us with regard to medicine as a moral art in an era when we need to determine whether or how new biomedical technologies fit into the pursuit of a good and worthy life?

Assuming that his arguments up to this point can be defended, Kass has shown us how medicine is a moral art. But we do not yet know enough about the standards of bodily excellence or (more broadly) the appropriate kinds of human functioning to make concrete judgments about what medicine should aim at, what should guide discernment of which desires medicine should fulfill, what constitutes an adequate level of flourishing for a particular patient, or how to minister to vulnerability while encouraging resistance. These are not yet criticisms of Kass since he never claimed that medicine is sufficient to answer questions like these. He claimed only that medicine contains implicit knowledge of human nature even if only in the terms of ordinary experience that needs to be articulated, and that medicine has moral commitments even if these also require further elaboration. By way of transition to the following section, I will briefly summarize the implicit knowledge and ethos of medicine according to Kass.

In its cooperation with the body's own powers of self-healing medicine implicitly knows what modern biology denies, namely that the body is not neutral with regard to the difference between health and unhealth. In its efforts to promote and maintain health medicine knows that health is a finite and mortal good that is destined eventually to fail. More generally, medicine knows that humans are vulnerable and necessitous beings who are also capable of resisting necessity. In ministering to the degradations and indignities of illness medicine knows the reality of shame and the human pursuit of the noble in appearance and performance (Kass, 1985, p. 221). The physician's encounter with human nature in these forms is also the source of the moral ethos of medicine. The prohibitions against participation in killing, sexual relations with patients, and breaches of confidentiality mark the boundaries of medicine as an art directed to the health of the patient and prevent abuses of the power over and intrusion into the lives of patients and families. These boundaries are "fixed, firm, and nonnegotiable." But within these boundaries "no fixed rules of conduct apply; instead prudence—the wise judgment of the man on the spot—finds and adopts the best course of action in light of the circumstances" (Kass, 1989, p. 36). Here medicine faces not the dilemmas of standard bioethics but the need to judge the proper relation between the universal end of health and the particularity of need, desire, and vulnerability in the individual patient. The task of biology, accordingly, is to develop a broad understanding of human nature that articulates this implicit knowledge and grounds this ethos. Without such articulation medicine will be caught between modern biology, which shuns the kind of implicit knowledge medicine represents, and modern ethics, which complements modern biology by its assumption that ethics is purely conventional. Wed to a science that seeks to control nature for the sake of a will that seeks to transcend nature, medicine will be unable to accomplish its limited but vital role in genuine human flourishing.

THE PROFUNDITY OF THE SUPERFICIAL

Is nature a source of knowledge about the human good? More specifically, can natural science articulate and develop the knowledge of human nature implicit in medical practice and determine which uses of the new biomedical technologies are in accordance with human fulfillment and which are dehumanizing? Kass seeks to develop an Aristotelian ethic capable of deriving from nature an ethical content substantive enough to ground a view of human flourishing.[4] For Kass this effort hinges on one's success in returning teleology to nature, or rather in finding there the teleology modern science drove from our ordinary conception of nature.

Exactly how does modern science make it impossible to derive moral significance from nature? According to Kass it does so by concentrating on efficient and material causes (how things work or happen) while ignoring formal and final causes (what and why things are). While applauding the insights of modern science into the former, Kass argues for the primacy of form, the "what" of a being, and finds in form the telos (the "why") of individual beings.[5] In so doing he faces two challenges from modern science. The first is the attempt to dismiss the importance of form by explaining it as the accidental product of more elementary mechanical or chemical dynamics of matter. The second is Darwin's explanation of form as the preservation by natural selection of chance variations. Beginning with the materialist challenge, Kass adapts Jonas's arguments regarding metabolism in order to establish the primacy of form over matter. Although material properties are in part responsible for its changes, the organism persists through these changes while its matter does not, and thus maintains a degree of independence from its matter. Moreover, while the organism persists due to transfers of chemical energy from molecule to molecule, metabolic exchange occurs only as the function of an organized whole (Kass, 1994, pp. 40–42).

Turning to the second challenge, Kass denies that Darwin's theory refutes the teleological nature of organisms. This becomes clear when one understands what form is. Form is the visible order of a being, its "looks." "'Looks' perserves the etymological insight that both the *fact* of a thing's wholeness and, more important, the distinctive *kind* of whole that it is are generally evident in its visible appearance" (Kass, 1994, pp. 36–37). In living organisms visible order is more than shape or figure: an organism is "a structure not a heap," and to be a structure is to be organized for a function and thus to be purposive. Form makes a being a unified whole through time while also giving it singularity as an individual and identity through its natural kind (species). And organisms are realized as living forms by development into a completion or a whole—the form into which they develop constitutes a goal, not just an outcome. Form also involves the internal organization of an organism: all of its parts contribute to the whole. There is teleology in the contributions of the parts to the whole and in the way in which the whole maintains itself through its powers to regenerate missing parts and to heal wounds or breaks. Form is not identifiable with the boundary of the organism constituted by its surface or skin. This is so for all living things due to metabolism, but is especially the case with animals (including humans), who through their form interact with the world in complex ways and whose form communicates inwardness. Not surpisingly, then, organisms as wholes function beyond simply maintaining themselves. They display concerns for various activities as ends in themselves (e.g., looks, play, even ceremony) and also participate in the ends of the group (Kass, 1985, pp. 254–256; 1994, pp. 36–39). Finally, the form of an organism is not only the goal of its development, but also involves standards. "When considering the functioning of an animal, we ask not only whether it functions in a characteristic way, but whether it functions well or normally as such and such an animal. . . . Teleological analysis will be concerned both to identify the end and to evaluate how well or badly it is achieved" (Kass, 1985, p. 257).

Kass insists that a "view of living beings as purposive, as self-producing, self-maintaining, and self-reproducing, is in no way undermined by Darwin's theory" (Kass, 1985, p. 259), though Darwin reduced this internal teleology to self-preservation. But Kass agrees with Jonas that if the survival or permanence of individuals or species were the good that nature seeks, life would never have begun in the first place. And like Jonas, Kass considers whether nature as a whole might have a purpose in bringing forth such a variety of forms—a purpose that eludes us if we look only to individual organisms and species.

> Though not his intent, Darwin makes us wonder whether the principle of survival is sufficient to account for nature's prodigality. Has Darwinism adequately identified, much less explained,

the immanent native "strivings" of organic life? Might appearance, show, diversity, even beauty be independent and additional "concerns" or "principles" of nature? (Kass, 1985, pp. 268–269)

Moreover, as for Jonas nature for Kass seems to produce not only variety of form but a hierarchy in which progressively greater complexity makes possible increasing richness and diversity of experience. In Kass's terms, "the processes of evolution not only produced more and more organisms, new species and new forms . . . but also *higher grades* of soul" (Kass, 1985, p. 270). He develops this observation along Jonas's lines, referring to the emergence of sensitivity and awareness followed by locomotion and desire and finally speech and intellect. Hence "[t]he ascent of soul has meant the possibility both of an ever-greater awareness of and openness *to* the world, and an ever-greater freedom *in* the world. . . . The hierarchy of soul is a hierarchy of openness and purposiveness" (Kass, 1985, p. 271).

Kass's understanding of form differs from Jonas's in a way that makes it possible for him to claim a more robust teleology. For Jonas form is identified with the self-performing activity of the organism which is not reducible to mathematical descriptions and physical explanations of its matter, or alternatively (and less dualistically) self-performance is the continual self-becoming of the organism that constitutes form and matter. In either case, purposiveness itself—the striving or self-concern of the organism—is logically prior to form. Hence Jonas does not designate realization of form as the telos to which the organism strives; rather the telos is constituted either by form simply as the continuing self-performance of the organism or by the playing out of the polarity of form and matter. In contrast Kass highlights the priority of form to purposiveness in the sense that an organism strives for completion or perfection of its form (just as evolution apparently aims at richer and more varied forms). Kass can therefore speak not only of continuing self-performance or living out polarities, but also of standards and of greater and lesser approximations of perfection or well-functioning. In other words, Kass is an Aristotelian at the very point where Jonas is, as I pointed out in chapter three, a modern. If Kass's view is defensible, nature provides in form itself—regardless of its origin or its future—a standard to measure the degree of fulfilment of beings. Even at this point, therefore, Kass's biology accounts for what medicine knows implicitly: that the body is not neutral with regard to disease and health; that in its powers of self-healing the organism strives to be a well-functioning whole.

Another difference between Kass and Jonas accounts for a radical difference of method and for Kass's explanation of why science has ignored form. Because purposive striving or concern for being is onto-logically primary for Jonas, form, or the polarity of form and matter, is for him knowable only through an ontology of the living body in which form is a result of purposive striving. Kass agrees that form is the his-torical product of purposive natural processes: there are no eternal Aristotelian forms. But for him form is readily knowable as a surface phenomenon, and its significance can be grasped apart from empirical questions regarding its origins, metaphysical questions regarding its status vis-à-vis matter or as a natural kind, and epistemological ques-tions regarding the relation of description (which grasps surfaces) and explanation.[6] Rather, the significance of form can be readily grasped in the ways in which it appears, and of course appearances are accessible to our ordinary experience of nature. This sets Kass against modern science, and modern culture more generally, both of which involve a "depreciation of surfaces and distrust of appearances" (Kass, 1985, p. 320). In any case, an investigation of what is primary in nature (i.e., form) will involve a return to "what is immediately and manifestly evi-dent" (Kass, 1985, p. 320). Ordinary experience, given sufficient reflec-tion, turns out to be "the privileged road to the deepest truth" (Kass, 1994, p. 8).

To understand the moral significance of nature, then, we must according to Kass attend reflectively to the profundity of the superficial, that is, to form, rather than to the more hidden material and efficient causes of things. What does the human form tell us? We saw above that for Kass nature produces forms that make possible an increasingly richer and more diverse experience of the world. The apex is the human form. Borrowing from a famous essay by Erwin Straus, Kass reflects on the upright posture of human beings as the condition for unique human characteristics and ways of relating to the world. First, the upright posture confers the capacity to stand. Standing is, like many other distinctively human traits, an accomplishment, and one that must be attained by repeated struggle against the forces of gravity. This itself is significant, for in Straus's words "[i]t seems to be [man's] nature to oppose nature in its impersonal, fundamental aspects with natural means" (Kass, 1985, p. 286; 1994, p. 65). Effort against natural forces and attainment of a special standing, yet also a precariousness in that one is always in danger of falling—the upright posture indicates the basic human stance of resisting or withstanding, a natural opposition to nature that according to Straus may make society itself possible (Kass, 1985, p. 286; 1994, p. 65). Perhaps because this stance could imply that humanity is destined to transcend nature (e.g., by technology), Kass quickly points out that such opposition is always incomplete; after all, standing itself is possible only because of gravity. However, the capacity to stand is an ambivalent characteristic. It expands our range of inter- action by making possible a stunning richness of cognitive, affective, and locomotive means of responding to and overcoming what is dis- tant. But it also trades the immediate commerce with things that crawl- ing beings have for a world relation in which our new powers and new kind of sociality are accompanied by a distance and aloofness from oth- ers and from things (Kass, 1985, pp. 286–287; 1994, pp. 65–66).

The upright posture frees the arms and hands for a variety of cog- nitive, practical and expressive functions. The free-swinging arms define a sphere of action or "action space." The hands, also liberated, enrich our experience through a developed sense of touch. The arms and hands are freed to express affection, desire, need, and so on. Pointing makes it possible to share our openness to the world with another (Kass, 1985, p. 287; 1994, pp. 67–70). Other features of Straus's reflection figure in Kass's account, but enough has been said to lend some plausibility to his claim that "[t]he dumb human body, rightly attended to, shows all the marks of, and creates all the conditions for, our rationality and our special way of being in the world" (Kass, 1994, p. 75). Although Kass does not carry out such a project, one begins to understand that careful and thorough attention to the human form might yield a fairly com- prehensive list of what Kass would consider the functions that count in the assessment of human flourishing. Once again, it appears that biol- ogy articulates the knowledge medicine presupposes.

Kass is aware, however, that Straus's account can be overly opti- mistic—in the same way, interestingly enough (though Kass does not mention this), in which Kass's initial description of medicine as an art was overly optimistic, namely by forgetting that with all their capacities human beings are still vulnerable and necessitous. Or as Kass puts it, "man is not a simple metaphysical success story" (Kass, 1994, p. 77). If the upright posture makes possible rationality and self-consciousness, is not the biblical story of the Garden of Eden on track in suggesting that the first discovery was not what was anticipated—"that his eyes would be opened and he would be as a god—that is, self-sufficing, autonomous, independent, knowing, perhaps immortal, and free at last"—but rather human nakedness? "The first human knowledge rel- evant to life is knowledge of our nakedness and knowledge that naked- ness is shameful and bad" (Kass, 1985, pp. 290–291).

Why shameful and bad? To be naked is to be vulnerable and exposed. Moreover, human awareness of nakedness is awareness that we are neither complete nor whole in ourselves but "have need for and are dependent upon a complementary other, even to realize our own

bodily nature." Furthermore, we are internally divided. "We are possessed by an unruly or rebellious 'autonomous' sexual nature within . . .
which embarrasses our claim to self-command." Finally, our nakedness
signifies our mortality: "the genetalia are also a sign of our perishability,
in that they provide for those who will replace us." The humbling of
pride occasioned by these four features is compounded by a result of our
awareness itself. "For a doubleness is now present in the soul" as a spon-
taneous, unself-conscious participation in life is replaced by seeing ourselves through the judgments of others. "Self-scrutiny, self-absorption,
attention to ourselves being seen by others, vanity, and . . . self-loathing"
are all "coincident with self-consciousness; and self-consciousness is coincident with learning of our nakedness" (Kass, 1985, p. 291).

We are now in a position to understand Kass's central claim
regarding ethics, namely that the human animal is a moral animal *by
nature* and not only as a result of society. Ethics, in other words, is not
simply a social invention; nature itself poses the problem of morality
that custom or convention in all its variety and diversity seeks to solve.
How does nature pose the problem of morality? First, as the survey of
the upright posture indicates, "our form—that is, our given nature—
points in a variety of directions and all at once, even before these directions are explored, pursued, and shaped by culture" (Kass, 1994, p. 76).
Our unique capacities can be exercised in various ways and for various
ends. We are capable of both autonomy and community, contemplation and action, rivalry and cooperation. Our nature is left open and
undetermined by its form; it must be made determinate by the contingency of choice. That human beings are by nature moral but that the
content of the moral is not determined by nature is also clear in the
case of our vulnerability and necessity. When Adam and Eve sew fig
leaves to cover their nakedness they indicate, in the first place, that the
human form is by nature completed by convention. "Man's look is
partly of his own making. It reveals that he is by nature an animal that
lives by art, that he is also by nature an animal that lives by convention"
(Kass, 1985, p. 338). Clothing dignifies necessity and thus transforms
into nobility our potentially degrading discovery of our likeness to
other animals and our distance from the divine (Kass, 1985, pp.
338–339). If the choice of a way of life gives direction or determinacy to
the fundamental openness of nature, the conventional here may be said
to transform or dignify the potentially degrading necessity and vulnerability of nature.

Clothing also shows human beings to be concerned with their looks.
This brings us to a more internal concern, apparent in shame, with how
one appears to others. Shame is knowable through the uniquely and uni-

versally human phenomenon of blushing. Blushing is first of all entirely involuntary (Kass, 1985, p. 334). This is significant because shame is, as noted above, connected with what we do not control (Kass, 1994, p. 147). But blushing also indicates an important duality. On the one hand it is social. The blush communicates to others and involves the sense of one-self as capable of being judged by others. It tacitly acknowledges shared conventions. On the other hand, the blush displays a concern with one's own looks and how one appears to others. The blush, in other words, signifies our social but also our aesthetic nature and combines them in our sense of self-esteem.

Once again, biology in this broad sense articulates what medicine in Kass's view implicitly knows. Medicine knows persons as vulnerable and necessitous beings and also as beings concerned with a self-esteem that is easily threatened by the effects of illness on self-presentation. The need to cover what is potentially degrading is, it seems, implicitly known by medicine in the Hippocratic injunction regarding confiden-tiality. Similarly, the physician's knowledge of the patient's capacities for courage and for resistance to fear, shame, and degradation seem to con-stitute a tacit knowledge of the capacity of human beings to elevate and dignify necessity.

The nature of morality according to Kass and its relation to nature and convention is now clear. As blushing indicates, shame is natural. It also involves sociality insofar as it requires, at least in imagination, one's awareness of the judgment of the other. Tracing the etymology of shame in the Greek language, Kass argues that one feels shame in relation to what is beautiful or venerable. Shame, then, is felt when one does what is base or disgraceful. Yet the standards for the beautiful and venerable are all determined by convention, so that one always feels shame with reference to a conventional standard. If that with reference to which we feel shame is therefore always conventional yet the capacity to feel shame (as the phenomenon of blushing implies) is natural, then it appears that we are by nature concerned with morality—that is, that custom provides standards that, however conventional, form or shape a natural concern with attaining individuation and distinction in the eyes of the community and thereby gaining self-esteem. "At the bottom of shame, for all its conventional trappings, lies a natural concern for self-respect, a concern grounded in self-consciousness and an aspiration to be worthy" (Kass, 1985, p. 342). An Aristotelian ethic of human flourishing as excellent activity or performance according to the standards of the community is thus shown to be ultimately grounded in nature.

For Kass, then, morality is rooted in nature: law or custom (*nomos*) completes, elevates or transforms nature (*physis*). Because human nature can be completed, and so forth in a variety of ways that human nature itself does not determine, morality is inevitably conventional yet is still grounded in the natural. Nevertheless Kass seems to operate with a complex view of the relation of convention to nature. I will try to order the complexity by distinguishing three types of morality that, I believe, fall for Kass on a spectrum between the limit cases of pure nature and pure convention. The grounding of morality in the natural is most clear in the case of taboos such as cannibalism and incest, where the close connection of morality to nature leaves little to convention or, by the very nature of a taboo, to reflective criticism. Cannibalism is ultimately the reduction of the human being to mere body—a denial of the difference between human beings and other animals and of the importance of this difference for human flourishing (Kass, 1985, p. 113; 1994, pp. 109–110). This understanding leads Kass to view the tendency to reduce embryos to mere fodder for experimentation as a form of cannibalism (Kass, 1985, pp. 108, 113). The incest and adultery taboos "defend the integrity of marriage, kinship, and especially the lines of origin and descent" (Kass, 1985, p. 113). This point is relevant to issues surrounding in vitro fertilization, to be discussed below. It is notable that taboos address both aspects of our nature according to Kass: our dignity and our necessity.

At the other end of the spectrum from taboos are customs in the strict sense. Customs address the aspiration to the noble. Unlike taboos, they leave much room for variation and are not universal. As conventional, customs can be criticized; but as grounded in the natural, they are criticized with reference to their adequacy to the natural.

> To be sure, much of the particular content of the cultural forms will be a matter of human agreement—that is, strictly conventional—and relative to time and place. But this does not necessarily mean that there cannot be better and worse customs. Some customs . . . might be more conducive than others to human flourishing. Some customs might be more fitting to the truth about the world. (Kass, 1994, p. 98)

As we will soon find out, Kass does not hesitate to criticize customs of other cultures when he believes that they are not adequate to the truth about human nature.

Between taboo and custom stand law and justice. Like customs their content varies, but like taboos they involve prohibitions rather than aspirations. Kass follows Aristotle for whom law and justice are necessary because the capacities of human beings make them potentially the worst of beings. "If [man] is not to become the worst of the animals, he must be restrained by law and justice. And if he is to become the best of the animals, he must be perfected by rearing in customs that bring out and complete what is best in his nature" (Kass, 1994, p. 98).

The foregoing account suggests that the task of a conventional morality is to complete our undetermined nature and to elevate our necessity into nobility. It is precisely this reference of convention to nature that is lost when morality or custom is thought of as purely conventional—as a matter of individual or intersubjective invention. The divorce of ethics from nature encourages the view, expressed so clearly in the Baconian project, that human flourishing consists in transcending—not transforming—natural necessity. "It is tempting to suggest that nobility consists in 'rising above' or 'transcending' our animality, through acts of what one might call 'self-levitation'" (Kass, 1994, p. 158). For example, Kass seems to view the biomedical quests to increase the human life span and to overcome the tie of procreation to lineage as efforts to transcend our natural mortality: one by extending life indefinitely, the other by declaring ourselves autonomous and independent of any connection to a lineage that reminds us of our mortality. In the face of these quests the task of bioethics is to present a more adequate—a more natural—conception of human nobility. "'Nobility' is not so much a transcendence of animality as it is the turning of animality into its peculiarly human and regulated form" (Kass, 1994, pp. 158–159).

Nature has a role not only as a criterion for our customs but also in determining what degree of criticism and reflection is appropriate to bring to our customs. Kass is keenly aware that critical reflection is potentially as damaging to our moral and political opinions as it is to our opinions about the nature of the world—in all cases inquiry is the enemy of the rule of opinion (Kass, 1985, pp. 4–7). He apparently would agree with Bernard Williams that reflection can destroy the immediacy and confidence with which we live out our own morality (Williams, 1985, pp. 167–171). But simply to take our morality as it is given is to ignore that we are by nature self-conscious beings. Our awareness of our nature can and should influence our customs and practices (Kass, 1994, p. 93). This indicates that Kass would find inadequate the first type of morality discussed by Michael Oakeshott in his famous essay, "The Tower of Babel," namely "the unreflective following of a tradition of conduct in which we have been brought up" (Oakeshott, 1989, p. 187). For this type of morality ignores the fact that by nature we reflect on our nature. It fails to treat convention as conventional, namely as a human construct designed to fulfill or transform the natural.

However, a morality that is grounded in reflective criticism itself can lead us to forget or deny altogether that we are natural beings. In a blistering critique, Kass attacks standard bioethics for being as far removed from ordinary experience as is modern science. It formulates its principles in abstraction from the deliberation and practice of concrete agents, ignores ends, treats human beings rationalistically rather than as embodied, substitutes rational analysis for prudence, and focuses on solving quandaries while ignoring entirely the moral formation of agents (Kass, 1990, pp. 6–9). Standard bioethicists begin with these abstractions, Kass argues, because they assume that we can get from thought to action via the application of principles. As such, standard bioethics reflects Oakeshott's second type, in which "a special value is attributed to self-consciousness, individual or social; not only is the rule or the ideal the product of reflective thought, but the application of the rule or the ideal to the situation is also a reflective activity" (Oakeshott, 1989, p. 191). For Kass this ignores the way morality is connected with our nature. Standard bioethics, and modern moral philosophy in general, fail to realize that mind and desire become grown together not through the application of principles, which never reaches desire, but through "the direct but unreflective education of our loves and hates, our pleasures and pains, gained only in practice, through habituation and by means of praise and blame, reward and punishment." This means that in ethics "the true route begins with practice, with deeds and doers, and moves only secondarily to reflection on practice" (Kass, 1990, p. 9). Kass therefore calls for Oakeshott's third type, a mixture of the first two in which the first is dominant.[7] A bioethics of this type, Kass argues, will attend first and foremost to the cultivation of self-esteem and to the appropriate moral content to give to this natural concern with the noble. It will therefore concern itself with how the passions of the souls of physicians and others are cultivated and instructed, and will recognize that resolving bioethical issues is more a matter of the kind of people our institutions produce than the kind of theories we generate (Kass, 1990, pp. 10–11).

What status does this nature-grounded, reflective customary morality have in law and policy? For the most part Kass accepts the legitimacy of liberal democracy and its laissez-faire approach to scientific research and to markets, though he worries that modern science and ethics have led to the inability to defend liberal democracy rationally (Kass, 1985, pp. 4–7, 133–138). In addition to legal protections to uphold basic rights Kass does argue for a regulatory role for the government with regard to potentially dangerous technologies, though he gives no criterion for this except a vague appeal to the public interest or the common good (Kass, 1985, pp. 41–42, 138–144). However, inculcation of and reflection on custom is not for the purpose of enacting laws and policies but for forming the kinds of citizens and institutions that Kass believes are required if liberal democracy is to survive and flourish (Kass, 1985, p. 348; 1992, p. 81).

Kass's view of the relation of nature to convention and the proper role of reflection in morality is cogently summarized in his discussion of a famous episode in Herodotus' *Histories*. Herodotus tells how the Persian King Darius asked a group of Greeks what he should pay them to eat the bodies of their fathers when the latter died. They replied that they would not do so for any sum. Darius then called in a group of Indians who ate their deceased fathers and asked them what he should give them to burn their corpses. They responded with outcries urging Darius not to use such language. Herodotus concludes: "Such is men's custom; and Pindar was right in my judgment, when he said, 'Law [or 'custom' or 'convention' or 'mores': *nomos*] is king over all'" (Kass, 1985, p. 281).

Kass begins with the divergent responses of the Greeks and Indians to the practices of the other. Both express unwillingness to adopt the practice of the other, but while the Indians respond with abhorrence and refuse to answer the question, the Greeks answer Darius and then stand by calmly to listen to the exchange with the Indians. For the Indians, who are more pious or superstitious than reflective, "the undoable is also unthinkable, or at least unspeakable. . . . Their customs completely dominate their thought. They will never attain to the insight that *nomos* is king over all, thereby discovering the difference between convention and nature. . . ." In short, they fit Oakeshott's first type. The Greeks, by contrast, "though closed in their practice, are open in thought. . . . The Greeks are pious, but mindfully so" since they know the difference between custom and truth. They are therefore able to countenance the reality of different customs while still adhering to their own. "The Greeks, far more than the Indians, behave as rational animals" (Kass, 1985, p. 296). They exhibit Oakeshott's third type. Kass notes, however, that there is a third party in the story: the Persians. Darius has seen through the conventionality of customs. "Indeed, he revels publicly in his discovery. He compels people to look upon ways that are not their own, to confront what must be seen from his detached and enlightened view as the simple arbitrariness of their own way." The Persians conform to Oakeshott's second type: "Strict rationality is the Persian way" (Kass, 1985, p. 297).

Kass goes on to speculate on possible relations between the different attitudes toward reflection and differences in attitudes and practices regarding the body. In ingesting the bodies of their ancestors, the Indians engaged in "a death-defying and even death-denying act, inasmuch as they swallowed much of the evidence of its occurrence." They reduced their ancestors to mere body (cannibalism) and denied mortality by having their ancestors live on inside of them (Kass, 1985, pp. 296–297). "The Greeks, in contrast, knew the difference between the father and his mortal remains" and thus maintained their connection with the ancestors through speech and symbolic deed rather than ingestion and incorporation (Kass, 1985, p. 297). The Persians, as their rationalistic morality would indicate, seperated the person from the body and displayed contempt for the body. For Herodotus reports that their male bodies were buried only after they were mutilated by dogs or birds and that they also mutilated their living bodies to shape them according to their own will and taste (Kass, 1985, p. 297).

It is clear that Kass favors the Greeks, who are reverent but neither superstitious nor autonomous, reasonable but not hyperrational, and respectful of the body rather than contemptuous of it or in denial of its mortality. It is also clear where he thinks modern medicine places us in the story.

> We, on the other hand, with our dissection of cadavers, organ transplantation, cosmetic surgery, body shops, laboratory fertilization, surrogate wombs, gender-change surgery, "wanted" children, "rights over our bodies," sexual liberation, and other practices and beliefs that insist on our independence and autonomy, live more and more wholly for the here and now, subjugating everything we can to the exercise of our wills, with little respect for the nature and meaning of bodily life. . . . Rational without wonder, willful but without reverence, we are on our way to becoming Persians. (Kass, 1985, p. 298)

This brings us to Kass's major practical concern: Can a bioethics informed by a proper understanding of nature and taking up a critically reflective stance toward convention enable us to distinguish uses of technological medicine that complete our nature and dignify our necessity from uses that degrade our humanity? Can bioethics become "Greek" or is it destined to remain "Persian"?

NATURE, MEDICINE, AND THE TECHNOLOGY OF CONCEPTION

Kass has addressed several concrete bioethical issues, including euthanasia, the buying and selling of organs, and the effort to retard the aging process. In all three cases he points to the intrinsic commitments of medicine or to the price we pay by sacrificing nature and well-founded custom to autonomy and expediency to respond to the increasing expectation that medicine empowered by technology should eliminate suffering and deliver humans from finitude. Any of these issues would illustrate how Kass wants medicine to deal with its technological powers. However, the issue of in vitro fertilization and embryo transfer is ideal for several reasons. First, Kass has addressed it in more detail than any other issue. Second, he treated it in two essays written several years apart that indicate changes of mind and approach. Third, infertility has an ambiguous status as a disease or a departure from well-functioning and is thus a good test case to explore what Kass means by health.

For standard bioethics the new reproductive technologies (NRTs) primarily raise issues of rights (usually those of the adults involved) and harms (usually to the potential child). Feminism and religious traditions, sometimes in alliance, expand the range of concerns. Many feminists argue that due to social factors and the entrenched interests of biomedicine the NRTs do not increase the autonomy of women, and that in their almost exclusive emphasis on the potential child standard bioethics and public policy eclipse both the role of and the risks to women in NRTs. Catholics and many Protestants argue that many or most NRTs violate norms and ideals that constitute the moral integrity of marriage. Both feminists and religious writers argue that at least some NRTs (especially commercial surrogacy) exploit women. Kass is often grouped with feminist and religious opponents of NRTs due to his deep reservations about in vitro fertilization (IVF). However, he disagrees with both groups on crucial issues, and where there is agreement it is often on different grounds. The picture is even more complicated since Kass started out opposing IVF in general but ended up accepting it (though not without reservations) as legitimate in the context of marriage.

In his major essay devoted to IVF Kass considers two of the issues most commonly addressed in standard bioethics, namely the right of a couple to have a child and the risks to the potential child. Neither issue plays a major role in his account. He quickly dismisses rights claims by pointing out some of the ambiguities in the language of rights (whose right, and to what?) and concluding that since infertility involves relationships between mother, father, and child, the language of rights is inappropriate (Kass, 1985, pp. 44–45). Risks to the potential child receive more attention. Kass considers Paul Ramsey's view, published several years before the first live birth of a baby born through IVF in 1978, that any IVF experiment conducted on embryos is morally wrong since it constitutes nontherapeutic experimentation on the unborn. He originally agreed with this argument but eventually changed his mind, noting that Ramsey assumes that having children is for the benefit of the parents and that therefore such experimentation does not benefit the child. If instead "we have children not primarily for ourselves but for our children . . . then this clear benefit to a child-to-be . . . could justify the risks taken because they are taken in the child's behalf" and thus are analogous to therapeutic experimentation, for which nonexcessive risks are justified (Kass, 1985, p. 55). As long as the risks are not significantly greater than in normal childbirth, IVF is not morally impermissible on these grounds.

Kass also rejects an argument, offered by the Catholic Church and by some Protestants and Jews, that IVF is morally illicit because the process produces embryos who are not transferred back into the womb.[8] Because Kass believes (more as an opinion than as the result of an argument) that the early embryo at the blastocyst stage is only potentially a human being it may be allowed to die, but because it is nevertheless potentially human it must be treated with respect, which means, concretely, that as long as the deaths of preimplantation embryos are not significantly more than those that occur naturally in procreation it is permissible to let them die, though not to conduct experiments on them (Kass, 1985, pp. 102–110).[9]

In short, no right of the couple to have a child justifies IVF, and no nonexcessive risk to the future child or limited loss of embryonic life prohibits it. In place of these standard arguments, Kass opposes IVF on the grounds that it is dehumanizing. Why? Because it delivers procreation over to calculative rationality and manufacture.

> [H]uman procreation is not simply an activity of our rational wills. Men and women are embodied as well as calculating creatures. . . . [Human procreation] is a more complete human activity precisely because it engages us bodily, erotically, and even spiritually, as well as rationally. . . . Before we embark on new modes of reproduction, we should consider the meaning of the union of sex, love, and procreation, and the meaning and consequences of its cleavage. (Kass, 1985, p. 72)

At first glance Kass seems to have adopted the official Roman Catholic conclusion that IVF is morally wrong because it violates the unity of conjugal love and openness to procreation that must not be separated (Congregation for the Doctrine of the Faith, 1988, pp. 161–164). But he has no objections to the separation of conjugal love from openness to procreation; he readily accepts contraceptives. His concern is rather with the subjection of procreation to calculative rationality, or "the attempt to supplant nature with rationality in the very mystery of life . . ." (Kass, 1985, pp. 71–72).[10] Still, one may ask exactly why sub-mission of procreation to rationality is dehumanizing. The reason is that Kass understands rationality in a way that recalls Jonas's equation of technology with artificiality and of artificiality with power unlim-ited by any respect for the value of what it controls.

> With *in vitro* fertilization, the natural process of generating becomes the artificial process of making. . . . To lay one's hands on human generation is to take a major step toward making man himself simply another one of the manmade things. Thus, human nature becomes simply the last part of nature that is to succumb to the modern technological project, a project that has already turned all of the rest of nature into raw material at human disposal, to be homogenized by our rationalized technique according to the artis-tic conventions of the day. (Kass, 1985, p. 73)

The shadow of this disenchanted world falls across Kass's whole account of IVF. In its "service of producing only wanted, willed, and flawless babies," IVF paves the way for cloning, positive and negative eugenics, and in general the capacity for human beings to create them-selves according to their own arbitary wishes—a capacity that, as with Jonas, portends the end of humanity itself (Kass, 1985, pp. 45–46, 69, 72, 77–78).

Of course this sounds like a classic wedge or slippery slope argu-ment, but Kass, like many feminists who are wary of the scientific-med-ical establishment, understands that new technologies do not only bring new forms of rationality but combine them with new forms of power (Kass, 1985, pp. 11, 69–70; see Corea, 1987). It is true that feminists are more concerned about power over women's lives while Kass, though he mentions this, worries more about power over children of future gen-erations. In any case, Kass's general point seems to be not only that nature has given way to calculative rationality in the service of arbi-trary ends, but that with the intervention of the scientist-physician a new partner and new forms of control have entered the sphere of pro-creation, and that this power, combined with calculative rationality, makes possible the more serious threats.

These ultimate consequences for our humanity are the major but not the only reason for the rejection of IVF. Two additional reasons are especially important. The first concerns both commercial and altruistic surrogacy and, to a lesser extent, oocyte donation. Since standard bioethical arguments for IVF based on autonomy often justify surrogacy as well, Kass considers the latter as an extension of the former. Both commercial and altruistic surrogacy risk adverse psychological consequences to the gestational mother who must give up the child at birth, and involve exploitation of women and their bodies. Altruistic surrogacy has the advantage of greater distance from the notion of children as property to be bought and sold but may put female relatives of infertile couples under intense pressures to lend wombs or donate eggs (Kass, 1985, p. 61). Many feminists and religious writers would applaud Kass for recognizing potential exploitation here, but feminists would question why Kass never considers that married women may be under similar familial and social pressures to participate in IVF.

Michelle Stanworth argues that NRTs are controversial in part because they crystallize contested social and political issues regarding sexuality, gender, and the family (Stanworth, 1987, pp. 4, 18–35). The second additional reason Kass opposes IVF—a reason that sets him against many feminists—regards its potential for the undermining, and even elimination, of the traditional family. The permissibility of the separation of procreation from sexual intercourse also permits the separation of procreation from kinship—unless, of course, there is a principle that can distinguish intramarital from extramarital uses of IVF. While Kass does not wish to idealize the traditional family, his condemnation of those who welcome its demise is unwavering, even to the point of an allusion to the Nazi Holocaust: "Are we to accept as desirable the final solution that eliminates biological kinship from the foundation of social organization?" (Kass, 1985, p. 74).

As long as the primary reason for opposition to IVF was its artificiality and the control of human nature it makes possible, the distinction between intra- and extramarital IVF was relatively unimportant. The submission of procreation to calculative rationality and the intervention of the physician-scientist, with the cost this exacts in terms of dehumanization, occur in both cases; the difference is primarily in the additional consequences for the family that occur with extramarital IVF. Perhaps more important, as I noted above, separation of procreation from sexuality is seen to extend, in the absence of an additional principle, to the separation of procreation from kinship. Kass's later work on IVF identifies, in the natural importance of lineage, a principle that would distinguish these. In effect, then, the concern with the family replaces the concern with artificiality and rational control as the determining issue. And the primacy of the concern for the family follows from the conviction that lineage or biological kinship is essential to human nature.

How does this change Kass's analysis of IVF? First, in accordance with Kass's biology the meaning of the natural shifts from a narrower concern with the relation of sex and procreation to consideration of what human aspirations and desires are natural. Among these is the desire of couples to have a child of their own (Kass, 1985, pp. 110–111). In what sense is this natural? Kass argues that our bodily form manifests our connectedness with the past and future, thus indicating both our mortality and our potential for self-perpetuation. "In the navel are one's forebears, in the genetalia our descendants. These reminders of perishability are also reminders of perpetuation; if we understand their meaning, we are even able to transform the necessary and shameful into the free and noble" (Kass, 1985, p. 293). Kass now believes the desire of couples like the parents of Louise Brown, the first IVF baby, legitimately express this meaning of embodiment. "People like Mr. and Mrs. Brown, who seek a child derived from their flesh, celebrate in so doing their self-identity with their own bodies, and acknowledge the meaning of the living human body by following its pointings to its own perpetuation" (Kass, 1985, p. 113). This use of IVF affirms the importance of lineage and connectedness that define the family, and Kass argues that there would be no objection to IVF if this were its only use (Kass, 1985, p. 111).

In contrast, in cases of embryo transfers outside of marriage (whether directly or through gestational surrogacy) "the new techniques will serve not to ensure and preserve lineage, but rather to confound and complicate it. The principle . . . is not to provide married couples with a child of their own . . . but to provide anyone who wants one with a child, by whatever possible or convenient means" (Kass, 1985, pp. 111–112). The same technology that enabled the Browns to affirm the importance of lineage allows others "to declare themselves independent of their bodies. . . . For them the body is a mere tool, ideally an instrument of the conscious will, the sole repository of human dignity" (Kass, 1985, p. 114). As the first quotation indicates, the problem is not only the denial of lineage but also its confusion. Hence while couples and single persons who make use of a heterologous gamete or contract with a surrogate may claim that they are attempting to approximate the ideal of a child of one's own and affirm the importance of lineage in the only way available to them, Kass would argue that they nevertheless technically violate taboos against incest and adultery that "defend the integrity of marriage, kinship, and especially the lines of origin and descent." The threat to the family comes not only from those who seek to avoid having children but also from those who deny the importance of a clear lineage for identity. "Clarity about your origins is crucial for self-identity, itself important for self-respect" (Kass, 1985, p. 113). Lineage, then, is not only a parent-centered concern for a child of one's own but also a child-centered concern for identity and self-esteem.[11]

Up to now the verdict on IVF seems to follow exclusively from Kass's biology; medicine as a moral art seems to play no role. Now I hope to show that IVF is a paradigm case of how Kass believes medicine should deal with new medical technologies. First, Kass's later stance toward technology exhibits a crucial difference with Jonas: while not morally neutral, IVF technology is capable of both fulfilling and degrading our humanity. This opens the possibility that technology may serve as well as threaten our moral identities. By contrast, when Kass previously interpreted IVF technology in terms of calculative rationality alone, its use for good was precluded. Second, medicine plays a vital role in determining whether IVF technology is used for good or ill. A crucial question is whether infertility is a disease. While repairing a blocked oviduct seems to be a clear case of restoring functioning, Kass questions whether other kinds of infertility or other medical responses qualify. Certainly IVF, which in effect creates a new life to heal an existing one, is a strange way to treat a disease—it seems rather to treat the desire to have a child (Kass, 1985, p. 121). Moreover, infertility often involves a relation rather than simply an individual. On balance then, Kass seems to hold that repairing a blocked oviduct is consistent with the end of medicine because, unlike IVF, it responds to an underlying somatic condition rather than the desire to have a child (Kass, 1985, pp. 45, 51–52). If instead IVF were justified on the grounds that involuntary infertility is a disease, then medicine quickly becomes the servant of the patient's wishes and desires. Whether infertility occurs in or out of marriage is immaterial, and whatever techniques produce a healthy child would be presumably permissible (Kass, 1985, p. 118).

This line of argument would clearly lead to the conclusion that physicians should not perform IVF. However, the reader will recall that medicine for Kass is not merely a *techne* that produces health, but also deals with actual patients whose desires often express a broader understanding of human flourishing than somatic functioning alone can capture. Within the boundaries set by the three Hippocratic prohibitions, physicians exercise prudence, and one task of prudence is to determine what desires of patients are legitimate objects of medicine even though they do not involve somatic health in the strict sense. On these grounds, the natural desire of married couples to have a child of their own, which is so well grounded in Kass's biology, can be a legitimate concern of medicine (Kass, 1985, pp. 118, 121). By exercising prudence shaped by the appropriate attitudes and reflections on human nature, medicine directs new technologies such as IVF toward their potential for human flourishing and away from their potential to degrade our humanity.

Nevertheless there is more to be said, for in this case medical prudence is surrounded by three qualifications and a final reservation. One qualification is that in light of more pressing medical needs IVF is a low priority item. In fact it is even a low priority relative to other ways of dealing with infertility (Kass, 1985, pp. 120–122). Another qualification is that legal prohibition of IVF even for unmarried persons is unwarranted. This would indicate that for Kass the medical profession itself, or perhaps individual physicians, should restrict the procedure to married couples, rather than doing so through public policy. Finally, IVF involves too many features that are morally questionable to many (such as the disposal of embryos) to warrant federal funding (Kass, 1985, pp. 124–125). The reservation follows from Kass's oft-repeated point that individual technologies must be evaluated in the context of the broader Baconian effort to master nature and all that this effort may involve. This this brings us back full circle to Kass's initial point: despite the justifiability of IVF for married couples, by subjecting procreation to calculative rational control we have opened the door to the tyranny of calculative rationality over our humanity and to all that may result from it (Kass, 1985, pp. 125–127).

EVALUATION

According to Kass, whether or not we can avoid the technological utopianism of modern medicine depends significantly on whether we can uphold medicine as a moral profession. This in turn depends on whether medicine is defined by an internal end. We therefore begin with Kass's view of health and its relation to medicine.

If the case of IVF is representative, the concept of health as excellent bodily functioning seems to be less important in determining what is legitimate as Kass moves beyond medicine as a *techne* to its concern with the patient. However, I believe that when Kass shifts from medicine as a *techne* with health as its end to medicine as a complex practice directed to the patient he abandons his original concept of health as somatic functioning in favor of a concept of health as wholeness. According to the original concept health is simply excellent bodily functioning, or the well-functioning of an organic whole. The major strength of this concept is its clarity about medicine as a moral art. Medicine as Kass describes it pursues an internal good (health) in accordance with standards of excellence and within the boundaries of certain rules (the Hippocratic prohibitions)—the major components in Alasdair MacIntyre's description of a practice (MacIntyre, 1984, pp. 187–197). At the same time, medicine is limited by the subjection of health to higher goods of life. A second strength is that Kass gives us, in principle at least, a criterion for the use of new medical technologies. However, the criterion depends on our ability to distinguish what leads to organic well-functioning from what is done for other reasons, and to make this distinction requires a more precise conception of organic functioning than Kass admittedly can supply.

This original account of health and medicine has two problems. The first problem involves the relation between health and virtue. Because Kass assumes that health is a necessary (though not sufficient) condition for virtue, he neglects ways in which sickness can be morally significant and ignores virtues that may be cultivated through suffering. One wonders what Kass and the Aristotelian tradition in general would make of John Donne's meditations on illness, Simone Weil's disturbing yet profound description of the moral and religious insight that comes only through affliction, or other spiritual or ascetic practices (Donne, 1987; Weil, 1951, pp. 117–136). The claim that some kinds of suffering can serve a moral project is treated in the following chapter. Here I simply note that while Kass does not explicitly rule out such a possibility, the body is morally significant for him only insofar as its healthiness is a necessary condition for virtue.

The second problem is Kass's lack of clarity about the standards of bodily functioning. He assumes, wrongly in my view, that what counts as a healthy body is roughly the same for everyone and that physicians therefore do not need to take account of a patient's way of life. He largely ignores the possibility that what is healthy for a scholar may be unhealthy for an athlete. Kass is wary of venturing too far out onto this terrain because the very reason he appealed to health as a standard was to avoid the suggestion that the physician is simply the servant of whatever lifestyle choices the patient brings to his office. The standard of health was designed to reassert the authority of medicine based on its knowledge of, commitment to, and skill in maintaining a well-functioning body. And indeed, as long as medicine is chiefly occupied with dietary and hygienic concerns well-functioning may not differ much from one person to the next. But medicine has become much more complex, and unless Kass wants to reject not only the use of medical skill for ends extraneous to health but also its use to enhance the well-functioning body, he must face the possibility that there may be multiple versions of the healthy body. Sports medicine has already made possible diverse senses of well-functioning; genetic medicine may greatly expand these in the future. If I am correct, the well-functioning body can no longer serve as a criterion to direct and limit medicine; rather, we must now decide which lifestyles are worth pursuing—and this is not a matter on which medicine qua medicine can pronounce.

It may have been problems similar to this last one that led Kass to formulate a second concept of health. In sharp contrast to the first one, this concept is not limited to the body. "To conserve health and cure disease . . . implicitly carry a natural reference: the healthy, normal human being, fit both in body and soul" (Kass, 1985, p. 11). Kass is not simply being careless in his language here. Echoing the phenomenological analyses of illness carried out in recent years, he now turns from somatic health as an end to "[t]he patient [who] presents himself to the physician . . . as a psychophysical unity," a unity that is disturbed by illness.

> Yet the patient aspires to have the disturbance quieted, to restore the implicit feeling and functional fact of oneness with which we freely go about our business in the world. The sickness may be experienced largely as belonging to the body as something other; but the healing one wants is the wholeness of one's entire embodied being. . . . This human wholeness is what medicine is finally all about. (Kass, 1989, p. 40)

Kass continues to treat health as a natural good. But perhaps because he is aware that different persons naturally value different life-functions, he now finds at least plausible the claim that the meaning of health depends on individualizing characteristics, while still arguing for a basic nonrelativity.

> Because of our powers of mind, our partial emancipation from the rule of instinct, our self-consciousness, and the highly complex and varied ways of life we follow as individuals and as members of groups, health and fitness seem to mean different things to different people, or even to the same person at different times of life. Moreover, departures from health have varying importance depending on the way of life one follows. Yet not everything is relative and contextual; beneath the variable and cultural lies the constant and organic, the well-regulated, properly balanced, and fully empowered human body. (Kass, 1989, p. 39)

While not a retreat from his earlier position—health and fitness only "seem" to mean different things and the "constant and organic" still lies "beneath the cultural and variable"—the emphasis has changed. First, the individualizing features are taken as given; in light of them it must be asserted that "not *everything* is relative and contextual." Second, even if Kass still means to argue that standards of health are in fact universal despite an appearance of difference, particular ways of life may attribute different degrees of importance to being healthy.[12] Third, if health as wholeness or human functioning is now the end of medicine, the "constant and organic" is less important relative to the "highly complex and varied ways of life" than it was when health was defined in terms of organic functioning.

This new view of health, I suggest, is what enables Kass to carry medicine beyond the limitations of a *techne* in the ways I described above. Only if human wholeness rather than somatic well-functioning is the end of medicine can physicians legitimately meet certain desires and wishes not immediately relevant to somatic health (such as IVF for married couples), concern themselves with maintaining and restoring valued life-functions, and address the senses of vulnerability and disruption that accompany illness. This new understanding of health is also much more consistent with the broad understanding of function and wholeness that emerges from Kass's phenomenological biology.

This new concept of health does not, however, provide a clear principle to limit the technological ambitions of modern medicine. If organic functioning itself was insufficiently precise, how will Kass restrict medicine by appealing to human functioning? He must show how this view can prevent medicine from serving any desirable human function in whatever way a patient requests. Here, I believe, Kass's view of medicine as a moral art ultimately depends on the kind of reflection on nature and the type of moral reasoning he recommends. Medicine is now limited not by a restriction to somatic functioning but by a view of wholeness that observes the proper relation of nature and convention.

Like Gustafson (and revisionist natural law theologians) Kass disavows "the intent of seeking and hope of finding precise rules of conduct deducible from even the fullest knowledge of nature . . ." (Kass, 1985, p. 347). Instead he calls for reflection that seeks to determine (e.g., from the significance of the human form) what human beings by nature desire and aspire to. This kind of reflection "might inform not the prescription of rules but an ordering of lives, according to a full standard of human flourishing . . ." (Kass, 1985, p. 347). In the absence of rules or even a principle (such as the earlier restriction to organic well-func-

tioning) to guide concrete choices on particular technologies and procedures, the physician must exercise prudence—a virtue that becomes
increasingly prominent in Kass's descriptions of medicine. If physicians
(and others) are formed by the attitudes that follow from proper reflection on nature and capable of exercising prudence, a general concept of
health is apparently all that is necessary.

The problem, of course, is that this position assumes that any
rightly reflective person will find the same meanings of embodiment
and exercise prudence the same way as Kass does. Kass assumes that
reasonableness demands taking the stance of the Greeks in Herodotus'
story. Against the "Indians" our natural repugnance about mutilation
should be able to yield to organ transplantation, but against the
"Persians" our reverence for the body should stop us short of buying and
selling organs (Kass, 1992). We should be neither too pious nor too critical but should think always with the respect for *tradition* and distanciation from *traditions* that marks Kass as a member of the University of
Chicago Committee on Social Thought. But Kass's confidence can be
questioned on several levels. First, we have now examined three authors
who argue for the significance of nature for ethics and arrive at three
very different views of nature and of ethics. While there are significant
agreements (especially between Jonas and Kass) there are major disagreements on method, content and even what is to count as "natural."

Second, even if we accept the priority of form, Kass's self-confi-
dent universalism is unwarranted. Feminist phenomenologies of the
female human form yield descriptions of time, space, motility, comport-
ment, and the self-other relation that reveal how thoroughly Kass's (and
Straus's) descriptions presuppose the male form as normative (Irigaray,
1991; Young, 1990). The striking differences in these phenomenologies
lead many feminist thinkers to deny what Kass assumes, namely that
there can be a single view of the human body (cf. Rothfield, 1995). Kass
also displays an individualistic bias when he treats interdependence
with others as a feature of human necessity rather than dignity.

The third problem is Kass's unargued assumption that the question of ethics is the question of nature and convention. The reason the
"Greek" answer is so self-evidently reasonable to him is that he assumes
the "Greek" question. He never considers the "Judaic" problem of ethics
as Emmanuel Levinas poses it, namely that the space occupied by the
human form in its natural innocence is revealed in the face of the Other
to be a space of moral guilt (Levinas, 1969, pp. 82–84, 197–201). Nor
does he consider that the nature-convention rubric rules out another
"Judaic" perspective in which revelation challenges the authority of
the natural in defining the significance of the body. From this perspec-

tive it is not self-evident that the basis of the family or the meaning and transcendence of mortality is found in biological lineage. But that does not make it "Indian" or "Persian."[13]

However, even if Kass could defend the universal validity of his "reverent reasonableness," the basis for the authority of medicine is not clear. Medicine may possess implicit knowledge of human nature, but there is no reason to assume that physicians will be more adept than others at reflecting on the meaning of nature or at exercising prudence. Kass simply attributes such prudence to physicians on the basis of their familiarity and experience with embodied humans. One could argue that the familiarity and experience of *modern* medicine renders physicians less adept than others at discerning human functioning, and Kass might agree. But one makes fewer counterfactual assumptions when one simply recognizes the capacity of medicine to facilitate life-functioning and leaves to moral inquiry (whether Kass's or some other kind) the question of what functions persons and their communities ought to value. This does not mean that medicine simply cures and restores organic functioning so that patients may pursue whatever way of life they choose. Medicine also tells people what ways of life their bodily conditions are suited for and what risks to their health follow from particular ways of life. In its knowledge of the mortality of all bodies, of the capabilities and limitations of particular bodies, and of the bodily conditions for human functioning medicine constitutes a tradition of knowledge of the body. But its knowledge does not enable it to answer questions of what functions are good for humans to pursue or what role their bodies ought to play in pursuing them.

Similar questions may be raised with regard to other roles required of medicine by the concern with the wholeness and vulnerability of the patient. For example, in most cases human well-functioning will depend heavily on matters of diet, healthy habits, and so on. Moreover, it is likely that, as Kass argues, the support of healthy life-functioning in the case of the chronically ill or the otherwise incurable "becomes less a matter of fighting disease and more a matter of physical therapy and rehabilitation; of hearing aids, dentures, and glasses; and especially of addressing habits of life and patterns of social arrangements" (Kass, 1985, p. 202). Surely physicians should participate in all of these activities, if for no other reason than because, as Kass points out, they often assist curative efforts (Kass, 1985, p. 203). But do they as physicians possess the training, the skills, the interest, or even the time to carry out these activities? And should they even try to do so when there are already other health professionals who specialize in dietetics, health maintenance, optimization of life functions, and addressing problems of life situations? Ironically, and quite unintentionally, in the very act of trying to maintain the status of physicians, Kass makes a strong case for diminishing it. Put simply, if these noncurative activities are as important as Kass says they are, physicians may not be nearly as important as he thinks they are. Once again, perhaps medicine should be more narrowly defined while realizing that, for those who hold to a view of health as well-functioning, curing and restoring are only a small part of a much larger pursuit of wholeness, or better, of the meaning of embodiment, attainment of which requires arts other than medicine.

What about the efforts of medicine to deal with the meaning of illness and the experience of vulnerability and necessity? Can the physician qua physician perform the roles of caring, encouraging, and "mediat[ing] between the patient's understanding and his own mysterious and silent body" that Kass assigns them? Here Kass recognizes that the physician is capable of addressing vulnerability "not only because the *techne* of medicine rubs his nose in the multifarious fragilities of the flesh, but also because of his own humanity" (Kass, 1985, p. 219). It is not only the physician's knowledge of the body but the fact that he or she and the patient share mutually and equally "in the ever-precarious, necessarily finite, yet daringly aspiring and hope-filled venture called human life" that enables the physician "to synthesize the abstract scientific knowledge of bodily workings with the concrete human experience of living in health and in sickness" (Kass, 1985, p. 220). Similarly, "when reasonable hope of recovery is gone, [the physician] acts rather to comfort the patient and to keep him company, as a friend and not especially or uniquely as a physician" (Kass, 1985, p. 163). The implications are that (1) because medicine deals with patients in their vulnerability, curing and restoring must be accompanied by and often replaced by caring; and (2) the capacity for caring belongs not only or especially to medicine as a *techne* (though medicine does possess its own knowledge of human vulnerability) but to one's ability as a human being to embody and express a way of understanding and dealing with vulnerability.

My criticisms should be obvious by now. Kass wrongly assumes that the meaning of bodily life must have the content supplied by his biology and can be developed only through the relation of nature and convention as he understands it. He wrongly assumes that medicine itself constitutes a single moral tradition, and one that is able to determine the relation of the body to the human good. And he expands the authority of medicine into areas in which physicians must cooperate with others. Much of what I find wrong with Kass on the first two counts is epitomized in his treatment of the oath sworn to the gods at the beginning of the Hippocratic Oath. Since Kass is determined to show how the Oath still expresses the moral content of medicine, he must make sense of this appeal to the divine. After showing how Apollo, Asclepius, Hygeia, and Panaceia form a sacred lineage and transmission, Kass goes on to point out that medicine indeed receives its capacities from beyond itself. The body's power to heal itself, the abundance of pharmacological agents in nature, minds equipped to discover—for all of this

> [o]ne can do worse than credit some higher-than-human power. . . . Apollo—or whatever its name is—brings wholeness to mind and us to wholeness, and further, in the art of medicine, brings us beyond *awareness* of wholeness to a divinelike overflowing into action, permitting us to help make the wounded whole. (Kass, 1985, p. 246)

Apollo, or whatever its name is. . . . Naming God is unimportant for Kass because he assumes that the meaning of healing can be cashed out in terms of nature without worrying about how traditions form and transform understandings of the natural. But as Allen Verhey argues, when Christians swore the Hippocratic Oath under a different name, they inscribed it into a different sacred history that led to different priorities and a different understanding of the ends of human life (Verhey, 1987). The lesson I draw is that the physician's skill and knowledge of the body require a particular view of the good of bodily life if medicine is to avoid serving whatever ends its technological capabilities throw open to human choice.

To avoid these problems will require us to abandon the assumption that a phenomenological biology can provide a single normative view of the body that can underwrite a comprehensive practice of medicine. Rather, with some feminist and religious thinkers we will have to turn our attention to the ways in which different practices form bodies differently and thereby form us as subjects. I argue for this approach to the body in chapter seven. However, that view by itself cannot address the question of the relation of health to a morally worthy life. By articulating this question and placing it at the center of his agenda, Kass makes an indispensible contribution to the kind of bioethic I am proposing. This project is deeply indebted to Kass on two additional grounds. First, he recognizes that the Baconian project is fueled by a view of the body made possible by modern science, and that modern ethics, including standard bioethics, perfectly complements and therefore does not challenge this view. One denies that the body has meaning or reduces its meaning to survival value, while the other views medicine as the means to fulfilling wishes and desires ungrounded in any respect for the body as a source of insight about genuine human aspirations. Kass therefore recognizes that the alternative to what he sees as the dehumanization of the Baconian project rests on a richer understanding of embodiment. Second, Kass realizes that the most important issues raised by the new technologies, and indeed the most vital issues in human life more generally, are not matters for law or public policy to resolve and cannot be reduced to principles and rules. The most vital task of bioethics is to shape our attitudes and postures toward ourselves as embodied beings rather than to regulate our behavior as citizens or to govern our lives according to principles. These attitudes and postures in turn make us capable of exercising prudence, and prudence alone enables us to choose wisely with regard to what role medicine and its technology will have in our lives.

CHAPTER 6

Medicine and the Reconciling Community

"The primary argument of this book, put in its simplest terms," Stanley Hauerwas writes in the Introduction to his collection of essays on ethical problems in medicine, "is that a humane medicine is impossible to sustain in a society which lacks the moral capacity to care for the mentally retarded" (Hauerwas, 1986, p. 18). The care for the mentally challenged may seem to be an unusual criterion for medicine, but I will argue that from this vantage point Hauerwas issues a stinging rebuke and calls for a provocative alternative to the entire Baconian project in medicine. His alternative seeks not to limit that project, but to overturn it. To this end, the concentration on the mentally handicapped constitutes a double gesture. On the one hand, there is a subversive or deconstructive (in a nontechnical sense) gesture. Hauerwas shows how the effort of modern medicine to cure all diseases and to produce a humanity free from suffering is built on the marginalization of what resists curative medicine. The mentally handicapped are marginalized by curative medicine in at least two senses. First, the burden of their care does not primarily fall on the medical profession. There is nothing improper in this—Hauerwas does not want to turn the care of the mentally handicapped over to physicians—but the privileged position of curative medicine depends on the overvaluation of specialized knowledge and technological expertise and the undervaluation of other forms of care. Second, the mentally handicapped cannot be cured by contemporary medicine. Hence the privileged role of curing must be maintained by eliminating or marginalizing those who cannot be cured, such as the chronically ill and the mentally handicapped. By bringing the marginalized to the center Hauerwas challenges the aura of moral necessity with which the Baconian project surrounds the ideal of eliminating suffering. On the other hand, there is a restorative gesture to Hauerwas's work. Hauerwas wants medicine to return to certain traditional commitments that are threatened by the Baconian direction of scientific medicine.

Like a city designed around a hub, there are many avenues into Hauerwas's thought but they all lead sooner or later to the key concept of the church as a community that embodies a story (or alternatively as a set of discursive practices) that constitutes an alternative to the world, which for Hauerwas is secular liberal society. Medicine, which in its ideal form, as we will see, is for Hauerwas characterized by certain substantive moral commitments, occupies an ambivalent place in this relation of church and world. On the one hand, its moral commitments distinguish it from liberal society. On the other hand, medicine requires a community like the church in order to sustain its commitments in the face of threats the liberal ethos poses to them. The church's practices of forging community with the mentally challenged expose the liberal or modern virtue of compassion—the virtue that for Hauerwas underwrites the Baconian project—as inadequate and ultimately cruel. In so doing, the church provides the kind of support medicine needs if it is to resist the liberal ethos and its drive to eliminate suffering even if this means eliminating the sufferer. In short, the place of the mentally challenged in the practice of medicine and the place of medicine in the relation of church to world not only indicate, because of the ambivalent status of medicine, a complexity in Hauerwas's thought that is less apparent from other perspectives, but (more important) expose the problematic moral ethos of the Baconian project and constitute a striking alternative to it.

MEDICINE: THE FRAGILITY OF A
PRACTICE IN A LIBERAL SOCIETY

One of Hauerwas's persistent themes is that liberalism relies on moral commitments and forms of life that its own presuppositions cannot account for. The problem is that liberal moral convictions and practices undermine these very commitments and forms of life (Hauerwas, 1981a, p. 79; 1994, pp. 190–91). This provides, I think, a helpful point of entry into Hauerwas's view of medicine. Medicine as a viable practice is constituted in part by certain moral commitments. The problem is that the moral discourse of modernity, of which bioethics is an instance, does not allow medicine to understand itself as the significant moral practice it in fact is (Hauerwas, 1986, p. 6; 1994, p. 162). This is largely because that discourse lacks the capacity to deal with the limits and tragic features that are inherent in medicine as a moral practice. Lacking a story that can make intelligible the tragic character of its commitments and a community that can sustain those commitments in spite of the tragedy, medicine is vulnerable to the ambitions of the Baconian project, which is premised on the denial of tragedy and limitation. In short, there is a vital and necessary connection between the moral commitments of medicine and the capacity to accept tragedy. In the absence of this capacity, medicine is enlisted in the effort of liberal society to eliminate the tragic features of the human condition. Hence the Baconian project of modern medicine is for Hauerwas a product of the liberal denial of tragedy. To the extent that medicine remains a viable practice, it still holds to its moral commitments, but the discourse and practices of liberal society with its Baconian ambitions make this hold ever more tenuous.

That the moral commitments of medicine make it a tragic profession is no anomaly for Hauerwas, since all substantive moral commitments are susceptible to tragedy. We may begin, therefore, with a discussion of tragedy in general. Unfortunately Hauerwas never clarifies his understanding of tragedy; it remains vague and unexplained, and his use of it as a category may not be fully consistent. Nevertheless, Hauerwas's major point seems to be that all substantive moral commitments "make us and others pay for our adherence to them" (Hauerwas, 1977, p. 12). Unless, that is, we are to reduce our moral lives to a commitment to survival or the avoidance of all harm, we must be willing to let ourselves and others suffer for our moral commitments, or be willing to forego opportunities to avoid harm, remove evil or do good. "Being unwilling to make others and ourselves suffer for our principles is but to admit that nothing in this life is worth ourselves or others making a sacrifice for" (Hauerwas, 1981b, p. 122).[1] Tragedy, then, refers to the inevitability of suffering and lost opportunities for accomplishing good that follow from having substantive moral commitments in a finite and fallen world.

This view of moral tragedy departs from a long philosophical tradition that denies that this kind of conflict is tragic at all since it does not involve a conflict between two or more valid and binding moral requirements. In other words, for this tradition there is no dilemma here, and neither blame nor moral regret (as opposed to nonmoral anguish) is appropriate since there appears to be no moral requirement to avoid the evil or bring about the good that is incompatible with our moral commitments. Against this position Hauerwas seems to agree with Martha

Nussbaum on two points: that significant commitments and not just moral duties in the narrow sense may have their own kind of valid and binding status, and that the (for Hauerwas) survival goods foregone or the harms done by adhering to such commitments are, if not binding, then at least morally significant (Nussbaum, 1986, pp. 27–32). Hauerwas is clear enough on the first point but because he does not say in what sense the survival foregone or the harm inevitably done in living according to those commitments is morally significant, it is not clear in what sense choices involving these results are tragic.[2] Another source of confusion is that for Hauerwas tragedy sometimes involves not conflicts but limitations. For example, he refers to the inevitable limits of knowledge and technique in medicine as a tragic element intrinsic to any endeavor to develop a science of the particular (Hauerwas, 1977, pp. 197–200).

Despite these theoretical problems, Hauerwas makes it clear why the moral commitments that in part constitute medicine require a sense of the tragic and what happens to medicine when a society and its moral theories lose this sense. Hauerwas's descriptions of the moral commitments of medicine bear significant resemblances to Kass's description of medicine as a moral art, though the emphases differ. As such, they stand in sharp contrast to the moral commitments of the Baconian project. In general, the moral commitment of medicine is to the care, protection, and health of the individual patient. This general formula expresses several commitments. First, medicine is committed to caring. The emphasis on care is directed against efforts to define medicine as successful only to the extent that it cures the patient. Hauerwas does not deny the obvious point that sick people turn to medicine to make them well. But he is aware of the limits of cure: in addition to the limits of medical knowledge and technique with regard to certain diseases and conditions, medicine, as we noted above, unlike natural science requires knowledge of the particular patient, which is always potentially inadequate even in cases of diseases for which cures exist (Hauerwas, 1977, pp. 197–200). "Yet the fact that medicine through the agency of physicians does not and cannot always 'cure' in no way qualifies the commitment of the physician. At least it does not do so if we remember that the physician's basic pledge is not to cure, but to care through being present to the one in pain" (Hauerwas, 1986, pp. 78–79). The major problem is that when medicine is defined in terms of its capacity to cure, patients who cannot be cured are abandoned in their illness. Hauerwas criticizes this because it perpetuates illness as an essentially alienating experience. "Our pains isolate us from one another as they create worlds that cut us off from one another" (Hauerwas,

1986, p. 76). It is difficult or impossible for the healthy, even those who have once been ill, to understand the experience of the ill; moreover, they do not wish to share the experience of those who are ill. But this is not all: "Pain not only isolates us from one another, but even from ourselves" (Hauerwas, 1986, p. 77). For these reasons, "[i]t is the burden of those who care for the suffering to know how to teach the suffering that they are not thereby excluded from the human community. In this sense medicine's primary role is to bind the suffering and the nonsuffering into the same community" (Hauerwas, 1986, p. 26) so that "illness does not quarantine a person from the human community" (1986, p. 6). It is already clear that reconciliation is central to the moral meaning of medicine.[3]

Second, medicine is committed to the individual patient. The emphasis on the individual patient is directed against consequentialist and utilitarian efforts to treat diseases, families, populations, and the human race rather than individual patients (1977, p. 181; 1986, p. 69). "The doctor's duty remains to the patient, not to secure the overall health of society" (Hauerwas, 1981b, p. 185). The task of medicine is not to eliminate diseases, secure the well-being of families or maximize the health status of populations.

However, Hauerwas qualifies this individualism. It holds for a society in which the only alternative is a utilitarian concern for the maximum well-being of society as a whole. But in a community with a shared account of the ends and values that science and medicine ought to serve, it might be appropriate for physicians to expect patients to undergo certain risks for the sake of the community (Hauerwas, 1977, p. 129). These ends and values would provide "the grounds to say why each of us should be willing to serve as research subjects for the good, not of mankind, but of the communities in which we exist" (Hauerwas, 1986, p. 117). Hauerwas's major interest is to show how a viable community will train its members to regard the good of the community above their individual interests.[4] When the commitment to the individual or to the good of a viable community is replaced by a commitment to bringing about the greatest good for families, populations or humanity, it becomes thinkable to carry out a utopian program, such as the elimination of suffering or ensuring the genetic health of future generations, that justifies overriding the protection of individuals.

Third, medicine is committed to bodily health, not to the task of freeing us from the constraints of nature or securing our happiness (Hauerwas, 1977, p. 181; 1986, pp. 46–50). For Hauerwas "medicine as a profession inherently carries the wisdom of our finitude" (Hauerwas, 1986, p. 13). Both physician and patient are subject to "a prior authority—the authority of the body" (Hauerwas, 1986, p. 48), and it is part of the task of medicine not to control but to teach us the limits of our bodies (Hauerwas, 1986, p. 51). Both of these comments are designed to restrict medicine to the goal of securing bodily health with a recognition of the inherent limits of the body (we will all get sick and die) and of our efforts to free ourselves from nature. When medicine is connected with a broad definition of health that includes general well-being rather than minimal human functioning human beings expand their expectations of medicine and medicine expands its control over human lives.

All three of these commitments involve tragedy insofar as they require some persons to suffer for them. For example, caring for individual patients may mean that energy and resources are taken away from curing, from the elimination of diseases and from caring for other patients, while the concern for the protection and care of the individual patient and for goods of a community may cause individuals and families and society to suffer.

> For to attend to one in distress often means many others cannot be helped. Or to save a child born retarded may well destroy the child's family and cause unnecessary burdens on society. But the doctor is pledged to care for each patient because medicine does not aim at some ideal moral good, but to care for the needs of the patient whom the doctor finds before him. (Hauerwas, 1977, p. 37)

Similarly, the concern for health may mean opportunities for general happiness and control over the body are passed up, which may put strains on individuals and communities. Finally, the limits of medicine in dealing with particularity may mean that some will suffer even though no one has acted negligently or incompetently. In these respects medicine serves as a paradigm of any moral practice that is rooted in substantive commitments. Like any such practice, medicine needs a story that enables it to deal with tragedy truthfully rather than by denial.

> The practice of medicine under the conditions of finitude offers an intense paradigm of the moral life. For the moral task is to learn to continue to do the right, to care for this immediate patient, even when we have no assurance that it will be the successful thing to do. To live morally, in other words, we need a substantive story that will sustain moral activity in a finite and limited world. Classically, the name we give such stories is tragedy. (Hauerwas, 1977, pp. 37–38)

Put more abstractly, since the virtues of medicine conflict with our tendencies to pursue other valuable goods and states of affairs,

> it is not sufficient simply to recognize that medicine as an activity entails certain virtues, but that those virtues require still other virtues necessary to sustain the activity of medicine itself. Such virtues must obviously be carried by a community that protects medicine from being perverted by goals not intrinsic to its task. (Hauerwas, 1985a, pp. 353–354)

The claim that medicine requires a story and a community distinct from medicine itself distinguishes Hauerwas from Kass in spite of their general agreement on the moral commitments of medicine themselves. I return to this below, but here I simply note that for Hauerwas this kind of story and this kind of community is precisely what liberal societies lack. Hence medicine in these societies is based on a denial of tragedy. Incapable of bearing the inevitable losses involved in the moral commitments of medicine, liberal societies replace these commitments with a commitment to "free us from our natural and self-made fates" (Hauerwas, 1977, p. 197). In this respect medicine mirrors modern moral theories for which the sphere of the moral is identical to the sphere of freedom and control.

Why, according to Hauerwas, do liberal societies deny tragedy and thereby undermine the moral commitments of medicine? And what happens to medicine under the dominion of the liberal ethos? These questions bring us to Hauerwas's interpretation of the Baconian project as the theodicy of liberal society. The task of the Enlightenment (which the Baconian project heralded and with which it became inextricably linked) is "to make society a collection of individuals free from the bonds of necessity other than those we choose" (Hauerwas, 1990, p. 108). In other words, its task is to increase our freedom. The problem is that when medicine is charged with carrying out this task in a society that lacks any agreement on what necessities we should choose to live with, "there seems to be no limit to the ends that medicine can be asked to serve. In such a context, medicine is in danger of being used as a means to eliminate all those 'evils' which we believe are arbitrary because we presume that it is our task as humans to make our existence free from outrageous fortune" (Hauerwas, 1990, p. 102).

Hauerwas suggests that by assuming this task medicine became the successor to theodicy. We (referring to post-Enlightenment people) accept its explanations of suffering and look to it to provide not consolations but elimination of suffering. "Our questions about suffering are asked from a world dominated by a hope schooled by medicine—a world that promises to 'solve' suffering by eliminating its causes" (Hauerwas, 1990, p. 35). Traditional theodicies, Hauerwas argues, were based on the assumption of God as having infinite power. The assumption of infinite power remains in medicine as a posttheological theodicy (what Hauerwas, following Ernest Becker, calls an "anthropodicy"). "Ironically, this god of infinite power . . . becomes the god that legitimates the Enlightenment project of extending human power over all contingency." Since the god of most theodices is a deistic god who after designing the world leaves affairs to natural laws and to creatures, "the view of an all-powerful but basically deistic god fits nicely with the understanding of the necessity of humankind's taking control of its destiny" (Hauerwas, 1990, p. 48). The problem now is how to account for those evils that allow for human intervention. Here medicine plays a leading role: it deals with something (illness) we believe we can intervene into and eventually eradicate. The result is that in our very effort to gain control over necessity by means of medicine we give medicine virtually unlimited control over our lives. This control takes two forms, both of which I return to in more detail below. First, we empower it to impoverish our moral lives by defining all of our suffering as pointless and thus subject to elimination by medicine. Second, because we have only arbitrary conceptions of what purposes and goods our lives should serve but share in common only a fear of death, we rely on medicine to extend our lives even when we have no idea what such an extension of life is good for.[5] As a result it would not surprise Hauerwas that we in the United States cannot resolve our systemic health care allocation crisis. "Our problem is simply that in the absence of any good beyond our basic physical survival, we lack any sense of what limits might be placed on the good that medicine serves. . . . Any attempt to limit medical care in such a context cannot help but appear arbitrary and cruel" (Hauerwas, 1994, p. 162).

The problem with medicine as a successor to theodicy is that medicine's technological capacity to guarantee control over suffering is as subject to counterevidence as was theology's metaphysical capacity. For, as we have seen, medicine is a tragic profession insofar as knowledge of the particular is always highly fallible. But this means that tragedy is inescapable since the very effort to escape tragedy through the offices of medicine makes us more subject to this final tragic feature (Hauerwas, 1977, p. 201). Like the mentally challenged, the chronically ill and others who resist cure remind us of the limits of medicine. But to be reminded of the limits of medicine is to be reminded of the limits of our control over nature. And this renders the traditional commitments of medicine even more vulnerable in a society that cannot accept limitation of control. "It would almost be better to eliminate the subjects of such illness than to have them remind us that our project to eliminate illness has made little progress" (Hauerwas, 1990, p. 63).

In conclusion, medicine for Hauerwas constitutes one profound way in which society gestures care for one another. However, setting aside that role in a society that lacks a sense of the tragic is a monumental task. For Hauerwas it requires a community distinct from medicine (1977, p. 202; 1986, p. 13). Here we arrive at the most important and controversial feature of Hauerwas's alternative to the Baconian project, a feature that distinguishes him most sharply from others who have sought to uphold similar interpretations of medicine. First, medicine for Hauerwas does not require either Christian commitments or theological presuppositions (Hauerwas, 1986, pp. 8, 14). This distinguishes Hauerwas from Paul Ramsey for whom medicine is unintelligible apart from the commitments and theological presuppositions inherent in covenant bonds. Second, the moral commitments of medicine cannot be derived from a natural teleology inherent in medicine as a practice since we now live in a morally incoherent society that lacks agreement on what ends are natural (Hauerwas, 1986, p. 51). Third, Hauerwas rejects the idea that bioethics can sustain or even comprehend these commitments. In fact, medicine as a moral practice is threatened by bioethics because bioethical theories overlook and distort the commitments the practice of medicine presupposes (Hauerwas, 1986, p. 4; 1994, p. 162). Rather than a theological grounding, a natural teleology or a bioethical theory, medicine needs a community in order to sustain its commitments and to qualify some of them. But which community? Hauerwas does supply some formal criteria. Medicine needs a community with differentiation of functions so that physicians can fulfill their commitment to individual patients confident that there are other roles in the community that can address the inevitable suffering that will sometimes result (Hauerwas, 1977, p. 181). And medicine needs a community that places practices like medicine in a narrative shared by people in an ongoing tradition (Hauerwas, 1985, p. 353), since without such a tradition the broader account of a life within which the goods of health and the limits of medicine have a place will be lacking. Hence, while Hauerwas insists that medicine and its moral commitments may exist independent of the church, it is already becoming clear that medicine needs something like a church. This places medicine somewhere in the dialectic of church and world that constitutes the structure and the hermeneutical key to Hauerwas's work. To that dialectic I now turn.

CHURCH AND WORLD:
THE DIALECTICS OF ENGAGEMENT

When one turns to Hauerwas from theologians of Gustafson's generation, one is acutely aware of a massive cultural shift. No longer is it the task of Christian social ethics to seek the moral maintenance and improvement of the world under the heading of natural law, vocation, or covenant, all of which assume that church and world share a common reality that has been formed or is capable of being transformed by Christian convictions. It is clear at the end of the twentieth century that the church no longer plays this role in culture. Hauerwas recognizes that the engagement with the world (he is not the kind of separatist he is often taken to be) must take a new form.

> Put starkly, the first social ethical task of the church is to be the church—the servant community. Such a claim may well sound self-serving until we remember that what makes the church the church is its faithful manifestation of the peaceable kingdom in the world. As such, the church does not have a social ethic; the church is a social ethic. (Hauerwas, 1983, p. 99)

What distinguishes Hauerwas is his insistence that the content of Christian social ethics cannot be separated from the church as a community that continues the story of Jesus. The nature and existence of the church as formed by that story is the content of Christian ethics, not any norm or ideal that can be abstracted from that story or any effort to find some means (e.g., natural law or orders of creation) by which Christian ethics can be made relevant to the task of ordering and governing the larger society.

By rejecting these alternatives, Hauerwas definitively breaks with the problematic so eruditely expressed by Ernst Troeltsch, namely the question of how such a purely religious ethic as the "ethic of Jesus" and so "spiritual" a community as the early church could supply the content to resolve the social issues facing a complex society—a problematic that itself reflects the needs and assumptions of Christendom (Hauerwas, 1981a, pp. 37–40). Rather, Hauerwas argues that the ethical task of the church is to be itself—to become a community capable of being formed by the story of Jesus in such a way as to embody an alternative to the world and to resist the totalizing ambitions of the latter. "We have almost forgotten that the church is also a polity that at one time had the confidence to encourage in its members virtues sufficient to sustain their role as citizens in a society whose purpose was to counter the unwarranted claims made by other societies and states" (Hauerwas, 1981a, pp. 73–74). The failure to resist the world in these ways has prevented the church from carrying out its positive social task, namely to "help the world understand itself as world" (Hauerwas, 1983, p. 100). "Christians have lacked the power that would enable themselves and others to perceive and interpret the kind of society in which we live" (Hauerwas, 1981a, p. 74).

To summarize, the church for Hauerwas is a community whose members are trained to develop the virtues and skills necessary to be capable of being the continuation of the story of Jesus. The church is also a set of practices that resist the knowledge-power-subject relations that constitute liberal society. As such the task of the church is to form a discourse and practices so that the world can understand itself through confronting a genuine alternative. These claims, drawn variously from the work of Alasdair MacIntyre, Hans Frei, Iris Murdoch, Michel Foucault, and John Howard Yoder, indicate the complexity and dialectical character of the relation of the church to the world.

One major point on which the church challenges the world is the effort of modern moral theories to abstract morality from particular communities. The problem is not only the fragmentation of once-coherent moralities or the liberal fear that violence will erupt from expressions of moral disagreement, but rather the standard response to these phenomena, namely, the effort to avoid the historical and community-dependent nature of all moral convictions either by reducing the content of morality to autonomy or choice or by attempting to secure a universal foundation for morality (Hauerwas, 1983, pp. 2–12). In both cases morality is abstracted from all particularity.

Hauerwas's descriptions and criticisms of this effort occur at three levels: the metaethical, the ethical, and the political. On the metaethical level Hauerwas denies that moral notions and convictions can be abstracted from particular communities and ways of life. He disagrees with the account that modern moral theories give of themselves—that they are free from particular moral convictions. In their efforts to portray themselves as such, these theories abstract from the very conditions that enable agents to have moral concerns in the first place and to describe moral situations.

Hauerwas rejects metaethical positions according to which normative terms differ from descriptive terms by the kinds of properties of objects they pick out (e.g., natural vs. nonnatural as in G. E. Moore) or by categories (such as factual vs. evaluative and its companion, descriptive, and prescriptive uses of language). Rather, following

Julius Kovesi's Wittgensteinian position, he argues that both descriptive and normative terms group together "some of the significant and relevant recurring aspects of our experience" that we have reasons for grouping together (Hauerwas, 1981b, p. 16). As such, moral terms involve grouping together and distinguishing features of acts and situations communities find it necessary to group or to distinguish in order to understand their moral experience and to carry out their moral practices. Some terms such as "murder" are quite restrictive in the features they group together while terms such as "good" are quite open. Sometimes communities develop new notions, such as "saving deceit," to mark off features of moral experience that are important for understanding and maintaining valued features of their moral life (Hauerwas, 1981b, pp. 14–22). The result is that morality is largely a matter of learning to "see" (the metaphor of vision dominates Hauerwas's texts) the world in a certain way, that is, of being trained to make certain groupings and distinctions among features of experience. Since the very meaning of moral notions occurs in this way, vision is a presupposition of identifying any moral problem (Hauerwas, 1977, pp. 21, 170; 1981b, pp. 30–47).

This analysis enables Hauerwas to show how moral notions are fully understandable only within a way of life: fully to interpret a moral notion requires a description of the way of life in which it serves as an important way of grouping features of acts or cases. "The objectivity of moral argument is ultimately dependent on the shared commitments and values of a community. There is no heavenly realm of values that exist independent of their embodiment in human agents and institutions" (Hauerwas, 1981b, p. 107).[6] The assumption of modern moral theories that their principles and concepts transcend particular communities simply conceals their own status as products of an unacknowledged way of life that is therefore accepted without criticism. This leads Hauerwas to one of his most persistent and important claims: that moral theories that isolate reasoning from particular communities and traditions underwrite the assumption that the way things are is the way they must or ought to be. By not making explicit the interests and purposes that underlie moral and descriptive notions, these theories implicitly accept the givenness of reality and thus perpetuate the hegemony of the conventional. The result is that, given the "nature" of the "world as it is," certain actions and policies are viewed as morally "necessary": the use or threat of violence for survival, the suppression of otherness to avoid conflict, the nontreatment of newborns to avoid suffering, and so forth. Ignored in this perspective is that agents or communities can form an alternative set of discourses and practices that constitute an alternative "reality." For "the world is not simply *there*, always ready to be known, but rather is known well only when known through the practices and habits of community constituted by a truthful story" (Hauerwas, 1994, p. 180). As such, the world is not simply a given to which all agents and communities must conform. "It is not enough that we as moral agents take into account all that is in the situation objectively understood, for what is also 'in' the situation is the possible change we can make by the fact that we are certain kinds of persons" (Hauerwas, 1981b, p. 64).[7]

On the ethical level, Hauerwas argues that efforts to abstract morality in this way involve self-deception made possible by the resulting indeterminacy of moral notions. Principles abstracted in this way lack the determinacy provided by a community or tradition and thus "easily can be and are divorced from the original insights that gave them substance, forming ideologies for quite a different set of practices" (Hauerwas, 1977, p. 165).

Accordingly, one of Hauerwas's chief strategies in treating concrete moral issues involves showing how principles are used to conceal certain features of actions or policies. One example is the principle of beneficence, which may be invoked to to describe nontreatment of Down syndrome newborns as relief of suffering. But Hauerwas shows how this involves an expansion in our understanding of suffering. "What the retarded child and its family are now to be spared are the difficulties occasioned by an indifferent and cruel society which rejects those who fail to meet its requirements of 'normality'" (Hauerwas, 1977, p. 165). The principle shields society from its own cruelty and allows it to describe its act of killing as beneficent, thus forestalling criticism of the society's convictions and practices and denying the need for changes in these convictions and practices. Moreover, it conceals the absence of a story and community that support a capacity to live with tragedy and care for those who suffer such tragedies. A second example is the use of the term "person" in medicine. Used by Paul Ramsey to provide deontological limits to utilitarian tendencies in medicine, the term now becomes a way to avoid certain moral quandaries. By designating individuals as persons or nonpersons, caregivers can justify decisions to treat or not to treat and thereby avoid accountability for socially and contextually contingent features of events and relationships. For example, in questions regarding what treatments, if any, are appropriate for severely impaired newborns, the designation of person or nonperson allows parents to avoid questions regarding their attitudes about children, their responsibilities as parents, and their convictions about the limits of medicine (Hauerwas, 1977, pp. 127–131).[8]

On the sociopolitical level Hauerwas argues that the abstraction of morality from communities serves the liberal assumption "that we all live in the same world, we all want the same thing, we all see the same things" (Hauerwas, 1994, p. 6). Hence narratives that are different cannot be understood as different since all experience is fundamentally the same (Hauerwas, 1992, p. 481). This assumption itself is rooted in the central concern of liberalism. For Hauerwas, the "liberalism of fear" as Judith Shklar calls it is fundamentally fear of conflict; hence the task of liberal societies, to put it perjoratively, is "to reduce all significant disagreements between communities to differences in opinion in the interest of producing the kind of bland souls necessary to sustain the 'peace' of liberal social orders" (Hauerwas, 1994, p. 15). Liberalism therefore lacks the means for the expression of significant histories of trust, suffering, and struggle such as one finds, for example, in the African-American tradition, except insofar as it can translate them into the expression of interests or victimization or the struggle for liberal freedom and equality (Hauerwas, 1981a, pp. 83, 252–253, n. 36; 1994, p. 13). As a result, however, liberalism domesticates conflicts and deprives them of their rich narrative contexts in the interest of sustaining peace. Fearing difference with its potential for conflict, and having no substantive narrative and view of the good of its own, liberal society lacks the skills and moral resources to understand those who do. It is therefore unable to understand the conflicts that define contemporary culture and to avoid suppressing difference.[9]

Hauerwas seeks to show how the church constitutes a contrast model that challenges these modern and liberal assumptions. The problem is that liberal Protestantism has accepted too many of these assumptions to serve as an alternative. Its endeavor has been that of Christendom in general, namely to legitimate the social order and to seek its transformation in accordance with moral and religious ideals to the extent that this is possible in a fallen world. The key to Hauerwas's strategy is his denial that the moral point of the church's story of Jesus can be disarticulated from the story itself, and that the story can be recounted apart from the practices and way of life that embody it. For it is precisely these assumptions that constitute the identification of Protestant liberalism with modernity and ground its effort to continue the project of Christendom in an age of unbelief. For example, if love can be disarticulated in this way, it can be useful in supporting notions like respect for persons that are necessary to maintain liberal societies.

Hauerwas's rejection of these assumptions is hermeneutical: the narrative character of the church's story of Jesus does not allow abstraction of the "point" of the story from the story itself. He adheres closely to Hans Frei's notion that much of the Bible consists of realistic narrative, in which the meaning of the story (what it refers to or represents) cannot be separated from the story itself (the depiction or representation). Under the pressure of empiricism and deism, however, narrative and reality were uncoupled; the narrative was now viewed as referring to something external to it. Consequently, biblical interpretation reversed the heremeneutical order of realistic narrative: rather than inscribing the experienced world of the present into the world depicted in the text, the world as known by empirical science and history was taken as the reality into which the story must be inscribed, or against which its reality claims must be tested (Frei, 1974, pp. 1–16). Frei's historical account is significant for ethics insofar as it may illuminate a similar reversal, so forcefully and unapologetically carried out by Kant, according to which the moral teachings of the Bible and the exemplarity of Jesus were to be measured by the rational moral law, and not vice versa (Kant, 1960). The same phenomenon occurs when certain ideals or norms (e.g., "covenant" or "love") are interpreted as the moral point or moral "upshot" of biblical stories and given the status of independently valid moral truths. This hermeneutical move assumes that there is a larger, shared moral world that the story is "about" and that the task of Christian ethics is to provide moral insight and direction for this larger public world. Hauerwas believes that this has happened with most Christian approaches to biomedical ethics, notably in the case of Paul Ramsey. Because Ramsey assumed that the ideal of covenant loyalty and the canons implied in it could be disarticulated from the story in this way and identified with a commitment to the individual, he could assume that medicine with its commitments is already implicitly Christian and, having identified the source of those commitments in scripture, could proceed to employ them as basic premises in casuistical arguments without articulating them any further in theological terms (Hauerwas, 1986, pp. 71–72; 1995). The result is that, as Leon Kass observes, "most religious ethicists entering the public practice of ethics leave their special religious insights at the door and talk about 'deontological vs. consequentialist,' 'autonomy vs. paternalism,' 'justice vs. utility,' just like everybody else" (Kass, 1990, p. 7).

Hauerwas thoroughly rejects this strategy. For him the story of Jesus already is a social ethic, which "means that there is no moral point or message that is separable from the story of Jesus as we find it in the Gospels" (Hauerwas, 1981a, p. 42). Hauerwas is aware that Jesus as portrayed in the Gospels is the product of the early church, but this is not the theological problem it is for many theologians since the "identity" of Jesus for Hauerwas is inseparable from the community he forms.

I am quite content to assume that the Jesus we have in Scripture is the Jesus of the early church. Even more important, I want to maintain that it cannot or should not be otherwise, since the very demands Jesus placed on his followers means he cannot be known abstracted from the disciples' response. . . . For the "real Jesus" did not come to leave us unchanged, but rather to transform us to be worthy members of the community of the new age. (Hauerwas, 1983, p. 73)

Following Frei (Frei, 1975), this theological claim is for Hauerwas first of all a hermeneutical claim. The question of the identity of Jesus Christ is inseparable from the narrative in which it is imbedded. And "if we pay attention to the narrative and self-involving character of the Gospels . . . there is no way to speak of Jesus' story without its forming our own. The story it forms creates a community which corresponds to the form of his life" (Hauerwas, 1981a, p. 51). Hence "there is no 'real Jesus' except as he is known through the kind of life he demanded of his disciples" (Hauerwas, 1981a, p. 41). In other words, one cannot identify Jesus without narrating the story in which that identity is present, and one cannot rightly narrate that story without being formed by the community it calls into existence. In narrating the story, the church inscribes itself into the story; teller and tale become one (Hauerwas, 1987, p. 186). What does this mean for Christian ethics? Simply put, it means that Christian ethics consists in the church's telling of the story, that is, continuing the story by inscribing its life and practices into the story. "The social ethical task of the church, therefore, is to be the kind of community that tells and tells rightly the story of Jesus" (Hauerwas, 1981a, p. 52). Hence Christian ethics does not consist in the determination of ideals and norms or in striking the proper balance between adjustment to and transformation of the "reality" of which the church is a part. Rather, the existence of the church as the community that continues the story is itself the content of Christian ethics.

There are complex issues at stake here. Hauerwas like Frei assumes the biblical narratives are realistic in the sense that there is a transparency between narrative and identity. But some argue that the narrative form of the synoptic Gospels conceals identity (Kelber, 1988).[10] Moreover, while Hauerwas and Frei reject a hermeneutics in which an external world or a metanarrative determines interpretation, both assume that the Bible itself can be rendered as a grand narrative encompassing the stories of Israel, of Jesus, and of the church (Frei, 1975, pp. 159–164; Hauerwas, 1987, pp. 179–187; 1983, pp. 81–87).

These controversial assumptions are worked out in what resembles a classical (i.e., Peircean) pragmatist account of mimesis. First, the biblical story is neither self-referential nor does it refer to a world outside the text. Instead its reference is ultimately grounded in the community that the story forms. Meaning thus occurs at the pragmatic level; the story refers to the habits and practices of the community that it should call forth (Hauerwas, 1981a, p. 37; 1987, pp. 191–193). Second, Hauerwas accepts the irreducible diversity of "the many-sided tale" that is the story of Jesus (Hauerwas, 1981a, p. 52; 1983, p. 166, n. 2) and the consequent impossibility of reducing the church's mimetic continuation of that story to a single, final form.[11] There is therefore a need for ongoing testing of the story in a diverse community of inquirers.

> The remarkable richness of these stories of God requires that a church be a community of discourse and interpretation that endeavors to tell these stories and form its life in accordance with them. The church, the whole body of believers, therefore cannot be limited to any one historical paradigm or contained by any one institutional form. Rather the very character of the stories of God require a people who are willing to have their understanding of the story constantly challenged by what others have discovered in their attempt to live faithful to that tradition. (Hauerwas, 1981a, p. 92)

Hauerwas echoes Alasdair MacIntyre's well-known description of a living tradition: "In effect the church is the extended argument over time about the significance of that story and how best to understand it" (Hauerwas, 1983, p. 107). Hence "[t]he church must always remain open to revision since the subject of its narrative is easily domesticated" (Hauerwas, 1987, p. 193). As a result, the ethical task of the church requires its capacity to form members who possess the virtues necessary to remember and tell the story (Hauerwas, 1983, pp. 103–106), exemplary figures who especially ground the reference of the story (Hauerwas, 1981a, pp. 232–233, n. 1; 1987, pp. 192, 197, n. 22), a polity that can sustain the differences necessary for discussion (Hauerwas, 1981a, p. 96), and a community that welcomes the other who challenges its current interpretations (Hauerwas, 1981a, pp. 92–93).

Formed by its story in this way, the church challenges the assumptions that reality is given in the form in which the world construes it and that the moral "necessities" that follow from the way the world "is" really are such. From this perspective moral reasoning is not an activity an agent or community engages in once its identity has been formed, but is essential to the formation of that identity. So whereas modern morality assumes a self and a community free from historical determination and external impediments as in Kant's kingdom of self-legislators, for Hauerwas

> to be an agent means I am able to locate my action within an ongoing history and within a community of language users. . . . My power as an agent is therefore relative to the power of my descriptive ability. Yet that very ability is fundamentally a social skill, for we learn to describe through appropriating the narratives of the community in which we find ourselves. (Hauerwas, 1983, p. 42)

Similarly, casuistry is a process by which a community forms itself by discovering previously unrecognized implications of its narrative commitments as it seeks to live them out under new circumstances, and by which it tests whether its practices are consistent with its habits and convictions (Hauerwas, 1983, pp. 119–120). Moral freedom is the capacity to redescribe the world in accordance with the convictions and practices of the community and to act from the redescription. "For the idea that the moral life is the examined life is but a way of saying that we can choose to determine ourselves in terms of certain kinds of descriptions rather than others" (Hauerwas, 1981b, p. 66).

This means that Christian ethics will refuse to accept the descriptions of situations and cases offered by other forms of ethics and the moral necessities implied in such descriptions.

> Our "freedom" in regard to our decisions depends exactly on not having to accept the determinism of those who would encourage us to assume that we have to "make" a decision because "this is the way things are." Such determinism can be defeated only if we have descriptive skills provided by a truthful narrative to see the "situation" in a new light—that is, in a light that enables us to do what we do or not do in a manner consistent with our moral commitments." (Hauerwas, 1983, p. 125)

Hauerwas is referring in this context to cases in which resort to force is regarded as "necessary" for the defense of the victim, but it also applies to cases in which nontreatment of impaired newborns is regarded as "necessary" to spare them a life of suffering. The major point is that cases like these often assume a description of the "way the world is" that (1) assumes certain actions or responses of others are inevitable and thus forecloses the possibility that our alternative action could make a difference, and (2) makes violence or nontreatment a necessity while the question of whether we or the world ought to be changed by forming communities and practices within which the given descriptions no longer hold and the contemplated actions are thus no longer necessary is never raised. "[T]hose 'necessities' too often simply assume that among the givens are my limits or the limits of my community, and never think of suggesting ways in which the community or myself might be asked to change our lives" (Hauerwas, 1983, p. 124). Hence, to follow up on a point made above, the church's casuistry stands in much the same relation to modern moral theory as revolutionary practice stands to philosophy in Marx's famous eleventh thesis on Feuerbach. Those theories "always end up underwriting our assumption that the way things are is the way they ought or have to be; but our task, through the power of practical reason, is to change the way things are by changing ourselves" (Hauerwas, 1988, p. 142). Hence the power to redescribe cannot be merely a cognitive power. It is rooted in the habits and practices of the community that carries it out as part of its own moral formation.

The foregoing analysis explains why for Hauerwas the church must exist concretely and not only in the form of witnessing to an ideal that transcends it. "If Christian convictions have any claim to being considered truthful, then my church has to exist as surely as the Jews have to be God's promised people" (Hauerwas, 1994, p. 20).[12] The analysis also explains both Hauerwas's method in moral reasoning and the importance of narrative in that method. In regard to method, Hauerwas consistently begins by identifying and challenging the description of the issue at hand. Moral reflection begins, then, with the issue or case as it has been constituted by the world. He then proposes a redescription in terms of Christian convictions and practices. The significance of this method is that it does not distinguish the process of moral reasoning from the process of transformation by which agents and communities are trained to see the world in terms of the discourse and practices of the church. The process of moral reasoning is the process by which one becomes part of the community that resists the world and serves as an alternative. Moral reasoning is therefore inseparable from becoming a moral agent of a certain character. Narrative is essential to this process because redescribing a case or an issue involves inscribing it into the progression of the convictions and practices of the community as it confronts new situations. And carrying out this task involves two tasks that MacIntyre also proposes. First, it presupposes a narration of the progression of the community's convictions and practices up to that point. Second, the skills required in order to redescribe issues in this way are acquired and cultivated in an ongoing process by which the agent is formed by the stories and practices of the community. Hence the capacity to reason morally presupposes the narrative of the one who reasons.

A church so formed resists the normalizing reality-descriptions of the world and shows the world what it means to be the world—that is, to lack a narrative and community that can live without violence and welcome the stranger without fear—by constituting a contrast model. One salient characteristic of such a church—a characteristic that marks a radical and decisive break with the most fundamental commitments of the Protestant ethics of vocation—is that its moral action seeks to be exemplary rather than effective in the world. ". . . Christians insist on service that may appear ineffective to the world. For the service that Christians are called upon to provide does not have as its aim to make the world better, but to demonstrate that Jesus has made possible a new world, a new social order" (Hauerwas, 1981a, p. 49). The chief task of the church is not to make the society in which it finds itself more just or to meet survival needs—or to rid individuals or the world of all conditions that cause suffering. When its task is conceived in this way the church must align itself with the political, bureaucratic, and technological processes of modern societies since it can fulfill this task only by being effective, and effectiveness requires the use of these means. To the extent it is successful—that is to the extent that it effectively serves the world as it is—the church loses its capacity to form a contrast model that challenges the violence that is done in the name of the "peace" and "justice" of liberal societies, and the world loses an opportunity to see how abnormal is the violence and fear of the other that it regards as "normal." Moreover, when it commits itself to an ethics of improvement of the world, the church also commits itself to an incrementalism that both accepts the basic structures and practices of the world as it is and must rest satisfied with piecemeal reforms of these existing structures and practices. Hauerwas, then, rejects the ethics of vocation on two grounds. One is its assumption that the world as it is is implicitly or potentially Christian, the other is its contentment with incremental change.

The foregoing interpretation of the church allows us to indicate more directly the relation between medicine and the church discussed above. Medicine possesses its own moral integrity, indeed, exemplarity, apart from the church. "Yet exactly to the extent that medical care has remained committed to those it cannot cure, medicine provides one of the more profound practices on which we can draw in our culture for moral experience" (Hauerwas, 1994, p. 162). Nevertheless, the demands of caring and the pressures to reject and abandon the ill who cannot be cured point to the need for another community.

> To learn how to be present in that way we need examples—that is, a people who have so learned to embody such a presence in their lives that it has become the marrow of their habits. . . . Thus medicine needs the church not to supply a foundation for its moral commitments, but rather as a resource of the habits and practices necessary to sustain the care of those in pain over the long haul. (Hauerwas, 1986, pp. 80–81)

Insofar as Christian ethics is not primarily concerned with accomplishing good results in the world, it is not surprising that Hauerwas focuses on caring rather than curing as the defining characteristic of medicine. In principle, therefore, medicine stands against the secular version of the Baconian project in exactly the same way the church stands against its religious roots in the ethics of vocation. But in practice, medicine is subject to the world as described by the speech and practices of a liberal society ruled by the fear of death and the need for control that feed the desire for curative medicine. In order to sustain its commitment to caring, medicine needs the example of a community that is strong enough to resist these discursive practices and to form its own. The church as a community that both resists the speech and practices of modern liberal societies and forms an alternative shows medicine the character of the modern society that is destroying its commitments and provides an example of resistance and counterpractice. The next task is to show how the church's care for the mentally handicapped forms such an alternative and thereby shows the world what it means to be the world.

SUFFERING, RECONCILIATION, AND THE MENTALLY HANDICAPPED

As a community formed by the story of Jesus' death and resurrection, the church deals with suffering in a way that both resists and challenges the world. Its willingness to live with certain kinds of suffering, even meaningless suffering, reveals the moral vacuity and even cruelty of a world that would eliminate suffering in part through the office of medicine. In this respect the suffering of the mentally challenged serves as a hermeneutical key. Hauerwas's point of departure is the effort to eliminate mental retardation, an effort supported by the deepest humanistic motives and connected with other efforts to eliminate suffering.

> For there is no question that the most compassionate motivation often lays [sic] behind calls to eliminate retardation, for helping the old to die without pain, for insuring that no unwanted children are born, and so on. Such policies seem good because we assume compassion requires us to try to rid the world as much as possible of unnecessary suffering. Those born retarded seem to be suffering from outrageous fortune, cruel fate, that if possible should be eliminated. (Hauerwas, 1994, pp. 164–165)

Hauerwas thus connects these efforts to the Baconian project. The problem with that project is that "in the name of responding to suffering, compassion literally becomes a killer" (Hauerwas, 1994, p. 165). Mental retardation is especially important in this context since it is not like some other diseases, such as cancer, polio or heart disease, which can or may be eliminated without eliminating the patient. "We can care for the cancer patients by trying to alleviate their cancer without destroying the patient, but you cannot eliminate retardation without destroying the person who is retarded" (Hauerwas, 1994, p. 164). This leads to a paradox that Hauerwas often points out and to which I have already alluded: by selective nontreatment of newborns, we eliminate the sufferer in order to save him or her from a life of suffering (Hauerwas, 1977, p. 165; 1986, pp. 23–24). The cure or elimination of the disease, not the care of the patient, is the focus of Baconian medicine, and this subjugation of the person to the disease may easily lead to elimination of the person as incidental to the elimination of the disease (Hauerwas, 1977, p. 167).

For Hauerwas this is what happens when love or compassion is disarticulated from the stories and practices of the Christian community. He describes the compassion that would eliminate suffering as "charity run wild and gone crazy because it is unable to totally relieve the world of its suffering" and thus "is willing to destroy some in the name of the 'quality' of life" (Hauerwas, 1981b, p. 193). By contrast, love in the Christian story and community is formed and disciplined by practices of cultivating a morally worthy life and welcoming the mentally handicapped—practices to which concerns for survival and overall well-being are subordinated. But disarticulated from this story and these practices, love serves the aims of the Baconian project, in which the effort to expand choice and eliminate suffering by controlling nature leave no room for such practices.

We are now prepared to understand the precise sense in which the church as a community supports and sustains the commitments of medicine and constitutes an alternative to the Baconian project. I believe the key to the church's alternative to the Baconian project in Hauerwas's thought is his interpretation of suffering in terms of alienation. Alienation calls for concrete practices to overcome it, practices that in the radical reformation tradition are known as reconciliation. Indeed, concrete reconciliation practiced by the community plays the same role in Hauerwas's thought that vocation plays in Gustafson's thought. Suffering, Hauerwas argues, alienates us from ourselves and from one another (Hauerwas, 1986, pp. 25, 76–78). Suffering is self-alienating not only insofar as pain causes us to objectify regions of the body that are the source of the pain, as Hauerwas mentions briefly and as physicians have often noticed. More generally, suffering is self-alienating because, by definition, it *happens* to us; it is not the product of our agency. It is this affront to the agent's control that appeals to the Baconian project of eliminating suffering. "From this [Baconian] perspective, medicine can be interpreted as the attempt to have us view our suffering as pointless, thus making it subject to therapeutic intervention." Medicine impoverishes our moral life by severing the link between suffering and our moral projects (Hauerwas, 1986, p. 33). In other words, for Hauerwas medicine that is bent on eliminating all suffering deprives agents of the opportunity to cultivate a moral life in which suffering is subject to the goods and virtues that make that life the kind of life it is.

As his attention to tragedy as the inevitability of ill results that come from living according to substantive convictions would indicate, Hauerwas agrees with Martha Nussbaum and others that efforts to guarantee a life devoid of suffering remove us from the very endeavors that make for a morally worthy life. At the very least, recognition of this fact should lead us to distinguish those forms of suffering that merely happen to us from those that are inseparable from our moral projects (Hauerwas, 1986, pp. 165–166; 1990, p. 85). This would enable us to give an account of unnecessary suffering or untimely death that we would look to medicine to prevent (1986, p. 26). However, as we saw above, an essential aspect of the moral life and human freedom of the Christian is his or her capacity to redescribe situations by inscribing them into a narrative. The effort of the Baconian project to define all suffering as pointless in the name of expanding the realm of human freedom over that of fate in reality deprives persons of the freedom to make even what merely happens to them their own (Hauerwas, 1986, pp. 33–34). Hence the assumption that whatever merely happens to us aside from our moral projects should be subject to elimination or cure can easily truncate our moral projects. "The task is to find the means to make that which is happening to me mine. . . . No doubt our power to transform events into decisions can be the source of great self-deception, but it is also the source of our moral identity" (Hauerwas, 1986, pp. 166–167).

This last remark indicates that there is some suffering that cannot be transformed into our narratives and that we can be self-deceived. "Our refusal to accept certain kinds of suffering, or to try to interpret them as serving some human purpose, is essential for our moral health" (Hauerwas, 1986, p. 168). In this connection Hauerwas mentions Auschwitz and Hiroshima. He may also have in mind those who accept suffering in neurotic and pathological ways. It is dangerous "to make suffering an end in itself or to acquiesce to kinds of suffering that can and should be alleviated" (Hauerwas, 1990, p. 85). Nevertheless, the alternative is to allow medicine to control our lives by defining all our suffering as pointless. In the end there is no substitute for a narrative that enables a community to reclaim medicine as a part of its moral project (Hauerwas, 1986, p. 36). "If medicine is to serve our needs rather than determining our needs, then we must recover a sense of how even our illnesses fit within an ongoing narrative. The crucial question concerns what such a narrative is to be, so that we can learn to live with our illnesses without giving them false meaning" (Hauerwas, 1990, p. 108). This enables Hauerwas to surmise that the reason the suffering of children and the mentally handicapped (the same would apply also to those who suffer dementia) is so troubling is that we assume they lack a narrative by which their suffering can be inscribed into a life project, an assumption that is closely linked with our fear that we too lack such a narrative (Hauerwas, 1986, p. 171; 1990, p. 67). Certain that they are suffering yet unable to understand how they can make their suffering meaningful, we "rob them of the opportunity to do what each of us must do—learn to bear and live with our individual sufferings" (Hauerwas, 1986, p. 175). Thus Hauerwas explains our desire to eliminate the suffering of the mentally handicapped and of children as the result of our own tendency to regard our suffering and that of others as pointless. Hauerwas is careful to insist that we cannot perform the task of transforming the pointlessness of suffering into a moral project on behalf of others. "When we do that we can force pointless suffering and pain into a teleological pattern that cannot help but be destructive" (Hauerwas, 1990, p. 89). But it does not follow that we are justified in depriving others of their own capacity to make that suffering meaningful.

But surely there is a great deal of suffering that we cannot transform into our moral projects *and* that medicine cannot cure; suffering, in other words, that really is pointless. This kind of suffering presents special problems insofar as medicine is committed in principle (Bacon: "call no disease incurable") and often in practice to the denial that such suffering exists. The overwhelming temptation in the face of pointless incurable suffering is to seek to gain control over it. Hence, for example, terminally ill children are often subjected to treatments that entail further suffering and cannot cure because our only way of dealing with this kind of pointless suffering is by efforts at medical control. But in such cases Hauerwas argues that the proper task of medicine "is to help us go on in the face of an illness that may not finally be curable" (Hauerwas, 1990, p. 65). The task, in other words, is to help us place pointless suffering in the context of care. Here medicine both parallels and depends on the church. Like medicine, the task of the church is to be a caring community whose speech and practices enable others to "go on" in the face of pointless suffering (Hauerwas, 1990, p. 89). But since these practices of caring follow from the narrative the church embodies, the church has a resource that medicine lacks. What is needed "is the wisdom and skills of a community constituted by a truthful narrative that can comprehend" the deaths of children, for example, "without denying their pointlessness. . . . We have no theodicy that can soften the pain of our death and the death of our children, but we believe that we share a common story which makes it possible for us to be with one another especially as we die" (Hauerwas, 1990, pp. 147–148). The church's narrative can absorb such suffering because it teaches us that "our lives are located in God's narrative—the God who has not abandoned us even when we or someone we care deeply about is ill" (Hauerwas, 1990, p. 67).

Hauerwas's ultimate warrant for this last claim about the church's narrative is its christology. "For we believe, on the basis of the cross, that our lives are sustained by a God who has taken the tragic into his own life" (Hauerwas, 1977, p. 12). A community whose practices are formed by a narrative in which Christ absorbs even pointless suffering overcomes self-alienation because it understands that the inability to claim one's life as one's own—that is, to "go on" even in the face of pointless suffering—is overcome only by the confidence that one's life is claimed by such a narrative.[13] But this reconciliation with God does not occur apart from the reconciling presence of a community that embodies the story in its concrete practices. Such a community may serve as a resource for medicine, which like the church is committed to being present with those who suffer pointlessly.[14]

But suffering not only alienates us from ourselves. It also alienates us from others. Again, there is an obvious sense in which others cannot and do not seek to share one's pain. There is also a sense in which remaining silent about one's pain in order to avoid alienating others only increases alienation: to the extent to which one is successful, one creates a narrative that others cannot share (Hauerwas, 1986, pp. 77–78). But Hauerwas's major point is that the suffering of others threatens our efforts to deny our subjection to illness and death as well as our dependence on others for our existence and identity—in other words, our efforts to maintain our illusion of self-possession (Hauerwas, 1986, pp. 168–170). This brings suffering in general, and the suffering of the retarded in particular, into the economy of alterity in Hauerwas's thought.

According to Hauerwas, our lives consist of a frantic search for security, which is achieved by self-deception regarding our sense of self-possession and is maintainted by violence and coercion against the other or stranger who reminds us that we are not masters of our existence (Hauerwas, 1983, p. 47). The other is therefore a threat.[15] The mentally handicapped appear to present a threefold challenge to our illusion of self-possession according to Hauerwas. "Exactly because we are unsure they have the capacity to suffer as we suffer, we seek to avoid their presence in order to avoid the limits of our own sympathy" (Hauerwas, 1986, p. 174). This first challenge reminds us of our own limits in overcoming the alienation of suffering. Hence, "we perceive them . . . as beings whose condition has doomed them to a loneliness we fear worse than suffering itself, and, as a result, we seek to prevent retardation" (Hauerwas, 1986, p. 176). Second, we are especially reluctant to enter into the suffering of others when we believe we can "do nothing" to relieve it. The mentally handicapped challenge our self-delusions about our capacity to relieve the suffering of others. The third challenge refers to the fact that the mentally handicapped, unlike some others who suffer, do not hide their suffering from us and therefore do not allow us to maintain our self-deceptions about our own neediness and powerlessness to avoid it. "[W]e 'naturally' disdain those who do not or cannot cover up their neediness. Prophetlike, the retarded only remind us of the insecurity hidden in our false sense of self-possession" (Hauerwas, 1986, p. 169). From these perspectives, then, the effort to eliminate mental retardation is an effort to eliminate the other or stranger who challenges our illusions. The policy of preventing or eliminating suffering is itself based on our self-deception about the limits of our capacities and the kind of mortal and interdependent beings we are.

The task of medicine is to overcome the alienation from others that suffering involves by means of "the physician's vocation . . . to serve as a bridge between the world of the sick and the world of the healthy." Physicians "stand as a constant reminder that the worlds of the sick and the healthy are actually one world joined by common destiny"—that is, a destiny bounded by the inevitability of sickness and mortality (Hauerwas, 1986, p. 49). Once again, medicine both parallels and depends on the church, which has story-formed practices that serve as a resource for medicine. In this case, health professionals like the rest of us must overcome their deeply rooted fear and rejection of the suffering other as well as the institutionalized practices of shielding the sick from the healthy. The church's speech and practices in this regard derive from the familiar Lutheran moral psychology. Just as for Luther God's forgiveness liberates human beings from anxiety over their salvation and thus enables them to concentrate on what is best for their neighbor, so for Hauerwas God's forgiveness liberates human beings from their quest to gain security through power and violence and thus enables them to renounce violence against the other and to welcome him or her.

> In Jesus we have met the one who has the authority and power to forgive our fevered search to gain security through deception, coercion and violence. . . . But by learning to be forgiven we are enabled to view other lives not as threats but as gifts. Thus in contrast to all societies built on shared resentments and fears, Christian community is formed by a story that enables its members to trust the otherness of the other as the very sign of the forgiving character of God's Kingdom. (Hauerwas, 1981a, p. 50)

Because forgiveness enables Christians to shed their self-deceptions about their lives, it removes the threat others pose to a life founded on those self-deceptions. Reconciliation with God issues in concrete reconciliation with the other who challenges those self-deceptions. Hence for Hauerwas the church is the community that allows its practices to be disrupted by the mentally handicapped not because the church is so charitable toward those in need but because the church could not exist as a community of reconciliation without the mentally handicapped (Hauerwas, 1994, pp. 181–186). The other who disrupts our lives is essential to our lives—not to our self-fulfilment but to our moral identity; this is what the speech and practices of the church witness to in the case of the mentally handicapped and those who suffer from other signs of our finitude and mortality.

In conclusion, Hauerwas's work shows how the Baconian project embodies the effort of modern morality to make our moral lives immune to the play of contingency and vulnerability. What happens to us outside of our agency and the other whose suffering challenges our fragile sense of control both alienate us from our allegedly "true" selves and must therefore be eliminated. But Hauerwas recognizes that the effort to render ourselves immune to these forces impoverishes our moral lives. It restricts our freedom and power to make what happens to us our own and deprives us of the skills and practices of caring that are the only appropriate response to suffering that cannot be cured. It is also destructive to others. It subordinates persons to diseases, subjects patients to further (avoidable) suffering by its unwillingness to accept the inevitability of some pointless suffering, and is willing in the interest of eliminating suffering to eliminate also those who suffer. In short, far from solving the problem of alienation, the Baconian project, by replacing the traditional moral commitments of medicine with its utopian and illusory dream of eliminating suffering, merely perpetuates it, since the inevitable limits of medicine as a tragic profession guarantee that there will always be some pointless suffering and some sufferers who will remind us of our subjection to contingency and fortune.

In contrast, by believing that some suffering can be given a point and by accepting the inevitability of other kinds of suffering, the church resists the efforts of Baconian medicine to eliminate suffering and expand the sovereignty of choice, and shows the world the illusory and dangerous nature of its reliance on these efforts. Moreover, the church's story and practices of reconciliation—the support of a community that helps its members give a point to their suffering, the care of a community that absorbs pointless suffering, and the welcome of a community that finds in the suffering of the other not a threat to its moral identity but the source of it—form a set of counternarratives and counterpractices that can for Hauerwas sustain the true moral life of medicine in the face of the fate and fortune it cannot master.

EVALUATION

One of the most surprising features of Hauerwas's thought is his willingness to accept traditional descriptions of the moral commitments of medicine more or less on their own terms. One would expect from his rhetoric about the church and the society in which it finds itself a clearer endorsement of the "sectarian" medicine he sometimes advocates in passing (Hauerwas, 1977, p. 131; 1981b, p. 182). This may lead one to wonder whether Hauerwas's contrast between church and society applies only to society insofar as it is characterized by liberalism, but it also raises questions about the independent moral status medicine enjoys. Of course, we have seen that Hauerwas sharply qualifies this independence. The moral commitments of medicine require support from outside to maintain them in a liberal society, and a broader account of the good, also from outside, in order to direct them toward the goods health itself serves. Nevertheless, according to Hauerwas the moral commitments I summarized near the beginning of this chapter are inherent in medicine as a profession and tradition. As we have also seen, Hauerwas rejects previous ways of accounting for these commitments: Ramsey's theological grounds, Kass's natural teleology, bioethics itself. In fact, it is partly the failure of all of these accounts that leads Hauerwas to view the church as an external resource to sustain, limit, supplement and direct them.

Nevertheless, Hauerwas can no longer simply assume that the moral commitments he identifies are inherent in medicine (if indeed they ever were); the utilitarians, managed care specialists, and Baconians have had their say and more. But if we can no longer assume, as Ramsey still thought he could, that medicine itself possesses these moral characteristics—if they have now become contested—then Hauerwas owes us a stronger account than Ramsey needed of how medicine (counterfactually) still rests on these commitments. We saw in the last chapter that Kass's effort to supply such an account ultimately fails. If Hauerwas wants to retain these commitments, it would seem that he must either supply some such account or admit that what he once found to be inherent in medicine itself is actually the moral self-understanding of medicine in the Christian community only. The second alternative would force Hauerwas to recognize what H. Tristram Engelhardt, Jr., has recognized: that there is now no substantive tradition of medicine of the kind Ramsey, Kass, Hauerwas, and others assume (which need not entail that there is no tradition at all, only that any such tradition must be diverse and contested). Hauerwas would then have to cash out his hints about a "sectarian" medicine that would differ from Engelhardt's version primarily by virtue of its stronger (Protestant) prophetic thrust directed toward the liberal, Baconian practice of medicine. In other words, Hauerwas has three options: to revise his description of medicine as a tradition to accomodate its currently contested moral terrain; to show how medicine, apart from any outside tradition and in spite of its current state, is still normatively bound to the moral features he identifies; or to concede that those features are in fact Christian and were all along.

A second criticism goes to the heart of Hauerwas's project. Hauerwas argues that his church must be actual (though not, it must be kept in mind, already perfect). It is important to keep in mind what is at stake here. Hauerwas's ethic rightly convinces us that significant moral commitments sometimes require ourselves and others—including those who from other moral perspectives it is our first duty to protect—to suffer. It therefore demands that prospective parents of a Down syndrome child, family members of a sufferer of Alzheimer's disease, a person with a painful and incurable disease contemplating suicide, and others consider placing profound burdens on themselves and others. Hauerwas may be right that we consider such things burdensome less because of the requisites of an incorrigible human nature than because a liberal society has forced us into a moral identity based on self-interest. But in a society with the moral practices and social institutions of our society, these can be profound burdens nonetheless. This makes it all the more imperative that there actually be the counterpractices and contrast community that form its members in the skills and virtues (including courage, patience, and caring) needed to live according to Hauerwas's convictions. If we are morally formed and guided only in real communities, and if Hauerwas claims that his church must therefore exist as a real community, then it is imperative that he be able to describe the community in which his moral stance is in the process of being realized.[16]

However, Hauerwas's descriptions of Christian moral convictions and practices often articulate their deviation from American liberalism much more thoroughly than their derivation from an ongoing tradition carried out by an identifiable community. In other words, in his effort to portray the church as a counterpractice to liberalism Hauerwas often articulates his moral convictions as responses to failures of liberal discourses and practices. Is Hauerwas then simply playing the role of a Socratic gadfly with regard to the moral minimalism of contemporary American liberalism—a role that for all its differences still has some striking similarities to the role Niebuhr played with regard to the moral optimism of an earlier stage of American liberalism? In both cases Christian convictions and practices seem primarily to be directed against false and dangerous American presumptions about its own moral soundness. Does this make Hauerwas by his own criterion (namely an obsession with America) the last great Social Gospel thinker? I have argued this (McKenny, 1995), but the issue may be more complicated.

Hauerwas repeatedly reminds his audience that they are deeply influenced by liberalism in ways they do not suspect—even (perhaps especially) in what they wrongly believe is the Christian content of their speech and practices. Hauerwas's first task is therefore to show his audience how they have been formed by liberal speech and practices, then to offer Christian redescriptions as counterpractices. Those who follow him in this exercise find themselves resisting liberalism and rein-scribing themselves into the Christian story. However, while Hauerwas can and does identify actual counterpractices and thus points to real-izations of his church, these realizations are scattered throughout com-munities that are in other respects still characteristically liberal. This is to be expected if Hauerwas is right about the pervasiveness of liberalism. The problem is that his own view of what a community must be in order to form the moral identities and habits of its members requires more than these (impressive but) scattered realizations. Persons can be formed in the church's story of Jesus only in a community which over time identifies and measures itself by the convictions and practices imbedded in this story. Hence partial or scattered realizations of these convictions and practices are not sufficient for Hauerwas to conclude that his church is actual. It seems rather that Hauerwas is urging his church (which is primarily Protestant but includes others insofar as they too are characterized by the fusion of Christendom with American liberalism) to resist their moral formation in American liberalism by forming themselves in the Christian story. Because his church is still so deeply formed by liberalism it is still in the early stages of forming the practices that embody its redescriptions and training its members in the skills and virtues necessary to carry out those redescriptions and practices. Since these are not yet well developed, Hauerwas must con-centrate on teaching his hearers to recognize the ways liberalism forms them and identifying the scattered points at which liberal formations are being resisted.

This characterization of Hauerwas's church explains, I think, why his treatments of concrete moral issues often seem to stop short of their destination. He typically begins by skillfully showing how allegedly neutral descriptions of actions can serve the self-deceptive tendencies of agents, as we saw above. For example, he shows how the distinction between killing and letting die in the case of Down's syndrome new-borns with life-threatening conditions enables both parents and doc-tors to avoid difficult moral questions about whether there are limits to parental sacrifice and the physician commitment to protect life and if so, what these limits are. The distinction allows parents and doctors to maintain their self-deceptions about their own roles in a society that has no way of raising such questions (Hauerwas, 1977, pp. 178–181). Similarly, the effort to understand suicide and euthanasia as morally neutral enables us to conceal the fact that one may be doing away with others who bother us rather than caring for them, or may be pretending to make a heroic self-sacrifice to avoid being a burden to others. Moreover, the morally neutral language of suicide and euthanasia can, in a way I detailed in chapter two, serve to shield a society from its abandonment of others and its unwillingness to bear burdens for the ill (Hauerwas, 1977, p. 114). What follows in both cases are interpretations of the deeper societal understandings of the meaning of children or the reasons for living that underlie the meanings of the moral language used. Up to now Hauerwas has offered persuasive accounts of the moral limitations of a liberal society—accounts in which his hearers can recognize the limitations of their own moral formation insofar as it too is liberal. But his alternative in both cases is disappointing. In the discussion of Down syndrome newborns Hauerwas posits a principle of justice according to which such newborns should be treated or not treated according to the same criteria as "normal" newborns since they have an equal claim to our care, but provides no distinctively Christian ground for this claim. As for the chief question he raises, namely the understanding of parental care that would enable us to determine what requirements and limits we can expect of parents and doctors, he simply concludes that we lack a community to determine such things (Hauerwas, 1977, p. 182). The treatment of suicide and euthanasia initially fares somewhat better. Hauerwas opposes to secular views the Christian understanding of life as a gift sustained by the care and trust of others which backs an obligation to live in order to keep faith with this care and trust (Hauerwas, 1977, pp. 107–111; 1986, pp. 105–106).[17] Suicide is therefore prohibited, with two caveats. First, the blame for suicide should often fall on the community rather than the individual. Second, since life is not of absolute value to Christians, it is not to be preserved at all costs. What is lacking, however, is anything resembling the rich description Gustafson gives of the powers and limits of the kind of care that sustains life. It is ironic that Gustafson says far more than does Hauerwas about the moral requirements and limits real communities face regarding suicide.

In both cases, the chief moral issue for Hauerwas is the requirements and limits of care. And in both cases these requirements and limits are apparently known only in a particular community. But in both cases there is no description of the discourses and practices of the actual community that seeks to discover and live according to these requirements and limits and to support one another as they face them together. The reason, I have argued, is that such discourse and practices only emerge over time in a real community that identifies and measures itself by them. But the community that identifies and measures itself by the discourse and practices Hauerwas describes is still forming itself in resistance to the liberalism that has formed it in the past. For this reason Hauerwas is necessarily more clear about the limitations of liberal discourses and practices than about the details of the contrast model.[18]

My third criticism concerns Hauerwas's effort to break with theodicy. Here I take an explicit stance within Christian theology. According to Hauerwas, theodicy and the Baconian project are linked in a common effort to place suffering in the context of control, whether by God or by technology. The church's recognition that some suffering is (morally or otherwise) inevitable breaks with this ethos of control. But Hauerwas's alternative ineluctably reinforces some of the very assumptions that characterize theodicies. For example, he claims that the Christian community and its narrative are able to absorb pointless suffering without giving it a false meaning (Hauerwas, 1990, pp. 53, 117). But it is difficult to understand how suffering can be absorbed without denying the very features that make it pointless, namely its unshareability and its absurdity. Hauerwas even refers to "a truthful narrative that can comprehend [the deaths of children from incurable diseases] without denying their pointlessness" (Hauerwas, 1990, p. 147). But to comprehend something is to make it intelligible—thus denying that it is pointless. Hauerwas ironically ends up in the company of theodicy and the Baconian project, denying pointless suffering.

Hauerwas clearly wants to avoid this company, so where does he go wrong? The problem lies, I believe, in a need to exonerate God from suffering and a consequent misunderstanding of reconciliation. Hauerwas sets himself a twofold task in his attempt to deconstruct theodicies. One task is to show how "our only hope lies in whether we can place alongside the story of the pointless suffering of a child . . . a story of suffering that helps us know we are not thereby abandoned" (Hauerwas, 1990, p. 34). I defend the legitimacy of this task below. But another task is to answer the question of "What kind of God it is Christians worship that makes intelligible the cry of rage against the suffering and death of our children" (Hauerwas, 1990, p. 35). Hauerwas recognizes that the cry of rage searches for meaning and he rightly refuses to reward this quest with an explanation of suffering. Moreover, he recognizes that the cry of rage or lament delegitimates theodicies by breaking with the assumptions of order and control they preserve and exposing the false comforts they conceal (Hauerwas, 1990, p. 83). He notes that God "is not a God who insures that our lives will not be disturbed" and "may not be the God we want." But in the end "it is a

God whose very complexity is so fascinating that our attention is cap-
tivated by the wonder of the life God has given us—a life that includes
pain and suffering that seem to have no point" (Hauerwas, 1990, p.
83). Like a theodicist Hauerwas here mutes the cry of rage, absorbing it
into a narrative of adventure in which a people discover a wondrous
God. Could Hauerwas say this to Job, much less to a victim of the Nazi
holocaust?

The problem is that the only God who can make the cry of rage
intelligible is some version of either Gustafson's or Jonas's God—a God
who will have no place in any theodicy. Because Hauerwas does not
accept either Gustafson's or Jonas's God, he confuses a narrative that
absorbs (and thus denies) pointless suffering with a narrative that
enables a community to care for those who suffer pointlessly because it
is grounded in the story of the cross and resurrection that assures them
that God has not abandoned them even in their pointless suffering.
Because of this confusion Hauerwas risks losing hold of the best
response to Gustafson, the response implied in his first task. What the
reconciling community does is place its narrative and the practices of
caring that it enables alongside the narrative of suffering and the legitimate rage against God. Reconciliation is by juxtaposition rather than
absorption; it denies the finality of pointless suffering by showing that
while God for whatever reason (whether Gustafson's, Jonas's or some
other that is beyond our knowledge) does not prevent pointless suffering, neither does he abandon those who are its victims.

In conclusion, Hauerwas's attack on the technological utopianism
of medicine is thoroughgoing and uncompromising. Its strengths are
clear. His insight into the Baconian project as a continuation of theodicy
enriches the account I give in chapter one, and his recognition of the
centrality to the Baconian project of control and of the illusions and
self-deceptions this involves constitute the sharpest critique yet. While
some would argue with Hauerwas's portrayal of liberalism, his connection of the Baconian project with the latter and his recognition that
alternative to the Baconian project must break with central features of
liberal societies are persuasive.

More positively, Hauerwas initiates a geography of suffering,
which is precisely what any tradition needs to do in order to resist and
counter the Baconian project. As I see it, the phenomenon of suffering
from a Hauerwasian perspective would be mapped as follows. First is
suffering that has a point because it either (1) fits into or at least does not
disrupt our moral projects (which may mean that it is not suffering in
the strict sense), or (2) occurs as a result of our moral convictions.
Second is suffering that is pointless and which either (3) cannot be cured

without violating one or more moral convictions, (4) cannot be cured at all (whether in general or for a specific individual) due to the limitations or the tragic nature of medicine, or (5) can be cured and does not fit into our moral projects. The Baconian project is grounded in a moral scheme that ignores (1) or denies that it applies to some classes of persons (e.g., children or the mentally handicapped), rejects the moral convictions that constitute (2) and (3) as instances of moral tragedy, and denies (4). It thus reduces all suffering to (5) and, since everyone agrees that this kind of suffering should by be cured, thereby seeks to justify the reduction of medicine to its technological and curative powers. In contrast, Hauerwas understands the importance of (1) and (2) to any morally worthy life and recognizes that (3) and (4) will always be with us. But if this is so, then the Baconian project, which gains so much of its moral authority from its effort to eliminate suffering, will either fail to address the most wrenching kind of suffering or will address it only by immoral means, such as the elimination of the sufferer. By breaking with the illusions and self-deceptions of the ethos of control, the church's practices of reconciliation with and care for the victims of these kinds of suffering (such as the chronically ill and especially the mentally handicapped) therefore undercut the Baconian project at the very point where it claims moral superiority. At the end of chapter one I argued that one barrier to seeking an alternative to the Baconian project is its moral claim regarding suffering and the authority it derives from it. By divesting the Baconian project of its superiority with regard to suffering, Hauerwas removes this barrier.

Hauerwas also shows how the ethos of control destroys the moral soundness of the agent by eroding the capacity to care.

> It is ironic . . . that what people fear is not illness itself but loss of control. That fear is so all-consuming is an indication of the common misunderstanding of what control of the body entails. . . . By learning to live as embodied beings, that is, as people subject to disease and ultimately death, we learn how significant it is that we be capable of caring for one another through the office of medicine. (Hauerwas, 1986, p. 50)

When the mentally challenged and others challenge our illusions of control, they also awaken our capacity to care. Here Hauerwas takes a first step in the direction I will pursue in the final chapter by challenging the Baconian understanding of the body and replacing it with one that finds moral significance in the subjection of the body to natural necessity. Only the body that is receptive to disease and death is also receptive to the suffering of the other, and thus capable of responding with care to "the call to humanity this one retarded child offers me" (Hauerwas, 1981b, p. 191).

Finally, the centrality of the church's practices of caring accomplish two other significant purposes. First, precisely because they are mundane and seemingly trivial (when compared to the allure and power of technology) and because nearly everyone (not just experts) is capable of participating in them, they offer a version of the ethic of ordinary life that breaks with the economy of efficiency and enhancement that supports the reign of technology. Second, the attention to practices and the portrayal of caring as a counterpractice that resists the reign of technology anticipates an important set of issues that is essential to our topic and is treated in the next chapter.

If these virtues commend Hauerwas's alternative to the Baconian project to us, the vices that qualify our acceptance must also be acknowledged. Hauerwas's failure to convince us that his church is an actual living tradition nullifies some of the advance over Kass constituted by his recognition that medicine requires a distinct tradition. The argument that medicine does require such a tradition is sound; the claim that Hauerwas's church fills the requirement is not yet substantiated. For much the same reason, Hauerwas has not shown that Gustafson's effort to limit the Baconian project more or less from within or that at least some measure of his and Jonas's attention to nature are not the wiser or more likely successful route to take. If Gustafson and Jonas underemphasized the role of tradition and thereby unwittingly contributed to the ethos that supports the Baconian project, Hauerwas has underemphasized the ways in which living traditions construe the natural, social and historical constraints of real communities. As we have seen, this leads Hauerwas to make grandiose claims about the capacity of a narrative or community to absorb suffering and thus ironically supports the very tendencies he so rightly seeks to avoid in the Baconian project. As a result, his alternative to that project is not fully persuasive.

The task of an alternative to the Baconian project is, following Hauerwas, to determine how suffering and also bodily health fit into our moral projects. Hauerwas has not yet told us what those projects are. One reason may be that they depend on our understandings of the moral significance of the body, its capacity for health, and its subjection to suffering and mortality. To complete Hauerwas's alternative to technological utopianism therefore requires that we turn our attention to the body. But if Hauerwas is right, our Baconian society has already formed the body in ways that we do not suspect and that our moral convictions (embedded in our bioethics) both reflect and help to sustain. In the spirit of Hauerwas I now turn to the task (in chapter seven) of bringing to our attention the body as the Baconian project has constructed it, followed by the task (in chapter eight) of beginning to redescribe the body as an alternative to the Baconian project.

CHAPTER 7

Modernity, Medicine, and the Body

I turn now to the third way of addressing the technological utopianism of medicine, reflection on the body. The body is not a new topic in bioethics; aside from the figures I treat in this chapter it figures strongly in both Jonas and Kass, as we have seen, and in discussions of the inviolability of the person and the analogy between the body and property in standard bioethics. When addressing, for example, the inviolability of the body or its alienability or inalienability from the person standard bioethics usually considers the body only in terms of the moral status of persons, their rights, and so on. In contrast Kass along with Paul Ramsey and Roman Catholic thinkers such as Germain Grisez believe that the modern tendency to reduce the moral significance of the body to that of personhood is a major source of what they see as the degradation of the body in modern thought and culture. The two schools of thought treated in this chapter raise new sets of concerns. Both emphasize the view of the body that began with Descartes and became enshrined in western medicine at the end of the eighteenth century with the development, by Xavier Bichat and others, of clinical-laboratory medicine, which is still very much with us though it may be nearing the end of its long hegemony. Phenomenologists of medicine such as Drew Leder and Richard Zaner implicate this view of the body in the "dehumanization" that according to many critics characterizes contemporary medicine. To frame an alternative they draw on and extend the work of phenomenologists such as Maurice Merleau-Ponty and Alfred Schutz and physicians such as Eric Cassell. For critical theorists such as Michel Foucault and his followers, by rendering the body analyzable and manipulable modern medicine allocates to itself the problem of (and the solution to) human finitude. At the same time this analyzability and manipulability subjects the body to various kinds of disciplinary control in order to optimize its capacities and increase its usefulness in accordance with societal interests. Medicine thereby becomes part of a complex knowledge-power-subject configuration that can be resisted only by self-formations that transgress against it.

My purpose in this chapter is diagnostic: I show how certain interpretations of the body underwrite technological utopianism. (My purpose in the final chapter is therapeutic: I hope to show how a view of the moral significance of the body might resist technological utopianism and provide an alternative to it.) Unlike the authors I have discussed in the previous four chapters, neither the phenomenologists nor Foucault and his followers take up technological utopianism as a major theme. Therefore my central thesis, that the Baconian project is best exposed and resisted by recovering the moral significance of the body, cannot rely directly on their work. Rather, this chapter works through the authors I treat with an agenda in mind that is only indirectly their own; it therefore dispenses with a thorough investigation of their work as a whole. Nevertheless I have found both the phenomenologists and Foucault and his followers to be indispensible sources for understanding the body as it is constructed by modern medicine and the problems this presents for reclaiming the moral significance of the body.

THE CARTESIAN BODY AND THE LIVED BODY

Neither Drew Leder nor Richard Zaner develops a conception of dehumanization or defends the thesis that modern medicine is dehumanizing, but both take this widespread criticism as the point of departure for their work (Leder, 1992a, pp. 1–3; Zaner, 1988, pp. 95–96). The term "dehumanization" easily becomes a slogan but it nevertheless captures the phenomenon described by Stanley Reiser, in which medicine has gradually substituted diagnostic judgments based on "objective" evidence such as laboratory procedures and mechanical and electronic devices for judgments based on "subjective" evidence such as the verbal testimony of the patient and the physician's own natural sensory experience. The result has been a gap "between the physician as healer and the patient as human being"; a gap which despite certain unquestionable gains has also inflicted losses—not only in humanistic terms, insofar as the personal relationship between doctor and patient is diminished, but also by confining medical judgment to quantitative factors and thereby constricting the physician's capacity to respond to illness (Reiser, 1978, pp. ix–x, 227–231).

For Zaner the charge of dehumanization constitutes a "historical irony": how is an intrinsically moral enterprise, in which distressed or damaged persons constitute in their very condition a moral demand or appeal to medicine as a form of caring for such persons, so often found in practice to be dehumanizing? Zaner locates the problem in the speech situation of the clinic. The patient typically interprets his or her illness to the physician in a rich texture of significations that links illness to the patient's lived world and its disruption by illness. For the physician, however, the patient's interpretation is significant only as an "initial *locational* index" that indicates where in or on the patient's body his or her experiences are rooted. The physician therefore substitutes a scientific and technical interpretation for the patient's richly textured interpretation. Since the patient's interpretation is also a self-expression the substitution constitutes a "linguistic displacement of the patient," whose communicative intent is narrowed to a somatic location (Zaner, 1988, pp. 95–97).

The problem for Zaner is hermeneutical: he begins with a conflict of interpretations and the displacement of one by the other. But the hermeneutical displacement is the linguistic surface of a deeper displacement of the patient's relation to the lived body by the physician's diagnostic relation to the body. The alternative interpretations of illness, in other words, reflect alternative kinds of relation to the body. In an earlier work Zaner draws on a well-known distinction made by Jean-Paul Sartre in order to give these two kinds of relation a phenomenological grounding. One encounters one's own body as "my body," which is "for-itself" (*pour soi*); it is one's embodied subjectivity. By contrast the body as the object of the gaze of the Other is "in itself" (*en soi*); it is the body as strange, as a material object, and as apprehended by and for the Other (Zaner, 1981, pp. 48–50). In keeping with this earlier analysis, the patient's interpretation is the expression of his embodied subjectivity which meets the objectifying gaze of the physician. The latter is censorious and directive: it is designed to persuade the patient to distrust his lived body and to replace it with the body as object for the physician, which is backed by considerable social power and authority (Zaner, 1988, pp. 104–105).

Leder largely agrees with this phenomenological analysis of the clinical setting but argues that illness itself, and not only the gaze of the physician, can turn the lived body into a thing, and that it may for different reasons be salutory for both patient and physician to regard the body as a thing in order to distance themselves from it (Leder, 1984,

pp. 33–34).[1] Leder also draws out an interesting implication of the reduction of the body to thingliness. When taken as a machine rather than as
one's essential self the body, like the tool in Heidegger's analysis of the
ready-to-hand, is ignored when functioning well. Hence the tendency of
modern persons to focus on the body only when ill rather than cultivating its health (Leder, 1984, p. 35).

Both Leder and Zaner follow Foucault and others who have found
the origins of the body assumed by modern medicine in the late eighteenth century, as described above. But like Foucault both also believe
that Bichat and his colleagues inherited central features of their view of
the body from Descartes. However, Leder and Zaner differ sharply in
their interpretations of Descartes and in the lessons they draw from
him. Their divergent interpretations of Descartes will lead me to draw
two different conclusions about the relation of the modern view of the
body to the technological utopianism of medicine.

Zaner argues from a wide reading of his letters as well as his
published writings that the key to understanding Descartes lies not in
his famous dualism between body and soul but in a different dualism
between nature as understood in daily life, ordinary conversation, and
experiences of pain, hunger, thirst, and feelings on the one hand, and
nature as an object of mathematical science on the other hand. This
distinction runs through Descartes's medical writings, which for Zaner
hold the key to his view of the body. Thus the understanding of the
body in Descartes's medical advice to Princess Elizabeth and to others
appeals to nature in the first sense while nature in the second sense is
presupposed in his writings on anatomy and physiology. The body in
the first sense exhibits the composite union of body and soul that for
Descartes is plainly evident in our ordinary experience but which cannot be understood by mathematics or metaphysics. The body in the
second sense may be described in mechanistic metaphors, but these
are inappropriate for the body in the first sense (Zaner, 1988, pp.
115–118). Hence for Zaner Descartes's dualism is not between soul and
body—a dualism which is foreign to ordinary experience and results
only from the inability of mathematics or metaphysics to understand
their composite union—but between two ways of understanding the
body. And if one takes Descartes's medical advice seriously, one who
wishes to treat patients must understand the body in the first way
rather than the second.

Zaner thus finds Bichat's dualism between symptoms and anatomical lesions and the gap between the lived body and the diagnostic body
prefigured in Descartes's dualism between the ordinary experience of the
body assumed in "clinical medicine" and the body assumed in "scientific

medicine" that makes use of fictions such as the body as a machine. (The scare quotes reflect my view that to attribute the distinction between clinical and scientific medicine to Descartes is anachronistic.) But crucial to Zaner's case is his conviction that for Descartes the ordinary experience of the body is primary while nature in the mathematical sense is something of an abstraction that makes use of mechanistic fictions for heuristic purposes related to a scientific knowledge of the body. For Bichat, as Zaner recognizes, it is quite the opposite; the body of pathological anatomy is primary while the body of ordinary experience is unreliable and ephemeral (Zaner, 1988, pp. 135–137).

Zaner's discussion of Descartes raises two questions: If the body as understood in ordinary experience was sufficient for "clinical" purposes, why did Descartes need the heuristic notion of the body as machine? And why did this notion of the body as machine eventually triumph over the body of ordinary experience? Zaner does not answer the first question, though he speculates that it has to do with Descartes's pride in his anatomical and physiological studies and with the history of dissection from the thirteenth century onward, which by Descartes's time no longer viewed the corpse as still haunted by the presence of the recently departed soul but as mere inanimate matter like the rest of nature (Zaner, 1988, pp. 120–123, 164–168). This means that to the extent that mechanism could function as the truth of nature the inanimate corpse could function as the truth of the living body, so that only when the body is dead can one know what it really is (Zaner, 1988, p. 123). Zaner's most original point, however, is implicit in his answer to the second question. If one is to understand the composite union of body and soul and to treat patients, one must for Descartes "turn to ordinary life and discourse and study them for their own sake. But this could only be a positive embarrassment, an epistemic nightmare, so far as genuine knowledge is concerned—especially for Descartes, but also for much of subsequent medicine and philosophy" (Zaner, 1988, p. 125). The mechanistic view of the body, Zaner implies, assumes priority when medicine becomes interested in gaining a type of knowledge to which ordinary experience contributes little. Zaner goes on to remind us of the irony in Descartes's work: only in ordinary experience can illnesses be treated and the composite union of body and soul be known, yet the domain of ordinary experience is in the *Meditations* the first to fall under his famous methodical doubt. It seems that for Zaner Descartes embodies a tension between the primacy of the everyday that phenomenology seeks to recover and the demand for theoretical certainty that fuels modern thought—a tension eventually resolved, in Descartes and in his followers, in favor of the latter. We have arrived at a chief, though largely implicit, thesis of Zaner's work: that the gap between the lived body of the patient and the objectified body of the physician is rooted in a conflict between phenomenology and epistemology that spans the history of western medicine.

Zaner, in effect writing the history of medicine backwards, traces this conflict from the hermeneutical gap found in contemporary medicine to its roots in Descartes and then to the conflict in ancient Hippocratic and Hellenistic medicine between the empirics and dogmatics that anticipates Descartes. Zaner admittedly relies heavily on historians such as Harrison Coulter (whose articulation of the "divided legacy" strongly shapes Zaner's account of the dispute between the empirics and dogmatics), Ludwig Edelstein, and Oswei Tempkin. But his summary of the conflict is marked by his own phenomenological perspective. Without pretending to be exhaustive, I will summarize Zaner's account (Zaner, 1988, pp. 137–150, 177–184). The fundamental issue between the dogmatics and empirics was hermeneutical: how are physicians to interpret symptoms? Are they signs of inner bodily parts and processes that are the proximate causes of disease, or do they refer to the patient's past experiences and conditions and suggest the body's own efforts to correct itself? The dogmatics argued for the former; the empirics the latter. For the dogmatics the relation between the symptom and the underlying proximate cause was a matter for theoretical knowledge. The physician does not attend to all the patient's symptoms but filters them through this theoretical framework which, prior to any encounter with the patient, tells the physician which symptoms are important. The individual patient was thus subordinated to a disease classification. The elements in this classification were the humors: contraries which, when imbalanced, cause disease. Therapy consisted of active intervention to restore balances.

Empiric medicine, by contrast, required attention to all the patient's symptoms without any exclusion or filtering based on an a priori theory. Empiric physicians engaged in semiosis, the interpretation and careful weighing of all the symptoms presented by the patient, rather than diagnosis of a proximate cause of the symptoms. They rejected classifications on the grounds that disease is inseparable from the patient and every patient is unique. Signs are commemorative of past events in the patient's embodied life rather than indicative of hidden causes, and therapy intensifies symptoms in order to support the body's own self-healing powers rather than intervening against symptoms to restore balances.

On the one hand, Zaner begins by viewing dogmatic medicine through the lens of a phenomenological critique of epistemology: the

dogmatic subordinates concrete experience and particularity to a theoretical framework that determines what counts as knowledge. The
empiric, on the other hand, is a good phenomenologist who restricts his
attention to what appears. But this initial picture is too simple. Later
Hellenistic empirics found their own way to bring prior knowledge to
the encounter with the patient and thus came to resemble their dogmatic counterparts. This knowledge was cumulative and historical
rather than a priori, and analogical rather than syllogistic, but it nevertheless led these later empirics to stress what is common to different
patients and thus to blur (though not to efface) their differences with the
dogmatics. The problem once again was the demand for knowledge.
The earlier Hippocratic empirics, whose stance was continued in the
Hellenistic period not by the later empirics but by the skeptics, neither
affirmed nor denied the knowledge claims of the dogmatics but simply
bracketed them (*epoche*) in order to grasp what appeared at the moment
(*ta phainomena*). This skepticism was not offered as a theoretical position
(in which case it would be subject to its own critique of the dogmatics)
but was derived from medical experience which, the Hippocratic empirics and the skeptics believed, deals always and only with unique individual patients.[2] Because patients are so variable, no cumulative knowledge of either the dogmatic or the Hellenistic empiric kind is possible; in
order to cure one must be attentive to everything about the patient and
try various remedies while noting their effects. At best, however, this
approach yields *doxa*, opinion, not *episteme*, knowledge. But medicine
always involves a tension between the need for knowledge and the
therapeutic needs of the individual patient. The Hippocratic empirics
seemed unable to accommodate the need for knowledge, but the skeptics who succeeded them proposed a solution that seems to be the one
Zaner himself endorses: the law or rationale of treatment "is derived
from the afflictions, experiences, and self-understanding of the patient
himself." The rationale for treatment resides in the patient's bodily
experiences and self-interpretations as grasped by the physician, and
thus in the *phainomena* rather than, as the Hellenistic empirics believed,
in the cumulative subjective experience of physicians or, as the dogmatics insisted, in theory (Zaner, 1988, pp. 183–184).

   While Zaner argues that the mechanized body was for Descartes a
heuristic abstraction necessary for anatomical and physiological knowledge but secondary for medical practice, Leder argues that it is at the
very center of Descartes' view of medicine and its purpose. Leder concentrates not on Descartes' medical advice but on his own expressions
in the *Discourse on Method* and in the Prefatory Note of the *Meditations* of
his motivation in pursuing metaphysical and scientific inquiries. The

independence of soul from body served Descartes as a sought-after metaphysical assurance that the soul does not die with the body, and he concludes the *Discourse* by devoting himself to the attainment of a knowledge of nature that would free human beings from diseases and from the infirmities of old age (Leder, 1990, pp. 138–141). Leder therefore describes Descartes's metaphysical and scientific work as a kind of therapy. "He seeks a way to overcome bodily illness and aging and to prove that death can not capture the soul. Just as he sought a treatment for the deceptiveness of the senses and the passions, so for the body's fragility" (Leder, 1990, p. 141). As with classical philosophy the treatment in all three cases is reason, but in the third case (the fragility of the body) the role of reason is twofold: it forms the core of the soul that is destined to survive the death of the body and serves as an instrument for conquering nature, eliminating disease, and increasing the life span.

The multiple threat posed by disease, decay, and death leads Descartes to view the living body from the anatomical standpoint as merely an animated corpse. But to stop here, as many interpretations of Descartes do, is to miss the radicality of Descartes's strategy. For as Leder points out, the body as corpse is also part of our ordinary experience of the lived body. Phenomena such as the sheer weight of the limbs in exhaustion, viewing an X-ray that reveals one's skeleton, and perceiving the loss of faculties and skills in aging bring to appearance an anticipation of one's body as a corpse that is ordinarily absent. In Leder's terms, "[t]he corpse is always approaching from within." Yet it never arrives: where I am as a living body, the corpse is not; "it necessarily withdraws from the egoic self" (Leder, 1990, p. 144). For the "I," therefore, the corpse never arrives, and in this sense the corpse never comes to full presence even when it "approaches from within." Descartes's thinking, however, exhibits a shift from the corpse approaching yet withdrawing—the corpse as my corpse—to the corpse of the Other. What motivated him, as we have seen, was the preoccupation with disease, decay, and death that constitutes the anticipatory corpse. "Yet his strategy for overcoming this first-person threat is precisely to capture the body fully in the third person. It is the body of the Other that Descartes anatomizes, his own body then reconstructed on such a model." In contrast to my own corpse which withdraws from self-experience, the corpse of the Other is brought from its absence into visibility and objectification by the autopsy (Leder, 1990, pp. 145–146). So understood, the corpse is no longer the source of the first-person threats of disease and decay, which can be overcome by the proper knowledge of nature, or of death, since the soul cannot be the captive of such a body. Thus science and metaphysics, in Leder's terms, constitute for Descartes precisely the practical and hermeneutical therapies needed to resolve the existential problematic of the body-as-mortal (Leder, 1990, p. 141).

Leder describes the profound implications the shift to the third person has for medicine when the latter takes the corpse of the Other as the truth of the body. The corpse, Leder argues, conceals even as it reveals. Since the dead body is no longer an operational whole, discrete organs and tissues can be studied in isolation. This makes atomistic conceptions of disease and therapy possible, but ignores the functioning of the body as a whole. Since diagnosis and therapy aim at what can be observed and quantified the patient's intentionality can be ignored, but at the expense of ignoring certain kinds of evidence, prescribing inappropriate treatments, and courting the noncompliance of the patient (Leder, 1990, pp. 147–148).

In short, whereas Zaner tries to portray Descartes as a (proto-)clinician caught in a tension between the demands of scientific knowledge and the ordinary experience he knew to be fundamental to medical care, Leder (more plausibly in my judgment) views Descartes as a metaphysician and scientist motivated principally by the existential threats of disease, decay, and death.[3] These threats are met by treating the body as capable of objectification and quantification. Like Zaner, Leder may be reading too much of Bichat and his contemporaries into Descartes at this point. But his portrait of Descartes seems also to capture the motivation behind the Baconian project. Burdened with existential anxiety in the face of the mortality of the body and its subjection to suffering and disease, Descartes inaugurates the process that will, with Bichat and his contemporaries, bring the hidden and absent truth of mortality and disease into visible presence, and thus under the mastery of the seeing eye and the intervening hand, while also distanciating the essential person, the soul, from the body that, despite the power of medicine, is destined to decay and die.

While Zaner and Leder both criticize the hegemony of the Cartesian body in medicine, neither wishes to do away with it entirely. Despite his sharp contrast between the phenomenological and epistemological approaches Zaner agrees with Leder that under certain conditions the body "reveals itself as a nexus of semi-autonomous biological processes" (Leder, 1984, p. 33). Following Freud, Zaner terms this "the uncanny." Because I am embodied by this and not another body, certain desires, wishes, and ideals are not within my scope. Moreover, I am exposed to whatever affects my body and am forced to attend to it in cases of pain, hunger, injury, disease, and death. Finally, involuntary aspects of the body occur without my awareness or control. In all these respects the body is uncanny: both mine and other, both familiar and strange. Hence "the Cartesian equivocation [between the ordinary and scientific body] has its basis in the embodying organism itself" (Zaner, 1981, pp. 50–55). Leder extends this type of reflection into a phenomenology of the various modes of absence that characterize the lived body, both on the surface of perception and action and in the depths of the viscera. Accompanying this is an analysis of the way forgotten or hidden aspects of embodiment, like Heidegger's tool, appear and can be thematized when dysfunctions such as pain, disease, error, the disruption of passion, and death occur or are anticipated (Leder, 1990, pp. 69–86, 130–146). This analysis underlies Leder's discussion of the presence/absence of the first-person corpse. But even the body of scientific knowledge—the corpse of the Other—is one manner in which the body shows itself, inasmuch as the third-person perspective of science itself arises out of lived experience (Leder, 1990, pp. 6–7).

All of this suggests that for Zaner and Leder the problem with Cartesian medicine is not the scientific approach to the body itself, but its primacy. For Zaner the subsequent history of the "divided legacy" of empiric and dogmatic medicine, as played out in Descartes, Bichat, and contemporary medicine, is the history of the effort of the successors of the dogmatic tradition to absorb the empiric stress on the individual, embodied patient (the phenomenological) into their own system oriented around knowledge and intervention. By finally making it possible to develop a science of the individual, Bichat seems at last to have incorporated the central argument of the empirics—that the patient is a unique individual—into the dogmatic framework. And if pathoanatomy succeeded here, today's diagnostic and radiological technologies seem to have inscribed empiric medicine even further into the dogmatic framework since these technologies capture not the corpse but the living body itself (Zaner, 1988, pp. 152–153). Finally, the contemporary version of dogmatic medicine seems to have incorporated the empiric emphasis on the patient's bodily experience and self-interpretation in its own theory of clinical judgment. According to this theory, clinical judgment involves three stages: the diagnostic, the therapeutic, and the prudential. The first two stages answer, respectively, the questions, "What is wrong?" and "What can be done?" Both questions are answerable by reducing the patient's discourse to a locational index in accordance with scientific-dogmatic medicine. At the third stage, however, the question, "What should be done?" requires taking the patient's discourse in its referential plenitude (and thereby incorporating the empiric's emphasis) since the patient's lifestyle, environment, and values may override what is medically indicated or logically consistent at the first and second stages (Zaner, 1988, pp. 99–102). In sum, Edmund Pellegrino's claim that contemporary medicine success-fully fuses Hippocratic empiricism into the neo-Cartesianism of clinical-laboratory (dogmatic) medicine seems unassailable (Zaner, 1988, p. 170).

However, Zaner refuses to accept this claim and argues that the fusion or incorporation is unstable. One reason is that the reduction of the body to the corpse cannot account for the reflexive experience of the anatomist herself.

> As a relic of a man once alive and communicating, the corpse is a haunting presence of that once-alive man as he was or might have been in actual, living relationships to us and is therefore a haunt-ing presence of the anatomist to himself—a faint but telling reminder of intimacies now foreclosed, fellow-feelings now for-bidden, impossible, or irrelevant. . . . That former life, once with us, is now no longer and, theory tells us, was really never there in any quantitative, measurable way anyway, yet it compellingly does remind us of that formerly alive, once-communicating per-son. (Zaner, 1988, p. 170)

Zaner's point seems to be that while the perspective of my lived body can (perhaps because of my own experiences of the uncanny or of the gaze of the Other) include the reflexivity that haunts the encounter with human corpse, this experience is foreign, even absurd, for the scientific account of the body. The scientific-dogmatic framework cannot account for my lived experience of its own paradigm of the body, and thus fails to absorb the empiric perspective into itself. A second reason Zaner refuses to accept the dogmatic absorption of the empiric is that the abstraction of diagnosis and therapy from the lived body can succeed only if acute and infectious diseases are the paradigms of all illness. Following Eric Cassell, Zaner points out that chronic and degenerative diseases now constitute the vast majority of illnesses (including arte-riosclerotic heart disease, hypertension, diabetes, degenerative joint dis-ease, perhaps cancer). But these diseases do not accommodate the notion that empiric elements can be absorbed into a scientific-dogmatic framework, since in their case even the diagnostic and therapeutic stages depend on individuating features of the patient and thus require attention to the patient's self-interpretation (Zaner, 1988, p. 103).

Zaner seems to want the reverse of what contemporary medicine claims for itself, namely to inscribe dogmatic medicine into an empiric framework such that the mechanistic body would hold primarily for infectious diseases and some conditions treated by surgery. Nevertheless,

Zaner does not tell us how diagnosis and therapy would actually be carried out under the empiric framework. On the contrary, his concrete examples reproduce the very Cartesian dualism he argues against. For example, in the treatment of pneumonia he seems to accept a straightforward distinction between the physician's response to the affective and social dimensions of the lived body on the one hand (illness) and killing the bacteria or bringing down the fever of the mechanistic body on the other hand (disease) (Zaner, 1988, p. 204). We seem to be left with parallel or complementary forms of diagnosis and treatment with no rationale for any priority of the first over the second.

By contrast, a major strength of Leder's account are his descriptions of how the primacy of the lived body alters diagnosis. Leder redescribes illnesses as biological expressions of bodily intentionalities. For example, a person who tacitly grasps the world as overpowering or overbearing may years later suffer from chronic back pain resulting from the stooped body posture he has assumed. Another person may take up the stance of fight or flight under stressful conditions. Over time a condition of internal hypermobility may result in gastritis or hypertension. Yet another person who experiences a primordial emptiness may attempt to fill it with food or smoke, resulting in obesity or cancer. "Such examples could continue indefinitely. They all exhibit illness as a disordered being-in-the-world. A certain preconceptual grasp of enworldment, e.g. as threatening, is expressed in a bodily stance that leads to illness" (Leder, 1984, p. 39). This etiology of disease seems to serve Leder as a paradigm for the relation of the lived body to the uncanny body of biological processes. Bodily intentionality, he argues, expresses itself in biological mechanisms and disruptions (Leder, 1992b, p. 29). Leder admits that there are some illnesses in which the uncanny so dominates that a purely physicalistic etiology is sufficient. These illnesses would presumably fall within Zaner's categories of infectious diseases and acute conditions treatable by surgery. At the other extreme are conditions that are mental in origin. But just as Zaner seeks to describe the dogmatic's paradigm diseases as limit cases of the empiric framework, so Leder views these as limit cases of the expression of bodily intentionality which, he argues, characterizes the diseases he and Zaner agree now constitute the vast majority of illnesses.[4]

I do not know whether research or clinical experience would confirm Leder's view that pathological processes form and develop along these existential-physiological pathways, but if they do, he has succeeded in showing how diagnosis requires his phenomenology. But when he turns to therapy, Leder like Zaner reintroduces a dualism between the mechanistic body and the lived body that contradicts his previous analysis. Leder's example is a patient who presents with headaches and dizziness resulting from hypertension. In mechanistic terms therapy would consist of readjustment of the body's circulatory dynamics through diet and medications. But perhaps the patient is involved in a difficult marriage or a stressful job. She inhabits a constricted world in which limitation and frustration are expressed in a constriction of the arteries. The dietary and drug treatments do little to address these preconditions of disease which require therapies ranging from counseling to meditation or visualization (Leder, 1992b, pp. 28–30). Since hypertension is not a limit case but a paradigm instance of a disease expressing a bodily intentionality one would expect Leder's therapeutics to mirror the relation between the lived body and its material or biological expression found in his etiology. Instead Leder leaves the mechanistic therapy intact. "The existential account does not replace the biological account, but rather places it within a broader perspective" (Leder, 1992b, p. 29). This broader perspective, however, merely adds a second set of therapies (counseling, meditation, visualization) alongside the physiological interventions (diet and medications): it treats the biological as independent of the existential, not as an expression of the latter as Leder's analysis of the etiology of disease would seem to require. Far from the biological being an expression of the existential, Leder now claims that "[t]he anatomy and physiology of the lived body are always intertwined with the body's intentionality in ways that undermine facile claims of priority" (Leder, 1992b, p. 29).

One reason why Leder and Zaner reintroduce dualism at the crucial point is that both remain fully wedded to western allopathic medicine, at least in the domain of therapy. Since therapy in allopathic medicine attempts to cure dysfunctions by treating the body as a mechanism, Leder and Zaner are left with only two options: a reductionism that obscures the lived body or a dualism that supplements mechanistic interventions with other kinds of therapy. It may be that therapeutic dualism is overcome only in systems such as traditional Chinese and Tibetan medicine, in which concepts such as *qi* and *lung* function in both lived experience and anatomophysiology.[5] But within a western context Leder's and Zaner's failures may instruct us further on a point I first raised with regard to Leon Kass, namely that we should understand the kind of therapy in which western medicine trains its practitioners as a very limited aspect of health that must be supplemented by the care and skills of others. Leder and Zaner's recognition that the biological body is one possible mode of the lived body should have led them to a more limited role for medicine, whose specialization in the biological would find its place within the care for the lived body of which the biological body is a mode. Rather, they simply assume that physicians are or could be as adept at diagnosing and determining appropriate treatments for "illness" (lived body) as they are for "disease" (biological body). But there is no reason to believe this, nor to expect it of them so long as other professional and lay caregivers of various kinds already attend to these broader dimensions of illness. It may be that diagnosis and therapy in the broader sense Leder and Zaner seek will have to be carried out in various formal and informal networks of caregivers in which the physician is one, and not necessarily the most important, member.

A second shortcoming is that by not reflecting on the problem of dehumanization that is their point of departure, the direction and outcome of Leder's and Zaner's inquiry is determined in a way they never make clear but which involves problems. Dehumanization as a critique of medicine usually carries with it a Marxist conception of alienation: the patient's self-expression in a narrative of illness is appropriated by the physician's narrative which is inaccessible to the patient and out of her control. The solution is for diagnosis and therapy to remain within the patient's narrative; the return to the lived body recovers the essential, nonalienated humanity of the patient. Leder and Zaner are sophisticated enough to avoid the assumptions that the lived body is the essentially human and that the alienation of the body as Other is all bad. But because they allow the problem of dehumanization to set the compass of their inquiries, they assume that dehumanization is the worst thing modern medicine does to us and that to confess one's lived world to health professionals and to bring it under the discipline of a now greatly expanded range of therapeutic techniques is therefore unambiguously liberating. Closely connected with this is their assumption that the world is disclosed to (and concealed from) bodily intentionality without being mediated through the discourses and practices that always constitute the particular ways in which the lived body is formed and that therefore always constitute experiences of body, illness, and healing in the concrete. Because they are convinced that dehumanization is the true threat and because they ignore the discourses and practices that constitute even the lived body, they are unable to realize that a medicine that is no longer "dehumanizing" may in the name of liberation subject the body to relations of power that would then inscribe even the patient's lived world into the processes of normalization that serve the requisites of a certain kind of society. Just as important, they are unable to identify discourses and practices that may form part of a way of life that exposes and resists these normalization processes.

This last criticism suggests that the most important issue is not dehumanization and the recovery of the lived body as the basis of a more authentic medicine, but rather the discourses and practices which form us as subjects at least in part by forming our bodies. Here the work of feminist thinkers not only challenges the assumption of many phenomenologists that the body is one (as I pointed out in criticism of Kass in chapter five), it also shows how the lived body and its intentionality are themselves formed by complex and pervasive discourses and practices designed to form women as subjects. The issue here is not the eclipse of the lived body but rather the ways in which modalities of female embodiment (e.g., body shape and weight, pregnancy, "breastedness") are bound up with interpretations of the body (e.g., as sexually appealing or not), interventions and disciplines (e.g., breast augmentation or dieting), and monitoring techniques (e.g., imaging techniques in prenatal care), all of which fundamentally form the lived body and its intentionality (Spitzack, 1990; Young, 1990).

This leads us to Foucault. But before turning to him, it is necessary to point out how Leder and Zaner deepen our understanding of the Baconian project and standard bioethics. First, they both provide a rich description of a phenomenon we first noticed with Kass, namely the close correlation between the body as modern science and technology treat it and modern moral theories that abstract from the body. If in Zaner's terms the Cartesian body as machine has replaced the lived body of ordinary experience, this helps us to understand the process I sketched in chapter one according to which the discourse that affirmed the moral significance of the body, with its finitude and subjection to suffering and its place in a morally worthy life, was replaced by a discourse that affirmed the values of expansion of choice and elimination of suffering. If we take the lived body to be concretely formed by particular discourses and practices, as I just suggested, we can now understand how the replacement of the lived body by the body as machine makes it possible to ignore the moral significance of the body. For if the body is merely a machine then moral theory will understand it as the property of the "person" and the instrument of his desires and preferences. Standard bioethics (and modern moral theory in general) perfectly reflects and supports (and may even depend on) the modern scientific and technological view of the body. Small wonder that it is unable to raise serious questions about the moral implications of this view of the body.

This picture is incomplete, however, without Leder's portrait of Descartes as a representative modern for whom disease, the decay associated with aging, and death itself become problems to be eliminated by technological and metaphysical strategies that rely on the mechanization of the body. Thanks to Descartes the problems of disease, decay, and death are now located in the dead body, the corpse of the Other. Interventions into the body to eliminate disease and postpone decay and death are thus no longer haunted by the trace of the living person or by the moral meanings that make lived embodiment determinate. The body as machine is the moral as well as the cognitive condition of the Baconian project.

THE BODY, POWER, AND RESISTANCE

Because of the triumph of the Cartesian view, most of us view the body as a biological substratum whose characteristics are best described in physical and biochemical terms. Fixed with regard to the naked will that stands over against it, the body is nevertheless alterable by technology, which promises to bring the body under the dominion of the will. Phenomenologists, as we have seen, argue that this Cartesian body is one mode of the lived body, grounded in the third-person perspective or in my experience of the Other. In contrast, Michel Foucault challenges us to understand the Cartesian body in its complex circular relations to a range of practices and techniques designed to manipulate, manage, control, correct, and calculate the body. While not denying the validity of questions about the epistemological status of the Cartesian body, Foucault is interested in how the latter is constituted as a system of knowledge about the body and bound up with forms of power and techniques of self-formation.[6] I will begin with Foucault's analysis of clinical-laboratory medicine, which can be viewed as the culmination of the Cartesian view of the body.

Foucault's task in *The Birth of the Clinic* is to trace the transformations in language, technologies, institutions, forms of evidence, and kinds of reasoning that structure modern clinical-laboratory medicine as a form of knowledge. Foucault states in his Preface that while modern medicine accounts for its own rise by attributing the transition from classificatory medicine to clinical-laboratory medicine to a return to perception after a long reign of theory and speculation, he will instead attribute it to a redistribution in the relationship of the visible to the invisible (Foucault, 1973, pp. xii). For classificatory medicine, following the epistemology of Descartes and his followers, things become visible to perception by virtue of the light of ideality wherein they are adequate to their essences. Diseases in classificatory medicine are understood accordingly as systems of relations and resemblances that form an intelligible order—nosological essences that are grasped in their ideal light by abstracting from the accidental features of the patient's body. Only after identifying the disease in its ideal form are the qualitative variations which mark the transposition of the disease entity into the individual organism identified (Foucault, 1973, pp. xii–xiii, 3–16). Classificatory medicine is thus a paradigm instance of what Foucault will later refer to as classical representation, in which the light of ideality enables the perceiver to represent the true order of reality, in this case the nosological table that represents the true order of diseases (cf. Foucault, 1970, pp. 46–77).

By contrast, for clinical-laboratory perception things become visible in their very opacity and as closed in on themselves beneath the surface of the body. Rather than identifying nosological essences and their qualitative variations, the clinical gaze reconstructs the progress of a disease by locating it in tissual lesions, thereby spatializing disease by mapping it onto the body of the sick person. Diseases are no longer distinguished from their particular modulations in individual bodies; rather than dissolving its objects into their essential ideality, the gaze now establishes them in their very corporeal particularity. One now arrives at the disease not by abstracting it from the presenting patient but by grasping its modulations in the tissue systems of individual patients; clinical-laboratory medicine thus makes possible for the first time a science of the individual (Foucault, 1973, pp. xiii–xiv, 127–132, 195–196). In contrast to the age of representation, medicine is a paradigm of a new kind of language that must deal with the opaque and individual rather than the transparent and universal; it is a question "of opening words to a certain qualitative, ever more concrete, more individualized, more modelled refinement" in order to grasp things in their opacity, individuality, and concreteness (Foucault, 1973, p. 169).[7]

Foucault's interest in the transition to clinical-laboratory medicine is fueled by his conviction that in European culture "medical thought is fully engaged in the philosophical status of man" (Foucault, 1973, p. 198). Clinical-laboratory medicine for Foucault articulates the very anthropological structure that sustains the human sciences in the nineteenth and twentieth centuries. This structure is grounded in the central place death occupies in the knowledge of individuality that clinical-laboratory medicine makes possible. Because clinical-laboratory medicine arrives at knowledge of disease through the corpse, its early proponents had to distinguish at autopsy which alterations in the corpse follow from death and which from disease. In their effort to do so they began to recognize death not as an absolute moment that simply marks the end or limit of life, but as a process that insinuates itself into the living body and is thus immanent in life itself. Since life is thus inseparable from the processes of degeneration that result in death, disease no longer appears as an accident that strikes the body as it were from outside (Foucault, 1973, pp. 155–159). Because death itself is now embodied in the living organism, it is no longer merely the end of life and disease is no longer an accident. Clinical-laboratory medicine thus inverts the relation of humanity to finitude: no longer merely the negation of the infinite (as reflected in the view of death as the end of life), finitude is now the characteristic mark of human beings, which they bear within their bodies. By discovering this embodiment of death, clinical-laboratory medicine discovers the ontological possibility of humanity as subject and object of knowledge: finitude (as Kant recognized) is for the knower both the critical limit and the founding origin of knowledge, and is the very being of "man" as object of knowledge (Foucault, 1973, p. 197; 1970, pp. 312–318).

Foucault's major point is that the discourse of the body that characterizes clinical-laboratory medicine makes it possible for human beings to know themselves as objects of the various human sciences, and that this knowledge, human beings' first knowledge of themselves as individuals, is intimately bound up with death. In this context medicine both confronts us with the finitude that is now inseparable from our identity and dispels the threat finitude poses to our identity. "Medicine offers man the obstinate, yet reassuring face of his finitude; in it, death is endlessly repeated, but it is also exorcised; and although it ceaselessly reminds man of the limit that he bears within him, it also speaks to him of that technical world that is the armed, positive, full form of his finitude" (Foucault, 1973, p. 198). As a result, suffering and death and the crises of meaning they impose are now problematized in terms of medicine rather than religion. "Disease breaks away from the metaphysic of evil"—where one responded to the crisis of meaning it provokes in terms of various spiritual practices or disciplines—"and it finds in the visibility of death the full form in which its content appears in positive [i.e., positivistic] terms"—where one responds to the crisis of meaning in terms of scientific explanation and technological control (Foucault, 1973, p. 196). The result is that "health replaces salvation": in place of the moral and spiritual significance one sought when suffering or death was unavoidable, medicine through its techniques and practices aims at eliminating or postponing suffering and death (cf. Rose, 1994, p. 68).

Thus far Foucault has given us yet another version of the transition I sketched in chapter one from traditional to modern discourses of suffering and the body. However, as I pointed out in drawing on his work in that chapter, he gives us more than this: Foucault's archaealogical method is designed to show how a certain knowledge or discourse, in this case that of clinical-laboratory medicine, constitutes a system of procedures, types of evidence, norms of reasoning, and so on that determines what is problematized and how, and what objects and truth claims are admissible—all to the exclusion of other, for example, religious, knowledges or discourses. Of course, Foucault's archaeology is not constructed around the displacement and exclusion of religious discourse; my interpolations in the previous paragraph presume (though not implausibly) that his brief hints support my account in chapter one. In any case, Foucault's genealogical method goes beyond archaeology by showing how discourse and knowledge stand in complex relations to systems and effects of power. Hence a Foucauldian analysis of technological utopianism requires showing how the discourse of clinical-laboratory medicine is related to processes of normalization and techniques of self-formation that constitute us as embodied subjects.

Foucault's analysis of power rests on his claim that beginning in the eighteenth century power began to assume new forms to which our standard theories of power, of rights, and of the subject have still not caught up. Foucault argues that since medieval times the question of power in the West has always been that of royal or sovereign power. Whether it takes the form of the articulation and defense of the legitimate rights of sovereignty and the obligation of obedience or that of limiting and challenging the prerogatives of sovereign power, "[r]ight in the West is the King's right" (Foucault, 1980, p. 94). Sovereign power is judicial in nature and suppressive in its dynamics. It therefore takes the form of law or prohibition (Foucault, 1980, pp. 119, 140). In what does the power of the sovereign consist? Ultimately, in his right to decide the life and death of his subjects. From early modern times this is the right to require them to defend the state and to punish by death those who threaten his rule or transgress against his laws. This right is the ultimate exercise of a more general power of deduction or suppression. "Power in this instance was essentially a right of seizure: of things, time, bodies, and ultimately life itself; it culminated in the privelege to seize hold of life in order to suppress it" (Foucault, 1978, p. 136).

As the past tense of the last quotation indicates, Foucault believes that the sovereign is no longer the primary paradigm of power or, more accurately, that the power of the state is now carried out in a different and more effectual form. Hence those analyses of power that take sovereign power as their paradigm—and this includes virtually all analyses, whether liberal, Marxist, or Freudian—are unable to understand the kind of power that came into prominence beginning in the eighteenth century. In conjunction with new economic forces, this new form of power "begins to exercise itself through social production and social service. It becomes a matter of obtaining productive service from individuals in their concrete lives." Power therefore

> had to be able to gain access to the bodies of individuals, to their acts, attitudes and modes of everyday behavior. . . . But at the same time, these new techniques of power had to grapple with the phenomena of population, in short to undertake the administration, control and direction of the accumulation of men. . . . [H]ence there arise the problems of demography, public health, hygiene, housing conditions, longevity and fertility. (Foucault, 1980, p. 125)

In short, "the old power of death that symbolized sovereign power was now carefully supplanted by the administration of bodies and the calculated management of life"—the life of both individuals and populations—". . . marking the beginning of an era of 'bio-power'" (Foucault, 1978, pp. 139–140). Concretely speaking, biopower evolved in two interrelated forms. The first centered on the body as a machine whose forces and capabilities can be extorted and maximized and its docility and usefulness simultaneously increased through an "anatomo-politics of the human body" in which power is exercised through various ways of disciplining the body. The second centered on the species body whose biological processes of propogation, mortality, health, and longevity were supervised by interventions and regulatory controls amounting to a "bio-politics of the population" (Foucault, 1978, p. 139).

Biopower differs from sovereign power in two crucial respects. The first concerns the locus of power. Foucault's genealogical studies claim to show that during the past two centuries power has shifted from the sovereign to various relations and networks such as the family, schools, hospitals and public health authorities, and prisons—relations and networks on which the power of the state increasingly depends—and is distributed throughout these relations and networks through increasingly complex technical and administrative "apparatuses" (*dispositifs*) (Foucault, 1980, pp. 121–123).

The second difference concerns the modus operandi of power. The new task of power is to optimize productive forces by simultaneously expanding and controlling them. Power thus becomes productive and administrative rather than suppressive; it is, unlike sovereign power, "a power bent on generating forces, making them grow, and ordering them, rather than one dedicated to impeding them, making them submit, or destroying them" (Foucault, 1978, p. 136). On one hand, the productive character of power is evident in shifts in the relations of power to desire and truth. Rather than repressing desire, power now invests itself in the body through various practices of mastery and awareness of the body amounting to a "control by stimulation" rather than by repression (Foucault, 1980, pp. 56–59). Similarly, while truth in the form of, say, the truth about the natural order or justice formerly set the limits to sovereign power, now power produces truth in the form of discourses about the body, human behavior and development, sexuality, and so on—in short, the sciences that generate the knowledge needed for the exercise of power throughout the social order. Truth therefore stands in a circular relation to power: power produces true discourses that in turn reinforce and extend power (Foucault, 1980, pp. 93–94, 133).[8] On the other hand, the administrative character of power substitutes norms for the laws and prohibitions of sovereign power.

> Such a power has to qualify, measure, appraise, and hierarchize, rather than display itself in its murderous splendor; it does not have to draw the line that separates the enemies of the sovereign from his obedient subjects; it effects distributions around the norm. . . . A normalizing society is the historical outcome of a technology of power centered on life. (Foucault, 1978, p. 144)

The bodies of individuals and populations are now measured against norms related to utility, amenability to profitable investment, capacity for being usefully trained, and prospects of survival, death, and illness (Foucault, 1980, p. 172).

Foucault argues that this new understanding of power requires a new understanding of the subject. For liberal and Marxist theories alike the subject is endowed with consciousness and already constituted as a subject before power comes along. Hence both liberals and Marxists believe that a fully liberated subject will emerge if all the influences of power can be stripped away. These assumptions enable liberal and Marxist critical theories to criticize society from the (albeit counterfactual) standpoint of a fully liberated subject as, for example, in the case of Jürgen Habermas. Chiding Marxists whose theory of ideology reproduces the liberal notion of power that siezes on an already-constituted subject endowed with consciousness, Foucault argues that it is more materialist to begin with the body and the effects of power on it (Foucault, 1980, p. 58). His genealogical studies of prisons and of sexuality are designed to show how we are constituted (objective) and constitute ourselves (subjective) as subjects by disciplines, practices, and apparatuses that act on the body. Objectively, these take the form of dividing practices that carve up the body (diseased parts/healthy parts) and the population (sick/healthy, sane/insane) into administrative and disciplinary categories, and of normalization which, as I noted above, measures bodies and populations against norms of utility, and so forth. Subjectively, human beings become subjects by internalizing these identifications and by acting on themselves in accordance with them (Foucault, 1983b, p. 208; 1987, pp. 10–11). Thus for Foucault there is no subject without power, yet as he emphasized late in his life the subject can never be purely the product of these objective and subjective forms of power since power cannot be exercised at all without exercising itself on something that resists it to some degree (Foucault, 1987, p. 12).[9]

Having sketched Foucault's general understanding of power, I now turn to its significance for medicine and bioethics. Biopower operates by seizing on bodies, and since medicine from Descartes to Bichat has articulated the anatamometaphysical understanding of the body as machine and developed both technicopolitical forms of altering and controlling the body and regulatory controls and interventions into populations that together constitute biopower, medicine appears to be a, perhaps the, primary network in which biopower is exercised (cf. Foucault, 1977, p. 136). When one turns to standard bioethics, however, one finds that power is discussed almost exclusively in terms of sovereign power. The state, the medical profession, and other institutions are viewed as suppressing choices and desires. The assumption is therefore that self-determination liberates us from power. Because the state, the medical profession, and other institutions continue to exercise power in this way—sovereign power for Foucault does not by any means diminish—this concern of standard bioethics is entirely legitimate. But its exclusive concern with sovereign power blinds standard bioethics to the ways in which biopower operates.

The question from the perspective of biopower is how does society through medicine produce the bodies it needs? One way is by stimulating the desire for a certain kind of body that serves as a norm against which individuals measure their own bodies, are identified and identify themselves as, for example, overweight or double-chinned or at risk for cancer, and are persuaded to monitor themselves and orient their behavior. The need of society for healthy and productive bodies gives rise to forms of knowledge ranging from information about health risks to studies detailing the kind of facial features and body shapes that are statistically correlated with success in business. These knowledges are disseminated everywhere from health pamphlets in doctor's offices to articles in airline flight magazines. They are correlated with practices ranging from diet and exercise programs to cosmetic surgery.

Some interesting research from this perspective has been carried out by feminists and other critics with regard to body size and eating practices (Spitzack, 1990; Winkler and Cole, 1995). Rather than summarizing this research I will illustrate the forms and effects of biopower in a different context, that of eugenics. Earlier in this century, most abominably in Nazi Germany but also in the United States and other countries, governments in various ways and to various degrees implemented or considered implementing eugenic policies that involved or would have involved various kinds of coercion. Standard bioethics has formulated principles that would (if combined with political effectiveness) limit or prevent this kind of exercise of power over individuals. However, standard bioethics is blind to the ways in which biopower achieves what sovereign power would not or could not achieve in the case of eugenics. The goal of an optimally healthy and productive population no longer requires suppression of the desire of some to procreate but now operates through stimulation (by means of everything from health information to advertising) of the desire of couples to have perfect children, through myriad forms of prenatal and neonatal monitoring and screening, and through the fear of having an imperfect child in a normalizing society that values persons according to their usefulness and that constantly measures their chances of success according to societal standards of success. Power no longer requires draconian policies but operates through our choices. As expressions of biopower eugenic goals produce new genetic knowledge as the truth about our bodies which we, well schooled by our society to fear imperfect babies, are eager to seize on. With the new knowledge come new screening techniques that require us to qualify, measure, and appraise our future baby against still more standards. Eventually gene therapy may add the possibility of correcting or mitigating unproductive conditions and enhancing productive traits. The result in any case is that due to our fear of the consequences of being abnormal in a normalizing society the genetic truth about the body becomes the operative truth for our choices. This truth is disseminated through physicians and genetic counselors, whose "nondirective" approach confirms us in the choices that normalization requires us to make.

These remarks, though brief and admittedly intuitive, nonetheless indicate the direction a genealogy of standard bioethics might take. Such a genealogy would show how the emphasis of standard bioethics on expansion of choice and elimination of suffering unintentionally promotes the reign of biopower, insofar as the choices of those formed by the practices of modern societies and their efforts to eliminate suffering produce by stimulation of desires and by normalization the bodies and populations needed by such societies. Foucault would then serve as a highly effective critic of technological utopianism—not because he directly criticizes the Baconian project (he does not) but because, in continuity with his other studies, he shows us how the utopian and humanitarian plan for a world free from fortune and suffering in fact inscribes us more deeply into the way our society seeks to form us. Standard bioethics is blind to biopower because in its exclusive focus on sovereign power it ignores the moral significance of the discourses and practices that form the body.

However, the limited scope of any such genealogy must not be forgotten. Genealogies show how subjects are formed and form themselves by practices that act on the body. A genealogy of bioethics would show how the latter's commitments to expansion of choice and elimination of suffering support the effort of modern societies through technological medicine to form subjects according to the needs of such societies for productive and efficient bodies and populations. The problem from the perspective of my project is that genealogy cannot answer the ethical question posed by technology, namely in what ways and to what extent should we allow medicine to form us by forming our bodies? To answer this question one must know something about what our bodies are for and how medicine may serve the purposes they embody.

Foucault is frequently misunderstood on this point. Critics often assume that his genealogies lead to a negative moral judgment regarding the practices they analyze. But this assumption is wrong. A genealogy of bioethics cannot justify the conclusion that because biopower is exercised through, for example, genetic screening or gene therapy we should therefore reject such diagnostic and therapeutic interventions. Nor can it justify the conclusion that we would be better off if genetic screening and gene therapy were never developed. At the same time it would be equally mistaken to assume that the genealogist has no moral task. Foucault's work exhibits two different moral tasks, both of which are problematic. The first task follows from the genealogist's recognition of the ubiquity (which is not to say the totality or finality) of power, namely that wherever there is a subject there are effects of power. Rejecting both the activism that would develop a full-blown alternative to present relations of power and thereby substitute one form of power for another, and the quietism that would resign itself to the inevitability of present relations of power, Foucault identifies the critical task. "My point is not that everything is bad, but that everything is dangerous, which is not exactly the same as bad. If everything is dangerous, then we always have something to do" (Foucault, 1983a, pp.

231–232). Every practice or social effect is dangerous because, whatever else it is, it is a way in which power is exercised and therefore may form us in unintended ways. The moral task is therefore, in the words of two commentators, to carry out a "permanent provocation" to the knowledge-power-subject relations that constitute the self in any particular historical situation (Bernauer and Mahon, 1994, pp. 153–154). Permanent provocation requires the continual formation of new practices that keep new permutations of power at bay by resisting their effects.[10] The second task stands in tension if not contradiction with the first. In his late work Foucault appears to endorse the central idea, though not the concrete content, of what he describes as a "care of the self" that that for him characterized Hellenistic attitudes and practices toward sexuality and the body (Foucault, 1984). Unlike the practices of control over the self that preceded it in Greek society, care of the self does not seek mastery over excesses that need to be mastered in order to dominate others but is concerned with supremacy over oneself so that one may take pleasure in oneself and form appropriate relationships with others. While he recognizes that to take care of oneself is to form oneself according to the power relations present in one's society, Foucault refers to the techniques it involves as "practices of freedom," thus implying that these exercises of power need not be permanently provoked.

Neither of these tasks is satisfactory. The first task, recognizing the ubiquity of power, seeks to escape the effects of power insofar as this is possible. But since any process of moral formation must subject persons to ongoing relations and effects of power, Foucault must recommend a way of life that consists in avoiding any enduring process of moral formation. One commits oneself not to a way of life but to resisting whatever new forms of power act on one. But this allows whatever power relations are in effect to set the agenda for one's moral life and offers no argument for its assumption that all relations of power ought to be deliberately resisted. The second task seems to presuppose that some or at least one form of power—that involved in caring for oneself—is not as dangerous as other forms or is worthy of being appropriated rather than resisted. It thus avoids the problems with the first task. But it does so at the price of arbitrariness: the genealogist qua genealogist has no business recommending one exercise of power or ruling out another. He or she cannot recommend an ethic of care for oneself over an ethic of self-renunciation, the alternative Foucault opposes to the former. He or she cannot even rule out the moral acceptability of a way of life that forms the self in exactly the way society through the offices of medicine and the principles of standard bioethics forms the self—the way of life that would use technology to produce as far as possible the bodies and babies modern societies regard as "perfect."

The inability of genealogy to answer the ethical question of the moral significance of the body and of technological control over it points to the need for a standpoint that can expose the workings of biopower while also constituting an alternative to it. One occupies such a standpoint when one participates in a set of convictions and practices that form the body in ways that resist the Baconian project.

CONCLUSION

Foucault and the phenomenologists both trace the effects of the Cartesian-Bichatian body on our self-understanding as embodied beings and its role in making the Baconian project conceptually and practically possible as well as morally desirable. If Foucault's account is superior to that of the phenomenologists, it is due to his recognition of the ways in which subjects are formed by practices that act on the body. The tendency of the phenomenologists to ignore the ways in which the lived body is a product of such practices in favor of an almost exclusive emphasis on what appears to (or withdraws from) cognitive awareness testifies to the continuing hold of the Cartesianism they claim to have superceded. (The phenomenologists are not the only ones who have slighted practices that act on the body. Such practices played an important role in ancient theories of virtue but are strangely ignored by many of their recent rehabilitators, perhaps because of lingering modern prejudices regarding asceticism.)

Beyond this, Foucault shows how the clinical-laboratory discourse of the body authorized medicine as the arbiter of the meaning of finitude or mortality and, conjoined in complex ways with forms of biopower, subjected the body to various kinds of control. A description of the body in terms of the practices that act on it, if correct, would make it possible to understand the role of standard bioethics in forming the body according to the needs of society. Such a genealogical investigation would thereby show how what appears to be a moral commitment to the expansion of choice and the elimination of suffering is also a way of producing a certain kind of body. But no genealogy can answer the ethical question of what practices should form us; it can only tell us how we have been formed by the biopower exercised in the Baconian project and how standard bioethics, with its commitments to expansion of choice and elimination of suffering, has supported and extended biopower. Bioethics therefore requires a new (or perhaps a very old) kind of inquiry that asks which discourses and practices—regarding what our bodies are for, how suffering relates to these purposes, and how technological medicine assists or hinders these purposes—should form our bodies and thereby form us as subjects.

CHAPTER 8

The Body after Utopia

We are now at the end of our discussion of the efforts to counter the technological utopianism of modern medicine. The case for an alternative is best made by working through the advantages and disadvantages of the three types of approach surveyed here. The first approach, that of Hans Jonas and James Gustafson, tries to counter the Baconian project by developing a normative conception of the human. Despite differences, their conceptions share three characteristics that unite Jonas and Gustafson in a common project. Both emphasize the embeddedness of humanity in nature, develop conceptions of responsibility (Jonas) or participation (Gustafson) designed to redirect human power over nature into a stewardship of nature, and deliver stinging criticisms of the ambitions of the Baconian subject as perilous to nature and humanity. Recognition of the embeddedness of humanity in nature leads both Gustafson and Jonas to consider issues neglected by standard bioethics and to preserve the initial understanding of bioethics as a field encompassing environmental and population issues as well as biomedicine. At the same time, their unwillingness to deny or retreat from the power modern technology has given human beings over nature leads both to reject a return to pretechnological ways of life (as advocated, for example, by deep ecologists) and to advocate instead an ethic of stewardship. Finally, their recognition of the perils of human actions under modern technology leads both to an ethic that is heavily consequentialist but that seeks to avoid certain features of consequentialism in modern ethics by emphasizing broader and longer range goods (Gustafson), intrinsic goods exempt from weighing of risks and benefits (Jonas), and moral values not subject to consequentialist considerations (both).

Of course, there are important differences of both method and content between Jonas and Gustafson. As for method, Jonas reformulates biology to account for what we know from our own human perspective to be integral to our nature as living bodies, while Gustafson reformulates our own human self-understanding to account for what modern biology and the other sciences tell us. Leon Kass, as we have seen, follows Jonas rather than Gustafson at this point. (It is ironic that the theologian—not the philosopher or the scientist—is most accepting of modern science as it is.) Both Jonas and Gustafson defend their views with highly informed and nuanced interpretations of nature, but both also bring extrascientific interests to their interpretations: Jonas seeks in nature an objective grounding for his humanism while one suspects that Gustafson accepts modern biology in part because it accords with his theological and ethical commitments to the ethic of ordinary life. As for content, his description of humanity in terms of intervention leads Gustafson to a more positive stance toward technology than Jonas, for whom modern technology represents the triumph of one feature of humanity, namely making, over all the rest. This would seem to render Gustafson less effective in countering the Baconian project. But such a conclusion would be misleading. Jonas's ultimate underlying concern is anthropocentric; he worries that technology will bring us to the point where any conception of human nature as it is will be obsolete. His emphasis on purposiveness and his insistence on understanding nature from the perspective of what comes to fruition in humanity reflect this concern. By contrast, Gustafson's ultimate underlying concern is the divine ordering of nature; he worries that our anthropocentric ambitions expressed in technology threaten the interdependent wholes in which all nature (including the human species) is ordered. Because for him the course of nature itself, and not merely purposiveness as an intrinsic good grounded in nature, possesses normative significance as a clue to the divine ordering, he is more willing than Jonas to place the moral concern for human beings in a broader context of concerns for larger wholes and less inclined to view the continued existence of humanity as an absolute good or obligation. For the same reasons he is also less troubled by the prospects of alterations to human nature as it presently is. In the end, however, both Gustafson and Jonas end up with an emphasis on the common good of humanity as the chief (though not exclusive) aim of most of our actions in the biomedical sphere. For Gustafson, the common good involves the most comprehensive set of patterns and processes of interdependence within the range of our most of our actions in this sphere, while for Jonas our duty in this sphere is to ensure the continuation of humanity as such.

However, this similarity is a thin one. It masks differing conceptions of the content of the common good and therefore does not extend to agreement on particular bioethical issues; for example, as I noted, Jonas is interested in preserving a conception of humanity as it is, while Gustafson is more willing to intervene into human nature for the common good under certain conditions.

This last remark brings us to the final point Gustafson and Jonas share in common—a point that illustrates the limitation of the effort to derive a normative conception of the human largely from nature. Despite their profound critiques of the Baconian project and the subject that carries it out, in the end both Gustafson and Jonas accept too many characteristics of the Baconian project and of modern moral discourse to formulate a convincing alternative to technological utopianism. Chief among these is a thin conception of the human. In the end Gustafson cannot say enough about the human to determine which kinds of interventions are and are not appropriate, while Jonas cannot tell us how we ought to balance freedom and necessity in coming to terms with our new powers. Of course, it is unreasonable to expect conceptions of the human drawn from modern interpretations of nature to resolve specific biomedical issues alone, which is why Gustafson is right to stress the need for communities of moral formation and moral discourse. But because neither Jonas nor Gustafson articulates the convictions and practices that would define such a community and render its prudence or discernment determinate, they are vulnerable to those whose commitments to freedom and to the elimination of suffering lead them to claim different prerogatives for choice and to weigh risks differently.

For the second approach, that of Leon Kass and Stanley Hauerwas, limitations to technological utopianism are given in the nature of medicine as a moral practice. For both Kass and Hauerwas medicine is morally committed to the well-functioning of individual patients and to caring for those whom medicine cannot cure or restore. The description of medicine in these terms follows not from general principles but from the role of medicine in attaining the goods or moral values appropriate to our embodied life. In other words, Kass and Hauerwas treat medicine as a means to, an expression of, and an element in a morally worthy life. However, they differ over the moral significance of embodiment. For Kass a morally worthy life is one that displays the excellences and elevates the necessities of human embodiment. Health is either a condition for or is partly constitutive of human flourishing as defined in these terms. Kass therefore begins with health or wholeness as the end of medicine. Given this end, he then recognizes that for particular patients it is realized approximately, under conditions of finitude and vulnerability. Hauerwas begins at the opposite point, namely with finitude and vulnerability. Medicine is a tragic profession whose very moral identity, which involves caring when curing is impossible, derives from its limitations. The moral tasks of our embodied life are to determine how our finitude and our subjection to suffering may become part of our moral projects and to care for those whose suffering is pointless and cannot be cured. This difference regarding the moral significance of embodiment is roughly the difference between an Aristotelian and a Christian (and also, I believe, a Jewish) view of the relation of the health and suffering of the body to a morally worthy life.

This difference correlates with several other important differences regarding the Baconian project and the moral purpose of medicine. For Hauerwas the Baconian project follows from the loss of the tragic; for Kass it follows from the loss of teleology. Hauerwas confronts the Baconian project as a denial of the tragedy medicine inevitably faces because it deals with particular and finite human beings. In this respect the Baconian project is the product of modern culture more generally: since we have no tradition that enables us to accept tragedy we are unable to find any moral significance in any kind of suffering and therefore call on medicine to eliminate it all. Bacon and his followers confirm the view that all suffering is pointless and, with their promise to eliminate it by technology, foster illusions about our finitude and subjection to suffering. For Kass the problem with the Baconian project is not its denial of tragedy but its denial of the ethical significance of the natural. The Baconian project is grounded in a modern science that seeks to control nature rather than to determine which human aspirations are natural, and in a modern ethic that manages our desires and wishes rather than determining which of them represent genuine human aspirations. Together, modern science and ethics remove us from the ordinary understandings of the meaning of embodiment embedded in our taboos and customs.

The results for medicine follow accordingly. For Hauerwas the denial of tragedy fosters illusions about the power of medicine that lead to its control over our lives, to the dangerous and impossible utopian quest for the elimination of disease, and to the abandonment of those medicine cannot cure—those who remind us of our own limitations and those of medicine. For Kass the disconnection of our desires and wishes from nature means that medicine is called on to exert ever greater control over the body in order to fulfil yet more arbitrary desires and wishes.

Of course, while Kass and Hauerwas believe medicine possesses certain intrinsic moral commitments, neither views medicine as self-sufficient. Medicine as Kass describes it requires both a biology that articulates its implicit knowledge of the meanings of embodiment and customs that fulfill these meanings. Medicine can flourish only in a society that has the institutions and practices that form physicians and others in those attitudes and habits that respect the meaning of bodily life. Ideally the physician's experience and training combined with his or her formation in these attitudes and habits equip him or her with the prudence necessary to carry out the moral wisdom of a broader community. For Hauerwas the role of medicine is more limited and its dependence on a particular community is more complete. Medicine can restrict itself to the bodily health and the care of individual patients only if there are other practices in the community that address the inevitable suffering that accompanies such a restriction. Both the demands of care and the pressures to reject and abandon those who remind us of our limitations require a community whose habits embody reconciliation with the suffering other. Finally, the role of medicine itself is determined by a community's understanding of what kinds of suffering fit into its moral projects and how.

I have argued that even with these major qualifications Kass and Hauerwas still assume more moral content than medicine by itself can or should try to deliver. Rather, I have argued for a more limited role that recognizes both the highly technical and specialized nature of modern medicine and the necessity of communities capable of caring for sick persons and directing their use of medicine and its technology to a view of the good. This amounts to questioning whether medicine is the tradition Kass and Hauerwas claim it to be or whether (as I think) it should instead be viewed as a *techne* which takes its place within a particular community's forms of caring and is directed to its understanding of the good. However, this does not mean that physicians should not be caring people; that they have no role in helping individual patients achieve their goods, in determining their capacities for pursuing their chosen goods, or in educating them about the likely effects on their health status of pursuing these goods; or that individual physicians may not also be experts or authorities on a particular community's view of the good (as, e.g., Moses Maimonides was for twelfth-century Jews in Egypt).

Neither Kass nor Hauerwas settles for an indirect challenge that seeks mainly to limit the development and exercise of the technological capacities of Baconian medicine; rather, they directly attack the central moral commitments of the latter. For Kass, to subjugate medicine to the expansion of choices however arbitrary and idiosyncratic they may be is to risk degrading our very humanity. For Hauerwas, the effort to eliminate suffering denies many the opportunity to fashion their suffering into a moral project while perpetuating dangerous illusions about the capacities of medicine and our control over suffering and death. However, Kass wrongly assumes that the account of (a nondegraded) embodiment his position requires is available for all in that fictive entity called "the Western tradition." Hauerwas is right to oppose to this the necessity of an actual community with its particular convictions and practices (though I have expressed my doubts that this community is already actual in the sense required by Hauerwas's view of moral formation and identity). However, Hauerwas tells us very little about the moral projects that at least some kinds of suffering are supposed to serve. A Kassian critique of Hauerwas would rightly insist that a description of these projects requires an articulation of the moral significance of the body that Hauerwas thus far has not supplied. This turn to the body would not only help identify the moral projects suffering is said to serve. Since (as Hauerwas rightly recognizes) any effort to carry out these projects must take account of how our society through medicine has already formed us in ways that ignore and exclude such projects, a deeper account of this formation would show the role played in it by our society's attitudes and practices regarding the body.

This brings us to those who have addressed more directly the place of the body in modern medicine. The significance of these approaches is twofold. It lies in their attention to the alterity involved in illness and in the body as object of technological control, and in their premise that technological control over the body is not merely an accidental feature of modern medicine but one with enormous implications for the way medical care is given and received and even for the constitution of modern persons as subjects. We become subjects in part by monitoring, acting on, and exercising vigilance over our bodies, and medicine, especially when it has the role and capacities it has in contemporary society, is a vitally important way in which we carry out these attitudes and performances on our bodies. From this perspective, it is possible to understand how the modern moral commitments to expanding choice and eliminating suffering depend in a twofold way on the formation of a subject who exercises control over the body. Most obviously, control over the body, as Bacon and Descartes saw so clearly, is necessary in order to realize the aims of expanding choice and eliminating suffering. But beyond this, those commitments require that one abstract one's moral identity from the body, which in turn becomes (through technology, it is hoped) simply the object of one's choices and desires. To the extent that one succeeds in abstracting one's moral identity from one's body, one is able to deny or ignore the way in which one's moral identity depends on one's attitudes and practices of control over the body, and the way in which this control is linked with forms of biopower. In short, one conceals the very process by which one is constituted as the moral subject one is. The price of this concealment is blindness to the ways in which one's choices and efforts to eliminate suffering both advance and result from the societal project of producing a certain kind of body.

However, as I argued in the previous chapter, there are problems with these approaches. Despite its brilliant account of the role of alterity in the phenomenon of illness and in the technological control of the body, the phenomenological approach overemphasizes the problem of dehumanization and the corollary assumption that a return to the "lived body" would necessarily be liberating. For the phenomenologists modern medicine is problematic insofar as it displaces a more wholistic and therefore more authentic experience of the body, but this assumes that the lived body constitutes a nonalienated experience that directly expresses the self and its everyday world. This assumption ignores the ways, often pointed out by feminist thinkers, in which our bodies are marked by the attitudes and practices of our society and of our particular communities and ways of life. The "lived body" too is in part a social body, and our ways of experiencing it mark us as members of a certain society or community. Modern medicine is one way in which a society forms its members; the disciplines and practices that attend to the lived body are equally so, and may even complement modern medicine in the task for which society employs it.

The task, therefore, is not simply to reorient health care toward the lived body, but to become aware of the attitudes and practices that have formed us in connection with the technological control of medicine over our bodies and to determine which attitudes and practices should form us—whether those of modern societies or some others. But as I argued near the end of the previous chapter, the genealogist cannot carry out this ethical task. The genealogist as exemplified and described by Foucault either strives to resist whatever forms of power are operative in forming him or her as a subject or recommends one process of subject formation as worthy of being appropriated. The first response gives no reason why we should make it our general project to resist power, while the second response is necessarily arbitrary since the role of the genealogist is to bring forms and relations of power to our awareness no matter where they occur. To advocate a way of life is to accede to one network of power as acceptable and thus to abandon this role. This leaves us with a problem: If the task is twofold, namely to recognize the attitudes and practices regarding the body that have formed us and to determine what attitudes and practices should form us, how are these two aspects (the critical and the constructive) to be combined?

If genealogy itself fails to combine these aspects, an alternative is to follow a hint of one of Foucault's interpreters and to look in those places that have not been fully formed by processes of normalization (Hoy, 1986, pp. 13–14). Presumably one would find here self-formations that by their very existence as alternatives expose the workings of biopower, but that also, precisely as alternatives, embody substantive convictions and practices regarding the body. The remainder of this chapter shows how Christian attitudes and practices regarding the body can be viewed as one such alternative, and one, moreover, that avoids the problems while also drawing on the strengths of the various approaches treated in this volume.[1]

It is clear from my evaluations of Jonas and of Leder and Zaner that the formulation of a Christian approach to the body will have to reject the ideal of a subject who can gain control of technology or whose nonalienated essence can be recovered from the capacities of technology to control the body. We in the West in the late twentieth century are always already formed by the discourse and practices of technology in a normalizing society; there is no possibility of a simple return to the kind of premodern moral formation whose replacement by the modern framework was described in chapter one. It is precisely here, however, that both Foucault and Hauerwas (at least as I have interpreted them) are most helpful. Foucault encourages us to focus on those points of resistance to normalization, while Hauerwas's entire approach is designed to show Christians how they have been formed by modern discourses and practices and to describe the hermeneutical and practical strategies by which they can inscribe themselves into Christian discourses and practices. By welcoming the mentally challenged into their midst, for example, Hauerwas's community shows modern societies the contingency of the normalization processes they accept as inevitable and the cruelty that lurks in what they consider to be compassion. At the same time, the welcoming is constituted by attitudes toward suffering and practices of caring that imply an alternative role for medicine and its capacities. As I hope will be clear below, Christian attitudes toward suffering and practices of caring do not require a subject who must control, reject, or transcend technology. Rather, they require a process of self-formation in which subjects are formed by both resisting and appropriating technology in accordance with an alternative (in this case, Christian) discourse and set of practices.[2]

What are this discourse and set of practices? Leder, Zaner, and Foucault show us how the Baconian project not only replaces attitudes and practices regarding the moral significance of the body, its pursuit of health, and its susceptibility to disease, decay, and death (as I argued in chapter one), but is itself a set of attitudes and practices regarding the body, and one that is pervasive in our self-formation. If we cannot entirely reject or transcend the processes by which we have been formed, it follows that our resistance and appropriation will also focus on the body. The problem is that those who have focussed on the body have left major problems in their wake. Leder and Zaner assume the sufficiency of a return to the lived body, while Foucault cannot, as genealogist, consistently endorse one process of self-formation over another. Kass develops a profound and nuanced view of the body but mistakenly regards it as universal. Hauerwas rightly understands that any such view must be particular but does not develop the view of the body that would have enabled him to articulate the moral projects that suffering, in his view, is alleged to serve.

It is therefore necessary to offer, however schematically and tentatively, a description of Christian discourse and practices regarding the body that is capable of resisting and appropriating technological control of the body and of answering Plato's questions regarding the attention or vigilance we should exercise over our bodies, the control we should give medicine over our bodies, the ends that should determine what counts as a sufficiently healthy body, and the limits we should observe in improving our bodies and eliminating suffering.

At the end of chapter six I reconstructed from Hauerwas's writings a typology of kinds of suffering in relation to moral projects and commitments (pp. 180–81). I will not repeat this typology (which is presupposed by what follows) but will simply underscore what I take to be its significance: that the conviction that some kinds of suffering can serve a moral project, and the correlative denial that all suffering is pointless, strikes at the very heart of the Baconian project and breaks the grip of the latter on the practice of medicine. Underlying it is a conviction that the attempt to render our bodies free from suffering and wholly subject to our choices is morally impoverishing in both self-regarding and other-regarding ways—that the kind of vigilance over the body it entails produces subjects who are incapable of understanding the nature and meaning of embodiment, of recognizing and accepting the limits of medicine, of caring adequately for those who embody those limits and fall victim to efforts to deny them, and of rightly ordering the goods of the body (including those made possible by technology).

As I argued above, this conviction that some kinds of suffering can serve moral projects requires a view of the body in order to articulate those projects. What distinguishes the Christian view from its modern counterparts is its refusal to separate the body of the Other from the self. Rather, it recognizes that the body of the Other is inextricable from the self, so that the self is separated from and within itself. This understanding of the body can be traced to Paul, for whom, as Rudolf Bultmann and a succession of later scholars have concluded, "the *soma* [body] is not a something that outwardly clings to a man's real *self* (to his soul, for instance), but belongs to its very essence, so that we can say man does not *have* a *soma*; he *is soma* . . ." (Bultmann, 1951, p. 194). There are two aspects to the body so understood. For Bultmann the first aspect refers to the self insofar as it can be the object of one's own action as subject or under one's control as subject. This reflexivity was asserted by Bultmann in order to contrast it to materiality, but it is possible to reject this contrast while retaining an understanding of *soma* as the outward expression of intentionality or will. In phenomenological terms, the body for Paul is a lived body; it could be described as will or intentionality "bodied forth" into the external world. But according to Bultmann, the body for Paul is also that in which one experiences oneself as "subjected to an occurrence that springs from a will other than [one's] own" (Bultmann, 1951, p. 196). The body, then, is that which resists or opposes one's will or intentionality; it is oneself as separated from oneself. Phenomenologically speaking, this is the body of the Other: oneself as subject to powers external to one's own willing or intentionality. According to Bultmann, for Paul this subjection to a power not one's own brings with it the temptation to allow the separation within the self to become a divorce in which, as in Gnosticism, the body becomes alien and foreign to the self (Bultmann, 1951, p. 199). Indeed, in view of the degree to which sin for Paul wrests away the dominion of will and intentionality, it is not difficult to understand the appeal of this solution. But Paul's refusal to resolve the problem of alterity by separating the body of the Other from the true self as alien to the latter is highly significant. For it means that for him the alterity recognized by many ancient writers does not occur between the self and something external to it, but within the self itself. Moreover, for Paul, in contrast to the Gnostics in his day and some phenomenological accounts in ours, the body of the Other is not altogether negative. While it poses the threat of wresting one from oneself (i.e., sin), it also harbors the promise, fulfilled in the resurrection of the body, of redemption, which is itself the work of a power that escapes one's will and intentionality (Bultmann, pp. 198, 201).

The body, then, is the whole person or self in a twofold determination, as that which, on the one hand, "bodies forth" our will and intentionality in the external world—the outward expression of our will and intentionality (the lived body)—and that which, on the other hand, resists or opposes our will and intentionality (the body of the Other). Hence a Christian view of the body will understand the body of the Other as integral to the self and will therefore interpret alterity—the body as it resists or opposes the dominion of will and intentionality—as the separation of the self from and within itself, a view that later Christian thinkers largely shared with Paul.[3]

Important implications for how Christians understand the body's imperfections and recalcitrance to our wishes, its susceptibility to disease and decay, and its mortality follow from this general view.[4] As phenomenological analyses of illness, aging, disability, and mortality remind us, all of these phenomena manifest the body of the Other that fractures the body as expression of will and intentionality, namely the lived body and the being at one with oneself that constitutes it. Within a Christian framework such manifestations participate in and point to sin as the ultimate power not our own that divides the self and controls us. And the healing that often follows such manifestations proleptically participates in and points to the eschatological resurrection of the body as the ultimate healing of the divided self. For this reason, as George Khushf and Robert Mordacci have pointed out, it is appropriate for Christians to view illness and healing in analogy (though not in a causal relationship, as some formulations imply) to sin and redemption, respectively (cf. Khushf, 1995; Mordacci, 1995). In accordance with this discourse of the body, one way in which illness, decay, and bodily imperfection have served the moral projects of Christians is as occasions for meditation on sin and the need for grace, and many of the disciplines and ways of monitoring the body Christians have developed have sought to form subjects accordingly.[5] These disciplines and practices are not masochistic. They do not lead one to seek out suffering. Still less do they try to justify suffering by putting it in a teleological framework ("This happened in order that . . ."). And as the long record of Christian commitment to healing indicates, they agree that much suffering is pointless and should be cured if possible.

From this perspective the effort to separate oneself as a subject from one's body prone to disease, decay, and death, or more generally, the quest to make the body perfect and perfectly subject to our choices, echoes the Gnostic attempt to divorce the body of the Other from the self. And the disciplines and ways of monitoring of the body and its processes that carry out this quest produce subjects constituted by their denial of the body of the Other. This denial prompts the use of medicine to eliminate all traces of the body of the Other in their own bodies, so that medicine is called on to postpone death, stall or reverse biochemical aging processes, restore youthful anatomical features, and in general eliminate or alter anything that is unwanted. Just as significantly, this denial of the Other equates the meaning of embodiment with control over the body. When the inevitability of the body of the Other is denied, the end of life may become a desperate quest to sieze control through physician-assisted death.

From a Christian perspective, therefore, when one monitors and acts on one's body in a way that denies the inevitability (this side of the resurrection) of the body of the Other, one becomes incapable of the use of illness and bodily imperfection to form oneself in an awareness of sin and grace. One wrongly supposes that medicine can resolve the crisis of alterity and overcome the division of the self by rendering the body the full expression of one's will and intentionality. But this denies the limits of medicine, which does not expel the Other but only delays his inevitable appearance, and which cannot dispel the deeper problem of sin or accomplish the resurrection of the body that is its solution. The effort to eliminate all traces of the body of the Other involves ways of monitoring, acting on, and exercising vigilance over the body that form subjects incapable of understanding, and thus coming to terms with, the deeper root of the divided self. Moreover, those who deny the body of the Other in this way end up affirming it in a most ironic way. For their efforts to perfect the body and bring it under the realm of choice do not restore the body to the willing and choosing subject but rather place it under the hegemony of a society that produces the subjects whose desires and choices enable it to accomplish its normalizing ambitions.

But more than self-regarding concerns are at stake here. Acceptance of the reality of the body of the Other that separates the subject from and within itself is the condition for receptivity to the body of the Other in a second sense, as the suffering of the Other. The Baconian project fails from this perspective because it does not address and in fact contributes to certain kinds of suffering. Just as the Baconian-Cartesian subject is formed by monitoring and acting on himself in accordance with societal standards for the body, so he internalizes his society's concern with producing other bodies that approximate these standards. His compassion for the suffering of others is thus formed by and expressed in these normalizing processes. The suffering of the other is elicited and responded to in terms of utility, efficiency, prospects of healthy survival, and so forth. Medicine exercises compassion by measuring individuals against these norms and helping them to approximate them to the highest degree possible. But as Edith Wyschogrod has argued (with respect to postmodern, not Christian, ethics), such a subject is incapable of responding to the pain of the Other because it never allows the Other to break through the codes (such as those of normalization) that inscribe the body in the text of society (Wyschogrod, 1990, pp. 98–99, 103–104; 1995, pp. 26–27). It is not surprising, therefore, that as Hauerwas argues, compassion for the suffering results in elimination of the sufferer who will never approximate the standards. It is also not surprising that as Baconian medicine keeps increasing the standards for a "normal" body in a society that measures and calculates bodies according to these standards, the marginalization of those whose bodies cannot meet the standards is increased and their worth in the eyes of society is diminished. By contrast, acceptance of the vulnerability of the body that separates the subject from itself opens up a receptivity to the Other that resists reducing the Other to social codes (Wyschogrod, 1990, p. 99). In Hauerwasian terms, a subject for whom the susceptibility of the body to suffering and death is integral to interpretations of and actions on the body may welcome the other who reminds us of the limits of medicine or whose body refuses to conform to the normalizing demands of society.

This, in rather traditional terms, is what I understand the Christian significance of the body to be. The remaining question is the one raised at several points in this study: What is the place of medicine, with its technological capacities, in a morally worthy life? I have argued against Kass and Hauerwas that medicine should not be viewed as a relatively independent tradition with its own implicit and fragile moral commitments and view of the good, but as a form of knowledge and set of techniques that must find its place within a larger understanding of the moral significance of the body. For Christians, then, the question is, what is the place of medicine in the space opened up by the divided self?

First, a community formed according to the understanding of the body sketched above is prepared to recognize and accept the limits of medicine and to reorganize health care around this recognition. It is becoming clear to many observers that the quest of medicine to find a "magic bullet" cure for every disease or unwanted condition has been founded on an exaggeration of certain accomplishments of medicine in this century (Golub, 1994). The prevalence and persistence of chronic diseases, the yawning gap between genetic diagnosis and effective therapy, the growing resistance of bacterial strains to antibiotics—these and many other similar factors assure us that the Baconian quest to eliminate suffering is not only being delayed but is an illusion. This is not to deny the many accomplishments of technological medicine—to the contrary, my point is that once we accept the limits of medicine in eliminating suffering, we will be in a better position to use technology, as part of a more general commitment to caring, in ways that help more and more people to live better with conditions that cannot be eliminated. But if chronic conditions, the gap between diagnosis and therapy, and the like will characterize medicine for the foreseeable future, then from a Christian perspective Baconian medicine has done those who suffer from these factors a double disservice. First, by defining all suffering as pointless and holding out the false promise of eventually being able to eliminate it all, it has discouraged them from coming to find in illness and imperfection the tragedy of sin and the hope of redemption. Second, in its devotion to the elimination of suffering it has grievously failed to provide adequate resources and other support for those who, due to the limitations of medicine in general or for a particular patient, cannot be cured. Because the Christian approach to the body and to bodily suffering as I have described it is committed to the transformation of suffering into the moral and spiritual projects I have identified, it is in a position not only to recognize and accept the limits of medicine in eliminating suffering but to form a practice of health care that assigns a much higher place to the forms of care and support that enable people to live with their conditions in such a way that they can accomplish the transformation.[6] While this need not, and should not, rule out efforts to eliminate disease, it should ensure that a high priority is given at every level of research and care to improving the conditions of those who cannot be cured.

Second, because a community formed according to this understanding of the body denies that all incurable suffering is pointless or that the worth of one's life is determined by how closely one conforms to societal standards of bodily perfection, it will see no "need" to eliminate those who suffer in order to spare them a life of suffering. It is necessary at this point to understand Baconian medicine in relation to the larger society that it makes possible but that also supports it. The Baconian project is bound up with an entire social and economic system that virtually demands that we be independent of the need to care for others or be cared for by them. Those who cannot or can no longer maintain their independence or control over their bodies are therefore abandoned to specialized forms of care which, due to the devaluation of this kind of care and support in view of the priorities of Baconian medicine criticized in the previous paragraph, are unable to meet their needs.[7] In these circumstances we are taught to value independence and control over our bodies and to fear their loss far more, I surmise, than our predecessors were. To the same extent we are inclined to deny the moral worth of those who cannot or can no longer exercise independence or control their bodies, including ourselves. In this context it is clear why many would kill others to spare them a life of suffering or call for assistance in dying as a way to regain control and independence. But for a subject constituted by the body of the Other, loss of control over the body may signal an occasion for oneself and others to understand the need for grace and to begin to experience it through the care of families, professional caregivers, and communities who recognize their duty to care in such circumstances. This is not to idealize or romanticize the loss of control; it can be a deeply troubling experience for everyone involved. Nor does it by itself resolve the status of those who are irreversibly incapable of responding to the care of others or whose incurable pain or tragic sense of abandonment at the end of life precludes accomplishment of any moral or spiritual transformation of suffering. My point is only that from a Christian perspective one does not lose one's moral worth or one's moral task in life simply because one has lost independence or control of one's body. A community committed to this perspective would form its institutions and order its health care priorities accordingly. In the case of the dying, this would involve a rather thoroughgoing redirection of resources from efforts to extend life to efforts to develop more effective comfort care, including pain relief, high-quality nursing care, and support of family caregivers.

Third, members of a community formed by this approach to the body would no longer measure themselves or others by the norms of a society bent on producing bodies designed for optimal levels of productivity, beauty, and success. Because the body is no longer measured, calculated and valued according to such norms, the need to reorder it in accordance with these norms disappears. In such a community, the uses of medicine to eliminate all traces of the body of the Other, some of which I referred to above, would simply disappear. This does not mean that all uses of medicine to enhance bodily functioning would disappear, but it does involve two implications. The first is that members of such a community will find the place of the pursuit of health and bodily excellence within the space opened up by the body of the Other and the moral and spiritual tasks and duties it entails for oneself and for others. The second is that it is clear how little is contributed to this task by efforts to draw lines between, say, treatment of a disease and enhancement of a trait. Rather, the process of discernment requires determination of how one's own body, with its capacities and limitations, best carries out the tasks and duties just mentioned and orders the rest of life in accordance with them.

In his study of sexual renunciation in early Christianity Peter Brown shows how "Christian attitudes to sexuality delivered the deathblow to the ancient notion of the city as the arbiter of the body" (Brown, 1988, p. 437). A subject formed by the body of the Other in the twofold sense I have described possesses both the self-regarding and other-regarding moral commitments to frame a way of practicing health care that is capable of rejecting as arbiters of the body Baconian medicine and the society that underwrites it. But this interpretation of the body is, of course, only the beginning. It indicates the attitudes and practices Christians should bring to occasions of suffering but is not sufficiently fine-tuned to specify what kinds of suffering should be eliminated or what choices should be made with regard to the capacities of technology. It tells us in general what priorities a health care system organized around these moral convictions should have but does not tell us in detail how to order the goods of the body. It shows how the twofold imperative of Baconian medicine fails on its own terms insofar as it delivers the body over to society rather than to human freedom and increases certain kinds of suffering in its effort to eliminate other kinds. But it does not offer a detailed alternative to the Baconian project. To overcome these deficiencies will require a description of the twofold alterity of the body, and the virtues and skills required to live it out, that is as rich as Kass's descriptions of the nobility and necessity of the body, and as capable of being articulated in view of the capacities and limits of technology. But if contemporary Christians are to reject Baconian medicine as arbiter of the body in the same way that their ancient predecessors rejected the Roman city, there is a final and much more important deficiency. That is the need for a concrete community (including health care institutions) to form subjects according to these attitudes and practices regarding the body as fully as the broader society forms subjects by the attitudes and practices of the Baconian project. That deficiency, alas, cannot be overcome by writing another book.

Notes

CHAPTER 1: TECHNOLOGY, TRADITION, AND THE ORIGINS OF BIOETHICS

1. Nothing that follows requires dismissal of concerns about autonomy, risks and benefit calculations, justice, and the like. But aside from questions about whether standard bioethics can avoid making autonomy a substantive principle or can measure risks and benefits without a more robust view of the good, one can protest against the narrowness of its agenda. Take in vitro fertilization as an example. Ideally, technical procedures and moral and legal safeguards could presumably be designed so that no one is harmed (for some, this would be impossible so long as there are extraneous embryos, a risk of psychological damage to the future child, or both), no one's self-determination is interfered with (except that of the future child, if this is deemed relevant), an acceptable risk-benefit ratio is operative (however risks and benefits would be weighed), and no injustice occurs. All the principal concerns of standard bioethics would therefore be addressed. Yet this ignores entirely the authority of medicine over a new area of our lives (one that does not immediately seem to involve disease or illness); practices relating to parenthood, children, sexual intercourse, and the body; and cultural constructions of gender and fertility, to name only a few.

2. Taylor distinguishes between historical explanation and interpretation. The former answers questions about the precipitating conditions of cultural phenomena in terms of diachronic causation while the latter discloses the appeal of its moral vision or its capacity to inspire. The latter kind of inquiry can never be separated from the former, since to understand the force of an idea is to know something relevant to how it came about and vice versa. But this kind of inquiry can be relatively independent. "We can say: in this and this consists the power of the idea/identity/moral vision, however it was brought to be in history" (Taylor, 1989, pp. 202–203).

3. Foucault's genealogical method is also of importance to this project, though I defer consideration of it until chapter seven. The genealogical task is to connect the principles and institutional practices of standard bioethics with the development of forms of domination and control of the body (cf. Foucault, 1984, pp. 76–100).

4. I do not carry out such an ambitious inquiry in this chapter or even in the volume as a whole. And I don't need to follow the exact methods or endorse all of the concerns of either Taylor or Foucault since my purpose in combining certain features of their respective approaches is limited. Specifically, I use Taylor's hermeneutical method to uncover the moral sources of standard bioethics, but with the quasi-Foucauldian purpose of showing how it constitutes a discourse that excludes, marginalizes, and distorts the moral convictions and aspirations of alternative moral discourses and thus prevents certain vital moral concerns raised by technological medicine from being adequately addressed. Nevertheless, readers who believe Taylor and Foucault pursue irreconciliable paths may wonder how I can combine them. Taylor's hermeneutical project is based on a conviction that only if we articulate the sources of our moral identity are we able to resist efforts to reduce morality to behavioral and other reductionist accounts while Foucault is often taken by both critics and followers to be engaged in a reductionist enterprise. However, the irreconcilability here is superficial. Taylor rejects the independence of ideas and recognizes that a complete account of our moral sources would have to include accounts of the cultural patterns and institutional practices that make them effective (as opposed to inspiring or convincing). And while Taylor's account of these patterns and practices would likely differ from Foucault's, he does not reject such an approach in principle. Similarly, Foucault repeatedly insisted that any effort to link ideas or knowledge with practices assumes that the two are not identical, and there is no reason why he would reject in principle Taylor's claim that ideas have some power to convince. A more crucial, and genuinely irreconcilable, difference is their radically different assessments of what constitutes the greater danger to human freedom. For Taylor it is reductionist social scientific accounts of human nature that deprive us of our moral identity, while for Foucault it is exercises of domination and control that our moral sources mask. Another crucial difference, also irreconcilable, is that Taylor believes that he can understand the formation of the self without direct reference to practices while Foucault believes that the self is formed by practices and cannot be understood apart from them. I return to this point in chapter seven.

5. Since I do not raise the question of whether standard bioethics is philosophically justifiable, I do not commit the genetic fallacy. However, I do arrive at two conclusions that are relevant to any such justification. First, I foreclose any assumption that standard bioethics is a rationally necessary response to technology or to the need for a common morality. Therefore, any justification of standard bioethics offered on these grounds is flawed. Second, I show how standard bioethics gains its content from moral and cultural values that are

widely shared in modern society but that are not universal. Consequently, those who do not share those values are not likely to accept justifications of standard bioethics that refer to such values.

6. For both Roman Catholicism and Protestantism this is a plausible strategy. Catholic theologians have traditionally framed many of their arguments in terms of a natural law doctrine of intrinsic goods that are knowable by everyone, and Paul Ramsey drew on a long Protestant tradition when he described his "ethics of a wider community" (of which the ethics of medicine is a subset) in terms of the Christian norm of covenant fidelity between persons (Ramsey, 1970b, pp. xii–xiii). It is also true that secular moralities are in many respects the offspring of these religious moralities. But the strategy has two limitations, both following from the abstraction of what is allegedly common from the full description of the Christian way of life. First, it is susceptible to misunderstanding when conclusions purportedly derived from common moral convictions turn out to be grounded in particularistic claims. For example, Ramsey's appeal to medical indications alone as opposed to quality of life considerations in decisions about whether to treat incompetents or impaired newborns and his rejection of in vitro fertilization as unethical experimentation on "possible future human beings" both follow from theological convictions rooted in a way of life that requires and fosters certain attitudes toward the vulnerable and relieves human beings from an exclusive concern with maximizing good consequences. However, as I argue below, apart from some such context—when viewed from another moral way of life or as independent injunctions that must stand alone before the bar of reason—conclusions such as these are likely to appear as arbitrary restrictions of human choice and to ignore certain kinds of suffering. Second, it is often unclear what theology actually contributes to bioethics in this strategy. For example, the Catholic doctrine of double effect has helped bioethicists sort out distinctions between intentional and unintentional killing. But the concern about intention is relevant only for those for whom intentions are morally decisive in certain cases.

7. Of course, there are many such narratives; the trick is to find one that neither exaggerates the differences between modernity and the middle ages nor trivializes them. In my judgment there are at least three distinguishing characteristics. First, while there was disagreement during the middle ages on the nature of the good, there was agreement that there are goods that are natural to human beings and that the common goods are the highest of these. This was challenged by nominalism in the late middle ages and met its strongest counterclaim with Hobbes, for whom goods are self-chosen (and thus nonnatural) and for whom the common good is derivative from individual goods. Second, the middle ages was characterized by enough agreement on who the moral authorities were that claims about the good did not require a bedrock of certainty and moral reasoning did not require fully rationalized or neutral procedures. But in the modern era the crisis of moral authority required a basis of certainty for morality as well as rationalized, neutral procedures. In this respect

Pascal's rejection of casuistry, and the grounds on which he rejected it, mark the beginning of the modern period in moral theory. Third, there is the process Charles Taylor identifies in which ideals of religiomoral perfection were replaced by the affirmation of ordinary life with its moral valuation of the efforts involved in the preservation and enhancement of human life. This third process is, I believe, most significant for my topic.

8. Both accounts reflect my own understandings of what medical and religious traditions are. However, my discussion of medicine as a practice is informed by descriptions of medicine by Leon Kass (1985) and by Edmund Pellegrino and David Thomasma (1981), and my discussion of the place of health and illness in religious traditions is informed by the views on the relation of health to virtue in Moses Maimonides (1975) and by John Bowlin's account of the relation of health, fortune, and virtue in St. Thomas Aquinas (Bowlin).

9. I leave aside for now the crucial question of whether medicine as a tradition can be complete without an adequate conception of what capacities and roles are conducive to a good or morally worthy life. I discuss this issue in my treatment of Leon Kass in chapter five. There I argue that medicine as a tradition is dependent on such a conception, and is therefore dependent on religious or moral traditions. In a response to an earlier draft of this chapter, Robert Veatch remarked to me that the notion of medicine as an independent tradition is a historical fiction. If I am right, then it is also a philosophical mistake.

10. Taylor's account thus shows how moral concerns gave credence and support to theories of ethics that abstract from all accounts of the way things are. His point is that such abstraction is not merely motivated by epistemic crises but also by the moral commitments rooted in the affirmation of ordinary life I have mentioned. The concern with ordinary life involves a new understanding of human dignity as consisting in self-responsible reason in addition to the moral valuation of human stewardship of creation for the preservation and cultivation of human life. Just as the latter required the shift from contemplation of a divine order to productive efficacy I have just referred to, the former required a form of rationality potentially accessible to everyone in place of the moral authority of a few. Both commitments therefore naturally favored disengaged reason as a proper way to realize moral ideals (Taylor, 1989, 231–232).

11. Of course, the humanist and existentialist critics may be right that any modern morality is woefully inadequate to provide the moral content capable of guiding technological action and of restraining the inevitability of technological progress and the will to power of technological ambitions, and is therefore only a rest stop on the road to moral nihilism. Nevertheless, if technological medicine itself expresses a moral agenda, the precise nature of this agenda and its influence on bioethics may be hidden if one jumps too quickly to the nihilistic implications. Standard bioethics may be dismissed too easily as an ineffective response to technological advance rather than an impetus to and a powerful legitimation of that advance. If so, the moral framework that confers

such overriding value on technology should be an important area of investigation even for these critics. I discuss technology and nihilism in my chapter on Hans Jonas.

12. Of course, this confidence extends beyond the practitioners. For moderns who have lived through the terrible evils of the twentieth century (most of which were aided by the technology Bacon hoped would "relieve and benefit the condition of man") but whose confidence in the relief of suffering and self-determination has remained intact along with a belief in the moral superiority of their culture, medicine serves as a persuasive *apologia*. The claims of modern medicine to have significantly reduced suffering and to have expanded the range of choices by arresting the play of fortune are a powerful ingredient in the moral self-confidence of such moderns, whether those claims are viable in the end or not.

CHAPTER 2: STANDARD BIOETHICS AND THE BACONIAN PROJECT

1. There has been much debate over whether there is any morally significant difference between assisted suicide and euthanasia. There is certainly a difference in who actually causes the death. But as Dan Brock argues, the notion that in assisted suicide the patient kills him- or herself while in voluntary active euthanasia the physician kills him or her is drawn too sharply, at least in those cases in which a physician prescribes the lethal medications and instructs the patient on how to use them. Clearly both are integral to the causal process that results in the patient's death. Similarly, in both voluntary active euthanasia and assisted suicide the patient chooses to die (Brock, 1992, p. 10). Hence with regard to causal responsibility and self-determination there seems to be little difference. This leaves the question of whether voluntary euthanasia is more liable to lead to abuses than is providing information and writing prescriptions (Quill, Cassel, and Meier, 1992, p. 1381). This is an empirical question that has not yet been answered. Since I generally agree with those who do not find morally significant differences between them, in what follows I will refer to both together under the heading of "physician-assisted death."

2. For example, it is possible to argue that the intention to remove a burdensome treatment differs from the intention to end one's life. Similarly, one could argue that a physician who places a patient on life support has a negative duty to remove it when it becomes too burdensome for the patient, but that he or she has no positive duty to ensure that the patient will die at a certain time.

3. In any case, the principles on which negative eugenics rest themselves depend on a line between disease and enhancement. They therefore would not be able to guard the line between therapy and enhancement since their formulation would itself depend on where that line is drawn.

CHAPTER 3: UTOPIA, NIHILISM,
AND THE QUEST FOR RESPONSIBILITY

1. Jonas's account of technology agrees with Heidegger's in key respects (Heidegger, 1977, pp. 283–317). For both thinkers, technology is not only an instrument serving ends posited by human subjects, but a pervasive phenomenon that determines human being, knowing, and doing. For this reason, both Jonas and Heidegger reject the confidence of modern humanism that human beings are or can be masters of technology. Moreover, both Jonas and Heidegger find technology implicit in modern physics and its view of reality, and therefore reject the idea that technology is only applied science. Finally, for both Jonas and Heidegger technology as a way of being triumphs over and eclipses other ways of being in the world. In Jonas's terms modern technology constitutes the triumph of *homo faber* over homo sapiens and becomes the exclusive vocation of humanity (Jonas, 1984, p. 9).

2. This insight led Jonas to reject standard views of the freedom of scientific inquiry. If, as in the model of antiquity, knowledge of the object were also knowledge of the good, the "territorial morals of the scientific realm" would suffice, but now that knowing takes the form of *techne*, "the alibi of pure theory and with it the moral immunity it provided no longer hold" (Jonas, 1976, pp. 15, 16).

3. Each element of Jonas's description is controversial, and one may question whether when taken as a whole they adequately mark off technological action from the assumptions of pretechnological theories. For example, human beings have always acted upon nature, including human nature, and began doing so in a radical way with the invention of agriculture. Similarly, the cumulativity referred to in the third distinction characterizes pretechnological action both phylogenetically and ontogenetically, and is also a feature of all actions that occur within the progression of a moral or political tradition. However, Jonas is not necessarily referring to characteristics of action per se, but to the assumptions about action implied by previous forms of ethics and now called into question by technology. Hence with regard to the first point Jonas argues that interactions with nature were considered morally neutral since previous cultures lacked any belief that nature could be significantly affected by human actions and because technology was a means of securing survival rather than the human project itself (Jonas, 1984, p. 4). With regard to the third point Jonas concedes that self-cultivation and education are cumulative but minimizes this cumulativity since primal nature may always break through to reinstitute the primordial conditions of action (Jonas, 1984, p. 233, n. 4). However, this denial of the significance of cumulativity for premodern ethics seems somewhat forced.

4. The relation of Judaism and Christianity to the modern materialist worldview in general and to modern technology in particular has been a controversial topic since Lynn White laid the blame for the ecological crisis at the

doorstep of these traditions (White, 1967). Jonas has a considerably more subtle view. He recognizes that the doctrine of the creation of the world in Judaism and Christianity substituted the contingency of the world for its rational necessity, which was entailed in the Greek doctrine of the eternity of the world, and thereby devalued the world in comparison with the classical view. But more positively, the doctrine of creation made God the direct cause of matter, which is the principle of individuation, and thereby upheld the value of concrete and individual beings in a way that classical thought could not. Nevertheless, the value of the world is dependent on the divine will; and when faith in the revelation of the divine will diminished, the voluntarism entailed in this position ultimately made the human will the arbiter of all value (Jonas, 1974, pp. 21–44). In my judgment, Jonas does not pay enough attention to the subtle ways in which the neoplatonic chain of being and its principle of plenitude infiltrated Jewish and Christian thought and mitigated the sheer voluntarism implied in the doctrine of creation.

5. Jonas argues that the rejection of final causes did not follow any failure to detect them in nature, and is an axiom rather than an empirical conclusion. Rather, he finds the reason for their rejection in the long struggle of modern science against Aristotelianism which began with Bacon, in which final causes were seen to be a hindrance to the causes science was interested in discovering (Jonas, 1966, p. 34). This involves a methodological ground. But Jonas also identifies a metaphysical ground in Descartes's rigid separation of *res cogitans* and *res extensa* in which all finality was segregated into the former while the latter was the realm in which mathematical and mechanical analysis held sway (Jonas, 1966, p. 35). That this separation continues even when we no longer accept Cartesian metaphysics is for Jonas a psychological fact: "No discovery about the laws and functions of matter *logically* affects the possibility that these very laws and functions may subserve a spiritual, creative will. It is, however, the case . . . that the *psychological* atmosphere created by science and reinforced by technology is peculiarly unfavorable to the *visibility* of that transcendent dimension which the biblical propositions [regarding creation and the image of God] claim for the nature of things" (Jonas, 1974, p. 177).

6. Jonas adheres to an existentialist interpretation of Nietzsche, finding in him the boldest articulation of the modern subject and its exaltation of arbitrary will over norm.

7. Two distinct accounts of nihilism appear in Jonas's writings. One is instrumentalist or Baconian, the other is existentialist or Pascalian. According to the Baconian interpretation, modern science and technology render all objects neutral to whatever value human beings may bestow on them. Lacking intrinsic value, they are necessarily lower than that by which alone they receive value, namely, human willing, and are thus reduced to objects of use by human beings (Jonas, 1966, p. 195). One of Jonas's most poignant insights is that Baconian charity, which I discussed briefly in the previous section, confirms rather than alters this reduction to use (Jonas, 1966, p. 196). For Baconian charity, as I

pointed out in chapter one, unlike the love of the good in ancient (and medieval) thought, is precisely concerned with rendering the world useful to one's fellow human being. Since it is rooted in the will and can not be derived from knowledge of the object, charity is for Jonas at best ephemeral and at worst nihilistic. According to the Pascalian interpretation, the discovery of the immensity of space and the purposelessness of nature lead to a sense of cosmic solitude in which human beings inhabit a universe utterly indifferent to human purposes. The sole divine attribute the world of modern science exhibits is power. Hence the only possible stance of human beings toward an indifferent cosmos is to meet power with power (Jonas, 1966, p. 216). It was Jonas's extraordinary insight to connect this existentialist nihilism with a similar estrangement from the world that characterized Gnosticism. From this perspective, modern technology plays a role analogous to that of the gnostic savior and his gnosis insofar as "the countering of power with power is the sole relation to the totality of nature left for man in both cases" (Jonas, 1966, p. 221). Jonas recognizes an important difference between existentialism and Gnosticism: both saw the world as alien to human aspirations, but while the former views the world as indifferent to these aspirations the latter viewed the world as hostile to them. What Jonas does not seem to recognize is that the latter is not really nihilistic at all, since the world is charged with value, albeit negative value. There is for Gnosticism at least one objective moral truth about the world, namely that the world is evil.

8. An example Jonas does not mention is the development of mechanical respirators in medicine. Initially designed as temporary devices (i.e., means) to facilitate a given course of treatment, they soon gave rise to new procedures (i.e., ends) that radically altered the entire practice of medicine and called forth yet more novel technological innovations and procedures.

9. Artificiality is not the only salient characteristic of technology. As we have seen, Jonas emphasizes the dynamics of endless progress as well. As technology develops, it requires additional objects to produce its artifacts (e.g., machines), which in turn require industries in order to build them—industries that themselves undergo technological development, and so on. This "syndrome of self-proliferation," as Jonas terms it, "exponentially increases man's drain on nature's resources" not simply by increasing ends for consumption but by the production of the means (Jonas, 1979, pp. 38–39). Moreover, Jonas is aware of the factor Albert Borgmann describes so persuasively, namely the ways in which the objects of technology form and alter the patterns of social interaction that comprise the lived world, and change the nature of society and politics (Borgmann, 1984, pp. 35–153; cf. Jonas, 1979, pp. 39–40). Nevertheless, Jonas's theme is the triumph of making; therefore, artificiality is the most significant feature of technology for him.

10. Jonas's analysis once again resembles a key element in Heidegger's discussion of technology. For Heidegger, when reality concerns humanity exclusively as "standing-reserve" and humanity is nothing but the orderer of the

standing-reserve, then humanity itself comes to be taken as standing-reserve. Nevertheless, humanity so threatened exalts itself to lord of the earth, maintains the illusion that everything that exists is a human construct, and fosters the delusion that humanity encounters only itself (Heidegger, 1977, p. 308). If one substitutes Jonas's "artificiality" for Heidegger's "standing-reserve," this train of thought matches Jonas's understanding of the relation of technology to the subject. Heidegger goes on to say that in fact humanity in this condition nowhere encounters its essence, since that essence does not consist in ordering the standing-reserve but in hearing ordering as a claim—which changes the relation of humanity to technology. Jonas will similarly define the normatively human in terms of responsibility for that which has come under human control, as I will show.

11. This narrative captures Jonas's position, but it also oversimplifies it in two respects. First, it implies that Jonas believed that a shift from Marxist utopianism to a utopianism without a metanarrative has already occurred, but in fact he continued to assume the historical viability of Marxism, as is evidenced by his extended argument against Bloch (Jonas, 1984, pp. 192–201). This seems to me to be inconsistent with Jonas's continual emphasis on the nihilism of modern technology and on its formal dynamics, which comprise a "new realm of necessity" that ultimately controls the will that would make use of it for a conception of its good—an emphasis that would seem to lead to the recognition of technology as another form of incredulity toward metanarratives (Lyotard, 1984). Second, in addition to the Marxist utopianism, the automatic utopianism of technology overpowers another form of utopianism (if indeed it is utopian): that of the arbitrary individual which Jonas finds in Nietzsche's writings (Jonas, 1966, pp. 209–210; 1979, p. 42; 1984, pp. 157–158).

12. The similarity with Levinas is primarily at the level of description of the object of responsibility and its distinction from the object of classical ethics, which roughly corresponds to Levinas's distinction between metaphysics and ontology. However, the account Jonas gives of this object as an object of responsibility is vastly different from the phenomenology of alterity in Levinas. As I argue below, Jonas grounds responsibility in an ontology in which the premodern identity of being and the good receives a postcritical expression. For Levinas this is to ground the other in being and thus ultimately to deny its alterity (Cf. Levinas, 1969).

13. The original German version of Jonas's major work was published before Derek Parfit pointed out the now famous paradoxes involving harm to future persons. Many efforts to avoid harming future persons will themselves determine which future individual persons will exist. Does it make sense to avoid harming a future person (for example, by adopting certain toxic waste or clean air laws) when the result is that the person in question will not exist as a result of the policy? Conversely, do we harm the individual future persons who will in fact exist when they would not have existed at all had we refrained from the acts that allegedly harm them (Parfit, 1984)? These arguments support

Jonas's point that existing (secular) moral theories are ill equipped to address the altered nature of human action in the age of modern technology.

14. This is somewhat conjectural since Jonas never mentions Husserl or Heidegger in connection with his own project. Moreover, in his last public lecture he seems to place his own concern with the organic over against the entire German philosophical tradition in the twentieth century (Jonas, 1994). Nevertheless, it seems clear to me that Jonas defines his approach over against these two figures. Like Husserl, Jonas seeks to return to the things themselves as they are given in concrete experience in order to overcome the epistemological bifurcation between nature as a realm of pure extension and our sense experience. However, Jonas rejects Husserl's reduction of concrete experience to pure phenomena given to intuition, viewing this as another, doubtless much more subtle, form of idealism and another effort to evade the ontological question posed by the failure of dualism. In this respect, Jonas's phenomenology is indebted to Heidegger. For Heidegger, the world is not a phenomenon given to intuition but is constituted in the factual concreteness of Dasein. Phenomenology as a general hermeneutic uncovers the being of Dasein as that being which is concerned about its Being, namely its actualization of its existence in its world-constitution. Jonas seems to accept this project in general, but seeks to expand Dasein to include organic existence as such rather than simply human Dasein. For Jonas, the organism exhibits concern about its own being, "decides" its existence by seizing or neglecting possibilities, and actualizes its being in its consitution of the world. All of these are characteristics Heidegger ascribes to human Dasein. In sum, we will see that Jonas begins like Husserl with my concrete experience, in his case the experience of my body, which defies reduction to an *eidos* and thus leads him away from what he views as Husserl's continuation of idealism and its philosophy of perception. Rather than a reduction, phenomenology is as with Heidegger an interpretation of Dasein, only now it is the Dasein of the living body, not of the being that raises the question of its Being. But here Jonas runs into problems. For Heidegger, the ontological question can be answered within the terms established by the starting point, namely Dasein as the being that asks the question of Being. But it is not clear how Jonas's starting point, namely my living body, can furnish an ontology of organism in general. Hence his move from my living body to an ontology of organic existence in general seems to take the form of inference or analogy and to draw on theory in precisely the ways phenomenology seeks to avoid. Richard Zaner arrives at a similar conclusion, though from a different understanding of Jonas's relation to the phenomenological tradition (Zaner, 1981, pp. 16–20).

15. Jonas's major point here is that the living body qua phenomenon, that is, *my* body, involves a transgression or trespass of the categories of idealism and materialism because inwardness and outwardness occur together in the phenomenon. More precisely, inwardness extends itself as itself into the outward. Compare Jonas on this point with Heidegger's explication of *physis* as "inward-jutting-beyond-itself ("in-sich-aus-sich-hinausstehen") (Heidegger, 1959, p. 14).

16. Jonas's overall argument against epiphenomenalism is much more complex than I have indicated and includes a thought experiment designed to show how the causal efficacy of mind is intelligible within the frameworks of both classical mechanics and quantum theory (Jonas, 1984, pp. 216–231). My justification for ignoring this thought experiment and restricting myself to mentioning only one part of the negative argument is that in developing it Jonas notes that he has made concessions to materialism and its conception of matter that he does not himself accept (Jonas, 1984, pp. 221–222).

17. One could compare this receptivity to the relation of the sublime to moral feeling in Kant, to Heidegger's analysis of guilt (*Schuldigkeit*), and to the recognition of one's violence against the Other that accompanies the epiphany of the Other in Levinas. In distinction to all of these, the feeling of responsibility is for Jonas a psychological disposition.

18. Of course, given Jonas's view of the dynamics of technology there may be little reason to distinguish uses of technology that put the existence of humans as responsible beings at risk from those that involve smaller scale interventions into human nature; in all cases modern technology is cumulative and irreversible. Moreover, when Jonas first became interested in biological technologies his apocalyptic perspective was widely shared. The enthusiasm over developments especially in genetics but also in behavior control that were the focus of much scientific discussion during the 1960s and early 1970s, the (as it turns out, misguided) optimism about the imminent applicability of many of these developments, and the sense that once developed, they would prove irresistible to the scientific community, led many scientists, theologians and philosophers to voice warnings similar to his.

19. Even here, questions could be raised. Are those who participate not because they identify with the cause but because they need or want money guilty of reducing themselves to things? They certainly express a purpose, but it could on Jonas's terms be a purpose that destroys their purposiveness, if only momentarily. But it seems awkward to call them mere samples or tokens; they are consciously expressing a purpose. However, it is possible to call them victims of injustice if they are poor single mothers or starving graduate students who have no other means of meeting needs.

20. One is entitled to ask why Jonas permits interference with nature at the individual level. Though he does not attempt to justify this kind of interference, the fact that it accomplishes good for the person and has no long-range consequences on the gene pool is an argument for it on consequentialist grounds.

21. This view is perfectly compatible, for example, with the view that humans ought to limit their population and consumption for the sake of other beings.

22. Jonas does attempt, admittedly without a conclusive verdict, to state the argument in the discourse of quantum mechanics (Jonas, 1984, pp. 222–231). Today he would also have to develop it against the new reductionisms of cognitive science.

23. This hunch is strengthened by looking at the way two of Jonas's Christian counterparts, Paul Ramsey and James Gustafson, have dealt with the possible future nonexistence of human beings. For Ramsey, Christian eschatology (Ramsey thinks he speaks for Judaism as well) assures believers that there will be a time when there are none like us to come after us. For this reason Christians can countenance, without denial or fear, any apocalypse nature may have in store for us according to the predictions of geneticists or astrophysicists. Knowing this, Christians are relieved of the need to succeed in preventing genetic deterioration or, one may suppose, in ensuring that humanity will exist forever. Thus freed from the need to ensure the success of our projects, Ramsey argues that our attention should focus instead on the moral rightness of the means by which we carry out our aims in, for example, negative eugenics or population control (Ramsey, 1970a, pp. 22–32). Gustafson is even less disturbed by the future disappearance of humanity, arguing that the findings of astrophysicists and others make it clear that there will be a *finis* to life on earth, and that human thinking about the place of human beings in the divine order and in the morality that follows from it should change accordingly. Concretely, this means that the horizon of moral concerns about the future is far broader than the future existence of human beings (Gustafson, 1981, pp. 82–83). It seems likely that these dismissals of the importance of human perpetuity would sound all too casual to Jonas's Jewish ears.

24. Richard Zaner has pointed this out in the case of Jonas's polarity between form and matter (Zaner, 1981, pp. 20–21). I believe that the criticism applies to the polarities more generally, though not in all of Jonas's formulations.

CHAPTER 4: MEDICINE AND THE ETHICS OF VOCATION

1. Gustafson's concise summary of the task of theological ethics—"to relate ourselves and all things in a manner (or in ways) appropriate to their relations to God" (Gustafson, 1984, p. 2)—conveys a strong role for human beings in the ordering activity of God that is consistent with the activist Calvinist ethic of vocation. Gustafson says, "relate ourselves and all things," not "relate *to* ourselves and all things"; human beings are to be active participants in the divine ordering, not quiescent conformers to it. Gustafson argues that this point distinguishes him from Stoics such as Epictetus (Gustafson, 1983, pp. 499–501).

2. The alert reader will have noticed a subtle and unargued shift from the descriptive "naturally" to the normative "properly." To some moral philosophers, of course, this is illicit, but even those who accept the "new naturalism" of Stuart Hampshire, Iris Murdoch, or Hilary Putnam may wonder what authorizes this move in Gustafson. I am anticipating a theme I address below, but in

my judgment the authorization is the notion of participation or vocation itself. In classical Protestant terms, God calls human beings to the service of God and others. Gustafson tends to replace the anthropomorphic language of "calling" with the cultivation and exercise of natural capacities in fulfilment of divine purposes for oneself and for larger wholes in which one participates. The ultimate backing is in either case the divine purpose for persons. In earlier writings Gustafson referred to divine intentions and the well-being of humans and the whole creation: "Since God wills well-being, the theological moral point of view is one which directs human action toward the realization of potentialities for value that are present in nature and in history" (Gustafson, 1975b, pp. 30–31). Hence biomedical research and practice are justified by their contributions to the well-being of creation, though within the limitations Gustafson is always sensitive to. Later, Gustafson refers neither to divine intentions nor to the well-being of creation but to the divine ordering, a less personalistic and less unambiguously teleological notion which justifies biomedical research and practice by how they "fit" into this ordering. Gustafson's metaethical naturalism is in general consonant with other similar positions in religious ethics (Cf. Geertz, 1973, pp. 126–141; Lovin and Reynolds, 1985, pp. 1–35; Stout, 1981).

3. In accordance with this conviction, Gustafson describes vocation itself in both self- regarding and other-regarding terms: vocation bestows dignity on an individual by virtue of her occupation, and vocations exist for the service to others and to the common good (Gustafson, 1982a).

4. Gustafson is particularly critical of Kant in this regard (Gustafson, 1984, pp. 116–141) but he also criticizes Catholic moral theology for its emphasis on the avoidance of sinful acts even when harmful consequences for others follow (Gustafson, 1990a). This same point was a decisive factor in Gustafson's criticism of the way health professionals handled the famous Johns Hopkins Down Syndrome case (Gustafson, 1973; cf. also 1984, p. 314).

5. Gustafson seems to hold a critical realist position that reality exists independent of language but can never be experienced or known as independent. It is impossible to separate experience of reality from its articulation in the language of particular communities, so that whatever common experience or experience of a common reality might mean for Gustafson (he does not clarify it) it does not mean that we can scrape off layers of particular articulations in order to identify it (Gustafson, 1981, pp. 120–128). But while he avoids a naive representationalism his formulations are subject to the standard criticisms of empiricist assumptions about the priority of reality to language.

6. The most basic disagreement here is over language: Gustafson, as I indicated, believes language articulates experience whereas Lindbeck and others believe that a particular language is the a priori that makes experiences what they are. For Gustafson a corollary is that religion shapes and transforms common human experience (Gustafson, 1975a, pp. 48–81; cf. also Niebuhr, 1941, pp. 114–139). Therefore the claim that there is discontinuity with the articula-

tions of scripture is in effect a claim that the natural is never fully transformed by the scriptural; for Gustafson this is an empirical claim. This sheds light on Gustafson's response (Gustafson, 1985) to criticisms of his work by Lisa Cahill (Cahill, 1985), Stanley Hauerwas (Hauerwas, 1985b), and Richard McCormick (McCormick, 1985). Gustafson insists that his interlocutors confront *evidence* from the natural and social sciences that dispute their claims about the extent to which biblical language absorbs the world. But central to his critics is the conviction that there is no evidence that is not always already a complex product of the language and practices of particular communities. Both Gustafson and his critics could agree that Christians do not fully succeed in absorbing their world into the world of scripture, but they would offer different explanations. Gustafson would argue that the concepts and symbols of a particular tradition are always mediated through a common experience and nature that they never fully determine, while his critics, or at least Hauerwas, would argue that the Christian life is a lifelong process of learning the cognitive and moral skills to reinscribe the world into the Christian story.

7. Even within Gustafson's critical realism there is good reason to quarrel with the requirement that theological claims must be consistent with or indicated by the sciences. This is appropriate when, in terms of Gustafson's scheme, questions about the divine ordering arise. If one agrees with Gustafson on participation as the central task of ethics, it is reasonable to expect the sciences to tell us a lot about how things are concretely related to God. But given the limits of nature in the strict sense in determining human life (nature itself leaves a great deal of room for culture in ordering human life, e.g.) and the limits of the kind of knowledge the sciences give us, Gustafson overstates the role of scientific methods and data in theology. He ordinarily does not have a naive positivistic view of the sciences, but unless one has such a view it seems absurd to hand over to the sciences issues regarding God's being and character, for example, or the question of whether God has intentions (Gustafson, 1981, pp. 269–271). There may be good theological and philosophical reasons for arriving at the same conclusion as Gustafson does, but to expect the sciences to pronounce on it indicates a misconception of what types of inquiry and what kinds of questions the sciences pursue.

8. This is somewhat ironic since Gustafson sharply criticizes those who simply develop a theological ethic to support a moral theory that stands independent of the theology. Gustafson's position is far more complex than most of these efforts since he begins with a theological question—What is God enabling and requiring us to be and do?—which itself leads him to the material that could stand independent of his theology; and as I show below, this material—his evaluative descriptions of nature—is developed in a strongly theological direction. Therefore many words have to be said before the last word, but the last word is that Gustafson is closer to those he criticizes than he is to, say, Karl Barth. Part of the reason for this is that Gustafson is a product of the predicament the Enlightenment emphasis on epistemology created for theology. Since

theology could not meet the qualifications for knowledge, it had to be grounded in something else: a postulate for morality as in Kant or a new category such as feeling in Schleiermacher. Gustafson's criticism of some of his theological colleagues is something of a Schleiermachian criticism of theological Kantians. In other words, he criticizes their use of theological claims as postulates that support a set of independently derived moral principles while proposing piety as a motive and rationale for granting moral significance to a set of descriptions about nature. A way out of the dilemma is to regard both theology and the sciences as ways of describing the world.

9. It is noteworthy that Gustafson's critique of natural law does not focus on the historical, dynamic, and interpersonal features of human nature that have occupied so many Catholic "revisionists." Nor does it focus on a neo-Aristotelian view of human nature as characterized by direction of virtues to their final end. Rather, natural law is revised due to the power and scope of human interventions into nature.

10. In recent editions of their *Principles of Biomedical Ethics* Tom Beauchamp and James Childress have recognized the inevitability of particularity in defining the circumstances in which principles are applied to cases, but they fail to describe either the process by which circumstances are described or the content of the description (Beauchamp and Childress, 1989; 1994). For Albert Jonsen and Stephen Toulmin description of circumstances is central to the move from paradigm cases to new cases but they seem to believe there is a single canonical description of a case that need not take account of particular sensibilities, perspectives, or beliefs (Jonsen and Toulmin, 1988).

11. H. Richard Niebuhr exhibits the critical, substantively agnostic position in his essay, "The Center of Value," which otherwise has a very strong influence on Gustafson. After a rich description of the irreducible relationality of value Niebuhr considers the unavoidability of taking a standpoint in or with some being as the center of value around which the various value relations are ordered. Niebuhr rejects such an absolute position for any finite reality on the grounds of its arbitrariness. God alone can serve as the center of value. But this theocentric standpoint is primarily critical: it prevents the absolutizing and even privileging of any finite center of value, though it also allows tentative and experimental orderings for limited purposes (Niebuhr, 1960, pp. 109–114).

12. This extreme is exhibited in the use the Catholic tradition has often made of Thomas Aquinas's discussion of natural law in the *Summa Theologica*. The issue is the status of the primary premoral goods in I–II, Question 94, article 2. According to one influential group of moral theologians these goods are intrinsic and incommensurable and thus not subject to weighing or prioritizing by prudential considerations. Acting against these goods is intrinsically wrong. This extreme also has at least two Protestant versions. One is that of Jonathan Edwards who like Augustine bases an order of love and justice on the order of being in which beings are proportioned by their degrees of being and goodness.

This metaphysical-moral order is at least in principle knowable, though Edwards gives only schematic descriptions of the order itself and says little about how one makes particular judgments on the basis of it (Edwards, 1989, pp. 550–560). A second, which Gustafson explicitly refers to, is that of Karl Barth (Gustafson, 1984, pp. 29–30). In an early volume of his *Church Dogmatics* Barth makes strong claims for the specificity and objective (though not subjective) certitude of divine commands (Barth, 1957, pp. 661–708). But as Gustafson realizes, for Barth there is no human certainty and the process of moral judgment is much more complex. Paul Lehmann, whom Gustafson discusses throughout his works, is probably a better example.

13. The degree of disagreement can be easily exaggerated. For example, while Niebuhr is skeptical about knowledge of any divine ordering however provisional he does allow for various provisional standpoints wherein goods are ordered around tentative centers of value. Hence while there is no effort to discern a divine ordering, moral reason apparently requires consideration of the goods of various parts and wholes and their complex relations to one another. In the case of Aquinas, the disagreement may be with one set of his interpreters rather than with Aquinas himself, since the latter could be construed as proposing an ordering of premoral goods subject to proportional considerations at all levels (provided no moral evil is committed) as the "revisionists" have argued (cf. Janssens, 1977; McCormick, 1978).

14. One of Gustafson's favorite hard cases involves consent in medical experimentation. Gustafson draws an admittedly weak yet interesting analogy between military conscription and extreme emergency cases when the consent requirement may be overridden (Gustafson, 1975b, pp. 45–46 [here the analogy is strained since justifiable military conscription occurs under conditions of unjust attack while for Gustafson at this earlier stage risks may be taken for the attainment of "new possibilities for the well-being of individuals, the human community, and the whole of creation"]; 1984, pp. 309–310). The analogy rests on the interpretation of a preventable disease as an aggressor against the health of a community. Gustafson hedges his case for the justifiability of overriding consent by setting weighty conditions on the degrees of risk of harm (less than that of death in combat or perhaps harm that falls short of death) that could be tolerated and requiring procedural fairness in the distribution of risks and the selection of candidates.

15. In the case of subjecting children to experimentation without consent, Gustafson asks, "Would one deprive the whole population of children susceptible to a communicable and life-threatening disease of a probably successful vaccine because children as an experimental population cannot give fully informed consent to participation?" If one gives a negative answer, as Gustafson presumably would under at least some circumstances, this does not eliminate the painful and potentially tragic feature of children put at risk for the sake of others without giving consent (Gustafson, 1984, p. 272) A strong deontological position might, in the manner of Charles Fried,

Michael Walzer, or Gilbert Meilaender, regard such a case as a "supreme emergency" wherein moral rules may be overridden. Meilaender denies this introduces a consequential element into morality since he gives no moral justification of such acts (Meilaender, 1991, pp. 106–108). But for Gustafson this seems to evade some troublesome implications of a rigidly deontological ethics and some uncomfortable conclusions about the nature of a God who does not order the world such that human beings can avoid such dilemmas. The most significant differences are Gustafson's willingness to give at least a conditional moral justification in some such instances and his unwillingness to shield God from human anger, as the last sentence of the quotation indicates.

16. Edward Farley touches on Gustafson's empiricism in his discussion of the relation of Gustafson's "commonsense ontology" to the naturalism of the 1930s and 1940s in American theology and philosophy (Farley, 1988). Lisa Cahill discusses the role of unrelieved suffering in Gustafson's project (Cahill, 1985).

17. A good example here is the recent stance of the Catholic Church. After repeating the traditional arguments against suicide, the Sacred Congregation for the Doctrine of the Faith notes that at times "psychological factors may lessen or even completely eliminate responsibility" for an act of taking one's life. It is clear that this is not a justification—suicide remains a mortal sin—but it seeks to account for a common conviction of the inappropriateness of moral blame for many suicides (Sacred Congregation, 1987, p. 442).

18. For Barth such judgments are inappropriate for two reasons. First, the person contemplating suicide believes he or she is abandoned by God. Such a person is radically alone and left to his or her own sovereignty. Moral injunctions are entirely ineffectual against such a self whose sovereignty and despair have carried him or her beyond good and evil. But there is a second reason. Moral injunctions can only deepen despair and mask its source in the solitary sovereignty of the self by forcing on such a self the "vain and godless notion that he must live." Such a person instead needs to hear the affirmation that he or she "may" live, not in his or her own sovereignty but in God's grace. Hence for Barth (whose discussion of affliction bears interesting resemblances to Emile Durkheim's notion of *anomie*) suicide is the spiritual sickness of modernity for which grace is the cure (Barth, 1961, pp. 400–413).

19. Chapter two addressed the tendency of many of these accounts to identify self- determination and certain consequential considerations as the only morally significant features. Even among physicians, who are more likely than philosophers to recognize other moral responsibilities, these are often confined to a duty to relieve the suffering that results from illness (cf. Brody, 1992; Cassel and Meier, 1990; Quill, et al., 1992). Most of these accounts wittingly or unwittingly assume with Aquinas and Kant that individuals are in control of the conditions that enable them to act from (self-chosen) reasons except when they are in great pain or clinically depressed.

20. Here Barth's account is helpful. Barth in effect links modern suicide to the solitariness of the modern self who, believing him- or herself to be abandoned by God finds him- or herself exercising sovereignty without content. Suicide as an exercise of this empty sovereignty is also the final confirmation of abandonment (Barth, 1961, pp. 400–413).

21. Indeed the accomplishments and shortcomings of medicine seem to have prompted many of Gustafson's central insights. Medicine is first of all a vocation in the precise sense indicated in this first section of this chapter. It is not first of all the living out of a covenant fidelity as it is for Paul Ramsey but an arena of life in which interventions into natural processes produce benefits for individuals and communities (Gustafson, 1984, p. 253). Moreover, medicine is a paradigm instance of the expanded scope of human interventions into nature, as its capacities to intervene into birth processes, to extend life, and now to begin to alter genes make clear. "Medicine is an area in which culture very dramatically 'stands between' human possibilities and the natural course of events" (Gustafson, 1984, p. 275). Medicine does not leave nature as it is; it intervenes into natural processes for benefits to human beings. Moreover, it confronts nature somewhat in Baconian fashion as a threat to human survival and well-being that must be overcome. "Nature is the enemy as well as the friend of man. . . . Medicine, as a part of culture, is a means of warding off the debilitating and death-dealing consequences of natural processes" (Gustafson, 1984, p. 273). Yet medicine cannot simply master nature in Baconian fashion. Rather, "interventions reorder natural processes that are occurring and thus there is still a basic dependence on the powers of life that are beyond human control" (Gustafson, 1984, p. 273). In an interdependent world medicine cooperates with natural processes. The success of medicine is one of the best evidences that nature and its laws are not immutable. For this reason, nature cannot serve as a fixed standard to judge the appropriateness of interventions. But there are limits to medicine. Not all legitimate human needs can be met by the available resources. Interventions create new social and moral problems. For example, the capacity to extend biological life leads to questions about the value of those lives to individuals and the consequences for an aging society. Beyond all this there is an ultimate limit to what medicine can do in the face of death and disease (Gustafson, 1984, p. 277).

22. In other words, if a consequentialist account gives one reasons for favoring research leading to prevention or to interventions early in the disease process, justice would require fair distribution under this criterion. But claims on behalf of justice would not be used to favor some criteria over others or to rule some out. Gustafson does, however, make one substantive claim about justice, arguing that distribution of therapies by the market alone is unjust since public funds support the research that leads to the therapies (Gustafson, 1984, p. 264).

23. See endnotes 14 and 15 above.

24. Here I am largely repeating what Aristotle and Aquinas said about the relationship between human nature and virtue. Both Stuart Hampshire (Hampshire, 1983, pp. 126–139) and Alasdair MacIntyre (MacIntyre, 1988, pp. 183–208) argue both in general and with respect to Aristotle and Aquinas, respectively, against the notion that morally relevant claims about nature are independent of a particular tradition. Clifford Geertz has argued from an anthropological perspective against the possibility of separating nature and culture (Geertz, 1973, pp. 55–83).

CHAPTER 5: MEDICINE AS A MORAL ART

1. Expansive definitions and narrow "disease" definitions are sometimes not as easily distinguished as Kass implies since it has (perhaps always) been the practice of medicine to define as diseases deviant social practices, hindrances to individual or societal aspirations, and conditions that are accompanied by mental anguish. Thus in the past masturbation and homosexuality were regarded as diseases; today infertility and "attention deficit disorder" are. In these and many other cases, the "narrow" disease model makes it possible to carry out the expansive WHO definition by redescribing undesirable conditions and practices as diseases calling for medical intervention.

2. Kass's universalism may not be as unyielding as it first appears. At one point he argues that the difference between being healthy and being unhealthy is what is nonconventional and thus universal, thus implying that there may be different concepts of health (though he may only mean that there are different concepts of diseases) (Kass, 1985, p. 169). In another place he holds that health is "to some extent" relative to individuals, though this falls well short of a subjectivist thesis (Kass, 1985, p. 173). Kass's affirmation of health as a natural and nonrelative good at first appears to make him an ally of Christopher Boorse, who has argued against relativistic and subjectivistic conceptions of health. Boorse defines health in terms of normality of biological function, where normality is understood in a statistical sense (Boorse, 1977). But given what I have already noted about Kass's favoring of ordinary experience over the abstractions of modern science, one would expect him to reject the key features of Boorse's account. For Boorse is rigidly committed to health as a value-free conception and to a view of nature in which the normal can be determined statistically. But since Kass rejects the rigid separation of fact and value, universality and objectivity do not for him require value freedom. Moreover, for Kass normality of function is determined by a general and somewhat intuitive conception of wholeness and well functioning grounded in ordinary experience rather than by biostatistics as Boorse maintains.

3. Maimonides, himself a physician as well as a rabbi and philosopher, articulates the traditional view of the relation of medicine to virtue that Kass develops here. He places medicine high above the other *technai*. "To study it dili-

gently is among the greatest acts of worship. It is, then, not like weaving and carpentry, for it enables us to perform our actions so that they become human actions, leading to the virtues and the truths" (Maimonides, 1975, pp. 75–76). Hence, "preserving the body's health and strength is among the ways of the Lord"—but not an end in itself, as Maimonides continues: "for to attain understanding and knowledge [of God, the highest end of human life] is impossible when one is sick" (Maimonides, 1975, p. 36). The health of the body is a genuine but subordinate good: health is valued not as an end in itself but because it is necessary to attain the highest good. Hence, "if [one] makes his goal solely the health of his body and its being free from illness, he is not virtuous." Such a person is no different from one who "prefers the pleasure of eating or sexual intercourse," for "neither has a true goal for his actions." As an end in itself health is not superior to other lesser goods. Its superior value is due solely to its being a condition for attaining the highest good. Therefore the proper reason to pursue the health of the body is so that "the instruments of the soul's powers—which are the organs of the body—remain sound. Then the soul can be directed toward the moral and rational virtues without any obstacle" (Maimonides, 1975, p. 76). As for the way to attain health, Maimonides emphasizes the elements of classical regimen: diet, hygiene, and sound eating and sexual habits (Maimonides, 1975, pp. 36–41).

4. Kass clearly views his own efforts, described below, to ground ethics in nature as Aristotelian (Kass, 1985, p. 319). But there is disagreement about whether or how Aristotle attempts to derive an account of human flourishing from nature. In Book I of the *Nicomachean Ethics*, after arguing that the good for human beings must be happiness since this is always chosen for its own sake rather than for something else, Aristotle goes on to argue that a less platitudinous conception of the good can be derived from the function that distinguishes humans from other beings, which turns out to be rational activity of which virtue is the standard (Aristotle, 1097a–1098a). But substantive appeals to nature play no role in the account that follows, though the arguments regarding pleasure and contemplation may imply some such appeal. Julia Annas argues that Aristotle uses nature in two senses, namely as the raw material for ethical development and as the source of a being's inner development toward its telos. The former, in which nature is not a moral guide, is most prominent in the *Nicomachean Ethics*, while the latter is most prominent in other works, notably the first book of the politics where Aristotle's notorious teachings about the natural status of the state, of women, and of slaves are found (Annas, 1993, pp. 142–158). If Annas is correct, Kass's claims about nature as a moral guide are not supported by the *Nicomachean Ethics*.

5. Kass's criticism of the emphasis of modern science is in no way a rejection of modern science. Instead he promotes his attention to form and teleology as a supplement to a science that leaves out the questions most important for human flourishing and the aspects of reality most accessible to ordinary experience. "[T]he teachings and discoveries of science are at best partial—indeed,

partial in *principle*" (Kass, 1985, p. 7). As a supplement rather than an alternative, Kass's biology with its focus on formal and final causes must be compatible with the findings of the sciences with regard to material and efficient causes (Kass, 1985, p. 8). This raises philosophical questions about the precise relation of Kass's biology to that of modern science—questions Kass does not answer, though he appears to favor a Kantian compatibilist account of, say, the relation between mechanistic and teleological accounts (Kass, 1985, p. 258 n.).

6. This does not mean that Kass considers these theoretical issues unimportant. In fact, on one of these issues—the relation of form to matter—Kass's formulation, which emphasizes the relativity and interdependence of form and matter, is actually superior to Jonas's formulation in that it breaks with the notion that form imposes order on matter. It thus overcomes the metaphysical dualism that still lingers in Jonas (Kass, 1994, pp. 35–36). Characteristically, Kass does not dwell on this or any other metaphysical point; he is convinced that what form can tell us about the functioning and flourishing of human beings and other organisms does not depend on the answers to such questions.

7. Kass himself presents his position as an instance of Oakeshott's first type over against standard bioethics as an instance of his second type. But he is certainly mistaken here, since he wants morality to be appropriately reflective. In contrast, under Oakeshott's first type "conduct is as nearly as possible without reflection" (Oakeshott, 1989, p. 187). Unlike Kass, Oakeshott is careful to point out that his first two types are in fact ideal extremes. Recent interpreters of modern morality often argue that the latter also has its habitual and dispositional elements. Oakeshott would seem to agree; for him the actual morality of the west conforms to his fourth type, which is a mixture of the first two types in which the reflective, not the habitual, is dominant but does not exclude habit and disposition altogether.

8. Numerous bioethical issues arise here, including embryo experimentation, cryopreservation, embryo selection, and potential germ-line gene therapy. Experimentation is the only one Kass discusses (1985, pp. 106–110).

9. Kass's most plausible argument turns on a distinction between the embryo, which is viable inasmuch as it can still be implanted into a womb, and the aborted fetus, which until late stages of pregnancy is not viable. Since the latter is absolutely nonviable experimentation on it is permissible, but not on the preimplantation embryo.

10. Commentators on official Catholic teaching often ignore the importance of this concern to the Church. The Vatican "Instruction on Respect for Human Life in its Origin and on the Dignity of Procreation," from which my remarks on the Catholic position are drawn, worries that IVF "entrusts the life and identity of the embryo into the power of doctors and biologists and establishes the domination of technology over the origin and destiny of the human person" (Congregation, 1988, p. 163). The reason for this concern is that "the ori-

gin of a human person is the result of an act of giving," which is inconsistent with the subjection of a future child "to conditions of technical efficiency which are to be evaluated according to standards of control and domination" (Congregation, 1988, p. 163).

11. In contrast to Kass, for the Roman Catholic Church the normatively natural is found not in lineage per se but in the inseparability of the unitive and the procreative meanings of the conjugal act. The dignity and self-esteem of the child therefore rest not on his or her place in a lineage, although this is obviously implied, but rather in his or her origin in an act of giving between mother and father (Congregation, 1988, pp. 162–163). The morally significant context is not lineage but marriage and the norms inscribed in the persons and their union (Congregation, 1988, p. 145, 147). For Paul Ramsey also, the unitive and procreative belong together by nature, though the context of their inseparability is the union of the two persons in the covenant of a marriage as a whole rather than each act of conjugal love (Ramsey, 1970a, pp. 32–35). In neither Catholicism nor Ramsey's traditional Protestant perspective is having a child of one's own viewed as natural in a normative way that would justify IVF. This leads me to wonder as I did with Jonas whether Kass's emphasis on lineage is due more to its relatively greater (though not absolute) importance in Judaism than to reflection on nature.

12. From the very beginning Kass has recognized that the question of what constitutes health is different from the question of the importance of health for a given patient. Initially this distinction indicated one obvious sense in which health is relative even when nonrelativity is claimed for it. Health, Kass admits, is relative to environment in the sense that persons with certain disorders may not suffer or may suffer only incidentally from them under particular conditions of climate, diet, occupation, or lifestyle. This means that such conditions can be ignored, overcome, or rendered less incapacitating by changes of lifestyle or environment. In such cases, Kass argues, the distinction between health and unhealth loses much or all of its importance, but nevertheless remains; a person without these conditions is still healthier than one who has them even when the latter may not actually suffer from them (Kass, 1985, pp. 167–168). Now, however, Kass implies that one way of life—a particular set of beliefs and practices regarding a worthy life—may not require health to the extent that another one does. What Kass does not seem to realize is that the claim that medicine aims at health has little force unless the physician knows what importance health has for the patient in front of him or her. In other words, even if health is universal the physician properly aims not at health as an end but at the importance of health, and the patient is the proper judge of this importance.

13. A profound Christian critique of Kass's primacy of biological kinship comes from Karl Barth. Barth argues from a survey of biblical parenthood that the meaning of lineage does not come from biological kinship. Rather, God commands human parenthood as a symbol of God's fatherhood over

human beings. This means concretely that while biological parenthood has weight and honor the meaning of parenthood can be fulfilled outside of it, and that the parental authority given by the fifth commandment is a spiritual authority that must be qualified by the first commandment and thus by the child's relationship to God (Barth, 1961, pp. 240–249). Because the meaning of parenthood has already been fulfilled in Christ as God's Son, there is no longer any unconditional command to propogate the human race. To have children is not a moral or natural necessity but a couple's confidence that God is offering the gift of a life through them. Both must believe they are capable of the task (Barth, 1961, pp. 268–273). Barth's disagreement with Kass is not on whether extramarital IVF is appropriate. Marriage is the proper context for having children for Barth—though he sharply rejects the notions that an unmarried mother has less dignity, that an unmarried father has fewer responsibilities, and that the former should be regarded differently from the latter (Barth, 1961, p. 277). The major difference is that Barth rejects the absolute claim of the natural, and thus of the primacy of lineage, as a false command (Barth, 1957, pp. 583–584). The natural for Barth is subordinate to the command of God because the true human is humanity as elected, justified, and sanctified by God in Jesus Christ (Barth, 1960, pp. 71–202). Hence the true meaning of biological lineage is its symbolic meaning, and its authority is qualified accordingly. However, it would be wrong to conclude that Barth ignores or denigrates nature as a moral source in the way that, say, Joseph Fletcher does. The natural is for him a sign or symptom of the truly human, which enables the biological to have the symbolic meaning it does, and Barth not infrequently appeals to the natural in his treatments of ethical issues. One unfortunate result of Kass's position is that it requires us to lump Barth and Fletcher together as "Persians."

CHAPTER 6: MEDICINE AND THE RECONCILING COMMUNITY

1. This may seem to contradict the chief moral commitment of liberalism if Judith Shklar is correct that the latter is founded on the avoidance of cruelty (Shklar, 1984, pp. 7–44). But for Hauerwas the most definitive commitment of the Christian community is to nonviolence, so that from the claim that substantive moral commitments are incompatible with the avoidance of all harm it does not follow that deliberate doing or causing harm is justified. Nevertheless, Hauerwas's substantive moral community—the Christian community—does not put cruelty first; it foresees that harm will inevitably follow from its moral commitments and is not willing to abandon its commitments to avoid that prospect, as one who puts cruelty first is willing to do (cf. Hauerwas, 1994, pp. 18, 197). However, as I show below, Hauerwas regards as self-deceptive the liberal claim to have avoided violence, since putting cruelty first does violence to all who have substantive moral convictions.

2. Because he fails to make clear what this moral significance is, Hauerwas's position ironically resembles a restatement (in the language of commitments that define a way of life rather than the language of narrowly moral duties) of the strict deontologist's position that denies tragedy because it denies that there is a valid and binding duty to bring about nonmoral goods or avoid nonmoral evils when doing so would require violation of a moral duty. If foregone survival and inevitable harms have no moral value, then if they are the result of living according to our moral commitments there is no tragedy involved. I do not think that Hauerwas agrees with this, but his failure to argue (as Nussbaum does so eloquently) for the appropriateness of moral regret or remorse at such results leaves the tragic element unclarified.

3. As I show below, this discourse of alienation and presence is, like nearly everything Hauerwas writes about medicine, rooted in theological claims.

4. On these grounds Hauerwas rejects Paul Ramsey's interpretation of covenant in the Kantian terms of respect for persons (Ramsey, 1970b, pp. xii–xv, 5–11). "To be a member of a covenant is to be loyal to the commitments of a community in a manner that renders suspect the placing of individual interests before those of the community and the object of loyalty that the community serves" (Hauerwas, 1986, p. 134). The difference between Hauerwas and Ramsey is theological: the question is whether being covenant partners means having mutual respect for one another as individuals prior to any determination of the good (Ramsey) or being members of a community largely defined by its commitment to shared goods (Hauerwas). Of course, Ramsey permits voluntary assumption of risks by competent adults for the benefit of others. But Hauerwas goes beyond this. "Given the Christian assumption that we are called to be of service to one another I see no reason why some might not be drafted to be of help to one another—e.g., to share blood—without their consent" (Hauerwas, 1995, p. 6). This stance has implications for cases of proxy consent: children may have moral standing in a community such that they may be expected to contribute to the good of that community. Hence Hauerwas sides with Gustafson (and with Richard McCormick) against Ramsey: "I am suggesting that sometimes communities can choose in a morally humane manner to assume that the child has moral standing in the community even when the child cannot choose that standing on his own." However, unlike Gustafson (and McCormick) he draws a line between the goods of a particular community and that of society as a whole, presumably because the latter has survival rather than richer convictions about a worthy life as its end. "As humans we share a moral capacity and needs, but such capacity and needs are not sufficient to ground concrete moral judgments; that requires the convictions and practices of specific actual communities" (Hauerwas, 1986, p. 137). Still, it is difficult to determine exactly what ends Hauerwas has in mind and thus difficult to determine how they differ from needs and capacities that human beings share by virtue of being human. It is also unclear how any particular community would determine which of its ends justify such risks and what criteria and procedures

would govern how they are carried out. Gustafson addresses these issues; without doing so Hauerwas raises the very concerns that lead many people to Ramsey's conclusions regarding consent in human experimentation.

5. There is a further irony here that Hauerwas does not make explicit. Having allowed medicine to try to eliminate all of our suffering as pointless, we then empower it to increase our pointless suffering by extending our lives in a way that usually involves significant suffering, but without our having any sense of the worth of our lives that would give such suffering a point.

6. The relation of Hauerwas's metaethics to other contemporary versions is complex, in part because Hauerwas's comments are sketchy, lack philosophical rigor, and are derived from a variety of probably incompatible sources. But the complexity in Hauerwas's writings as in those of others who work out of religious traditions may also be due in part to the fact that most metaethical theories are devised for modern moral theories and are ill-suited to robust religious traditions for which accounts of the way things are do constitute reasons for action (Lovin and Reynolds, 1985). In general, Hauerwas's account of moral notions seems to be realist insofar as moral notions group together features of events and situations, yet it also seems instrumentalist or constructivist insofar as communities construct moral notions by grouping together and distinguishing such features in accordance with their purposes. But this is contradictory only if one assumes that the purposes of a community stand apart from the real world. For Hauerwas, as I show immediately below, the speech and practices of the Christian community claim to show forth and embody the truth about the world, and the purposes of the community in describing the world are imbedded in these practices. The language of showing forth and embodying is not Hauerwas's but it serves as a shorthand way of saying that anything as complex as "the truth about the world" cannot be captured in a single tradition-neutral description or set of such descriptions, partly because, in a way I explain in the following note, our practice-embedded descriptions themselves form part of the world. In any case, I believe one could argue that Hauerwas's metaethics is realist in the nonempiricist Wittgensteinian sense that Sabina Lovibond has developed (Lovibond, 1983).

7. These remarks provide the occasion to pursue the question of Hauerwas's realism raised in the previous note. In one strand of his thought Hauerwas refers to the Christian story and practices as enabling Christians "to see the world as it really is." Yet I think that a careful reading would show that he is not referring to the world as given apart from any of our speech and practices. Rather, he has three major purposes in these contexts, largely derived from Iris Murdoch. The first is to deny that we create the good through our choices. "Even though the good is embodied in our choices, we do not create it through our choices" (Hauerwas, 1981b, p. 102). The second and third purposes have to do, respectively, with the rejection of the reality of the world as seen from our self-concern and from the conventional. In other words, realism in ethics demands that we purge ourselves of the illusion that the world as con-

strued from the perspective of the self or from the conventions of society is the real world. "Our vision must be trained and disciplined in order to free it from our neurotic self-concern and the assumption that conventionality defines the real" (Hauerwas, 1981b, p. 102). None of these claims requires the belief that there is a world independent of the speech and practices of any community. I believe Hauerwas's realism contains two elements. First, he argues that certain descriptions of the world are self-deceptive insofar as they maintain illusions about the self or reality. But to counter these illusions one does not match them up against an independent reality but against a story or practice from which their illusory character is apparent. The church serves this role for the world— this is part of what it means for the church to show the world what it means to be the world—and the stranger serves this role for the church—which is why the church must be that community that welcomes the stranger. The difference is that the church has a story that allows for tragedy and describes our self-delusions, which enables it to welcome the one who challenges its illusions. Second, Hauerwas argues that descriptions of reality are wrong or incomplete when they do not take account of the way events, situations or practices change due to the creation of a people who embody the story of Jesus. In short, the world is known only through one or another set of discursive practices, and the world as it is known through Christian speech and practices is different from the world as it is known through other speech and practices. To describe the world in the latter way and call it the "real world" into which Christian speech and practices must fit is to beg the question and to assume that the way things are— that is, the world as "normalized" through current discursive practices—is the way they must be. This rejection of the idea that Christians must accept the world as described outside of Christian speech and practices constitutes Hauerwas's rejection of Reinhold Niebuhr's Christian realism.

8. A third example Hauerwas frequently uses indicates the limitations of this critique of modern moral discourse. This is the distinction between killing and letting die or that between sustaining life and prolonging dying (Hauerwas, 1977, pp. 114–115, 166; 1981b, pp. 184–185; 1986, pp. 35–36). Hauerwas's major point in seeking to preserve these distinctions is that questions of how aggressively to treat patients or when to stop treating them can be answered only in terms of a narrative or life plan that reflects a community's understanding of the value and purposes of life. He is right that apart from such an understanding, the distinction could be used to allow health professionals to deny what they are doing, as in the famous Johns Hopkins case where a Down syndrome newborn was not treated for a bowel obstruction and then "allowed" to starve to death. But simply having such a narrative is no guarantee against similar self-deceptions on the part of Christians or others. What is needed is an ongoing historical process in which various self-deceptions are exposed and overcome. Pending the development of such processes, moral philosophers who challenge these distinctions by retaining an abstract meaning of the term "killing" have probably done more for the cause of truthfulness in medicine at this point than has Hauerwas.

9. To the extent that the foregoing criticisms depend on the claim that modern morality is abstract, they are no longer valid. Liberalism has shown itself as capable of redescription in the more substantive Aristotelian terms favored by communitarianism; hence much of what was once thought to distinguish them has disappeared. However, I do not think that Hauerwas's criticisms depend on the charge of abstraction. The problem with modern moral theories is not that they abstract from all content but that they claim a thin content (what Jeffrey Stout [Stout, 1988] calls a limited and self-limiting consensus on the good) that allegedly constitutes a common morality but that, as Charles Taylor has shown, is rooted in specific religious and secular traditions that formed the modern west. Hence modern moral theories assume their normalizing function (of underwriting the way things are) not by abstraction but by assuming that the world established by liberal practices is the real world. Self-deception occurs not because moral theories are abstract but because the content of modern moral principles and their specifications under liberal assumptions allow agents to ignore other features of actions they describe as doing good. Finally, the domestication of conflict and the suppression of difference that accompanies it are due not to abstraction but to the assumption that the world of liberal discourses and practices is a common world.

10. Hauerwas recognizes the ironic form of the Gospel of Mark and suggests that it indicates the difficulty of knowing how to identify Jesus correctly and thus follow him truthfully. But he goes on to argue that the crucifixion reveals the identity of Jesus and the nature of his kingdom (Hauerwas, 1983, p. 74). By contrast, Werner Kelber argues that the Markan narrative never allows its readers to arrive at this point of disclosure since the narrative itself has continually shown the old insiders (namely, the disciples) their limited and erroneous understanding, thus leaving them as outsiders. The new insiders (namely, the readers) may believe they have an advantage, but Kelber shows how the fact that Jesus dies forsaken by God, in which epiphany occurs at the point of the absence of God, subverts the reader. The narrative mechanism which assures that insiders will become outsiders thus also assures that those who think they now can understand the revelation of God in the cross will continue to stumble over the messianic secret (Kelber, 1988). Nevertheless Hauerwas may be able to claim Kelber's analysis of Mark for his project insofar as he interprets the mentally handicapped as outsiders who challenge the self-understandings of insiders and makes this challenge part of the identity of the church, as I show below.

11. There is an important difference, of course, between the diversity of scripture and the indeterminacy of its meaning. Recognition of diversity is compatible with the claim that the meaning of the various stories is fully determinate. I believe Hauerwas is committed to some form of indeterminacy. But indeterminacy takes a variety of forms. Charles S. Peirce held to the fallibility and revisability of any single scientific claim but only against the assurance of a finally determinate reference for all concepts in the "final opinion" as the telos of inquiry. Hans-Georg Gadamer similarly posits a "fusion of horizons" in

which indeterminacy is finally resolved. On the contrary, Jacques Derrida argues that determinacy is always deferred through the production of semiosis and that mimesis is accordingly the free play of signifiers. In my opinion, Hauerwas's indeterminacy is due to what he and Frei regard as the peculiar character of the biblical narrative. Since that narrative ultimately refers to the community that continues it in an ongoing tradition, it necessarily remains open insofar as the story is not complete as long as the tradition continues. Hence the resemblance to Peirce is superficial: determinacy for Hauerwas would have to be eschatalogical rather than teleological.

12. Although the church must exist concretely for Christian convictions to be truthful, Hauerwas insists that church and world are not ontologically distinct. "The world is those aspects of our individual and social lives where we live untruthfully by continuing to rely on violence to bring order." Similarly, Christians may discover that "people who are not Christians manifest God's peace" better than Christians do (Hauerwas, 1983, p. 101).

13. Hauerwas recognizes that the cross itself was not pointless suffering. "The cross was not inexplicable; it was the expected response to the political and moral challenge posed by Jesus' proclamation of the kingdom" (Hauerwas, 1990, pp. 86–87; cf. also Hauerwas, 1986, pp. 30–36). More positively, the cross was tragic suffering insofar as it resulted from living according to a set of moral convictions. However, the cross may still serve theologically as a sign that God does not abandon his people.

14. I believe there are serious problems with this position, some of which I take up at the end of this chapter. One may question, for example, how suffering can be comprehended by a narrative or community and still be pointless, or how suffering can be absorbed and still be pointless. More seriously, I argue below that the notion of a narrative and community that absorbs suffering commits many of the same errors as theodicies and their technological successors do and is in fact a theodicy.

15. Here the reader is left to determine exactly what Hauerwas is saying. Is this account of self-possession and alterity a social-psychological claim, a phenomenological claim, an experiential claim, or something else? The claim that our existence and identity are constituted by others is identical to the claim made by George Herbert Mead and adapted for theological ethics by H. Richard Niebuhr. The other as threat recalls Jean-Paul Sartre's analysis of having the meaning of one's being constituted by another—a decentering encounter. But is the other of Mead compatible with that of Sartre? Hauerwas's point may simply be a straightforward theological point: we are in fact (inter)dependent creatures whose sin consists in our assumption that we are independent and self-constituted, an independence that is called into question when we see others suffer.

16. Of course, for reasons I have given in previous chapters, we must be careful in asking Hauerwas to give more concrete descriptions of actually exist-

ing communities and practices not to expect him or anyone else to give exhaustive descriptions of the goods of life. These goods, as Hauerwas recognizes, can be specified only in the concrete choices of persons whose lives have been formed by the virtues and practices and guided by the exemplars and paradigm cases that constitute a way of life. But this makes it even more important that one describe the community or tradition and its relevant living practices, real exemplars and casuistry. What I am asking of Hauerwas is something like what MacIntyre has done in *Whose Justice? Which Rationality?* with regard to the traditions he treats there (MacIntyre, 1988). That is, I am asking him to describe a community that embodies a living tradition comprised of a development of speech and practices, though not necessarily to trace its historical development as MacIntyre has.

17. Since care and trust sustain us even amid suffering and disease and since care and trust always involve being a burden to those who care for us, Hauerwas rejects both suicides from pain, suffering and dismal life prospects, and altruistic suicides intended to avoid burdening others. He thus rejects the strongest justification offered by Gustafson and the motive (altruistic sacrifice) that Bonhoeffer excludes from blame (Bonhoeffer, 1955, pp. 170–172). The only suicides Hauerwas clearly exempts from blame are those that result from the failure of trust and care by others.

18. For another instance see my remarks on consent in experimentation, note 4 above.

CHAPTER 7: MODERNITY, MEDICINE, AND THE BODY

1. Neurologist Oliver Sachs describes his experience of a broken leg complicated by nerve damage that resulted in loss of movement and sensation. Lying in a hospital bed and suddenly aware that he cannot move his leg, Sachs describes the sudden experience of the body as Other: "In that instant . . . I knew not my leg. It was utterly strange, not-mine, unfamiliar. I gazed upon it with absolute non-recognition" (Sachs, 1984, p. 72). Eric Cassell documents extensively the tendency of his patients to refer to diseases or to afflicted body parts in impersonal terms as an "it" or a thing, and hints that this distanciation of the body or the disease may have salutory effects in enabling the person to live with his or her condition (Cassell, 1976; 1985).

2. Of course, the skeptic position is still vulnerable to its own criticisms of the knowledge claims of others if its assertion of the uniqueness of each individual is an empirical or metaphysical claim about the nature of human beings.

3. Leder's position is more plausible than Zaner's because he accounts for why Descartes devoted so much attention to his metaphysical and mathematical inquiries and invested them with so much importance. The attention and

importance given to these activities would be absurd under Zaner's interpretation. The value of Zaner's interpretation is his attention to ordinary experience and medical advice in Descartes's writings, but to propose them as the hermeneutical key to Descartes's project as a whole leaves too much of Descartes's work unintelligible.

4. If Cassell, Leder, and Zaner are right about the nature and preponderance of chronic and degenerative diseases as opposed to acute and infectious diseases, the era of Bichat—of the paradigm of the corpse of the Other—may now be over.

5. This does not mean, as is often assumed by devotees of non-Western methods of healing, that Ayurvedic or Chinese methods of healing treat the lived body of the ill person or empower patients rather than doctors. As Arthur Kleinman argues, every professional tradition of medicine abstracts from the lived experience of illness (what Kleinman terms the popular sphere) in order to produce a diagnosis, an etiology, and a plan of treatment that requires expert knowledge inaccessible to the patient (and thus occurs in the professional sphere) (Kleinman, 1986). This is as true when the explanation of the disease refers to *lung* or *qi* as when it refers to cells or genes. However, there is an important difference. The history of medicine in the west since Bichat exhibits an increasing localization of disease. Just as symptoms gave way to anatomical lesions as the location of disease, so cells replaced lesions and now genes may be in the process of replacing cells. Each step has made the location more specific and allowed for a more precise focus on the disease entity. But each step has also further isolated the body into its component parts and processes and removed diagnosis and therapy further from the patient's own experience of his or her body. Explanations of disease that refer to *lung* or *qi* still replace the patient's illness description with a technical disease description. But unlike their western counterparts they use concepts that connect with the patient's experience of the lived body. *Lung* and *qi* are terms not only in the medical lexicon but also in the lexicon of mental and spiritual practices. Hence while medical therapy involves specialized knowledge and techniques it nevertheless works on the same mental-somatic processes involved in spiritual discipline and attainment. As a result, healing may involve both the former and the latter without dualism. I am grateful to Anne Klein and Angela Shen for explaining aspects of Tibetan and Chinese medicine and spiritual practice to me.

6. My interpretation of Foucault is loosely based on a division of his career from the early 1960s into three periods dominated, respectively, by his interests in discourses as systems of truth, their transformations and radical disruptions, and their constraints and practices of exclusion (archaeology); forms of power that give rise to and sustain, express and extend, discourses (genealogy); and techniques of disclosing, forming, and acting on oneself. There are considerable tensions between the methods and assumptions that govern these three periods. Foucault himself admitted at least a substantive continuity between these three stages, claiming while at work on the analyses of power that mark his second

period that all of his work up to that point had actually been about power, and insisting at the end of his life that his concern all along had been the subject (Foucault, 1980, p. 115; 1988, pp. 1, 9). Others identify philosophical and methodological incompatibilities between, say, archaeology and genealogy (Dreyfus and Rabinow, 1983). Still others argue that archaeology and genealogy involve different though not incompatible accounts of systems of ideas and practices (Gutting, 1990). Since the methodological and epistemological questions Foucault's work raises are not directly relevant to my concerns here, I largely bracket them.

7. Readers of Foucault's text will know how inadequate this brief summary is. It ignores the sociopolitical and institutional conditions for the transition, and omits the earlier clinical stage that marks the first shift away from classificatory medicine. In partial compensation for the latter deficiency I offer the following summary of Foucault's account of the way each stage in the transition to clinical-laboratory medicine treats symptoms. In classificatory medicine the disease itself remains invisible to the gaze but symptoms make it possible to designate the pathological state in which the disease shows through, while somatic signs indicate the temporal progression of the invisible disease process. A sharp distinction between signifier and signified therefore marks classificatory medicine. In early clinical medicine this distinction largely collapses. Disease is now identified with a collection of symptoms visible to the well-trained gaze and therefore exists not in an invisible essence but in a successive order of symptoms. The gap between the object of medicine and the gaze that deciphers it thus disappears. In clinical-laboratory medicine the anatomy of tissues makes it possible to understand the chronological ordering of symptoms geographically, in accordance with a lesional location and its logic which is determined by the structure, properties, and functions of a tissue system. Disease is now understood by what is characteristic of its lesional space, and symptoms signify disease only within the questions posed by the medical investigation, itself informed by a detailed knowledge of pathological anatomy (Foucault, 1973, pp. 90–93, 138–140, 159–161).

8. Critics of Foucault often confuse this circular relation between power and truth with a claim that truth is reducible to power, that is, that truth claims are in fact only expressions of power. But Foucault does not make this claim. Power generates truth in the sense that forms of power give rise to certain types of knowledge. For example, knowledge of human behavior arose because certain forms of discipline and control of individuals were being implemented. From the fact that this knowledge arose due to these forms of power (if it did) and is necessary for extending that power (if it is) it does not follow that the claims about human behavior enshrined in this knowledge are any the less true or that accounts of truth necessarily must in all cases refer to power (Foucault, 1980, p. 133; 1987, p. 16).

9. Earlier Foucault had implied the opposite, namely that the subject is the product of power *simpliciter* (Foucault, 1980, p. 98). Foucault's later argument

may have been in response to critics who accused him of reducing the subject to power relations and thus leaving him with no perspective from which to criticize forms of power. The later argument, which is close in form to Augustine's argument in Book 7 of the *Confessions* that evil, as corruption, requires some degree of being that can be corrupted, does not signal a return to the liberal-Marxist subject that is constituted prior to power but rather locates the subject at the point where power meets resistance. For Foucault this point where power meets resistance, and not the perspective of a universal subject, is the standpoint of the critic.

10. This task of permanent provocation is closely linked to the task of genealogy itself. The genealogist speaks neither from the universal perspective of a theory of justice (Jürgen Habermas) nor from the ethnocentric solidarity of one's own web of belief (Richard Rorty). Rather, he or she speaks from the point where power meets resistance and thus is exposed as power (Foucault, 1980, p. 99). Permanent provocation requires the constant formation of new practices at the points where they can resist new effects of power.

CHAPTER 8: THE BODY AFTER UTOPIA

1. I am not implying that Christianity is the only way of carrying out this ethical task. But neither can I claim that Christianity is purely neutral in my formulation of the problem addressed in this volume. It was Christian convictions that led me to question the Baconian project, not a dissatisfaction with the Baconian project that now leads me to Christian convictions. I remain agnostic as to whether Christian convictions and practices are more or less effective than other ways of countering the Baconian project, but my commitment to them does not depend on their effectiveness here or on any other external criterion. Let this suffice as my "signature." Regarding the likelihood that there are other effective ways of carrying out this twofold ethical task, the field of bioethics as I envision it would in part involve conversations between these different ways, though such conversation will for their adherents often be a secondary endeavor that follows from their primary endeavor to form themselves in their own alternative. There are several reasons why particular communities would engage in such conversations with others. One reason is strategic: together such communities might be more effective in identifying and countering aspects of standard bioethics or bioethical policy that are incompatible with their pursuits of the good. Another reason is that in an era when communities constantly interact with each other, knowledge of the effects of one's discourses and practices on others is a moral task for all. Christians, and perhaps others as well, will have two additional reasons. One is their belief that by divine providence wisdom is found in many places and is there to be appropriated, though always and only under the authority of Christian convictions and practices. (Karl Barth is among recent theologians the one who best exemplifies the "no" and "yes," or in my terms, the resistance and appro-

priation, of this Augustinian hermeneutical practice.) The other is their Gospel narratives, which remind them that insiders can understand the gospel only through the challenge of outsiders.

2. The thesis that the subject is formed by attitudes and practices regarding the body is not only the property of feminists and Foucauldians. It is shared by ascetics in various traditions and, I believe, by Paul in his admonitions in Romans 6:12–13 and 12:1–5, and in I Corinthians 6:13–20.

3. Gedaliahu Stroumsa's study of the body in various patristric sources indicates that despite major conceptual differences this Pauline conviction of the divided self continued to define Christian attitudes and practices. Stroumsa also shows how this approach to the body formed in early Christians a new kind of moral subject. In contrast to the Greek subject, the Christian is integrated as a unity of body and soul but now divided in itself, a paradox of wholeness and division that gives rise to a reflexive attitude in which "the wounded and contrite self develops at once humility toward itself and compassion toward others" (Stroumsa, 1990, p. 49). The connection Stroumsa draws between humility and compassion figures strongly in my understanding of the two modes of the body of the Other, articulated below, though (in spite of important differences from this account) I have also been strongly influenced in this regard by Simone Weil's reflection on affliction (Weil, 1951, pp. 117–136), Emmanuel Levinas's later account of alterity (Levinas, 1981, pp. 61–129), and (as will become clear below) by Edith Wyschogrod.

4. The foregoing account does not authorize the view that acceptance of the body of the Other leads to the acceptance of all kinds of suffering, and especially suffering at the hands of another. The body of the Other as I have described it fractures the self from within, as it were, while the power or control another subject exercises over one is power or control over one who is already separated from and within oneself. If in theological terms separation from oneself is the ontology of sin, power or control over one by another is evil. This is why, as I argue below, illness or bodily imperfection are privileged as experiences that bring one to an awareness of one's spiritual imperfection and need for grace. But the power over or control of patients by physicians or by institutions (in the absence of a community with an agreed-on view of how such power should be exercised and what its limits are), while they may bring one to this awareness, exhibit a different structure of experience—one that constitutes evil rather than sin—and is thus a kind of suffering that ought to be eliminated if one can do so proportionately and without violating other moral convictions. Illness and bodily imperfection, in other words, can (often) serve our moral projects in a way that oppression (ordinarily) cannot. One of the most pernicious effects of the modern moral discourse that levels all distinctions between different kinds of suffering is that we are led to take the same stance toward illness and bodily imperfection that we take toward oppression.

5. The meditation on bodily suffering as a form of edification or a source of insight was familiar in earlier times and may be undergoing a revival. For

classical forms I have in mind especially John Donne (1987) and Blaise Pascal (1948). A post-Christian successor to this genre that has influenced my thinking on the body and the way I understand the challenge of chronic, incurable illness to Baconian assumptions that still govern medicine is Mark C. Taylor's philosophical reflection on diabetes (Taylor, 1993, pp. 214–255). I am indebted to Richard Gunderman for the reference to Pascal.

6. How much money that we now spend in quest of a genetic cure for certain conditions could have been spent in research that would have led to major improvements in the lives of those who suffer from these conditions? And so for any number of conditions. However, while I am committed to assigning a much higher priority to research and practice that enables people to live and function better, there are two caveats. One is that while much of the care and support I have in mind is interpersonal and therefore more labor intensive than technology intensive, this is not exclusively the case. Technological devices play vital roles in enabling patients to live at home rather than in the hospital and enable many patients to improve mobility and other basic functions, to mention only two obvious—though not entirely unambivalent—examples. My point is that technology should be assessed in these terms, not that it should be eliminated. The other caveat is that undoubtedly much of what enables those who suffer to live better under their conditions comes as a spin-off of efforts to eliminate their suffering. While I recognize this, I am unconvinced that this is the only or the most effective or efficient way to discover and develop the kinds of care and support I am speaking of.

7. The problem is compounded when so many of those who oppose abortion, selective nontreatment of newborns, and physician-assisted death fail to share the burdens of caring for those whose lives they claim to value so highly, and in fact enthusiastically support the very social and institutional structures that make such care impossible or force individuals (usually women) to bear it alone. Such opponents are perhaps the cruelest of all moderns, for they leave intact the modern social and institutional arrangements that cause so much suffering for those who bear ill or imperfect children and who die in dependence on others, while depriving them of the means modern liberal societies offer in order to make these arrangements bearable. This does not mean that a community should guarantee those who bring ill or imperfect children into the world or who die in dependence on others that they will not suffer from doing so, but it should set up institutions and practices that assign a high priority to supporting them and minimizing their suffering.

Bibliography

Anderson, W. French. "Human Gene Therapy: Why Draw a Line?" *Journal of Medicine and Philosophy* 14 (1989): 681–93.

Annas, Julia. *The Morality of Happiness*. New York: Oxford University Press, 1993.

Aquinas, St. Thomas, *Summa Theologica*.

Arendt, Hannah. *The Human Condition*. Chicago: University of Chicago Press, 1958.

Aristotle. *Nicomachaean Ethics*.

Bacon, Francis. *Works of Lord Bacon*, edited by Joseph Devey. London: George Bell and Sons, 1894.

Bacon, Francis. *The New Organon and Related Writings*, edited by Fulton H. Anderson. New York: Liberal Arts Press, 1960.

Barth, Karl. *The Doctrine of God, Church Dogmatics*, vol. II, part 2. Edinburgh: T & T Clark, 1957.

Barth, Karl. *The Doctrine of Creation, Church Dogmatics*, vol. III, part 2. Edinburgh: T & T Clark, 1960.

Barth, Karl. *The Doctrine of Creation, Church Dogmatics*. vol. III, part 4. Edinburgh: T & T Clark, 1961.

Beauchamp, Tom L., and James F. Childress. *Principles of Biomedical Ethics*, 3rd ed. New York: Oxford University Press, 1989.

Beauchamp, Tom L., and James F. Childress. *Principles of Biomedical Ethics*, 4th ed. New York: Oxford University Press, 1994.

Bernauer, James, and Michael Mahon. "The Ethics of Michel Foucault," in Gary Gutting, ed., *The Cambridge Companion to Foucault*. New York: Cambridge University Press, 1994, pp. 141–158.

Bleich, J. David. "Of Cerebral, Respiratory and Cardiac Death." *Tradition* (1989): 24, no. 3; 44–66.

Bonhoeffer, Dietrich. *Ethics*, edited by Eberhard Bethge. New York: Macmillan, 1955.

Boorse, Christopher. "Health as a Theoretical Concept." *Philosophy of Science* 44 (1977): 542–573.

Borgmann, Albert. *Technology and the Character of Everyday Life: A Philosophical Inquiry*. Chicago: University of Chicago Press, 1984.

Bowlin, John. "Health, Fortune and Moral Authority in Medicine," *Christian Bioethics* 2 (1996): 42–65.

Brock, Dan W. "Voluntary Active Euthanasia," *Hastings Center Report*, March–April (1992): pp. 10–22.

Brody, Howard. "Assisted Death— A Compassionate Response to a Medical Failure." *New England Journal of Medicine* 327 (1992): no. 19, 1384–1388.

Brown, Peter. *The Body and Society: Men, Women, and Sexual Renunciation in Early Christianity*. New York: Columbia University Press, 1988.

Bultmann, Rudolf. *Theology of the New Testament*, vol. 1. New York: Scribners, 1951.

Cahill, Lisa Sowle. "Consent in Time of Affliction: The Ethics of a Circumspect Theist." *Journal of Religious Ethics* 13 (1985): pp. 22–36.

Callahan, Daniel. "Can We Return Death to Disease?" *Hastings Center Report* (1989): January–February, pp. 4–6.

Cassel, Christine K., and Diane E. Meier. "Morals and Moralism in the Debate over Euthanasia and Assisted Suicide." *New England Journal of Medicine* 323 (1990): no. 11, 750–752.

Cassell, Eric. *Talking with Patients*, vol. 1: *The Theory of Doctor-Patient Communication*. Cambridge, Mass.: MIT Press, 1985.

Cassell, Eric. "Disease as an 'It.'" *Social Science and Medicine* 10 (1976): 143–146.

Clouser, K. Danner. "The Challenge for Future Debate on Euthanasia." *Journal of Pain and Symptom Management* 6 (1991): no. 5, 306–311.

Congregation for the Doctrine of the Faith. "Instruction on Respect for Human Life in its Origin and on the Dignity of Human Reproduction," in Thomas A. Shannon and Lisa Sowle Cahill, *Religion and Artificial Reproduction*. New York: Crossroads, 1988, pp. 140–177.

Corea, Gena, editor. *Man-Made Women: How New Reproductive Technologies Affect Women*. Bloomington: Indiana University Press, 1987.

Donne, John. *Devotions upon Emergent Occasions*, Anthony Raspa, editor. New York: Oxford University Press, 1987.

Dreyfus, Hubert L., and Paul Rabinow. *Michel Foucault: Beyond Structuralism and Hermeneutics*. Chicago: University of Chicago Press, 1983.

Edelstein, Ludwig. *Ancient Medicine: Selected Papers of Ludwig Edelstein*, edited by Owsei Temkin and C. Lilian Temkin. Baltimore: Johns Hopkins Press, 1967.

Edwards, Jonathan. *Ethical Writings*, edited by Paul Ramsey. New Haven: Yale University Press, 1989.

Emanuel, Ezekiel. *The Ends of Human Life*. Cambridge: Harvard University Press, 1991.

Engelhardt, H. Tristram Jr. "Content, Tradition, and Grace: Rethinking the Possibility of a Christian Bioethics." *Christian Bioethics* 1 (1995): no. 1, 1–10.

Farley, Edward. "Theocentric Ethics as a Genetic Argument," in Harlan R. Beckley and Charles M. Swezey, editors, *James M. Gustafson's Theocentric Ethics: Interpretations and Assessments*. Macon, Ga.: Mercer University Press, 1988, pp. 39–58.

Fletcher, John C. "Evolution of Ethical Debate about Human Gene Therapy." *Human Gene Therapy* 1 (1990): pp. 55–68.

Fletcher, John C., and W. French Anderson. "Germ-Line Gene Therapy: A New Stage of Debate." *Law, Medicine and Health Care* 20 (1992): nos. 1–2, 26–39.

Foucault, Michel. *The Order of Things: An Archaeology of the Human Sciences*. New York: Vintage Books, 1970.

Foucault, Michel. *The Archealogy of Knowledge*. New York: Pantheon Books, 1972.

Foucault, Michel. *The Birth of the Clinic: An Archaeology of Medical Perception*. New York: Vintage Books, 1973.

Foucault, Michel. *Discipline and Punish: The Birth of the Prison*. New York: Vintage Books, 1977.

Foucault, Michel. *The History of Sexuality*, vol. 1: *An Introduction*. New York: Vintage Books, 1978.

Foucault, Michel. *Power/Knowledge: Selected Interviews and Other Writings, 1972–1977*, edited by Colin Gordon. New York: Pantheon Books, 1980.

Foucault, Michel. "On the Genealogy of Ethics: An Overview of Work in Progress." Afterword to Hubert L. Dreyfus and Paul Rabinow. *Michel Foucault: Beyond Structuralism and Hermeneutics*. Chicago: University of Chicago Press, 1983a, pp. 229–252.

Foucault, Michel. "The Subject and Power." Afterword to Hubert L. Dreyfus and Paul Rabinow. *Michel Foucault: Beyond Structuralism and Hermeneutics*. Chicago: University of Chicago Press, 1983b, pp. 208–226.

Foucault, Michel. "Nietzsche, Genealogy, History," in Paul Rabinow, editor, *The Foucault Reader*. New York: Pantheon Books, 1984.

Foucault, Michel. *The History of Sexuality*, vol 3: *The Care of the Self*. New York: Vintage Books, 1986.

Foucault, Michel. "The Ethic of Care for the Self as a Practice of Freedom," in James Bernauer and David Rasmussen, eds., *The Final Foucault*. Cambridge, Mass.: MIT Press, 1987, pp. 1–20.

Frei, Hans W. *The Eclipse of Biblical Narrative: A Study in Eighteenth and Nineteenth Century Hermeneutics*. New Haven: Yale University Press, 1974.

Frei, Hans W. *The Identity of Jesus Christ: The Hermeneutical Bases of Dogmatic Theology*. Philadelphia: Fortress Press, 1975.

Geertz, Clifford. *The Interpretation of Cultures*. New York: Basic Books, 1973.

Golub, Edward S. *The Limits of Medicine*. New York: Times Books, 1994.

Gustafson, James M. *Christian Ethics and the Community*. Philadelphia: United Church Press, 1971.

Gustafson, James M. "Mongolism, Parental Desires, and the Right to Life." *Perspectives in Biology and Medicine* 16 (1973): 529–557.

Gustafson, James M. *Theology and Christian Ethics*. Philadelphia: United Church Press, 1974.

Gustafson, James M. *Can Ethics Be Christian?* Chicago: University of Chicago Press, 1975a.

Gustafson, James M. *The Contributions of Theology to Medical Ethics*. The 1975 Pere Marquette Theology Lecture. Milwaukee: Marquette University Theology Department, 1975b.

Gustafson, James M. *Ethics from a Theocentric Perspective*, vol. 1: *Theology and Ethics*. Chicago: University of Chicago Press, 1981.

Gustafson, James M. "Professions as 'Callings.'" *Social Service Review* 56 (1982a): 501–15.

Gustafson, James M. "A Theocentric Interpretation of Life," in James M. Wall, editor, *Theologians in Transition*. New York: Crossroad, 1982b, pp. 82–91.

Gustafson, James M. "Ethical Issues in the Human Future," in Donald J. Ortner, editor, *How Humans Adapt: A Biocultural Odyssey*. Washington, D.C.: Smithsonian Press, 1983, pp. 491–516.

Gustafson, James M. *Ethics from a Theocentric Perspective*, vol. 2: *Ethics and Theology*. Chicago: University of Chicago Press, 1984.

Gustafson, James M. "A Response to Critics." *Journal of Religious Ethics* 13 (1985): 185–209.

Gustafson, James M. "Theology Confronts Technology and the Life Sciences," in Stephen E. Lammers and Allen D. Verhey, editors. *On Moral Medicine: Theological Theological Perspectives in Medical Ethics*. Grand Rapids, Mich.: Eerdmans, 1987, pp. 35–41.

Gustafson, James M. "The Focus and Its Limitations: Reflections on Catholic Moral Theology," in Charles E. Curran, editor, *Moral Theology: Challenges for the Future: Essays in Honor of Richard A. McCormick, S.J.* New York: Paulist Press, 1990a, pp. 179–190.

Gustafson, James M. "Moral Discourse about Medicine: A Variety of Forms." *Journal of Medicine and Philosophy* 15 (1990b): 125–142.

Gustafson, James M. "Response to Hartt." *Soundings* 73 (1990c): 689–700.

Gustafson, James M. "A Response to the Book of Job," in Leo Perdue and Clark Gilpin, editors, *The Voice from the Whirlwind*. Nashville: Abingdon Press, 1992a, pp. 172–184.

Gustafson, James M. "Theological Anthropology and the Human Sciences," in Sheila Graves Davaney, editor, *Theology at the End of Modernity: Essays in Honor of Gordon D. Kaufman*. Philadelphia: Trinity Press International, 1992b, pp. 61–77.

Gustafson, James M. "A Christian Perspective on Genetic Engineering," *Human Gene Therapy* 5 (1994): 747–754.

Gutting, Gary. "Foucault's Genealogical Method," in Peter A. French, Theodore E. Uehling, Jr., and Howard Wettstein, eds., *Midwest Studies in Philosophy*, vol. 15. Notre Dame, Ind.: University of Notre Dame Press, 1990, pp. 327–343

Hampshire, Stuart. *Morality and Conflict*. Cambridge: Harvard University Press, 1983.

Hauerwas, Stanley. *Truthfulness and Tragedy: Further Investigations into Christian Ethics*. Notre Dame, Ind.: University of Notre Dame Press, 1977.

Hauerwas, Stanley. *A Community of Character: Toward a Constructive Christian Social Ethic*. Notre Dame, Ind.: University of Notre Dame Press, 1981a.

Hauerwas, Stanley. *Vision and Virtue: Essays in Christian Ethical Reflection*. Notre Dame, Ind.: University of Notre Dame Press, 1981b [1974].

Hauerwas, Stanley. *The Peaceable Kingdom: A Primer in Christian Ethics*. Notre Dame, Ind.: University of Notre Dame Press, 1983.

Hauerwas, Stanley. "On Medicine and Virtue: A Response," Earl E. Shelp, editor, *Virtue and Medicine*. Dordrecht: D. Reidel Publishing Company, 1985a, pp. 347–355.

Hauerwas, Stanley. "Time and History in Theological Ethics: The Work of James Gustafson." *Journal of Religious Ethics* 13 (1985b): 3–21.

Hauerwas, Stanley. *Suffering Presence: Theological Reflections on Medicine, the Mentally Handicapped, and the Church*. Notre Dame, Ind.: University of Notre Dame Press, 1986.

Hauerwas, Stanley. "The Church as God's New Language," Garrett Green, editor, *Scriptural Authority and Narrative Interpretation*. Philadelphia: Fortress Press, 1987, pp. 179–198.

Hauerwas, Stanley. "Reconciling the Practice of Reason: Casuistry in a Christian Context," Baruch A. Brody, editor, *Moral Theory and Moral Judgments in Medical Ethics*. Dordrecht: Kluwer Academic Publishers, 1988.

Hauerwas, Stanley. *Naming the Silences: God, Medicine, and the Problem of Suffering*. Grand Rapids, Mich.: Eerdmans Publishing Company, 1990.

Hauerwas, Stanley. "A Non-Violent Proposal for Christian Participation in the Culture Wars." *Soundings* 75 (1992): no. 4, 477–492.

Hauerwas, Stanley. *Dispatches from the Front: Theological Engagements with the Secular*. Durham, N.C.: Duke University Press, 1994.

Hauerwas, Stanley. "How Christian Ethics Became Medical Ethics: The Case of Paul Ramsey." *Christian Bioethics* 1 (1995): no. 1, 11–28.

Heidegger, Martin. *An Introduction to Metaphysics*. New Haven: Yale University Press, 1959.

Heidegger, Martin. *Basic Writings*. New York: Harper and Row, 1977.

Hoy, David Couzens. "Introduction," in David Couzens Hoy, ed., *Foucault: A Critical Reader*. New York: Basil Blackwell, 1986.

Irigaray, Luce. "Sexual Difference," in *The Irigaray Reader*, Margaret Whitford, editor. Oxford: Basil Blackwell, pp. 165–177, 1991.

Jacobovits, Yoel, translator and annotator. "[Brain Death and] Heart Transplants: The [Israeli] Chief Rabbinate's Directives," *Tradition* 24 (1989): no. 4, pp. 1–14.

Janssens, Louis. "Norms and Priorities in a Love Ethics." *Louvain Studies* 6 (1977): 207–238.

Jonas, Hans. *The Phenomenon of Life: Toward a Philosophical Biology*. New York: Harper and Row, 1966.

Jonas, Hans. *Philosophical Essays: From Ancient Creed to Technological Man*. Chicago: University of Chicago Press, 1974.

Jonas, Hans. "Freedom of Scientific Inquiry and the Public Interest." *Hastings Center Report* 6 (1976): no. 8 (August), 15–17.

Jonas, Hans. "Toward a Philosophy of Technology." *Hastings Center Report* 9 (1979): no. 1 (February), 34–43.

Jonas, Hans. "Response to James M. Gustafson," in Daniel Callahan and H. Tristram Engelhardt, editors, *The Roots of Ethics*. New York: Plenum Press, 1982, pp. 197–211.

Jonas, Hans. *The Imperative of Responsibility: In Search of an Ethics for the Technological Age*. Chicago: University of Chicago Press, 1984.

Jonas, Hans. "Ethics and Biogenetic Art," *Social Research* 52 (1985): 491–504.

Jonas, Hans. "The Burden and Blessing of Mortality." *Hastings Center Report* 22 (1992): no. 1 (January/February), 34–40.

Jonas, Hans. "Philosophy at the End of the Century: A Survey of Its Past and Future." *Social Research* 61 (1994): no. 4, 813–882.

Jonsen, Albert R. *The New Medicine and the Old Ethics*. Cambridge: Harvard University Press, 1990.

Jonsen, Albert R. "American Moralism and the Origin of Bioethics in the United States." *Journal of Medicine and Philosophy* 16 (1991): 113–130.

Jonsen, Albert R., ed. "The Birth of Bioethics." Special Supplement, *Hastings Center Report* 23 (1993): no. 6, 1–4.

Jonsen, Albert R., and Stephen Toulmin. *The Abuse of Casuistry: A History of Moral Reasoning*. Berkeley: University of California Press, 1988.

Kant, Immanuel. *Religion within the Limits of Reason Alone*. New York: Harper and Row, 1960 [1794].

Kass, Leon R. *Toward a More Natural Science: Biology and Human Affairs*. New York: The Free Press, 1985.

Kass, Leon R. "Neither for Love nor Money: Why Doctors Must Not Kill." *The Public Interest* 94 (1989): 25–46.

Kass, Leon R. "Practicing Ethics: Where's the Action?" *Hastings Center Report* (1990): January–February, pp. 5–12.

Kass, Leon R. "Organs for Sale? Propriety, Property, and the Price of Progress," *The Public Interest* 107 (1992): 65–86.

Kass, Leon R. *The Hungry Soul: Eating and the Perfecting of Our Nature*. New York: The Free Press, 1994.

Kleinman, Arthur. "Concepts and a Model for the Comparison of Medical Systems as Cultural Systems," in Caroline Currer and Meg Stacey, eds., *Concepts of Health, Illness, and Disease: A Comparative Perspective*. New York: Berg Publishing Company, 1986.

Kelber, Werner H. "Narrative and Disclosure: Mechanisms of Concealing, Revealing, and Reveiling," *Semeia* 43 (1988): 1–20.

Khushf, George. "Illness, the Problem of Evil, and the Analogical Structure of Healing: the Difference Christianity Makes in Bioethics," *Christian Bioethics* 1 (1995): 102–120.

Krimsky, Sheldon. "Human Gene Therapy: Must We Know Where to Stop Before We Begin?" *Human Gene Therapy* 1 (1990): 171–173.

Leder, Drew. "Medicine and Paradigms of Embodiment," *Journal of Medicine and Philosophy* 9 (1984): 29–43.

Leder, Drew. *The Absent Body*. Chicago: University of Chicago Press, 1990.

Leder, Drew. "Introduction," in Drew Leder, ed., *The Body in Medical Thought and Practice*. Dordrecht: Kluwer Academic Press, 1992a, 1–12.

Leder, Drew. "A Tale of Two Bodies," in Drew Leder, ed., *The Body in Medical Thought and Practice*. Dordrecht: Kluwer Academic Press, 1992b, pp. 17–35.

Levinas, Emmanuel. *Totality and Infinity*, Alphonso Lingis, translator, Pittsburgh: Duquesne University Press, 1969.

Levinas, Emmanuel. *Otherwise than Being or Beyond Essence*, Alphonso Lingis, translator. The Hague: Martinus Nijhoff, 1981.

Lindbeck, George A. *The Nature of Doctrine: Religion and Theology in a Postliberal Age*. Philadelphia: Westminster Press, 1984.

Lock, Margaret, and Christina Honde. "Reaching Consensus about Death: Heart Transplants and Cultural Identity in Japan," in George Weisz, editor, *Social Science Perspectives on Medical Ethics*. Dordrecht: Kluwer Academic Press, 1990, pp. 99–119.

Locke, John. *Two Treatises of Government*, edited by Peter Laslett. New York: New American Library, 1960.

Lovibond, Sabina. *Realism and Imagination in Ethics*. Minneapolis: University of Minnesota Press, 1983.

Lovin, Robin W., and Frank E. Reynolds, editors. *Cosmogony and Ethical Order: New Studies in Comparative Ethics*. Chicago: University of Chicago Press, 1985.

Lyotard, Jean-Francois. *The Postmodern Condition: A Report on Knowledge*. Minneapolis: University of Minnesota Press, 1984.

MacIntyre, Alasdair. *After Virtue*, 2nd ed. Notre Dame, Ind.: University of Notre Dame Press, 1984.

MacIntyre, Alasdair. *Whose Justice? Which Rationality?* Notre Dame, Ind.: University of Notre Dame Press, 1988.

Maimonides, Moses. *Ethical Writings of Maimonides*, edited by Raymond L. Weiss with Charles Butterworth. New York: New York University Press, 1975.

McCormick, Richard A., S.J. "Ambiguity in Moral Choice," in Richard McCormick and Paul Ramsey, editors, *Doing Evil to Achieve Good*. Chicago: Loyola University Press, 1978, pp. 7–53.

McCormick, Richard A., S.J. "Gustafson's God: Who? What? Where? (Etc.)." *Journal of Religious Ethics* 13 (1985): 53–69.

McKenny, Gerald P. "Whose Tradition? Which Enlightenment? What Content? Engelhardt, Hauerwas, Capaldi, and the Future of Christian Bioethics." *Christian Bioethics* 1 (1995): 84–96.

Meilaender, Gilbert. *Faith and Faithfulness: Basic Themes in Christian Ethics*. Notre Dame, Ind.: University of Notre Dame Press, 1991.

Munson, Ronald, and Lawrence H. Davis. "Germ-Line Gene Therapy and the Medical Imperative." *Kennedy Institute of Ethics Journal* 2 (1992): no. 2, 137–158.

Niebuhr, H. Richard. *The Meaning of Revelation*. New York, Harper and Row, 1941.

Niebuhr, H. Richard. *Radical Monotheism and Western Culture, with Supplementary Essays*. New York: Harper and Row, 1960.

Niebuhr, H. Richard. *The Responsible Self*. New York: Harper and Row, 1963.

Nussbaum, Martha C. *The Fragility of Goodness: Luck and Ethics in Greek Tragedy and Philosophy*. New York: Cambridge University Press, 1986.

Nussbaum, Martha C. *Love's Knowledge: Essays on Philosophy and Literature*. New York: Oxford University Press, 1990.

Oakeshott, Michael. "The Tower of Babel," in *Anti-Theory in Ethics and Moral Conservatism*. Stanley G. Clarke and Evan Simpson, editors. Albany: State University of New York Press, 1989, pp. 185–203.

Parfit, Derek. *Reasons and Persons*. New York: Oxford University Press, 1984.

Pascal, Blaise. "Prayer by Pascal Asking God to Use Illness to a Good End," in *Great Shorter Works of Pascal*, edited by Emile Caillet. Philadelphia: Westminster Press, 1948, pp. 220–227.

Pellegrino, Edmund D., and David C. Thomasma. *A Philosophical Basis of Medical Practice*, New York: Oxford University Press.

Plato, *Republic*.

Quill, Timothy E., Christine K. Cassel, and Diane E. Meier. "Care of the Hopelessly Ill: Proposed Criteria for Physician-Assisted Suicide." *New England Journal of Medicine* 327 (1992): no. 19, 1380–1383.

Ramsey, Paul. *Fabricated Man: The Ethics of Genetic Control*. New Haven: Yale University Press, 1970a.

Ramsey, Paul. *The Patient as Person*. New Haven: Yale University Press, 1970b.

Reiser, Stanley J. *Medicine and the Reign of Technology*. New York: Cambridge University Press, 1978.

Resnik, David. "Debunking the Slippery Slope Argument Against Human Germ-Line Gene Therapy." *Journal of Medicine and Philosophy* 19 (1994): 23–40.

Rose, Nikolas. "Medicine, History and the Present," in Colin Jones and Roy Porter, eds., *Reassessing Foucault: Power, Medicine and the Body*. New York: Routledge, 1994, pp. 48–72.

Rothfield, Philippa. "Bodies and Subjects: Medical Ethics and Feminism," in *Troubled Bodies: Critical Perspectives on Postmodernism, Medical Ethics, and the Body*, Paul A. Komesaroff, editor. Durham: Duke University Press, 1995, pp. 168–201.

Rothman, David J. "Human Experimentation and the Origins of Bioethics in the United States," in George Weisz, editor, *Social Science Perspectives on Medical Ethics*. Kluwer Academic Press, 1990, pp. 185–200.

Rothman, David J. *Strangers at the Bedside: A History of How Law and Bioethics Transformed Medical Decision Making*. New York: Basic Books, 1991.

Sachs, Oliver. *A Leg to Stand On*. New York: Summit Books, 1984.

Sacred Congregation. "Declaration of the Sacred Congregation for the Doctrine of the Faith (May 5, 1980)," in Stephen E. Lammers and Allen D. Verhey, editors. *On Moral Medicine: Theological Perspectives in Medical Ethics.* Grand Rapids, Mich.: Eerdmans, 1987, pp. 441–444.

Shklar, Judith N. *Ordinary Vices.* Cambridge: Harvard Belknap Press, 1984.

Spitzack, Carole. *Confessing Excess: Women and the Politics of Body Reduction.* Albany: State University of New York Press, 1990.

Stanworth, Michelle. "Reproductive Technologies and the Deconstruction of Motherhood," in *Reproductive Technologies: Gender, Motherhood and Medicine*, Michelle Stanworth, editor. Cambridge: Polity Press, 1987, pp. 10–35.

Stout, Jeffrey. *The Flight from Authority.* Notre Dame, Ind.: University of Notre Dame Press, 1981.

Stout, Jeffrey. *Ethics after Babel: The Languages of Morals and Their Discontents.* Boston: Beacon Press, 1988.

Stroumsa, Gedaliahu G. "*Caro Salutis Cardo:* Shaping the Person in Early Christian Thought." *History of Religions* 30 (1990): no. 1, 25–50.

Taylor, Charles. *Sources of the Self: The Making of the Modern Identity.* Harvard University Press, 1989.

Taylor, Mark C. *Nots*, Chicago: University of Chicago Press, 1993.

Troeltsch, Ernst. *Social Teachings of the Christian Churches*, 2 volumes. Chicago: University of Chicago Press, 1931.

Veatch, Robert M. *A Theory of Medical Ethics.* New York: Basic Books, 1981.

Verhey, Allen. "The Doctor's Oath—and a Christian Swearing It," in *On Moral Medicine: Theological Perspectives in Medical Ethics*, Stephen E. Lammers and Allen Verhey, editors. Grand Rapids, Mich.: Eerdmans, 1987, pp. 72–82.

Walters, Leroy. "Human Gene Therapy: Ethics and Public Policy," *Human Gene Therapy* 2 (1991): 115–122.

Weber, Max. "Politics as a Vocation," in Hans H. Gerth and C. Wright Mills, eds., *From Max Weber: Essays in Sociology.* Oxford University Press, 1958, pp. 77–128.

Weil, Simone. *Waiting for God*, translated by Emma Craufurd. New York: G.P. Putnam's Sons, 1951.

White, Lynn. "The Historical Roots of our Ecologic Crisis." *Science* 155 (1967): 1203–1207.

Williams, Bernard. *Ethics and the Limits of Philosophy*. Cambridge, Mass.: Harvard University Press, 1985.

Winkler, Mary, and Letha Cole, eds. *The Good Body: Medicine and Asceticism in Contemporary Culture*. New Haven: Yale University Press, 1995.

Wolf, Susan M. "Holding the Line on Euthanasia," *Hastings Center Report*, January–February (1989): 13–16.

World Health Organization. "Constitution of the World Health Organization," in *Concepts of Health and Disease: Interdisciplinary Perspectives*, Arthur L. Caplan, H. Tristram Engelhardt, Jr., and James J. McCartney, editors. Reading, Mass: Addison-Wesley Publishing Company, 1981, pp. 83–84.

Wyschogrod, Edith. *Saints and Postmodernism: Revisioning Moral Philosophy*. Chicago: University of Chicago Press, 1990.

Wyschogrod, Edith. "The Howl of Oedipus, the Cry of Heloise: From Asceticism to Postmodern Ethics," in Vincent L. Wimbush and Richard Valantasis, eds., *Asceticism*. New York: Oxford University Press, 1995, pp. 16–30.

Young, Iris Marion. *Throwing Like a Girl and Other Essays in Feminist Philosophy and Social Theory*. Bloomington: Indiana University Press, 1990.

Zaner, Richard M. *The Context of Self: A Phenomenological Inquiry Using Medicine as a Clue*. Athens, Ohio: Ohio University Press, 1981.

Zaner, Richard, editor. *Death: Beyond Whole-Brain Criteria*. Dordrecht: Kluwer Academic Press, 1988a.

Zaner, Richard M. *Ethics and the Clinical Encounter*, Prentice-Hall, 1988b.

Index